STORIES
OF THE PAST

STORIES OF THE PAST

Viewing History through Fiction

CHRIS GREEN

Published by Sidestone Press, Leiden
www.sidestone.com

Imprint: Sidestone Press dissertations

Lay-out & cover design: Sidestone Press
Photograph cover: Motizova (stock.adobe.com)

ISBN 978-94-6428-033-3 (softcover)
ISBN 978-94-6428-034-0 (hardcover)
ISBN 978-94-6428-035-7 (PDF e-book)

Contents

Biography

Dr Chris Green is currently Honorary Visiting Research Associate in the Department of History and Archaeology at the University of Chester. He obtained his doctorate from the University of Chester in March 2020, studying the uses of novels as resources for the study of History, having obtained his MA in Landscape, Heritage and Society from the same institution in 2006. Following his BA in Geography from the University of Sheffield in 1976, he worked for many years in the Information Technology industry. He is currently researching the history of Manchester's Hallé Choir, of which he has been a member since 2009. He lives in Chester.

1

Introduction

1.1 Stories of the Past

The book is an ungilded and sorrowful picture of the life of the class of workpeople in such a town as Manchester, with which circumstances seem to have made the writer more than ordinarily familiar... It behoves everybody to know more of the matter, and fiction may be allowed to enter where philosophy cannot well find its way. We defy anyone to read *Mary Barton* without a more thoughtful sense of what is due to the poor; without a stronger and healthier persuasion of the justice they have the right to claim, and the charity they have so many more reasons than the rest of the world to stand bitterly in need of.[1]

Thus writes the critic John Forster in a review of Elizabeth Gaskell's *Mary Barton*, following its publication in 1848.[2] Within the novel he believes he sees a truthful picture of working-class life in the industrial Manchester of the 1840s, the perceived injustices of which he sees as needing to be addressed. Francis Sparshott poses a question that is related, namely 'can truth be found in works of fiction?'.[3] He sets a series of objections to the idea of truth in fiction, based in part on Joseph Margolis' idea, contradicting Forster, that fiction 'cannot be construed as embodying claims to tell any truth about the real world'.[4] The gist of these objections centres on the imagined nature of fiction; novels are stories – a series of imagined events affecting imagined people in imagined places (even if those imagined places share their names and appearance with actual places such as Manchester), and any generalised inferences we may make from them about the 'actual' world are not part of the story. Within the story itself there can be 'no claim by a fictional utterance to embody any truth'.[5]

However, as Sparshott goes on to state in addressing the objections he has raised, 'an author does not imagine a world *ex nihilo*'. He sees fiction as an amalgam of 'remembered' and 'invented' aspects between which one cannot differentiate as they are 'but aspects

---

1   John Forster, '*Mary Barton* Review', *The Examiner*, Nov. 1848, pp. 708-9.
2   Elizabeth Gaskell, *Mary Barton: A Tale of Manchester Life* (London: Chapman and Hall, 1848).
3   Francis E. Sparshott, 'Truth in Fiction', *The Journal of Aesthetics and Art Criticism*, 26 (1967), pp. 3-7.
4   Ibid. Sparshott is summarising Chapter 11 of Joseph Margolis, *The Language of Art & Art Criticism: Analytic Questions in Aesthetics* (Detroit: Wayne State University Press, 1965), pp. 151-64.
5   Sparshott (1967).

of the whole'.[6] Forster's review is an example of this process in action; he knows *Mary Barton* is fiction, describing it as such, but behind the imagined surface he perceives the past world around which Gaskell is building her fiction, and those perceptions bring forth within him ideas of social change within that world, and a consciousness that fiction has the power to go further in describing the world than mere 'philosophy'.

Building on Sparshott's comments, this study looks in detail at how authors like Gaskell adapt elements from a past world into their fiction, and how the novel itself might, when consumed, be used as a resource for the historical study of that past world. This act of consuming a novel does not necessarily happen in isolation as a private transaction between us and the author. Especially with novels written in a time before our experience, there will have been an initial critical reception of the novel, but further layers of critical consensus that have accrued through time may affect our reading of the novel in the present day. Terry Eagleton, referencing the hermeneutic principles of Hans-Georg Gadamer, describes how our understanding of a literary work is a factor not only of the time it is written but also of cultural constraints of the time in which we are reading it.[7] We reach understanding when we reconcile our own set of cultural assumptions with those of the period in which the work was written, and all periods in between. Meaning constantly evolves through time and a reader's understanding of a literary work, and by extension the world within it, changes according to the period when that work is read.[8]

There are also ways other than reading the book itself in which a novel can be experienced. We may view an adaptation of the novel for the theatre, the cinema, or television, or we may first encounter the novel on a visit to a literary place devoted to the novel itself, to its author, or to an adaptation of it. Each of these stages in the novel's journey involves the creation of an imagined world that stands in some form of relationship to the past world that sits behind the novel, and can be thought of in terms of a process, a concept that will be enlarged upon as this study progresses. This introductory chapter examines the nature of the debate around the relationship between fiction and history, and between past worlds and their imagined versions within novels. It begins with a brief philosophical background to ideas around the nature of reality and how we perceive it, before examining views of how well the imagined worlds of novels are able to capture the essence of a past world. This is followed by a discussion of the role of fiction in historical research and historical understanding which examines in the first place whether novels can be considered useful historical resources, and if they can, the extent to which one can obtain valid insights about a past world from the imagined worlds created within them.

1.2 History and Fiction

Any discussion of past worlds and their imagined versions should begin with an acknowledgement of the difficulty of defining whether, in cognitive terms, there can be such a thing as an objective reality, at least in terms of our perception of it, within which a past world is framed. Alexander Miller, drawing on philosophical thinking from Plato onwards, summarises ideas of realism in terms of two concepts, the first being 'existence', that objects exist and possess certain facts (*e.g.* a table exists, and it is square). The second

---

6   Ibid. p. 6.
7   Terry Eagleton, *Literary Theory: An Introduction* (Oxford: Blackwell, 1996), pp. 61-2.
8   Ibid.

is 'independence', that the fact of an object's existence is 'independent of anything anyone happens to say or think about the matter'.[9] This study will make the basic assumption that a 'real world' containing such objective, independent objects does indeed exist, and that the past existed within it. However, its primary concern is with the way that past world is perceived and then reimagined in a fictional context. Bishop George Berkeley, writing in 1710, examines such links between reality and our perception of it, believing that the objects within it are 'but the things we perceive by sense'.[10] He cannot conceive an object 'distinct from the sensation or perception of it'; the 'real world' only exists inasmuch as we perceive it.[11] This expands on the view of reality described by John Locke, writing in the previous century to Berkeley. Locke describes a theory of 'ideas', in which 'everything existing or occurring in a mind is or includes an idea'.[12] Locke contrasts 'real' ideas, which 'have a Foundation in Nature; have a Conformity with the real Being, and Existence of Things, or with their Archetypes', and 'fantastical' ideas, which have no such connection with the 'reality of Being'.[13] Locke believes it is impossible to perceive a purely objective real world, only one's subjective idea of it, whilst at the same time acknowledging that such an idea can have a 'foundation' in the real world.

Berkeley and Locke were part of a wider debate about the nature of truth and reality that has stretched from the classical philosophy of Plato through to thinkers of the last two centuries such as Søren Kierkegaard and Jean-Paul Sartre. Kierkegaard introduced the concept that 'truth is subjectivity'. Whilst not denying the existence of an objective reality, he believed that real truth comes subjectively from one's own encounter with one's existence. He quotes the example of 100,000 people witnessing an event – their acts of witnessing the event are all individual, subjective encounters, and do not become something more objective simply because there are 100,000 of them.[14] Sarah Bakewell describes Sartre's ideas of 'being and nothingness' succinctly: Sartre thought of existence being divided into two groups, the *pour-soi*, ourselves and our human consciousnesses, and the *en-soi*, which is all other objects, whose main purpose is simply to exist. The *pour-soi* has no real being other than to observe the *en-soi*, as Bakewell describes: 'my consciousness is specifically mine, yet it has no real being: it *is* nothing but its tendency to reach out or point to things'.[15] Waldo Jewell-Lapan argues that this means that 'the objects of perception do constitute the "real world" because the "real world" *is* our perceptions'.[16] Either way, if we accept these views, it would follow that perception of the real world is a subjective thing, and that each of us experiences it differently. Jewell-Lapan goes on

---

9   Alexander Miller, *Realism*, (Stanford: Stanford University, 2016) <https://plato.stanford.edu/archives/win2016/entries/realism/>.

10   George Berkeley, *A Treatise concerning the Principles of Human Knowledge* (Philadelphia: J.B. Lippincot & Co., 1710 (1881 edition)), pp. 195-6, Principle 4.

11   Ibid. pp. 196-7, Principle 5.

12   Vere Chappell, 'Locke's Theory of Ideas', in *The Cambridge Companion to Locke*, ed. by Vere Chappell (Cambridge: Cambridge University Press, 1994), p. 26.

13   John Locke quoted in ibid. p. 50.

14   Søren Kierkegaard, 'Concluding Scientific Postscript (1846)', in *Philosophic Classics: From Plato to Nietzsche*, ed. by Walter Arnold Kaufmann and Forrest E. Baird (Upper Saddle River, N.J.: Prentice Hall, 1997), p. 1066.

15   Sarah Bakewell, At the Existentialist Café: Freedom, Being & Apricot Cocktails (London: Chatto & Windus, 2016), p. 154.

16   Waldo Jewell-Lapan, 'Perception and Reality', *The Journal of Philosophy*, xxxiii (1936), pp. 365-73.

to suggest that our perception is also influenced by 'a whole life-time of knowledge and experience', and that these affect 'the judgement implicit in every perception'.[17]

As we are interested here in how that perception of reality is taken a step further when adapted into the descriptive content of a novel, we must specifically address ideas of *literary* reality. If it is true that we perceive a past world via a combination of our senses and our past knowledge and experience, the way a novelist perceives that world will never be completely identical to other perceptions of the same world that exist at any one time, given each individual's differing knowledge and experience of it. Novelists' perceptions of the past world that informs their fiction can therefore never coincide exactly with those of readers of that fiction, even for those living at the same time as the author.

At this point it is important to state that not all fiction is written with a view to describing any form of reality. Margolis refers to the concept of fiction being the description of various 'possible' worlds. He differentiates between the 'possible' world of Honoré Balzac's *La Cousine Bette*, internally coherent and compatible with a certain portion of historical 19th century France, and the 'impossible' world of Lewis Carroll's *Alice's Adventures in Wonderland*, a world that is also coherent in terms of its own internal logic, but which does not, at least on the surface, reflect any sort of reality.[18]

Any fictional world is imaginary in the sense that it is made up by the author, but Margolis expresses the links between the imaginary and the real as follows. For him the 'truths' of fiction are not truths about reality as such, but truths illuminated by the 'imagined relationship' between the real and the fictional.[19] This reflects Locke's view of real ideas being those that have a foundation in an objective real world, as well as Sparshott's ideas of remembered and invented elements. If a past world is fictionalised by the author through such a combination of remembered and invented elements, then the reader can, as Peter McCormick says, 'historicise' the fiction by comparing it to his or her own experience of the world. McCormick sees this as a 'mediation' between the fictional world and the world of the reader.[20]

There is also the question of the novelist's intent regarding how we are to view their imagined world in relation to the elements of the past that inform the novel. Sparshott sees what he calls the novel's 'implication' about those elements as important. He compares Leo Tolstoy's *Anna Karenina* with P.G. Wodehouse's *Carry On, Jeeves*; in one he says the novel's implications can be taken as 'serious comments about life', and in the other as 'enjoyable fantasy'.[21] Importantly, the reader's response to the implications can affect how the novel is read. Sparshott makes it clear that as readers we have no obligation to view fiction in any realistic fashion; we can treat any fiction either as a 'jest' or as a 'solemn commentary on the world we live in'.[22] One should also not forget that novelists can have firm views on the matter of realism. George Eliot believed it the duty of the novelist not to portray an idea of the world as it ought to be, but of the world as it is. In terms of portraying the life of ordinary working people, she believed the reader should encounter not the 'heroic

---

17   Ibid. p. 371.
18   Joseph Margolis, 'The Logic and Structures of Fictional Narrative', *Philosophy and Literature,* 7 (1983), pp. 162-81.
19   Ibid.
20   Peter McCormick, 'Real Fictions', *The Journal of Aesthetics and Art Criticism,* 46 (1987), pp. 259-70.
21   Sparshott (1967).
22   Ibid.

artisan' or 'sentimental peasant', but 'the peasant in all his coarse apathy, and the artisan in all his suspicious selfishness.[23]

Linked with Sparshott's idea of 'implication' is the assumption that a novel would usually be written with the intention on the part of the novelist that the finished product is of commercial worth. Ranald Michie accepts that authors create novels based on their own experiences and those of friends and relatives, and on other contemporary sources, and that they then add to that their own 'prejudices, biases and opinions'. However, he also emphasises that a novel is not a 'factual report', but a 'literary creation' whose very existence is contingent on it achieving sales.[24]

By Sparshott's reckoning, when readers consume the novel, they may simply consume it as an enjoyable story without differentiating between the remembered and invented aspects of it. However, especially if the remembered elements resonate with their own experience or knowledge, in other words their own subjective view of the world, they may discern the remembered 'truth' that lies behind the fiction. However, while such an ability to discern through self-knowledge may be strong if we read a piece of present-day contemporary fiction, about whose world we may have some familiarity prior to reading it, it is weaker when we read a novel set in a place or time removed from our experience, and of which we have limited knowledge or first-hand experience. Take Ian McEwan's novel *Saturday*, which is set on the day of the mass demonstration in London against the impending war in Iraq in 2003.[25] Whilst many will have taken the novel at face value with little prior knowledge of its subject matter, many will have read it with knowledge obtained from having participated in the demonstration or from having seen or read about it, and with awareness of the political background to the march and the war that followed. They may also be aware of the other social issues that populate the novel and its portrayal of life in London on that day. We have certain shared cultural reference points with McEwan that are not there when we read the novels of authors like Jane Austen or Charles Dickens. We do not have the direct life experience of Victorian London or Regency England with which to test the 'truths' within their fiction that we might have with present-day authors like McEwan. However, the continuing popularity of Austen, Dickens and other writers of 'classic' fiction suggests that we are more than willing to enter Margolis' 'imagined relationship' between the real and the fictional.

Indeed, it may be that there is a need within us to be drawn into fictional descriptions of past worlds. Jerome de Groot recounts Hilary Mantel's visit to the house of Ralph Sadler, whom she describes in her historical novel *Wolf Hall*, and sees in her visceral reaction to the encounter a sense of a past experienced through place, that is at once both tangible but also nostalgically distanced. He suggests that the popularity of historical fiction, like the popularity of historical places, comes from a need to 'somehow raise the dead', and to

---

23   George Eliot, 'The Natural History of German Life', *Westminster Review,* XIX (1856), pp. 51-79. Note that George Eliot, the pen name of Marian Evans, only wrote one novel, *Daniel Deronda*, set in her own contemporary world, and because of this she has been excluded from specific consideration within this study. However, this statement regarding realism is important when discussing issues of truth and fiction.
24   Ranald Michie, The City of London in Literature: Place, People and Pursuits, (London: Gresham College, 2013).
25   Ian McEwan, *Saturday* (London: Jonathan Cape, 2005).

'put the flesh back on the skeleton that is history'.[26] If there is an inbuilt desire within us to commune in such a way with the past, the same should apply to contemporary fiction of a particular period as to historical fiction set in that period, given that the authors of such fiction can have a direct connection with the world they describe.

Given this sense of elements of the past present in many works of fiction, is it therefore valid to treat such novels as resources for historical research? Arthur Marwick is adamant that all novels should be treated as primary sources for the period in which they were produced, indeed he says that they are *never* to be accounted secondary sources.' For example, he quotes Dickens' *Pickwick Papers* being at one time quoted by historians as an example of politics of the period before the Great Reform Act of 1832. However, he sums up the problem with using fiction within historical research, as he sees it, as follows: 'Novels are always primary sources, though in many cases they may be thoroughly useless ones. Or when they do provide information, they may well not be the *best* source for that information...'.[27] For Marwick, using a fictional account of, say, living conditions in a particular era, would always be secondary to using actual statistics and information from that era. One of his tests for using fiction is 'does it tell us anything we couldn't discover more readily from a different source?'.[28] In a similar vein John Tosh, whilst saying that novels and plays 'cannot, of course, be treated as factual reports, however great the element of autobiography or social observation may be', grants that they can provide 'insights into the social and intellectual milieu in which the writer lived, and often vivid descriptions of the physical setting as well'.[29]

John Smith Allen echoes Marwick in warning of historians who 'read fiction for its historical detail without much consideration of its literary nature', and of the problems within fiction of 'mistaking intention for accomplishment and details for facts'.[30] However, as Beverly Southgate says, 'both [history and fiction] in short aim to provide a story that is meaningful, or (again in some sense) true',[31] which links with David Lowenthal's view that the difference between history and fiction, when both are essentially telling stories, is one of 'purpose not content'. Lowenthal does not see history as the only truth about the past; one can see truth in all stories, but in ways that 'are more specific in history and more general in fiction'.[32]

Lowenthal lists three constraints that limit what can be understood from historical enquiry: firstly, we cannot retrieve 'the virtually infinite sum total of past events', most of which went unrecorded or were fleeting; secondly, as the past is now gone, we cannot check our version of the past against it, only against other versions of the past; and thirdly, the knowledge we gain from history is subjective, both from the point of view of

26   Jerome de Groot, 'The power of the past: how historical fiction has regained its gravitas', *The Guardian*, 30th September, 2009. De Groot is quoting from Alessandro Manzoni, *On the Historical Novel*, trans. Sandra Bermann (Lincoln: University of Nebraska Press, 1984).
27   Arthur Marwick, *The New Nature of History: Knowledge, Evidence, Language* (Basingstoke: Palgrave, 2001), p. 187.
28   Ibid. p. 188.
29   John Tosh, *The Pursuit of History* (Harlow: Longman, 2015), p. 79.
30   James Smith Allen, 'History and the Novel: Mentalité in Modern Popular Fiction', *History and Theory*, 22 (1983), pp. 233-52.
31   Beverley C. Southgate, *History meets Fiction* (Harlow: Longman, 2009), p. 20.
32   David Lowenthal, *The Past is a Foreign Country* (Cambridge: Cambridge University Press, 1985), p. 229.

the historian and the audience.[33] With so much of the past therefore unknown, de Groot sees fiction being able to fill in the gaps in between the truths of history ('the verifiable fact'), which he describes as 'the spaces scholars have no idea about'.[34] Gabrielle Spiegel also makes the important point that in looking at historical sources we are looking at 'mediatory practices of past epochs (in effect, discourses)' and that the literary nature of those sources 'prohibits our access to any reality other than the codes inscribed in such texts'.[35] In other words, even with the potentially limited sources historians have, they also need to understand in the present day the past processes of mediation that produced those sources, and the various textual codes inherent within them before they can mediate with that past in the present.

Louis Mink compares the reliance on incomplete sources in history with scientific method, within which formal explanation and deduction using specific laws determine how, given prescribed conditions, a particular phenomenon will occur. In the study of history, by comparison, we cannot ascertain directly the exact causal factors for events because 'the general laws formally required have not been empirically discovered'.[36] By this reasoning, historical narratives may never be direct accounts of cause and effect, even if, as Fritz Stern reports, early 20th century historians such as J.B. Bury saw their role as using available sources to establish direct cause and effect in the same way as scientists investigate natural processes.[37] Rather, historians rely on available sources backed up by reasoned conjecture in a way that can more directly resemble storytelling than scientific method.

Continuing this idea of history as storytelling, Hayden White describes historical works as containing 'data', *i.e.* 'sets of events presumed to have occurred in times past', linked in their presentation by a 'narrative structure' that is 'generally poetic, and specifically linguistic, in nature'. He terms this the 'metahistorical understructure' to works of history.[38] If this resembles storytelling, the historian may also be influenced, as may be writers of fiction, by what Timothy Parrish calls 'the demands of the teller and the teller's audience'.[39] This suggests they tailor their account to fit in with their own and their readers' attitudes and prejudices in a way that resembles the way some authors tailor their fiction, as we will see with Elizabeth Gaskell (Section 5.3). This is reflected in White's use of the term 'emplotment' to describe 'the way by which a sequence of events fashioned into a story is gradually revealed to be a story of a particular kind'.[40] The different ways in which a single piece of history is plotted can therefore produce a number of different interpretations depending on the type of emplotment used. This storytelling aspect suggests that achieving historical truth is not as simple as achieving scientific truth. As

---

33 David Lowenthal, *The Past is a Foreign Country – Revisited* (Cambridge: Cambridge University Press, 2015), pp. 336-37.

34 Jerome de Groot, Consuming History: Historians and Heritage in Contemporary Popular Culture (London: Routledge, 2009), p. 217.

35 Lawrence Stone and Gabrielle M. Spiegel, 'History and Post-Modernism', *Past & Present,* (1992), pp. 189-208.

36 Louis O Mink, 'History and Fiction as Modes of Comprehension', *New Literary History,* 1 (1970), pp. 541-58.

37 Fritz Stern, 'Introduction', in *The Varieties of History : From Voltaire to the Present,* ed. by Fritz Stern (Cleveland: Meridian Books, 1956), p. 20.

38 Hayden V. White, *Metahistory. The Historical Imagination in Nineteenth-Century Europe* (Baltimore and London: John Hopkins University Press, 1975), p. ix.

39 Timothy Parrish, 'History and Fiction', in *The Cambridge Companion to Postmodern American Fiction,* ed. by Paula Geyh (New York: Cambridge University Press, 2017), p. 81.

40 White (1975) p. 7.

Jonathan Hart writes: 'History, like fiction, is a matter of point of view. Who is speaking to whom? Who is writing for whom?'.[41]

If the novelist and the historian are both storytellers piecing together a narrative, 'the difference between "history" and "fiction"', White says, may reside 'in the fact that the historian "finds" his stories, whereas the fiction writer "invents" his'.[42] Dorrit Cohn describes the qualitative difference between the 'constrained' processes that historians use to turn archival sources into narrative history and the 'free' processes novelists use to turn their sources ('autobiographical, anecdotal, or even historical') into narrative fiction.[43] Southgate, in pursuing the storytelling analogy, is of the view that truth is the primary concern of the historian, unlike the writer of fiction, and that indeed it is 'the only appropriate goal for any historian'.[44] He does though acknowledge Leo Braudy's view that novelists and historians are both interested in giving what he calls a 'compelling and convincing narrative shape' to their descriptions of human life.[45] De Groot develops this idea further in arguing that popular history might be seen as a form of re-enactment whereby one brings the past alive by reinserting 'the body and the emotion back into the stories of the past', and that thereby 'history is essentially a set of narratives performed by individuals in the present'.[46]

Southgate's idea of truth is developed by White, who in building on the ideas of Michel de Certeau, contrasts the 'truth' of history with the 'reality' of fiction, whereby a true historical account of a past world would be based only on 'what the documentary record permits one to talk about what happened in it at particular times', which may be only be a small part of the overall 'reality' of that past time, but a fictional account can cover the whole reality, *i.e.* 'everything that can be truthfully said about its actuality [the historical account] plus everything that can be truthfully said about what it could *possibly* be'.[47] The novelist Robert Penn Warren condenses this into a contrast between the historian, concerned with 'knowledge *about*' the past and the novelist whose concern is with a more immersive 'knowledge *of*' the past.[48] Like White and de Groot, he suggests 'real' fictional accounts, and in particular those contemporary to the times they are describing, might be capable of filling in some of the gaps in the documentary record, the 'true' historical account, of those times.

Proponents of the school of literary analysis that developed during the 1980s and became known as the 'New Historicism' suggest that all texts, be they literary or non-literary, are pertinent to the study of the cultural and intellectual history of a period. Such texts, in H. Aram Veeser's summation, 'circulate inseparably', and no discourse, be it 'imaginative' (*i.e.* 'fictional'), or archival (*i.e.* 'historical'), 'gives access to unchanging

---

41   Jonathan Hart, *Fictional and Historical Worlds* (New York: Palgrave Macmillan, 2012), p. 149.

42   Hayden V. White, *The Content of the Form: Narrative Discourse and Historical Representation* (Baltimore: Johns Hopkins University Press, 1987), p. 173.

43   Dorrit Cohn, 'Signposts of Fictionality: A Narratological Perspective', *Poetics Today*, 11 (1990), pp. 775-804.

44   Southgate (2009) p. 2.

45   Leo Braudy, *Narrative Form in History and Fiction: Hume, Fielding & Gibbon* (Princeton, N.J: Princeton University Press, 1970) Quoted in Southgate (2009) p. 4.

46   Jerome de Groot, 'Affect and empathy: re-enactment and performance as/in history', *Rethinking History*, 15 (2011), pp. 587-99.

47   Hayden V. White, 'Introduction: Historical Fiction, Fictional History, and Historical Reality', *Rethinking History*, 9 (2005), pp. 147-57.

48   Ralph Ellison, William Styron, Robert Penn Warren, and C. Vann Woodward, 'A Discussion: The Uses of History in Fiction', *The Southern Literary Journal*, 1 (1969), pp. 57-90.

truths, nor expresses inalterable human nature'.[49] All information from a period, by this estimation, is grist to the mill in terms of understanding that period, thus blurring the distinction between what would normally be the separate domains of, say, literary scholars, anthropologists, and social historians.[50]

Before discussing some of the practical ways in which fiction has been used in the study of history, one should emphasise that the historical 'story' is not fixed but is, as Marc Bloch describes it, 'an endeavour toward better understanding and, consequently, a thing in movement'.[51] Stern, referencing the 19th historian Henry Thomas Buckle's view that 'there must always be a connexion between the way in which men contemplate the past, and the way in which they contemplate the present',[52] reminds us that the historian has 'presuppositions which are deeply intertwined with the basic assumptions of his age'.[53] So, as more sources becoming available or existing sources are reinterpreted, as philosophical thinking about the past develops and transmutes and as new methods of interpreting the past develop, the nature of the historical narrative about any particular time develops. Bloch insists that any discipline that aspires, as he believes history does, to 'dignity of a science', should not insist purely on 'Euclidian demonstrations or immutable laws of repetition'.[54] Robin Collingwood, writing in the 1940s, saw belief that history followed general laws as a 'positivistic fallacy', and historical understanding, as it evolves, essentially involves a relationship between the actual past and constructions of that past made by historians in the present. As he describes it, 'history is nothing but the re-enactment of past thought in the historian's mind'.[55] And as David Carr reminds us, historians creating in the present what they might consider to be a 'once and for all' version of history need to be aware that 'the present point of view is somehow permanent and yet always changing, framed at each moment by a different past and future'.[56]

Fiction is also subject to constant reinterpretation and reimagining as it moves beyond the original novel, as it is criticised and re-criticised through time, as it is adapted for various different media, often multiple times, and as it is used to create interpretations for tourist destinations. What was once a single immutable historical artefact informed by its author's reaction to elements of the past becomes, to paraphrase what was written above, a series of reimagined versions that involve a relationship between the novel and constructions of that novel made by various agents in the present.

Such is the nature of some of the arguments around the use of fiction within the study of history. There is acceptance of fiction's place, *inter alia*, as a historical resource. However, there are disputes as to its efficacy as such, despite which fiction has often been used, by academics particularly, as a means of understanding social and geographical aspects

---

49   H. Aram Veeser, 'Introduction', in *The New Historicism*, ed. by H. Aram Veeser (London & New York: Routledge, 1989), p. xi.

50   Ibid. p. xv.

51   Marc Bloch and Peter Putnam (trans.), *The Historian's Craft* (Manchester: Manchester University Press, 1954 (1992 reprint)), pp. 10-11.

52   Henry Thomas Buckle, *History of Civilisation in England* (London: John W. Parker & Son, 1857). Quoted in Stern (1956) p. 15.

53   Stern (1956) pp. 15-16.

54   Bloch and Putnam (trans.) (1954 (1992 reprint)) pp. 14-15.

55   R. G. Collingwood, *The Idea of History* (Oxford: Clarendon Press, 1946), p. 228.

56   David Carr, 'Reflections on Temporal Perspective: The Use and Abuse of Hindsight', *History and Theory*, 57 (2018), pp. 71-80.

of the real world of which it is an imagined version. Examples include Harold Darby's placing of descriptions of Hardy's fictional Wessex as valid resources alongside historical land surveys of Dorset,[57] Amy Bell's use of fictional descriptions of wartime London from Graham Greene and Elizabeth Bowen to inform and to add resonance to the historical record of that time,[58] and the use of GIS techniques to merge real and fictional geographies, as for example with *A Literary Atlas of Europe*.[59]

Finally, what must not be forgotten is that, in Gabrielle Spiegel's words, 'literary text and historical context are not the same thing'.[60] A novel created in the past uses written language to mediate with the writer's perception of certain pieces of information about that past and, subject to particular influences, construct a narrative. As such it is therefore a step removed from the historical 'truth' of that past. When we receive that novel in the present, we are ourselves in turn mediating with the novel with our own perceptions and influences and attempting to deconstruct that narrative to extract the historical 'truth' with which the original novel was a mediation. Subsequently, as further actors create further artefacts based on the original novel, they are doing so by mediating with the novel using their own perceptions and influences and creating further layers on top of the original 'truth'. As Spiegel puts it, the problem is 'how we reach it [the truth] and what procedures permit us to do so in ways that respect its integrity'.[61] None of the actors within this process act neutrally as they all bring their own perceptions and influences to bear in the way they create or consume the various artefacts. In attempting to uncover the historical 'truth' we therefore need to remove the presumptions that the various actors bring to the text that they create. Understanding these processes of mediation and investigating procedures that would allow us to extract the historical background are therefore both substantial elements of this study. It is important at this stage to briefly outline what can happen to a novel beyond its publication to add these further layers.

1.3 Beyond the Novel

What complicates any discussion around history and fiction is the fact that many novels have associations that have moved well beyond the novel itself. The ways in which these associations have built up are many and various. Following the initial publication of the novel, there is the initial critical response to it, and the potential for a critical review to affect perceptions of the book. There has also been an industry working on behalf of certain novelists, an early example being when shortly after Charlotte Brontë's death, her friend and fellow novelist Elizabeth Gaskell produced the first biography of Brontë.[62] Biographies, autobiographies, and critical studies, such as the biographies of Thomas Hardy, Elizabeth Gaskell, and Jane Austen referenced within this study, interpret and reinterpret the lives of these novelists. Allied to this has been the growth of people wanting to visit the homes and haunts of their favourite authors. In terms of the British Isles, mass literary tourism began in earnest with tourism

---

57   H.C. Darby, 'The Regional Geography of Thomas Hardy's Wessex', *Geographical Review*, 38 (1948), pp. 426-43.
58   Amy Bell, 'Landscapes of Fear: Wartime London, 1939-1945', *The Journal of British Studies*, 48 (2004), pp. 153-75.
59   Various, *A Literary Atlas of Europe*, (Zurich: Institute of Cartography, ETH Zurich, 2018) <http://www.literaturatlas.eu/en/index.html>.
60   Gabrielle M. Spiegel, 'History, Historicism, and the Social Logic of the Text in the Middle Ages', *Speculum*, 65 (1990), pp. 59-86.
61   Ibid. p. 76.
62   Elizabeth Gaskell, *The Life of Charlotte Brontë* (London: Smith, Elder & Co., 1857).

based around the works of Walter Scott, and in particular the publication of his epic poem *The Lady of the Lake* in 1810, soon after which tourists could be found clutching a copy of the poem as they were rowed across the waters of Loch Katrine, the setting for the poem.[63] The influx in tourists even resulted in landscape features on the Loch being renamed after characters in the poem.[64] This desire to see the landscapes that inspired poets and novelists or which were featured in their works, or to experience places associated with the writers, expanded through the 19th century to novelists such as Jane Austen and Thomas Hardy. Literary houses, museums, and heritage centres such as the Brontë Parsonage in Haworth, the Charles Dickens Museum in London, and the Elizabeth Gaskell House in Manchester have grown up dedicated to interpreting and presenting the life and works of specific authors to a present-day audience.

Finally, the 20th century saw the growth, both in films and on television, of adaptations of novels, adaptations that are largely taken from an established, and limited, canon of novels that have gained classic status. It is possible through these adaptions to know the story, background, and setting of a novel without ever having held a printed copy of the novel. And again, the 'message' of the novel, as in the case of critical appreciation and heritage interpretation, is prey to the interpretation that the filmmakers put on the story.

To emphasise that familiarity with a novel's story does not necessarily equate to familiarity with the book itself, the research for this study required the reading of many novels for the first time, even though many of the stories were familiar from screen adaptations. In the same vein, some may visit a literary site such as the Brontë Parsonage with little or no direct experience of the Brontë sisters' novels, or their adaptations. Sarah Tetley and Bill Bramwell's study of tourism in Haworth and in particular what motivates visitors to the Brontë Parsonage, a prime site for literary pilgrimage, shows that whilst for the majority of visitors to the house the connection with Brontës was the reason for their visit, for 36% of visitors the connection with the Brontës was of 'low importance' in terms of influencing their visit – the suggestion being that for many it may simply have been the next place to visit.[65] The way that adapters and interpreters approach novels and novelists and the recreations of the world of the novel can therefore have as much effect on the consumers of the novel, in whatever form, as any decisions made by novelists in initially framing their novel. As each imagined world created by someone other than the novelist appears, so the process gains in complexity as the layers build up between the original novel and the elements of the past that lie behind it and our perception of it.

1.4 A Fiction 'Process'

The previous sections and the following chapters acknowledge the depth of research that has been undertaken in describing the nature of the processes of writing, reviewing, adapting, and interpreting of fiction, as well as the ways in which the novel has moved beyond the printed page. What this study attempts to do is to pull all these aspects together in the form of an overall process flow. A process flow in the context in which it is used within this study is a diagrammatic representation of the flow of information through a

---

63 John Towner, An Historical Geography of Recreation and Tourism in the Western World, 1540-1940 (Chichester: Wiley, 1996), p. 156.

64 Nicola J. Watson, *The Literary Tourist* (Basingstoke: Palgrave Macmillan, 2008), p. 151.

65 Sarah Tetley and Bill Bramwell, 'Tourists and the Cultural Construction of Haworth's Literary Landscapes', in *Literature and Tourism: Essays in the Reading and Writing of Tourism*, ed. by Mike Robinson and Hans Christian Andersen (London: Continuum, 2002), p. 160.

system. Process flows are used in a business environment to illustrate the movement of data through a particular business procedure, with all of the specific inputs, actions, and outputs at each step in the process. Within this context, the data are the elements of the past that an author perceives when imagining the world of the novel. Such a process flow would demonstrate the cumulative effect of the influences on each of the actors at each stage within the process and their ability to modify the information about the past that is depicted in the imagined world presented in the artefact produced at that particular stage. Such influences may be societal or cultural in nature, beginning with those that affect novelists when they create the first imagined world, that within the novel.

Further down the process flow we see the production of a succession of further imagined worlds connected to the original novel, such as those perceived and created by critics, adapters, and interpreters, each of whom has their own set of influences that bear upon them. Defining such a process flow also serves to illustrate the degree to which these actors interact with each other, how for example an adaptor making a version of the novel for film and television might be influenced not just by the novel, but by the critical consensus around the novel, by previous adaptations of the novel or of other novels, by general historical research of the period in which the novel is set, or by a perception of what the targeted audience expects from an adaptation.

What will be demonstrated below, via means of the process flow, is how this creates a layering effect between the ultimate consumer of the novel (in whatever form), and the imagined world they perceive within it, and the elements of the past used by the novelist to create the initial imagined world of the novel. Understanding the totality of this process flow helps us in determining the degree to which we can utilise the fictional information contained within the flow as a historical resource to stand alongside contemporary records and testimony, and both the potential benefits and drawbacks of such use. This helps provide answers to Sparshott's question posed in the opening paragraph: 'Can truth be found in works of fiction?'. This is especially important given the degree of public exposure to history that is not through historical studies as such, but through the pages of classic novels, or, in a more immediate way, their adaptation into a visual form for film or television, or their interpretation within a literary place.

The remainder of this study builds up this idea of a classic fiction process model. It describes how a past contemporary society and landscape that are the backdrop to the writing of a novel are variously adapted on their journey firstly into and out of the novelist's imagination and into the novel, then as the novel passes through other agents such as critics, adapters, and interpreters, until finally we consume the novel, or an artefact derived from it. It assesses how the imagined worlds thus created and the way we receive them affect a novel's utility, alongside contemporary records, and testimony, as a historical resource.

This study looks specifically at English novels of the period from 1800 to around 1930. The justifications for choosing this period are three-fold. Firstly, this was a period when realist novels were to the fore. John Baxendale describes Victorian realist novels making 'social and physical reality their subject matter, dealing with real events and offering a recognisable account of the social world'.[66] Add to this Rae Greiner's idea of the existence of what she calls 'sympathetic realism' in nineteenth-century fiction, where 'fellow-

---

66   John Baxendale, *Priestley's England: J.B. Priestley and English Culture* (Manchester: Manchester University Press, 2007), p. 13.

feeling', sympathy of the reader to the characters and situations within the novel, was more important than simple descriptions of objects with regard to the task of 'maintaining reality'.[67] We therefore see fiction within this period as capable of connecting us to the world both outwardly in terms of its purely descriptive elements, and inwardly in terms of these sympathetic elements.

Secondly, this was also the period in which the novel gradually became a truly popular art form. Dennis Walder, giving Jane Austen's *Pride and Prejudice* as his first example, describes 'realist prose fiction' becoming the dominant literary form during the first half of the 19th century.[68] As Section 5.1 shows in more detail, this can be backed up by sales figures showing the growth in popularity of the novel. The largest initial print run of any of Austen's novels was only 2,500 and no new editions of her novels emerged until 15 years after her death. The more popular Walter Scott could sell four times as many copies of his novel *Rob Roy* just in the first fortnight after publication.[69] Through the growth of, and improvements in, education and literacy which culminated in the introduction of free universal education through the late 19th and early 20th centuries, the publication of novels such as those by Dickens in serial form, the introduction of cheap popular editions, and the increasing availability of libraries, sales and readership of novels increased.

By 1928 a novel such as J.B. Priestley's *The Good Companions* saw its publishers sending out 5,000 copies a day, and it was still selling 1,000 copies a week a whole year after publication.[70] Priestley saw himself, in his own words, 'out-of-date before I began',[71] the inheritor of a tradition of 'breadth and vitality' in fiction that he saw as going back to Henry Fielding, Walter Scott, and, to an extent, Dickens, and that he saw as being under attack from a new breed of modernist writers and critics typified by Virginia Woolf and F.R. Leavis.[72] This idea of Priestley being, at least in his own estimation, one of the last inheritors of a tradition of which Austen was an early exponent, made them convenient authors to bookend the study period.

Thirdly, novels from this period, the so-called 'classic' novels, have since the early part of the last century been a fruitful source for theatrical, film, and television productions, with some novels being adapted many times over, as is shown in Chapter 3. This chapter also demonstrates, however, that as a canon of classic novels developed, it represented only a small proportion of the total number of novelists and novels published during that period. In addition, as Chapter 2 shows, places and settings associated with authors and novels from this period, and adaptations thereof, have formed a large part of the literary tourism industry. Novels from this period therefore allow one to test all the elements of the proposed classic fiction process. Because of their classic nature, these novels are those most likely to have been encountered by present day consumers as novels or in

---

67   Rae Greiner, *Sympathetic Realism in Nineteenth-Century British Fiction* (Baltimore: Johns Hopkins University Press, 2012), p. 10.

68   Dennis Walder, 'The Genre Approach', in *The Realist Novel*, ed. by Dennis Walder (London: Routledge in association with the Open University, 1995), p. 4.

69   B. C. Southam, *Jane Austen: The Critical Heritage Volume 1 1811-1870* (London: Routledge, 1968), p. 4 of Introduction.

70   Lee Hanson and David Joy, 'Priestley's 'Happy Daydream' – Biographical Background', in *The Good Companions (2007 edition)*, ed. by Lee Hanson and David Joy (Ilkley: Great Northern Books, 2007), pp. 23-25.

71   J.B. Priestley, *Margin Released: A Writer's Reminiscences and Reflections* (London: William Heinemann, 1962), p. 154.

72   Baxendale (2007) pp. 15-17.

the form of adaptations or tourist site interpretations. If they are going to gain insights into historical times through fiction, it is therefore likely to be through these novels. This has meant that many novelists of the period within whose works there may be much to interest the historian, such as, for example, Benjamin Disraeli and George Gissing, have of necessity been excluded from detailed study here because of their lack of present-day mass visibility as novelists.

Regarding the specific novels used as case studies within this study, they were chosen as examples of how the process model might have worked in practice. Many other novels could have been chosen to make similar points and would have if space had allowed. With the limitations that existed, the decision was taken to examine specific novels at length within the case studies and to reference other novels in summary form to help emphasise the particular points being made. Note also that this study does not examine the specific *literary* merits of the novels being examined within the case studies as such, other than in the context of their value as historical resources.

Note also that the novels under discussion are those whose subject matters were, at the time they were written, contemporary or near contemporary to their authors. This excludes fiction that is consciously historical fiction, where authors such as Hilary Mantel and George Eliot may use the same techniques as a historical researcher to produce the imagined world of their fiction, rather than their experience and perceptions of elements of their own worlds. De Groot describes many such works as being 'obsessed with paratexts: footnotes, additions, acknowledgements, bibliographies, author information, maps', thus giving the reader a 'sense of authority, and authenticity'.[73] However, this sense of authority and authenticity is essentially a product of research. Within the novels chosen for this study, it comes from the experience of the novelists themselves – historical novels give different sorts of insights and would provoke a different kind of study. One should also state at this point that in carrying out the research for this study the writer has become more familiar with the conventional historical sources that link to the fiction that will be discussed, which may produce a tendency to see the expected in the literature being studied. It is difficult to stand outside such a process and measure it objectively and the writer is to a degree an agent in the process that is being defined.

Much of the classic fiction from this period remains in print and is an important part of the National Curriculum and the examination syllabus, at least within the discipline of English Literature. Outside of the academic field, however, many of these novels are known more by reputation, from their adaptations, or from the literary associations of tourist destinations, than from actually being read. The paradox is that we think we know their worlds intimately. Mention *Pride and Prejudice* and a picture appears in our minds of Regency country estates, but Section 2.3 shows that for many the picture may also include an image of Colin Firth as Mr Darcy in the 1995 BBC adaptation of *Pride and Prejudice*, and more specifically an image of him emerging from a pond at Lyme in Cheshire. Similarly, when we think of *Wuthering Heights*, we may remember a hike across the Yorkshire Moors and a visit to Top Withens,[74] especially when the association is emphasised by both the

---

73   Jerome de Groot, *The Historical Novel* (Abingdon: Routledge, 2010), p. 63.
74   A ruined farmhouse on the moors close to the village of Haworth, home of the Brontë family, which has become associated with the eponymous house in Emily Brontë's novel *Wuthering Heights.*

Haworth village and Brontë Parsonage websites.[75] With regard to consumer reactions use has been made within this study of consumer reviews of both literary places and classic adaptations of novels. It should be noted at this point that as people consciously decide to post reviews on a site such as Amazon, the reviewers are essentially self-selected, with the result that these are not strictly random selections drawn from the complete set of visitors to the literary place or of viewers of the adaptation. It would be a useful further exercise to ascertain whether a formally polled random selection of consumers would come up with the same spread of views.

The research for this study began with the understanding that critics, adapters, interpreters, and consumers of a piece of literary fiction all share a direct common progenitor in the author and the piece of fiction itself. There was also an understanding that members of each of these groups are also part of a more complex process in which they interact not just with the author but with other groups, with others in the same group, and with various outside influences. Much of the research that followed was therefore aimed at uncovering the links, interactions, and influences within the proposed classic fiction process model.

The research carried out to test the initial concept of a classic fiction process model was of necessity both deductive and inductive, deductive in terms of discovering direct verifiable instances of authors using real-life examples within their fiction, but also inductive in terms of discerning instances where the evidence suggests authors using real life but does not provide direct proof. The research began with a basic framework of what the process flow within the model might involve. This was amended and enhanced as a developing theory emerged from the data, and further data examples were chosen accordingly.[76]

When examining the possibility of the use of a process-oriented approach note was also taken of work that has been done within the field of digital humanities, especially regarding how particular phenomena can be quantified and modelled. Examples found included Claire Battershill and Shawna Ross talking of using digital humanities techniques to 'study digital cultures, tools and concepts' and using 'computational methods to explore the traditional objects of humanistic enquiry', be that examining aspects of a present-day or historical city from digital mapping resources or carrying out analyses of digital texts.[77] In terms of a specifically process-oriented approach, Johanna Drucker notes the popularity of visualisations within the digital humanities, specifically 'network diagrams, directed graphs, and other depictions of relationships', and their ability to provide 'static expressions of complex systems'.[78] Finally, Gérald Péoux advocates the use of a flowchart approach to the study of past scholarly texts using a process definition approach borrowed

75   *Top Withens – Withins – Bronte Country*, (Haworth: haworth-village.org.uk) <http://www.haworth-village. org.uk/brontes/places/top_withens.asp>; *The Brontës and Haworth – Brontë Places*, (Haworth: The Brontë Society) <https://www.bronte.org.uk/the-brontes-and-haworth>.

76   As such, this approach mirrors what A.L. Glaser and B.G. Strauss call 'theoretical sampling'. A.L. Strauss and B.G. Glaser, *The Discovery of Grounded Theory: Strategies for Qualitative Research* (New York: Aldine de Gruyter, 1967), pp. 45-46.

77   Claire Battershill and Shawna Ross, Using Digital Humanities in the Classroom : A Practical Introduction for Teachers, Lecturers and Students (London: Bloomsbury, 2017), pp. 3-4.

78   Johanna Drucker, 'Graphical Approaches to the Digital Humanities', in *A New Companion to Digital Humanities*, ed. by Susan Schreibman, Ray Siemens, and John Unsworth (New York,: John Wiley, 2016). <http://ebookcentral.proquest.com/lib/uocuk/detail.action?docID=4093339>.

from an industrial context, through means of 'a proper translation', to uncover the decision processes followed by the historians in compiling the text.[79]

Within the area of adaptation Deborah Cartmell and Imelda Whelehan provide a visualisation of the sub-processes visible within adaptation theory that echo many influences on adaptation that will be described in Chapter 3, but which makes no attempt at mapping it as any kind of process. Similarly, Yvonne Griggs only hints at the existence of process within adaptation that could plausibly be mapped in describing an adaptation as evolving 'from a complex web of adaptive processes related to existing narratives, cultural mores, industrial practices, and to the agenda of those engaging in its construction', and thereby again implying the links and relationships that will be described in Chapter 3.[80]

Given this writer's background in Quality Management Systems (QMS) within the field of Information Technology, the approach taken in mapping the classic fiction process model was not therefore taken specifically from the field of digital humanities, but was largely influenced by quality standards within QMS, and specifically the ISO 9001 process standard defined by the International Organisation for Standardisation. As defined, the ISO 9001 process approach seeks to discover how an organisation's processes operate as an 'integrated and complete system'.[81] In terms of defining a process flow it talks about defining the network of processes and their interaction through consideration of the following:

- The inputs and outputs of each process,
- Process interaction and interfaces on which processes depend or enable,
- Optimum effectiveness and efficiency of the sequence,
- Risks to the effectiveness of process interaction.[82]

Of course, the writers of ISO 9001 were interested in how one defines flows that have tangible and measurable inputs and outputs, and within which processes are consistent and standardised. Such standardisation will not be found within the process that is defined here, and nor should it, given that the process is founded on the varying perceptions of, and influences on, individual actors within the process, and that the various actions within the process have largely happened in the past. However, the idea of information flowing through a system, the many links and interactions between the various actors in that system, from author to critic to adapter to interpreter to consumer, and the many influences that form the input to the various actions within the process, all chimed with describing the classic fiction process as a form of process flow. Within ISO 9001 a process is defined and measured in terms of 'optimum effectiveness and efficiency' with the potential outcome that the measurements be used to loop back into improvements in the system.[83] Within the classic fiction process, no such objective need be contemplated – the system of writing and developing fiction is what it is, and one is not seeking to improve it. The hope is, however, that by defining the process and all the potential links

---

79   Gérald Péoux, 'To Visualize Past Communities: A Solution from Contemporary Practices in the Industry for the Digital Humanities', *Digital Humanities Quarterly*, 11 (2017).

80   Yvonne Griggs, The Bloomsbury Introduction to Adaptation Studies: Adapting the Canon in Film, TV, Novels and Popular Culture (London: Bloomsbury, 2016), p. 5.

81   *The Process Approach in ISO 9001:2015*, (Geneva: International Organisation for Standardization, 2015).

82   Ibid. p. 4.

83   Ibid. p. 7.

and interactions within it, this study might help in an improved understanding of the historical information flowing through it and of the potential points at which that historical information might be enhanced, altered or compromised.

Because this study is concerned with descriptions of past and imagined worlds, most of the data collected and processed was descriptive and textual, and therefore of a qualitative nature. This qualitative data was, however, supplemented with the collection of small amounts of quantitative data to provide objective background data where required to measure specific phenomena such as the growth of readership for novels through the 19th century or the growth of a canon of classic novels. Because many of these data sources either informed, or derived from, an author's novel they can all be considered as primary sources for this study given that they form part of the process model being investigated. Such sources included:

- Novels,
- Diaries, letters, and other autobiographical information pertaining to the author,
- Adaptations of novels for film and television,
- Critical reviews of novels and adaptations,
- Expository information by adapters and filmmakers pertaining to the creation of specific adaptations,
- Interpretive schemes in literary places, including literary guidebooks,
- Expository information by interpreters pertaining to literary places.

The novels contain the initial descriptive elements that drive the process model forward, whereas the other sources, either directly or through induction, help in understanding how the imagined world within a novel is perceived, adapted, and interpreted.

Other primary sources were those that provided real-life background and corroboration to the imagined world presented within the fiction. These included contemporary accounts, reports, drawings, and photographs of the contemporary world in which the author lived. The only true secondary sources were those that provided third-party information on either the author, the novels, or the contemporary world. These included literary biographies (as opposed to autobiographies), and historical studies and surveys that provided information that could not be gleaned from the primary sources listed.

The various sources collected during the course of the research served to establish specific sets of components which would then develop and refine the classic fiction process model. The first set of components consists of the various actors that are involved within the process model, either actively or passively, including all who have the potential to be agents of change. For each of them there is an input, some form of activity or 'action', and various physical and mental outputs or 'artefacts'. The following list therefore comprises the generic terms that are used throughout this study to define those who engage in some form or another with the process model:

- **Novelists** – the writers of the original source material,
- **Critics** – initially the contemporary critics who review the original novel, but also later critics who review the various film and television adaptations of the novel,
- **Adapters** – those who take the novel and adapt it for the purposes of film and television productions. The focus is on the adapters who actually take the text of the novel

and recreate it within the text of the adaptation, but the category includes all those involved in the creative process of the adaptation such as directors, set designers and costume designers,

- **Interpreters** – those who curate, interpret, and present tourist sites devoted to literature, plus those who write literary guidebooks,
- **Consumers** – those who ultimately read novels, view adaptations of those novels or visit tourist sites devoted to literature.

The second component set within the model consists of specific mental actions made by the actors that layer the view of the world of the novel. Of these perception and reception are the means by which we obtain information about the world, and interpretation and adaptation are the means by which we take that information and modify it to suit the requirements of the artefact we are producing:

- **Perception** – the process of forming a mental image of a landscape and a society. The novelist forms that image from first-hand knowledge and experience, as can the contemporary critic, whereas the consumer in the present day forms the image second-hand from the reception of the artefacts associated with the novel and the novelist,
- **Adaptation** – the means by which an existing artefact, for example a novel, is edited, expanded, and generally changed to produce a new artefact, for example a film or television version of that novel. The author of the original novel may also use the processes of adaptation on their perception of the contemporary world for literary, dramatic, or social purposes,
- **Interpretation** – similar to adaptation, but in this case the means by which the essence of the artefact, and its creator, are extracted to produce a description of that artefact for use in a guidebook or at a heritage site,
- **Reception** – the process of consuming one of the artefacts associated with a novelist or a novel, be it the novel itself, an adaptation of the novel, or a literary guidebook or site.

The third component set consists of the worlds that are accessed or created by the actors during the course of the process model. These begin with the real past world perceived by the author in the writing of a novel and continue with the various imagined worlds that are created via adaptation and interpretation, linked to each of artefacts listed below. Each of the imagined worlds is then received by subsequent actors in the process model and forms a potential input into their own imagined world. The creation of each imagined world is, in effect, a mediation. For the author, the novel's imagined world is a textual mediation with elements of the author's contemporary world, and for subsequent actors the mediation with that world is of necessity via the novel and any other relevant previous artefacts in the process. The layers that thereby build up between these imagined worlds and the initial past world, as we will see, lie at the heart of this study.

The fourth component set consists of the specific artefacts produced by the actors that are relevant to the particular point in the process model, each of which, as suggested above, can create an imagined world. The concentration will be on the following artefacts:

- Novels,
- Critical reviews,
- Film and television adaptations,
- Interpreted literary sites.

The final component set consists of the external influences that have an effect on each actor's actions. If we take Jewell-Lapan's statement about perception being affected by a lifetime's knowledge and experience,[84] then one can assume that these are specific to each actor in the process model, and specific influences are described within the case studies. However, amongst those that are discussed are:

- Cultural mores,
- Level of education,
- Social and Political status,
- Gender.

Together with visits to the places and landscapes within which the individual authors lived and worked and within which their novels were set, use is made of all these sources in testing the validity of the process model.

1.5 Overall Structure

This introduction sets the groundwork for the following chapters in explaining how the ideas behind the study fit in with past and current thinking about the links between fiction and history and in particular the usefulness, or otherwise, of fiction as a historical resource. The contribution this study makes to such thinking is two-fold. Firstly, there is the definition of the end-to-end classic fiction process model. It describes how the production and consumption by various agents of the various artefacts and imagined worlds produced during the course of the process model are affected by certain specific actions carried out by the actors at each stage, and how those artefacts interact with each other. Secondly, by highlighting the complexities of the process model and the opportunities for it producing misleading perceptions on the part of consumers, this study assesses both the potential pitfalls and benefits of using fiction as a resource for history, either in the field of education or for the lay consumer.

To that end, the constituent parts of the process model are described through an examination of the actors involved, the imagined worlds perceived, and the artefacts produced at each stage in the process. The approach taken has been to begin the discussion at the point in the process that is furthest removed from the author and the novel itself and potentially has the largest number of layers separating the consumer and the novel, namely the area of literary tourism, and to then work back through the process towards the point at which the author actually writes the novel, removing layers in the process. The process model is therefore split into the following constituent steps, which are covered in the sections indicated:

- **Interpretation** (Chapter 2) – where curators and interpreters create interpretive com-mentary in a literary house or place associated with that author using the life of an

---

84   Jewell-Lapan (1936).

author, the past in which the author lived, and the imagined worlds that the author created within their novels,

- **Adaptation** (Chapter 3) – where filmmakers transform the imagined world of the novel into the imagined world of film or television adaptations, influenced by their own research into the past that the author perceived, and by previous literary adaptations of that novel, or of contemporaneous novels,
- **Criticism** (Chapter 4) – where contemporary critics receive the novel and compare the imagined world they perceive within the novel with their own perception (or lack thereof) of the elements of the past that the author used within the novel,
- **Writing** (Chapter 5) – where novelists perceive elements of the past in which they lived and adapt them into the imagined world of the novel.

Running throughout the process model is the action of reception, where consumers reading the imagined world of a novel or viewing the imagined world of an adaptation, may use their own imagined world perceived as a result of that reception to make judgements of the past world perceived by the author. Chapter 6 looks at various ways in which these various methods of reception could be enhanced to facilitate the use of the novel, in its various forms, as a historical resource.

Through Chapters 2 to 6 are threaded case studies of novelists chosen to illustrate the workings of the process model in practice. These are all authors whose novels are still in print, whose novels have been adapted for film and television, and who to varying extents are the subjects of literary tourism. Whilst each author is mentioned in most of these chapters, a major part of each chapter includes case studies based on the research carried out on one or two specific novels. Each case study was chosen to show how specific elements of the classic fiction process model work in practice and examine how worlds, artefacts and influences worked on actors to produce further artefacts. Any number of novels could have been chosen as case studies to illustrate the model. The intention is that the ones that have been chosen acts as exemplars for the wider set of fiction that was potentially available. Taken together, the case studies demonstrate how this overall study crosses the subject boundaries of pure literary or historical research by bringing ideas around the writing, critical analysis, adaptation and interpretation into a single overriding process within which these ideas can influence each other.

The case studies for Chapter 2 contrasts the literary tourism that has grown up around Thomas Hardy and Jane Austen. In the case of the former the descriptive depth of Hardy's writings, along with the identification of particular fictional locations within Hardy's writings with real locations in Dorset and the West Country, led to a novel-based tourist industry based around the idea of 'Hardy Country'. For Austen, an author in whose writings pure description paid a lesser part than for Hardy, the case study investigates how the author-based tourism that has grown up around her writings is linked less to a Hardy-esque sense of place, and more to a sense of Austen the person. Chapter 3 looks at adaptations of Hardy to show how filmmakers approach the task of creating an imagined world for their adaptations that is perceived by consumers as authentic. The success of their efforts is then tested against comments within newspaper and journal reviews of the adaptations. Taking the ultimate consumer's point of view, Chapter 3 also looks at how perceptions of the authenticity that the adapters strive for are expressed in customer reviews of the DVD of an adaptation of a novel by Elizabeth Gaskell. It places these alongside the perceptions of authenticity expressed in reviews of a current edition of the novel itself in order to understand the different influences that might bear on the consumer when viewing the adaptation as opposed to reading the novel. The case studies in Chapter 4 looks at contemporary critical reviews of novels by Gaskell and Thomas Hardy to ascertain how perceptions of the world can differ between writer and critic and therefore affect the critic's perception of truth within the fiction. Chapter 4 studies the descriptive content in novels by Elizabeth Gaskell and Jane Austen. It contrasts Gaskell's vivid descriptions of social and working conditions in industrial Manchester with Austen's relative lack of descriptive content within the imagined worlds of her novels, whilst asserting that examination of Austen's characters' interactions may make it possible to see the historical social geography of those landscapes within those worlds. The final case study in Chapter 6 takes the issues around the past and the imagined versions of it, the author's writing process, critical reception, adaptation, and literary tourism, and moves them one stage further. Using aspects of J.B. Priestley's novel, *The Good Companions*, it examines ways in which a novel and the artefacts that have developed around it and its author could be deconstructed in order to be used practically as a resource for the teaching and understanding of history.

Chapter 7 ties things together in two ways. It describes the completed classic fiction process model and return to both Sparshott's question about truth being found in works of fiction and the question of the use of novels as historical resources. It summarises the conclusions that can be drawn from the model regarding the usefulness or otherwise of the imagined worlds associated with a work of fiction. It suggests that examining any artefact from within the process model involves an assessment of the veracity of the links between the imagined world of the artefact and the past. The further away one gets from the original source, *i.e.* the novel, the greater chance that the layering effect of the various actors, actions, and artefacts in play at subsequent points in the process model creates in the mind of the consumer an imagined world that is increasingly further removed from the past world than was the original imagined world of the novel.

As a practical step, it uses these conclusions to suggest possible ways ahead in the use of the classic fiction process model as both an educational and a creative tool. As an educational tool this study proposes that knowledge of the intricacies of the process model along with use of various deconstructive techniques helps evaluate the usefulness of the historical insights one might get from the various artefacts within the model. As a creative tool the study suggests that adapters and interpreters could use the process model in the act of artefact creation to understand both the process build-up of which they are a part and the influences that affect the potential consumers of the artefact.

The Literary Tourism Process

2.1 Introduction

This chapter begins the task of uncovering the layers that translate the past that informed the imagined world created by an author in writing a piece of fiction into the imagined world that the general consumer perceives when receiving that fiction in the form of the original novel, a critical review, an adaptation, or the interpretation within a literary place, and placing the same within the context of the overall classic fiction process model. It concerns itself with the part of the process that has the greatest potential for complexity in the nature and variety of those layers, especially given its ability to be influenced by all of the other artefacts within the model, namely the area of literary tourism.

Interpreters of places associated with authors and their works seek to create visitor presentations that provide insights into the life of the author, the works that they produced during that life, and the historical context within which those works were created. What is of interest here is the degree to which the descriptive content of the novels themselves can assist with this interpretation, either directly or indirectly. To this end the chapter contrasts tourism that is a mediation between the tourist, the *novel*, and the world within that novel, and tourism that is more explicitly a mediation between the tourist, the *author*, and the world of that author. For the purposes of this study, these two types of tourism are referred to as 'novel-based' and 'author-based'. The chapter concludes by showing how novel-based tourism can be seen as part of the overall process model in that it can be the means by which readers of a novel, or consumers of an adaptation of a novel, can both immerse themselves in the imagined world of the novel or adaptation and attempt to place that imagined world in the context of a historical past. To begin, however, one should understand what one means by a 'literary place' in the context of novel- and author-based tourism, and how such a place may be viewed by a potential visitor.

John Tribe summed up tourism as having occurred if one has travelled from one place to another, has motives for undertaking that travel, and engages in activity at the place travelled to.[85] With reference to travel motivated by literature, that destination is likely to be a 'literary place', a place associated in some way, shape or form with a piece of literature and/or its author. A literary place can have many forms. Dallen Timothy lists the following candidates:

---

85   John Tribe, 'The Indiscipline of Tourism', *Annals of Tourism Research*, 24 (1997), pp. 638-57.

- An author's home
- Landscapes within which an author lived and worked
- Settings of the stories created by an author
- Museums associated with an author
- Sets and locations of films based on the author's work[86]

In terms of this study the third and the fifth types are of specific interest, as they directly put the place in the context of novel-based rather than author-based tourism. These are literary places that are, to quote Dallen Timothy and Stephen Boyd, 'fusions between the real world in which the writers lived and the illusory worlds depicted in the stories'.[87] To quote Mike Robinson, 'creative fiction does not exist in isolation from the "real world", it is part of it', and to a degree that is dependent upon the level of detail in the fiction, 'images of real places are absorbed into the consciousness of reader and tourist alike'.[88] The visitor desires to inhabit the 'real' world of the fiction. As Harald Hendrix writes, literary tourism emanates from a 'desire to go beyond' mere admiration for the work of an author, and a 'dissatisfaction with the limits of that very work'.[89]

Some literary places may of course contain elements of both author-based and novel-based tourism, and the tourist's motivations for visiting them may be similarly mixed. For example, tourists might visit Hill Top Farm, Beatrix Potter's Lake District home, because it is at the same time the former home of Potter, the setting for many of her stories, and a source of nostalgia for a childhood consuming those stories.[90] In the context of this study, the second of these motivations would be of prime relevance.

A visitor indulging in novel-based tourism may be someone to whom an author is a known quantity, appreciated over time, and who therefore has a conscious motivation to visit places associated with the novel and whose visits are effectively literary 'pilgrimages'. Dean MacCannell draws the parallels between literary pilgrimages and religious pilgrimages, with both being 'quests for authentic experiences.'[91] Conversely, the visitor could be one to whom the visit is based on a casual acquaintance with an author via, say, a film adaptation, or one to whom the literary place is simply the next place to tick off from a list in a guidebook or tourist brochure. An example of this is Lyme in Cheshire on the western fringes of the Peak District, which in external shots stood in for Pemberley in the 1995 BBC adaptation of *Pride and Prejudice,* and which makes capital out of this manufactured Austen connection, not least in the merchandise sold in the National Trust gift shop. Robinson was effectively talking about 'pilgrims' when describing 'tourists exploring the world as depicted

86   Adapted from Dallen J. Timothy, *Cultural Heritage and Tourism: An Introduction, Aspects of tourism texts* (Bristol ; Buffalo: Channel View Publications, 2011), p. 67.

87   Dallen J. Timothy and Stephen W. Boyd, *Heritage Tourism, Themes in tourism* (New York: Prentice Hall, 2003), p. 40.

88   Mike Robinson, 'Literature-Tourism Relationships', in *Literature and Tourism: Essays in the Reading and Writing of Tourism*, ed. by Mike Robinson and Hans Christian Andersen (London: Continuum, 2002), p. 54.

89   Harald Hendrix, 'From Early Modern to Romantic Literary Tourism: A Diachronical Perspective', in *Literary Tourism and Nineteenth-Century Culture*, ed. by Nicola J. Watson (Basingstoke: Palgrave Macmillan, 2009), p. 14.

90   David Herbert, 'Literary Places, Tourism and the Heritage Experience', *Annals of Tourism Research,* 28 (2001), pp. 312-33.

91   Dean MacCannell, 'Staged Authenticity – Arrangements of Social Space in Tourist Settings', *American Journal of Sociology,* 79 (1973), pp. 589-603.

in literature, discovering real locations used in fiction and seeking to correlate fictional locations with some markers of reality'.[92] There is a potential conflict in the way that literary places are curated and presented between catering for the needs of the literary pilgrim and those of the casual tourist. Herbert saw an increasing tendency to cater for the latter in that many literary places are now 'social constructions' designed to attract those who visit 'out of curiosity and general interest' rather than the dedicated pilgrims they now outnumber.[93]

The challenge for those who interpret literary places is to cater within that interpretation site for everyone, from the most dedicated of pilgrims to the least knowledgeable of casual tourists, and somehow make the place interesting to them all. If they take a deliberately specialist or a deliberately populist approach, they might risk either baffling the casual tourist in the first instance or alienating the literary pilgrim in the second. Herbert, in talking about the 'exceptional' versus the 'general' qualities of a literary place, is essentially talking about this challenge, balancing the exceptional needs of the pilgrim with the general needs of the tourist, and making the site equally attractive and saleable to both groups.[94] This balance may depend on who actually owns the literary place and presents it to the public. The National Trust or a local authority presenting a literary place such as Lyme may have a remit to inform a wider public than the curators of a literary pilgrimage site like the Jane Austen's House Museum, and the visitor presentations may vary in the degree of pre-knowledge expected of the visitor as a result.

The remainder of this chapter considers aspects of novel-based literary tourism as it has developed for the authors within the study period, with specific reference to two of those authors, Thomas Hardy and Jane Austen. Section 2.2 examines how literary tourism based specifically on the content of Hardy's novels began to develop in Dorset in the late 19th and early 20th centuries, and how Hardy tourism in the Dorchester area today is still intrinsically connected more to Hardy's novels than to Hardy the man. Section 2.3 demonstrates that whilst interest in Austen's novels has in general led to author-based tourism that concentrates on the author as a person and on the re-creation of the author's life, the growth of adaptations of those novels had resulted in a growth of a form of novel-based tourism based not on those past places that informed the novel, but on places that were the locations used within the adaptations.

The case studies also assess the degree to which the tourism around these two authors is biased towards the literary pilgrim or towards the more general tourist. The assessments in this regard, and more generally regarding the quantity and quality of interpretations, are based on the writer's personal observations as a consumer of the interpretations and on publicly available customer reviews on websites such as Trip Advisor and Amazon, and any conclusions are based on observations and data thus derived. Further assessment of the motivations of visitors, and the degree of their foreknowledge of authors and novels when visiting literary places, could involve customer surveying at literary sites, though the sheer quantity of data within the review websites exceeds what would be available from such surveying. Both to a large extent also involve respondents being self-selected, on the website in terms on the respondent making an active decision to review, and in customer surveys in terms of a candidate making an active decision to respond to the survey.

---

92   Robinson (2002) p. 40.
93   David Herbert, 'Place and Society in Jane Austen's England', *Geography*, 76 (1991), pp. 193-208.
94   Herbert (2001).

2.2 Thomas Hardy – Wessex and Dorset

Section 4.2 will outline Thomas Hardy's roots in the heart of the Dorset countryside, how the language and customs of rural Dorset fed into his descriptions of a fictional 'Wessex', the degree to which those descriptions were accepted as authentic by reviewers of his books, and the extent to which Hardy formalised the links between the fictional Wessex and the historical Dorset within his fiction. As Hardy's fiction developed, he increasingly saw that the Dorset he knew was changing, with increasing industrialisation of agriculture and improved transport links reducing the county's sense of isolation. Thus, Simon Gattrell talks of him believing himself to be 'the historian of a Wessex now passed, the recorder of a series of unique micro-environments, ways of life and speech, which together had formed a cultural whole'.[95] This case study draws on this sense within Hardy's literature of him being a recorder that caused Margaret Drabble to call the resultant Wessex 'one of the best known of literary landscapes', a place where the fictional names he gave to the many locations he described 'have sometimes confused themselves with their originals' such that 'fiction created fact'.[96] It endeavours to demonstrate, with regard to Hardy-based literary places, how important Hardy's novels are in the way those places are presented to visitors and the degree to which different interpreters attempt to use the fiction to mediate with the historical past.

Hardy wrote his last full-length piece of fiction, *Jude the Obscure*, in 1895. The following decades saw an expansion of interest in the idea of Wessex and of people actually visiting the locations that were supposed to have informed Hardy's Wessex locations. Examples from the early 20th century of books describing themselves as guides to 'Hardy Country', were works by Charles Harper,[97] R. Thurston Hopkins,[98] Hermann Lea,[99] and Bertram Windle.[100] Hardy's active espousal of the idea of Wessex is reflected in the fact that Windle's book actually acknowledges Hardy's 'generous assistance', without which the book's contents would have been 'much less complete than it is hoped they will be found to be'. Indeed, he believes this assistance has enabled him to speak with 'certainty as to the identification of certain of the spots.'[101]

In his preface, Harper expounds on the attractions of Dorset, 'a land of great dairies, of flowers and bees, of rural industries, where rustic ways and speech and habits of thought live long', to which he sees as having been added 'the romantic interest of Mr. Thomas Hardy's novels of rural life and character, in which real places are introduced with a lavish hand.'[102] He then proceeds to tour Dorset and the surrounding areas, looking specifically for the elements of Dorset that, he believes, have found their way into Hardy's novels, illustrating them both with extracts from the relevant novels and a degree of historical context. Here is part of Harper's description of the village of Puddletown, Hardy's

---

95   Simon Gattrell, 'Wessex', in *The Cambridge Companion to Thomas Hardy*, ed. by Dale Kramer (Cambridge: Cambridge University Press, 1999), p. 31.

96   Margaret Drabble, 'Thomas Hardy and Wessex', in *The Oxford Guide to Literary Britain & Ireland*, ed. by Daniel Hahn and Nicholas Robins (Oxford: Oxford University Press, 2009). <https://www.oxfordreference.com/view/10.1093/acref/9780198614609.001.0001/acref-9780198614609-e-2794>.

97   Charles G. Harper, *The Hardy Country: Literary Landmarks of the Wessex Novels* (London: Adam & Charles Black, 1904).

98   R. Thurston Hopkins, *Thomas Hardy's Dorset* (London: Cecil Palmer, 1922).

99   Hermann Lea, *Thomas Hardy's Wessex* (London: Macmillan & Co., 1913).

100 Bertram C. A. Windle, *The Wessex of Thomas Hardy* (London & New York: John Lane: The Bodley Head, 1901).

101 Ibid. p. xi.

102 Harper (1904) pp. v-vi.

Weatherbury, with a reference to the churchyard where Fanny Robin was buried in *Far from the Madding Crowd*, which is followed in the book with a reference to the real-life location of the model for Bathsheba Everdene's farm in the same novel.[103]

> This church of Piddletown, or "Weatherbury," is the scene of Sergeant Troy's belated remorse and of the acute misery of that incident where, coming by the light of a lantern and planting flowers on Fanny Robin's grave, he sleeps in the porch while the rain-storm breaks and the storm-water from the gurgoyles of the tower spouts furiously over the spot.[104]

What is noteworthy is that there is a sense in the guides that the world that Hardy describes is already one that is in the historical past, and that the tourist might use the guide to place the imagined world of the novel in a real-world setting, and to place that setting in a historical context. For example, in the section on Puddletown Harper writes of the beginnings of change in the village, that it is 'not the Weatherbury he [Hardy] once knew' being 'very largely rebuilt' with 'rather stern and prim limestone cottages'.[105] In the opening chapter of his guide Hopkins echoes Harper's comments about 'rustic speech and habits' by describing the 'mellow sound of the speech that was so dear to Raleigh and Drake', but laments that these are 'now giving way to the new order of life, alas'.[106]

Each of the guides contains copious information on the town at the centre of Hardy's world, Casterbridge, Hardy's version of Dorchester. With a copy of Hopkins' guide, one would have had access to the following information about the King's Arms Hotel in Dorchester's High East Street:

> The visitor will be interested in the old inns of Dorchester. In High Street East stands, just as described in *The Mayor of Casterbridge*, that fine and most comfortable of country hotels – the King's Arms. From a doorway on the opposite side of the street Susan and Elizabeth-Jane, amid the crowd, witnessed the dinner given to the mayor. Through the archway of this inn Boldwood carried Bathsheba, fainting at the news of her husband's death.[107]

Hermann Lea's 1913 guide would have enabled one to follow the plot of *The Mayor of Casterbridge* through the streets of Dorchester as Casterbridge, whilst at the same time linking this to both the history of Dorchester and the life of Hardy himself, as in this example:

> Returning to our wayfarers, we see them standing before "a grizzled church, whose massive square tower rose unbroken into the darkening sky". In this we recognise the Perpendicular Church of St. Peter, from whose belfry the curfew bell still rings... It is said

---

103   Note that at the time this book was written the village was known generally as Piddletown. That has since been bowdlerised to current name of Puddletown.
104   Harper (1904) pp. 56-57.
105   Ibid. p. 53.
106   Hopkins (1922) p. 14.
107   Ibid. p. 77.

Figure 2.1: Organ and West Gallery, St Michael's Church, Stinsford.

Figure 2.2: Damers House, Dorset County Hospital. The former Dorchester Workhouse.

by some archaeologists that St. Peter's Church is built on the site of a Roman Temple... Inside are some interesting effigies; the Hardy Chapel at the end of the south aisle brings back to us forcibly our author's connection with the town through his ancestors.[108]

These three guides assume the reader has some acquaintance with Hardy's novels in terms of the places described and the language used. They are works that would have appealed to those at the 'pilgrim' end of the tourist spectrum, and as such they were part of a wider interest at the time in locating fictional landscapes in the real world, exemplified by William Sharp's 1904 work *Literary Geography*. This attempted to set the literary landscapes of the likes of Dickens, Walter Scott, the Brontës, and Robert Louis Stevenson in the real world, illustrated by photographs and sketch maps.[109]

As described in the previous section, the rise of mass tourism since the publication of these early Hardy literary guidebooks has led to a distinction between the literary pilgrim who would have been the main consumer of those guides and the general tourist to whom a literary place may simply be one of a number of places to visit. The remainder of this section examines the types of tourist interpretations available to visitors to Dorset today, the types of historical insights that they give and whether they are geared towards the pilgrim or general tourist.[110] For the dedicated Hardy pilgrim visiting Dorset today, simply reading relevant passages from Hardy's novels whilst visiting the real-life locations that Hardy-sanctioned guidebooks have linked to those passages may do two things. Firstly, it may bring the novel to three-dimensional life for the visitor, and secondly it may provide through the fictional description a historical background for the real-life location. One such example is Hardy, in *Under the Greenwood Tree*, describing the village band playing for church services in Mellstock church:

> The gallery of Mellstock Church has a status and sentiment of its own... Old William sat in the centre of the front row, his violoncello between his knees and two singers on each hand. Behind him, on the left, came the treble singers and Dick; and on the right the tranter and the tenors. Further back was old Mail with the altos and supernumeraries.[111]

The model for Mellstock church was the parish church at Stinsford, near Hardy's birthplace. During Hardy's childhood, musical accompaniment came from a similar village band to that which Hardy describes, and in Stinsford they performed from above the west door. During the course of the 19th century the village bands were replaced by organs, as described in the novel. What the passage may therefore help one to do, when visiting Stinsford, is both to bring the novel alive in the context of its real-life location, and to recreate and visualise the historical antecedents of the current church setup (Figure 2.1).[112]

---

108 Lea (1913) p. 89. The quote is from Thomas Hardy, *The Mayor of Casterbridge* (London: CRW Publishing Ltd, 1886 (2003 edition)), p. 44.
109 William Sharp, *Literary Geography* (London: Offices of the Pall Mall Publications, 1904).
110 The observations that follow are based on a field trip to Dorset undertaken in 2014. As such they are, like the novels they reference, a snapshot in time.
111 Thomas Hardy, *Under The Greenwood Tree* (Ware: Wordsworth, 1872 (1994 edition)), pp. 26-27.
112 According to Legg, the gallery itself was remodelled to its current form in 1996. Rodney Legg, *Thomas Hardy's Dorset* (Wellington: Halsgrove, 2011), p. 24.

The fact that Hardy's grave is in the churchyard means that Stinsford church is an obvious destination for Hardy pilgrims.[113] However, there is little in the way of interpretation within the church to provide any sort of historical insights for the general tourist. When visiting for the purposes of research, the only item found was a print of a painting of the 'Mellstock Quire' from *Under the Greenwood Tree*, but no mention was made in its description of either the connection to the novel or to the significance of the gallery choir in terms of the history of the church.

Other pilgrimage locations that can be directly linked to Hardy's novels also pass without any formal on-site acknowledgement. The old Dorchester Workhouse, built in 1836, is now a wing of the Dorset County Hospital (Figure 2.2), and was the model for the workhouse in which Fanny Robin delivers her stillborn child and dies in *Far from the Madding Crowd*. A blue plaque simply states, 'Dorchester Workhouse 1836 – Architect George Wilkins – Chapel added 1870', making no mention of the link to Hardy. The general tourist passing by without a guidebook might simply notice a particularly distinctive NHS building. A dedicated pilgrim might, as did this writer, seek out the location and in the context of Hardy's description in the novel gain some insights into the historical appearance of the building when it was a workhouse, which one assumes is either accurate or prototypical depending on how much Hardy took from life:

> Masses of ivy grew up, completely covering the walls, till the place looked like an abbey... The stone edifice consisted of a central mass and two wings, whereon stood as sentinels a few small chimneys... In the wall was a gate, and by the gate a bell-pull formed of a hanging wire.[114]

What could be seen as bridging the gap between the Hardy pilgrim and the more general tourist is a pamphlet produced in 2014 by local councils in conjunction with the Thomas Hardy Society that the publishers believed would 'help you explore the area that inspired Thomas Hardy throughout his life'.[115] It contains a brief biography of Hardy describing how he used the locations and landscapes of the area as raw material of his fiction, as well as information on adaptations of Hardy novels that have been filmed in the area. The reverse of the pamphlet describes the 'Hardy Trail', a route through the region that explicitly links actual locations on the ground with their fictional counterparts. It gives the literary pilgrim the raw material for further investigation of Hardy Country and the general tourist a brief introduction to the idea of Hardy Country, especially by putting it in the context of adaptations they may have seen, particularly the new adaptation of *Far from the Madding Crowd* that had just been released at the time of the publication of the leaflet.

The idea of a mediation between the author and fictional and past worlds is bought out clearly in the place descriptions on the reverse side of the pamphlet where the historical origins of certain points of interest are emphasised by relating them to their appearance

---

113   Hardy always wanted to be buried here in the same grave as his late first wife, Emma. However, the executor of his will insisted he be buried in Poet's Corner in Westminster Abbey. The compromise was that his heart be interred here and the rest of him in London. The story of his two funerals is told in Claire Tomalin, *Thomas Hardy: The Time-Torn Man* (London: Penguin, 2007), pp. 370-76.

114   Thomas Hardy, *Far from the Madding Crowd* (Ware: Wordsworth, 1874 (1993 edition)), p. 212.

115   *Exploring Thomas Hardy's West Dorset*, (Dorchester: West Dorset District Council and Weymouth & Portland Borough Council / Thomas Hardy Society, 2014).

within Hardy's novels. For example, connections are made between the tithe-barn in Cerne Abbas and Bathsheba's barn in *Far from the Madding Crowd*, between Lower Lewell Farm in West Stafford and Talbothays Dairy in *Tess of the D'Urbervilles*, and between St Michael's church in Stinsford and the church in *Under the Greenwood Tree*.[116]

A similar approach with regard to Charles Dickens, but on a smaller scale, is made in a pamphlet in the City of London City Walks series, entitled *Dickens's Magic Lantern*, compiled by an academic who is also a trustee of the Charles Dickens Museum.[117] It describes a self-guided walk that starts at the Charles Dickens Museum in Dickens' former home in Doughty Street, travels through Clerkenwell and winds its way around the City of London before finishing at St Paul's Cathedral. The text gives historical information about Dickens and his life, but also points out particular locations, outlining their historical provenance alongside their appearance within specific Dickens novels. The pamphlet, for example, draws the connections between the old Central Criminal Court and scenes in *Oliver Twist*, *Great Expectations*, and *Tale of Two Cities*, between the One Tun pub and 'The Three Cripples' in *Oliver Twist*, and between Bleeding Heart Yard and *Little Dorrit*.[118] The pamphlet, whilst containing elements of author-based tourism, concerns itself predominantly with novel-based tourism in the same way as the Dorset Hardy pamphlet, by engaging in a dialogue between present-day London, Victorian London, and the descriptive elements within Dickens' novels.

Returning to Hardy, a similar dialogue between the modern, the historical and the fictional can be seen in some of the tourist interpretations in the streets of Dorchester, as seen on a study visit in 2014. As such these interpretations are from a particular point in time. Those visiting Dorchester now will probably find much of the interpretation described here either altered, enhanced or removed. Though they are of varying age and provenance, they supplement the historical narrative of Dorchester by providing word pictures of the historical town through the use of descriptions from Hardy's novels of the fictional Casterbridge. As such they are of interest to both the general tourist through their use of passages from Hardy's work, which are essentially treated as historical sources, and to the Hardy pilgrim to whom the quotes may enhance both their understanding of the history of Dorchester and of the novels and poems they know and love. Essentially, they do not require a detailed knowledge of the life and works of Hardy to provide valuable information about the town.

Examples of these interpretations begin with Dorchester's Roman roots. South Walks Road and West Walks are tree-lined streets marking the outer wall of the old Roman city of Durnovaria.[119] One small stretch of Roman wall survives at the top end of West Walks, forming part of the garden wall of a large villa. A panel here describes Dorchester's walls in terms of their history and construction. It also includes an excerpt from Hardy's *The Mayor of Casterbridge* describing the ways in which the fictional Roman Casterbridge infiltrated the 19th century town of Hardy's novel. By so doing it gives us information about

---

116   Ibid.

117   Tony Williams, Dickens's 'Magic Lantern' – Discover the city that was his home and inspiration, (London: City of London / Charles Dickens Museum, 2017).

118   Both *Oliver Twist* and *Little Dorrit* were written while Dickens was resident in Doughty Street, so his use of locations in the immediate vicinity can also be seen as examples of an author writing directly from life.

119   Hardy applied the Roman name for Dorchester to a small suburb of Casterbridge which he called Durnover. Durnover has been equated with real-life Fordington.

Figure 2.3: Plaque at Barclay's Bank, South Street, Dorchester.

Dorchester's Roman past that we can use to interpret the fragment of wall, but it also allows us to use Hardy's fictional description to produce a historical picture of Victorian Dorchester, and how even then the fabric of Durnovaria was still close to the surface, which we can then compare with the evidence of the Roman town that still shows today.

Nearby is a weather-worn and unattributed 'Hardy Trail' interpretive panel that links specific elements of Dorchester with Hardy's Dorchester and uses a further quote from *The Mayor of Casterbridge* to provide visual descriptions of the appearance of Casterbridge at the time of the novel, and by extension, of Dorchester at that time. Another interpretive panel sits outside All Saints' Church on High East Street and uses a quote from Hardy's poem *The Dance at The Phoenix* to provide a poetic insight to add to the historical record of, in this case, the military in late 19th century Dorchester.[120]

There are a further group of Dorchester tourist interpretations, usually older, that provide far less in terms of historical background to go with the literary connection. For example, there is a blue plaque on the wall of Barclay's Bank in South Street stating simply that the building is the 'reputed' site of the house of Michael Henchard, a character in Hardy's *The Mayor of Casterbridge* (Figure 2.3). To the general tourist who knows nothing of the novel or that Henchard is the eponymous mayor of the novel's title, this information might mean very little, and would certainly provide little in the way of historical insight. To the dedicated pilgrim, however, this would evoke memories of that character in the context of Hardy's novel, and in so doing might provide a historical insight into the sort of dwelling in which a wealthy inhabitant of Casterbridge/Dorchester might have lived in the mid 19th century.

Modern guidebooks continue to point up these direct correspondences between Casterbridge and Dorchester, and Wessex and Dorset. Rodney Legg's 2011 guide to Thomas Hardy's Dorset lists numerous *Far from the Madding Crowd* locations in Dorchester,

120   The Dance at The Phoenix, from Thomas Hardy, Wessex Poems and Other Verses (London: Harper, 1898).

Figure 2.4: Hardy's Cottage, Higher Bockhampton, Dorset.

especially those related to Fanny Robin's final scenes in the novel and their aftermath, including Grey's Bridge, Salisbury Walk, Napper's Mite, the Corn Exchange, and the White Horse Hotel.[121] His stated aim in his introduction suggests a desire to enable the tourist to see historic Dorset through the frame of Wessex, 'to revisit the Dorset heartland of Hardy's Wessex as if with the author on a pre-car age exploration of its path and byways'.[122] Steve Wallis, in his 2012 book, uses archive photographs of the Dorset locations that Hardy used in his fiction alongside their present-day equivalents, again creating a link between the historic, the modern and the fictional:

> I was intrigued... by the idea of using the format of the Through Time series to look at these places, with the added bonus that most of the old pictures would have been taken in Hardy's lifetime and so would show places as he saw them.[123]

Finally, Tony Fincham's 2016 guide invites the reader to 'follow in the footsteps' of Hardy's characters through an exploration of 'the rural landscape of the towns and villages which form the heart of Hardy's Wessex'.[124] It contains descriptions of a number

---

121 Legg (2011) p. 42.
122 Ibid. p. 7.
123 Steve Wallis, *Thomas Hardy's Dorset Through Time* (Stroud: Amberley, 2012) Introduction.
124 Publicity material for Tony Fincham, *Exploring Thomas Hardy's Wessex* (Wimborne, Dorset: Dovecote Press, 2016) <https://www.dovecotepress.com/shop/biographies/exploring-thomas-hardys-wessex-tony-fincham/>.

of literary walks that, in the same way as the Dickens walk combines elements of the author's life and of his fiction.

The two locations in the Dorchester area most closely associated with Hardy are Hardy's Cottage in nearby Higher Bockhampton, where Hardy was born, and Max Gate, the house Hardy built for himself on the outskirts of Dorchester and in which he lived for the last 40 years of his life. Both are now in the care of the National Trust. Of particular significance to this study is Hardy's Cottage, especially given that he wrote much of his early work here, including *Under the Greenwood Tree* and *Far from the Madding Crowd*. As the house was devoid of period furnishings when it came into their possession, the Trust have attempted to create a period feel by bringing in appropriate furnishings, specifically of the period when Hardy lived in the cottage.[125] However, little has been done to make the specific link between the house and Hardy's fiction, other than simple statements that certain works were written here and the presence of copies of his novels scattered throughout the house. This endeavour is evidenced by this quote from the Hardy's Cottage website:

> The garden reflects most people's idea of a typical cottage garden, with roses around the door, and the sound of birdsong, even in winter. Once inside you will discover that 19th-century rural life, with its open hearths, small windows, and stone floors, was not always idyllic.[126]

This is despite the fact that descriptive power of Hardy's novels can enable one to make a direct connection between the world described in those novels and Hardy's own life. Read, for example, the description of Dick Dewy's house in *Under the Greenwood Tree* and compare it with how Hardy's cottage appears today (Figure 2.4). The similarities between the two are striking, suggesting the one was a model for the other, with Hardy's description providing an almost photographic sense of how such a rural cottage might have appeared in Hardy's time:

> It was a long cottage with a hipped roof of thatch, having dormer windows breaking up into the eaves, a chimney standing in the middle of the ridge and another at each end. The window-shutters were not yet closed, and the fire- and candle-light within radiated forth upon the thick bushes of box and laurestinus growing in clumps outside...[127]

Other than showing a non-original table in Hardy's bedroom in the supposed position in which he wrote *Under the Greenwood Tree*, there is no attempt to link either interior or exterior descriptions of Dewy's cottage in the novel to the present-day cottage of which it is an echo. Such inferences would most likely be made by someone with knowledge of the novel and its provenance, a Hardy pilgrim if you will. During the research trip for this study, those connections were present not at Hardy's Cottage but at Hardy's other National Trust home, Max Gate, on the outskirts of Dorchester. The house itself has no specific connection with any of Hardy's novels and is presented largely as a piece of author-based

---

125   Notes from conversation with National Trust volunteer on 22nd June 2014.
126   *Hardy's Cottage: evocative cob and thatch cottage – birthplace of Thomas Hardy*, (London: National Trust) <https://www.nationaltrust.org.uk/hardys-cottage>.
127   Hardy (1872 (1994 edition)) pp. 5-6.

Figure 2.5: Max Gate, Dorchester. Tim Laycock performing.

tourism. The house was only opened to the public in 2010 having previously been occupied by tenants since being given to the Trust by Hardy's sister in 1940. In 2014, though much of the house was as it was when the last tenant left, with modern carpets, furniture, and wallpapers, some of the rooms were being refurbished in 'appropriate' style following a bequest in 2012, including the dining room, drawing room, hallway, and staircase.[128] The sense of novel-based tourism came not through the house or its fabric, which gave little sense of the wider Wessex/Dorset connection, but through the folk-singer Tim Laycock (Figure 2.5). Firstly, a video created by Laycock entitled 'The Master Storyteller of Dorset – Tradition, Truth and Fiction in Hardy's Cottage', was running on a loop in the tea room of the house. It was filmed at Hardy's Cottage and attempted to provide insights into his early life by dramatising some of the scenes described in his first novel *Under the Greenwood Tree*, providing the detailed link between the historical and the fictional that was lacking at the cottage. During the visit to Max Gate in 2014 Laycock arrived in person to play some traditional tunes in the Drawing Room.[129] Some of these were specifically mentioned as being performed at the sheep-shearing supper in *Far from the Madding Crowd*, and Laycock in his introductions drew out the significance of the tunes in the survival of the folk tradition in Dorset of which Hardy was himself a part, and the way in which at that supper Hardy gives a pure folk song, *Seeds of Love*, to the labourer Joseph Poorgrass to

---

128 Notes from conversation with National Trust volunteer on June 21st, 2014.
129 As was found from conversations with Laycock, he was at the time employed by the National Trust to perform at both Max Gate and Hardy's Cottage, and also at T.E. Lawrence's house at Clouds Hill.

sing, but a composed 'art song', *Banks of Allan Water*, to his social superior Bathsheba Everdene.[130] Thus through video and performance, Laycock put Hardy's novels in a specific geographical, historical, and social context, providing a novel-based interpretation to put alongside the author-based interpretation that is the dominant theme at Max Gate.[131]

In the way Dorchester and the area surrounding presents Hardy to visitors, we see a number of different methods of novel-based interpretation being created in different styles, at different times, by different bodies, which suggest that the links between Dorchester and the Casterbridge of Hardy's novels are deeply ingrained in the fabric of the town. There is a sense of Hardy as the creator of Casterbridge, and of setting that fictional place within the historical context of the town, thus enhancing the understanding of the general tourist visiting the town. The connections between Hardy and Dorset, and between Hardy's imagined descriptions of Wessex and the real history of Dorset feel so close that Hardy and his work can be presented as another historical source for the interpretations. For literary pilgrims, travelling around the various locations identified as specific models for locations described in the novels, with novel in hand or one of the many guidebooks to Hardy's Wessex, enables Robinson's correlation between fictional locations and 'markers of reality'. What these interpretations create in the mind of both the general tourist and the pilgrim is an imagined historical world based on Hardy's idea of Wessex that was itself a conflation of number of different elements, both historical and fictional. This is summed up succinctly by Rosemarie Morgan and Scott Rode, if one were to add 'or visitor's imagination' to the end of the quote, in their study of the way the idea of Wessex evolved through time:

> Wessex... seems to be located upon the margins, positioned somewhere between Hardy's literary revisions, his hand-drawn maps, British historical artefacts across the landscape, the actual counties of south-west England and the reader's imagination.[132]

2.3 Jane Austen – Interpretation through Association

At the time of her death Jane Austen was neither a particularly best-selling author by the standards of the day, nor identified in person as a novelist other than by those who knew her. A biographical note that prefaced the combined edition of *Northanger Abbey* and *Persuasion*, the year after her death in 1817, finally identified her, informing the readers that as 'the hand which guided that pen is now mouldering in the grave, perhaps a brief account of Jane Austen will be read with a kindlier sentiment than simple curiosity'.[133] Austen's fame was still slow to catch on, even after this 'unmasking'. Tomalin talks of 15 years passing after the remaindering of her last pair of novels before new English editions of any of her novels were published.[134] Slowly, however, awareness about her began to grow, helped by favourable diary entries about her fiction by Walter Scott being

---

130 The singing of the two songs is described in Hardy (1874 (1993 edition)) pp. 121-23.
131 At the time of this visit Laycock was employed by the National Trust to play at Max Gate, at Hardy's Cottage in Higher Bockhampton, and at T.E. Lawrence's cottage at Clouds Hill.
132 Rosemarie Morgan and Scott Rode, 'The Evolution of Wessex', in *The Ashgate Research Companion to Thomas Hardy*, ed. by Rosemarie Morgan (Farnham: Ashgate, 2010), p. 177.
133 Jane Austen, *Northanger Abbey and Persuasion* (London: John Murray, 1818), p. v.
134 Claire Tomalin, *Jane Austen: A Life* (London: Viking, 1997), p. 274.

Figure 2.6: Development of Jane Austen memorialisation in Winchester Cathedral.

quoted in J.G. Lockhart's *Life of Scott* published in 1837,[135] and by the publication of a full-length biography of Austen by her nephew James Edward Austen-Leigh, which provided this candid acknowledgement of the slow-burning nature of his aunt's reputation:

> Even her fame may be said to have been posthumous: it did not attain to any vigorous life till she had ceased to exist. Her talents did not introduce her to notice of other writers, or connect her with the literary world, or in any degree pierce through the obscurity of her domestic retirement.[136]

Many new editions started appearing in the latter half of the 19th century, and literary tourism based around Austen began to take off at the same time. Austen's fiction, unlike that of, say, Dickens or Hardy, does not contain huge amounts of descriptions of place, other than the simple naming of that place. However, Section 5.2 describes how, in the absence of any clear physical descriptive element within Jane Austen's fiction, one can gain historical insights into the society and landscape of Austen's Hampshire through studying the social geography of her novels, but that this required a degree of faith on the part of the researcher.

This lack of connection between the novels and the distinct physical world that we see in the novels of Hardy and Dickens may be connected with the way Austen tourism began to develop, which was by linking itself to sites specific to the life of Austen, as opposed to her work – author-based rather than novel-based. Typical of how this developed are the various Austen memorials that can be seen today in the north aisle of Winchester Cathedral, where she was buried following her death in Winchester, where she had gone in an attempt to recover from what proved to be her final illness. They praise Austen the person and, as time goes on, Austen the writer but make no attempt to make connections with her novels. They can be seen in Figure 2.6: top left is Jane Austen's gravestone from 1817, set into the side aisle followed chronologically by a memorial brass from 1870 (top right), the memorial window of 1900 (middle left), with a more recent description of its provenance (bottom right) and finally a 21st century display cabinet which details Austen's time in Steventon (bottom left).

The same is true when visiting the Jane Austen's House Museum in Chawton, her home for the last years of her life before her final journey to Winchester.[137] With the exception of the guest bedroom, which has been renamed the Admirals' Room and contains memorabilia associated with Austen's two sailor brothers, Francis and Charles, its rooms are presented in line with their uses at the time of the Austens (such as dining parlour, kitchen, Jane and Cassandra's bedroom and Mrs Austen's bedroom) and furnished accordingly. As far as connecting the house and Austen's fiction is concerned, in terms of

---

135   J. G. Lockhart, *Memoirs of the life of Sir Walter Scott, Bart* (Edinburgh: Robert Cadell, 1837) Quoted in Cheryl A. Wilson, *Jane Austen and the Victorian Heroine* (London: Palgrave Macmillan, 2017), p. 63. Lockhart recounts a diary entry by Scott where he describes Austen as displaying that "exquisite touch which renders commonplace things and characters interesting from truth of the descriptions and the sentiment.".

136   James Edward Austen-Leigh, *A Memoir of Jane Austen by Her Nephew* (London: Folio Society, 1870 (1989 edition)), p. 1.

137   As with the Hardy locations, these locations were visited by the author in 2014 and any observations represent a snapshot at that point in time.

Reviewer	Title of Review	Review Sample
BeverlyBelury	A Glimpse into Jane Austen's Life	I felt I had stepped into Jane's life and was awed by its apparent simplicity. Yet inspired by what she wrote on that tiny desk in the little house at such a young age.
steven h	Take a turn about the garden	It was a wonderful view into the past for both of us. Can't wait to re-read the 6 novels after seeing where the books were written.
Beth E	Loved it	There was first a short film depicting Jane's life which was very interesting and a good introduction to the life of Jane for those who are not fans...
angelicann	Learn more about Jane and her family	It was interesting to see the house Jane had lived in and where she wrote many of her novels.
emma_kristine	Absolutely brilliant!	The house contains a lot of the Austen's personal possessions, so it really feels like you have stepped back into time, giving you a good sense of how they lived.
marple5	Fabulous	Although having read some of Jane Austen's work it was extremely interesting to learn more about the author herself. It was wonderful to visit her home where she did her now famous novels.
jazmin07	Jane Austen essential	For Janeites worldwide, the Jane Austen's House Museum is the topmost pilgrimage site, being the cottage where Jane Austen lived in the most productive period of her short life... Jane Austen's presence lingers here.
KWUK	I'm not a JA fan – the visit to her House & Museum was Superb	I'm aware of Jane Austin and her place in literary history. But I have to say that I've never read any of her books, not even one paragraph, and have never seen the associated films... But – I enjoyed the visit to this house and museum. I'm now almost tempted to start reading one of her books.
mconnor042	Great place to visit and you don't have to be an Austen fan to appreciate.	Really good to see the house she did her writing in and what was for a large part of her life, her family's home.
CriscrisMicone	No need to be an Austen fan... one will convert as soon as the first step is taken!	The cottage is beautifully restored with all the needed information so as to help people understand the Austen's family timeline and how it informed and shaped Jane.

Table 2.1: Trip Advisor reviews on Jane Austen's House Museum. Extracts from the first ten reviews of the Jane Austen's House Museum on 14th February 2018.

describing the mechanics of production there is little beyond the writing desk displayed in the dining parlour. An introductory video shown on a loop in the Learning Centre outlines Jane's life and the locations associated with her life, especially this location, with long shots of an actress portraying Jane in the act of writing. The film concentrates on her life rather than the detail of the literature and ends with a brief filmed tour of the house. No attempt is made to relate her life to the content of the literature, other than one panel in Jane and Cassandra's bedroom pointing up the similarities in the relationship between Jane and Cassandra and that between Elinor and Marianne in *Sense and Sensibility*, and a panel in the Admirals' Room linking the lives of Austen's brothers to that of Fanny Price's brother, William, in *Mansfield Park*.

The main thrust of the interpretation at Chawton is therefore author-based, uncovering the background to the life of the writer rather than any landscapes associated with the fiction. In concentrating specifically on the life of the author, the interpretation is also geared towards the Austen pilgrim engaged in one of MacCannell's 'quests for authentic experiences'.[138] This appears to be substantiated by the list of Trip Advisor reviews of the house shown in Table 2.1, all of which suggest they visited with a desire to find out about Austen the person and Austen the writer, rather than any desire to uncover the historical background to the novels.

---

138 MacCannell (1973).

What we do get from Austen's novels are detailed descriptions of the makeup of her small slice of late 18ᵗʰ and early 19ᵗʰ century English society, the social conventions regarding conversations, meals, visits, courtship, balls, and parties, one's social superiors and one's social inferiors, money, and wealth, as well as the simple interactions between individuals. So, when one visits an Austen literary location, the historical books one is likely to take away from the gift shop are those that interpret these social insights within the novels. For example, in 2014 Winchester Cathedral gift shop included books that gave a wider historical framework to descriptions found within Austen's novels, books such as the social history *Eavesdropping on Jane Austen's England*, *Dinner with Mr Darcy*, a recipe book, and *Tea with Jane Austen*, a study of the serving and drinking of tea within the novels.

In his essay on tourism and literary places Herbert notes that for many of the visitors to the Jane Austen's House in Chawton who responded to a questionnaire, there was a sense that the historical world of the author and the imagined world of the author's characters fuse in their minds. When in Chawton they are interested not only in whether this 'was the small table at which Jane Austen wrote', but also 'whether any of her characters is placed in these settings'.[139] They are using the real-world setting in which the Austens lived as a source for building the worlds they imagine for her novels rather than, as in Hardy tourism, using the fictional descriptions and real-world settings together to create those imagined worlds.

A by-product of this emphasis within Austen tourism for it to be author-based rather than novel-based is that there has grown up a sub-element of Austen tourism which is based around places where Austen's stories have been filmed, where the descriptive elements that are largely lacking in the stories themselves have been realised via adaptations. One can regard this as novel-based tourism, but it is novel-based tourism where the novel is seen through the lens of the imagined world of the filmmakers within the adaption, which is itself a fleshing out of the limited descriptive world of Austen's original novels. The question then arises as to whether the visitor is seeking a historical experience, as informed by the novel, as might be the case with the novel-based Hardy tourism, seeking such an experience informed by the adaptation, a combination of the two, or simply a sense of experiencing the adaptation with no historical connotation at all.

An example is the way in which Lyme, a National Trust property in Cheshire, trades on its association with the 1995 BBC serial adaptation of Austen's *Pride and Prejudice*.[140] Within the serial, the exterior shots of Mr Darcy's home at Pemberley were shot at Lyme, with the interior scenes being shot at Sudbury Hall in Derbyshire.[141] One Lyme scene that became iconic was that of Lizzie Bennett encountering Mr Darcy, played by Colin Firth, emerging from a pond wet-shirted following a swim, a scene which does not appear in the novel but which was inserted by the adapter Andrew Davies.[142]

---

139 Herbert (2001).

140 *Pride and Prejudice*, dir. by Simon Langton (BBC / Chestermead, 1995).

141 Amy Noton, *20 famous film locations in Derbyshire and the Peak District*, (Derby: Derbyshire Life and Countryside, October 19th, 2015) <http://www.derbyshirelife.co.uk/out-about/places/20-famous-film-locations-in-derbyshire-and-the-peak-district-1-4148349>.

142 Davies discussed the genesis of the scene in the following article: Nicholas Barber, *Pride and Prejudice at 20: The scene that changed everything*, (London: BBC, 2015) <http://www.bbc.com/culture/story/20150922-pride-and-prejudice-at-20-the-scene-that-changed-everything>.

Figure 2.7: Pride and Prejudice merchandise on display in Lyme gift shop, September 2015.

Whilst the interpretation of the house itself, when visited in September 2015, concentrated on the history of the house and in particular, the period following the First World War, the fictional association of Lyme with the adaptation is emphasised in three respects. Firstly, the National Trust Handbook entry for Lyme makes explicit play on the connection, stating 'you may recognise Lyme as "Pemberley" from the BBC adaptation of *Pride and Prejudice*, starring Colin Firth'.[143] Secondly. the National Trust website advertises a 'Pemberley Walk', on which the visitor is invited to 'discover some of the idyllic filming locations from the 1995 BBC adaptation of Pride and Prejudice', including what they call 'Darcy's Pond'.[144] Thirdly, on a visit in 2015 a large section of the house's gift shop was taken up with merchandise associated with the adaptation including, more specifically, Colin Firth's role within it (Figure 2.7).

Sudbury Hall, though with less emphasis than Lyme, given its main role is as a Museum of Childhood, makes one reference to the adaptation within its description of the house's Long Gallery: 'Fans of the 1996 BBC 'Pride and Prejudice' adaptation will recall

---

143 *National Trust 2019 Handbook*, (London: National Trust, 2019), p. 318.
144 *Pemberley Walk at Lyme*, (London: National Trust) <https://www.nationaltrust.org.uk/lyme/trails/pemberley-walk-at-lyme->.

Reviewer	Review Title
Poly_Tribe	Seeking Mr. Darcy on a sunny day
Keith R	Oh, Mr. Darcy!
Girl36	Mr. Darcy here I come
LadyJules67	Oh Mr. Darcy! Fabulous house, gardens and history
Carole H	Hello Mr. Darcy
BlaydonBlunderer	Mr. Darcy wasn't at home, but we wish we lived closer to visit more times
Brooke N	Hoping to Run into Mr. Darcy!
bella D	Looking for Mr. Darcy and finding so much more

Table 2.2: Sample Trip Advisor reviews for Lyme extracted in September 2018.

the room being used as the place where Elizabeth sets eyes on Darcy's painting'.[145] Similar references are made at Chatsworth House in Derbyshire to the 2005 film adaptation of *Pride and Prejudice*, for which both exterior and interior Pemberley scenes were shot at that location, though the on-line interpretation adds a note of authenticity, alongside a picture of the actor Keira Knightley as Elizabeth Bennet, with the comment that 'it is believed that Jane Austen may have based her idea of Pemberley on Chatsworth House and written the novel while in Bakewell'.[146] This same webpage states that the house also holds a bust of the actor Matthew Mcfadyen, who played Mr Darcy, as a souvenir of the filming of the adaptation.

This reference to the link between Chatsworth and Pemberley is a rare example of interpretation at Austen literary places making the link between the author's fiction and a specific real-world location. The three properties could be said to be using a form of novel-based interpretation. However, the main driver for Lyme and Sudbury Hall, and to an extent for Chatsworth, is the promotion of their link not with the novel itself but the adaptation of the novel. The Trip Advisor comments made by visitors in Table 2.2 suggest that many visitors coming to Lyme for its literary connections come to the location not to view the three-way dialogue between the modern, the historical, and the fictional in the form of the novel, but to view the dialogue between the modern, and two fictional forms, that of the novel and that of the adaptation. Unlike with the Hardy and Dickens novel-based interpretation there is little sense of historical connection with the elements of the past that sit behind the novel, but rather a sense of connection with the world of the adaptation, regardless of where the location has any links to that past, which both Lyme and Sudbury Hall appear not to have.

If we now look at the type of visitor that the Austen literary places described above attracted, the sense whilst touring the Chawton house was that the author-based nature of the interpretation assumed a degree of knowledge about the life of Austen on the part of the visitor and that it was geared towards the pilgrim end of MacCannell's pilgrim/tourist spectrum.

145 *Explore Sudbury Hall*, (London: National Trust) <https://www.nationaltrust.org.uk/features/highlights-of-sudbury-hall>.
146 *Chatsworth on Film – Pride and Prejudice*, (Chatsworth: Chatsworth.org, 2018) <https://www.chatsworth.org/news-media/chatsworth-on-film/pride-and-prejudice/>.

The novel-based interpretations at Lyme, Sudbury Hall, and Chatsworth House, seem at first glance more geared to the passing casual visitor than the pilgrim. However, the comments in Table 2.2, when placed alongside the comments of the Austen pilgrims in Table 2.1, Suggest there amongst some of the visitors there may have been a subtly different type of pilgrimage involved. This pilgrimage is, however, not one based on a sense of experiencing the historical background of the writer, as in the case of the Austen author-based interpretations, or the historical background of the novel, as in the case of the Hardy and Dickens novel-based interpretations, but rather experiencing the world presented in an adaptation, filtered as that is through the lens of the filmmakers, and particularly a vicarious sense of being close the actors in that adaptation.

2.4 Conclusion: Literary Tourism and the Classic Fiction Process Model

Within Austen's fiction, descriptions of the physical makeup of the novel's world take second place to minute descriptions of the social interactions between her novels' characters, and hence of the social hierarchies, customs, and conventions that bound together her particular slice of late 18th and early 19th century England. As a result, the interpretations on offer at Austen literary places make little use of physical description of place from within her novels in the fusion of the historical and the imagined. This is inevitable with the Austen sites in Winchester given that there are no associations with Winchester in Austen's fiction, but it is also evident at the Jane Austen's House Museum in Chawton. At Chawton, the interpretation concentrates on Austen as a person, and at recreating the environment within which she lived from original family artefacts, carefully sourced period pieces, and a selection of other Austen family memorabilia. There is only the occasional reference to the world of the novels, but it is intuitive rather than directly taken from the pages of the novels.[147] As will be discussed in detail in Section 5.2, there is a degree to which the social geography of *Pride and Prejudice* and *Emma* can be seen reflected on the ground in Steventon and Chawton, but the casual visitor would not be expected to make such a connection, and none of these sites when visited in 2014 appeared to attempt to make such a connection.

Where there is a sense of Austen tourism being novel-based rather than author-based, it is often made via the prism of an adaptation of an Austen novel rather than directly from the novel. Lyme makes play of its connection with Austen's Pemberley via the 1995 BBC adaptation of *Pride and Prejudice,* part of which was filmed there. Similarly, at Chatsworth House connections are made with the same novel as much from its use in the 2005 adaptation as from the connection some have made between it and the Pemberley of the novel. The Lyme Trip Advisor reviews quoted in Table 2.2 demonstrate the degree to which visitors go to Lyme to create Herbert's fusion between real and imagined worlds, but that imagined world is the one dependent more on the creative decisions made by adapters than the descriptive power of the novelist.

In the interpretation of literary places associated with Hardy in the Dorchester area, there is a much greater use of novel-based interpretations, of using descriptive passages

---

147 For example, there were interpretations comparing the relationship between Austen and her sister Cassandra with that between Elinor and Marianne in *Sense and Sensibility,* and between Austen's naval brothers Francis and Charles and Fanny Price's brother William in *Mansfield Park.*

within his fiction and their links to real-life locations to both provide a real-life backdrop to the fiction, and to place the fiction in a historical context which it illuminates and by which it in turn is illuminated. For example, the descriptions of Dick Dewy's cottage in *Under the Greenwood Tree* help us understand specific details of Hardy's life. However, in actually visiting Hardy's Cottage, not only are those fictional descriptions brought to life, but we gain a historical context for the cottage, enhanced by supplementing the novel's descriptions with historical research of the period and of Hardy's life. Similarly, within Dorchester itself, the many references to Hardy's novels in interpretative panels provide real-life pictures for the words in the novel, but also enhance the historical interpretation of Dorchester.

Turning to the other two authors that are being looked at in depth in this study, for Elizabeth Gaskell, examples exist within the literary tourism connected to her of both author-based and novel-based interpretation. Despite the descriptive content of her two most important Manchester novels, *Mary Barton* and *North and South*, the location most associated with Gaskell in terms of literary tourism is Knutsford, the town where she grew up, and which she portrayed in fictional form in her *Cranford* stories. Around the same time as literary guides were being produced connecting Hardy's novels and their real-world settings, so guides were also being produced putting Gaskell's novels, particularly *Cranford*, in the real-world setting of Knutsford, books with titles such as George Payne's *Mrs Gaskell and Knutsford* and Mrs Chadwick's *Mrs Gaskell: Homes, Haunts and Stories*. For example, Payne echoes the Hardy guides in writing that *Cranford* 'while depicting life in almost any country town, is especially descriptive of some of the past and present social characteristics of Knutsford'.[148] In the present day the Knutsford Heritage Centre, the major tourist destination within the town itself, making use much of the town's connection with the descriptive elements of *Cranford*, offers a guided walk entitled 'Cranford and Elizabeth Gaskell', described on their website as follows:

> Travel back in time with our guide to discover Knutsford as the real Cranford. View the childhood home of Elizabeth Gaskell the church where she married and see the shops and residences that would have been frequented by the Cranford Ladies.[149]

The main literary house associated with Gaskell is however the Elizabeth Gaskell House in Plymouth Grove, Manchester, where Gaskell lived with her family for the last years of her life. On a visit in February 2016 there was a feeling that the house contained elements of both author-based and novel-based interpretation, but that it was weighted towards author-based. Frank Galvin, who was involved in the restoration of the house and the way it was subsequently presented to the public, whilst admitting when interviewed that some features of the house resemble those of the Hales' house in Gaskell's *North and South*, was also clear that the prime driver behind the presentation was to show it very much as a family home, rather than as a literary house. Specifically, the restoration attempted to present the house as it would have been when the Gaskell's were living there in the 1850s.[150] Whilst there was a touch-screen display in the reception room that put the house

---

148   George A. Payne, *Mrs. Gaskell and Knutsford* (Manchester: Clarkson & Griffiths, 1900), p. 30.

149   *Knutsford Heritage Centre: Walks*, (Knutsford: Knutsford Heritage Centre) <http://www.knutsfordheritage. co.uk/visitor-info/bookings/walks/>.

150   From notes taken during a conversation with Frank Galvin, consultant to the restoration of the house, and Dinah Winch, at the time the house manager, on February 3rd, 2016.

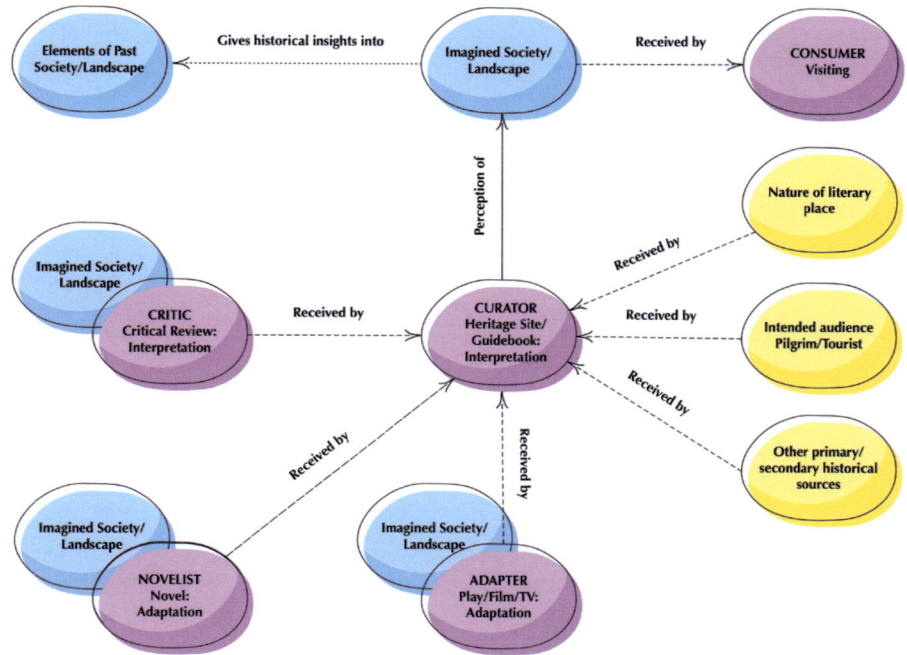

Figure 2.8: Classic Fiction Process – Interpreting the author and the novel in the context of Literary Tourism.

in the context of a wider Manchester, another that allowed one to see images of her work, and a display in an upstairs room (not created by the House itself) about Victorian Manchester, there was little attempt in the rest of the house to put the house in these two contexts, that of Manchester or that of her work.[151] As a recreation of a family villa of mid-19th century Manchester, it worked well in creating the sense of Gaskell and her family living and working there, but the interpretation created by the House essentially left it at that.

Literary tourism devoted to J.B. Priestley is minimal compared to the other three authors being studied here, as can be seen in detail in Section 6.6, which shows that acknowledgements of Priestley on the ground in his hometown of Bradford are few and far between. However, this section also demonstrates that such is the descriptive power of parts of novels such as *The Good Companions* and *Bright Day* that they can be used in and of themselves as an interpretive tool in evoking a sense of the Bradford that Priestley was born in and in which he grew up and began his working life.

What this means in terms of the classic fiction process model is shown in Figure 2.8. In the centre we see the interpreter/curator of a literary place receiving input from the novel and the imagined version of the past that its author has perceived within it, along with any critical layering that may have accreted to the novel since its conception and adaptations of the novel and their imagined worlds created by filmmakers. There are also a number of other external influences, marked in yellow. These include additional biographical, archival and historical sources, and also the nature of the literary place and who the perceived target

---

151 Observations taken from various visits between 2016 and 2018.

audience is for the interpretation – pilgrim, tourist, or a combination thereof. From an amalgam of these various inputs, they produce interpretations that are consumed by the visitor that can either, in the case of author-based tourism, use biographical information to place the author in an imagined historical setting, or, in the case of novel-based tourism, use an author's fictional descriptions in conjunction with historical sources to produce an imagined historical world where the one informs the other.

The author-based interpretations can provide true historical insights, but they are predominantly concerned with using the author's real life in a real location to create those insights, and only indirectly in using the author's novels. Within novel-based interpretation the emphasis is more on using the author's fictional descriptions in a specific landscape to create insights into the author's historical world, and only secondarily in linking those insights to the life of the author. The exception to this is where the connection between the place and the novel is second-hand, as for example in the places that are connected via their use in an adaptation of a novel. In these instances, the interpretation can, as is the case at Lyme, be biased more towards the adaptation than to the original source material and any descriptions therein, thus making historical insights more indirect, seen through the eyes of not just the interpreters, but also the adapters. The evidence from the comments of visitors to Lyme suggest that they are willing to receive the imagined world thus created by the interpreters and use it to inform their own imagined version of the world of Austen's novel, despite its lack of any specific historical accuracy.

Finally, one must consider the intended audience for the interpretation. Comparison of the author-based Austen interpretations and the novel-based Hardy interpretations suggest that the former is geared more towards its consumption by dedicated literary pilgrims. The Trip Advisor comments in Table 2.1 hint visitors to the Jane Austen's House Museum tend to come with a degree of foreknowledge of the author and her works and are interested in experiencing the author's world. Whilst Hardy's works have long attracted literary pilgrims, as evidenced by the various guides to Wessex produced over the years, and whilst some Hardy literary locations, such as Michael Henchard's house, would require the resources of a pilgrim to interpret, the gist of much of the Hardy interpretations in Dorchester is geared to general tourist consumption, in using Hardy's fictional descriptions of Dorset as Wessex to supplement historical sources in finding a version of a past world within the present-day landscape.

The suggestion is that the greater the descriptive power of a novel, the more willing interpreters are to use it as what is essentially simply one more descriptive resource to complement and illuminate the more conventionally sourced historical narrative. This provides a much more direct link to the novel's imagined world than the author-based tourism, where any such reference is generally tangential, or novel-based tourism based around adaptations, where the lack of historical accuracy combines with the extra layering effect of viewing the past through that adaptation to provide a potentially misleading view of a historic past.

3

The Adaptation Process

3.1 Introduction

The previous chapter looked at ways in which the curators and interpreters of literary places use both the content of an author's life and their novels to inform historical aspects of the interpretation they produce for that place. It discussed how at their best the novel-based interpretations can produce a mediation between the imagined world of the novel, the elements of the past that might lie behind that fiction and the present-day world within which the visitor is consuming the interpretation. However, it also emphasised how, as for example with the case of Lyme and *Pride and Prejudice*, novel-based interpretations in which the novel is filtered through the lens of an adaptation provide extra layering that may provide the visitor with misleading historical insights. This chapter goes back one stage in the un-layering of the classic fiction process flow and looks at what happens at the moment the story of the novel moves beyond the novel itself into adapted forms, and how the multiplicity of influences on those adaptations affect our perception of the worlds of the novel. It examines how the decisions made by filmmakers in adapting a novel for film and television, the visual nature of the adaptation, and the comparisons we make when viewing an adaptation with other adaptations, can influence our perceptions of what is significant about the past that sits behind the adaptation and its source novel. It also discusses the significance of the fact that those adaptations come, particularly regarding fiction written within the period covered by this study, from a restricted canon of novels, with the consequent restricted view of history that implies.

To begin, data confirms that the way in which fiction and history most obviously intersect for a mass audience is through film and television adaptations of so-called 'classic' fiction.[152] In the immediate aftermath of the BBC television adaptation of *Pride and Prejudice* in 1995, sales of the printed book in the UK increased to 35,000 copies a week.[153] However, such figures were dwarfed by the fact that around 11 million viewers would watch the

---

152 This section accepts the following general definition of 'classic' with regard to fiction: 'Classic (noun) In the singular, *classic* is usually applied to a piece of literature that by common consent has achieved a recognized superior status in literary history; also an author of similar standing', from William Harmon and C. Hugh Holman, *A Handbook to Literature* (New York: Macmillan, 1992).

153 Ronnie Jo Sokol, 'The Importance of Being Married: Adapting Pride and Prejudice', in *Nineteenth-Century Woman at the Movies: Adapting Classic Women's Fiction to Film*, ed. by Barbara Tepa Lupack (Bowling Green: Bowling Green State University Popular Press, 1999), p. 78.

adaptation each week on BBC.[154] Within adaptations we receive the filmmakers' version of the author's world directly, visually and aurally, and as is shown within this chapter, critical reactions to adaptations suggest that consumers may sense they are perceiving an authentic historical past.[155] David Herlihy writes of the dangers inherent in this, of a 'suspension of disbelief' when a historical adaptation invites us to become 'eyewitnesses' to history by creating an 'illusion' within which we as an audience are included. He contrasts this with the historian's use of primary sources to create a 'presumably critical' reconstruction of the past.[156] A similar view is taken by Natalie Zemon Davis, talking about the 'elements of historical authenticity in film', who argues that '*when rightly understood*, they allow a film to be an admirable way to tell about the past'.[157] However, she sees issues arising from the comparison between the historian's approach to history to that of the filmmaker. Historians are interested in ensuring images and events are firmly documented and where these may be 'speculative and imagined' they 'use *perhaps, may have been,* and footnotes to express their doubts and reasons'. This stands in contrast to film, where Davis believes 'such qualifications are difficult to maintain, so powerful is its direct evocation of "reality"'.[158]

Filmmakers can take great pains to achieve what they term 'authenticity'. The actor Stephen McGann, writing about the experience of creating the role of Dr Turner in the BBC drama series *Call the Midwife*, set in the East End of London in the late 1950s and early 1960s, recounts the steps taken to ensure accuracy in its depiction of the medical world of that time, including all the medical research the filmmakers undertook, the fact-checking undertaken with the assistance of experts in the field, and even the discussions about the correct way to pronounce a particular medical term or condition. He differentiates between the terms 'accuracy' and 'authenticity', the first being the means by which one identifies a character as a doctor through correct use of period procedures, and the second the means by which one creates 'a particular doctor – a unique human individual – within this social group'.[159] Essentially, McGann's use of the term 'accuracy' reflects a specific authenticity, namely an academic desire to *be* authentic by being as accurate as possible in the attention to historical detail within the adaptation. His actual use of the term 'authenticity' reflects a more general authenticity, a more aesthetic desire to *look* authentic, which may or may not have the same end result. For example, here is Françoise Fourcade, Assistant Costume Designer of the 2015 adaptation of Hardy's *Far from the Madding Crowd*, talking about a particular costume choice made within that adaptation, where the historically accurate was abandoned in favour of something with a less specific authenticity that was more aesthetically pleasing. She is quoted in full to show how the argument developed:

---

154 Ibid.

155 The term 'filmmaker' is used here as a general term for the main film-making roles responsible for bringing a production to the screen, particularly the adapter, the director, the art director, the costume designer, and the editor.

156 David Herlihy, 'Am I a Camera? Other Reflections on Films and History', *The American Historical Review,* 93 (1988), pp. 1186-92.

157 Natalie Zemon Davis, '"Any resemblance to persons living or dead": film and the challenge of authenticity', *Historical Journal of Film, Radio and Television,* 8 (2006), pp. 269-83.

158 Ibid.

159 Stephen McGann, 'From how to who: accuracy and authenticity in the portrayal of the medic in TV drama', *Journal of the Royal Society of Medicine,* 108 (2015), pp. 123-26.

What was very strong amongst the farmers of Dorset in this period was the smock. You get this beautiful actor, Matthias Schoenaerts [the actor playing Gabriel Oak], and he just, he couldn't put it on. You know, the accurate Dorset smock with big collar. On him, it was... And then when we said to Thomas [Vinterberg, the director], we were showing him, because we had bought an original one, and Thomas went, "Oh no, you're not going to put his chest in a dress." So, we ended up using a French one, original from the period, really beautifully broken down, but a very simple shape.[160]

Gil Bartholeyns describes this as a distinction between 'historicity', which he views as archaeological in nature, and 'authenticity' which he views not as historical realism *per se*, but rather 'the life of a moment of history'.[161] To him this type of authenticity can make up for the lack of historicity in a film, but not the reverse, with the result that 'in films the way facts are apprehended takes precedence over the facts themselves'.[162] The ultimate verdict on the authenticity of the adaptation is, however, that made by consumers of an adaptation. Consumers of an adaptation may base their view of authenticity on influences that are not necessarily those that affect the makers of the adaptation with regard to their approach to authenticity. This distinction between academic, filmmaker, and consumer mirrors three different aspects of the word 'authentic' given in the Cambridge Dictionary, that if something is authentic, it is 'real' (the filmmaker's view), 'true' (the historian's view), or 'what people say it is' (the consumer's view).[163]

Michael Kelleher, when writing about the way historical reconstructions have been presented to tourists at places such as Colonial Williamsburg, hints at the contradiction between these differing views. He talks about how such sites 'challenge visitors to differentiate authentic historical material from inauthentic, and accurate interpretations of history from nostalgic visions of the past'.[164] Alison McIntosh and Richard Prentice's research into the insights gained by visitors to historical theme parks found that for most the experience was a sensory and emotional one and that they retained little in terms of factual knowledge after their visit despite what interpretation may have been on offer.[165] Within filmed adaptations there are no guides or interpretations to help us make distinctions between the authentic and inauthentic, were we inclined to make them. We are presented with a picture of the past which we are invited to accept at face value, and our ultimate response may simply be that it *feels* authentic. Kelleher quotes Lowenthal's summation of this response, namely that 'visitors soon forget, if they ever note, differences between authentic and imitated, untouched and restored, specific and generic'.[166] Substitute 'viewers' for 'visitors' and we see how many consumers react to adaptations,

---

160 Francoise Fourcade, interviewed in 'The Look of *Far from the Madding Crowd*', (20th Century Fox Home Entertainment, 2015).

161 Gil Bartholeyns, 'Representation of the Past in Films: Between Historicity and Authenticity', *Diogenes*, 48 (2000), pp. 31-44.

162 Ibid.

163 *Cambridge Dictionary: Authentic*, (Oxford: Cambridge University Press, 2019) <https://dictionary.cambridge.org/dictionary/english/authentic>.

164 Michael Kelleher, 'Images of the Past: Historical Authenticity and Inauthenticity from Disney to Times Square', *CRM: The Journal of Heritage Stewardship*, 1 (2004), pp. 6-19.

165 Alison J. McIntosh and Richard C. Prentice, 'Affirming Authenticity: Consuming Cultural Heritage', *Annals of Tourism Research*, 26 (1999), pp. 589-612.

166 Lowenthal (1985) pp. 354-55. Quoted in Kelleher (2004).

with any academic or filmic claims of authenticity subsumed within a general sense of authenticity on the part of the consumer, as will be shown in the analysis of consumer reviews in Section 3.4.

As well as this tendency for consumers to view whatever they are presented with as 'real', one also needs to be aware of the way attitudes towards authenticity may change with time and fashion, or with the resources available. Linda Troost describes how different influences, social attitudes, and fashions may alter how authenticity is viewed for different adaptations of the same novel. She compares three different adaptations of Jane Austen's *Pride and Prejudice*, from 1979, 1995, and 2005, to investigate how their depictions of Elizabeth Bennet's visit to Pemberley differ, and detects differences between the three that she traces to a changed 'connection to the past' in the years between them that has been reflected both in heritage tourism and the way the past is filmed.[167]

The resources available to adaptations may also affect the look and feel of the adaptation. For example, the 1995 television adaptation of *Pride and Prejudice*, made on what was at the time a relatively high budget for television, cost roughly £6 million (£1 million for each of the six episodes).[168] Whilst this was considerably more than the £2.5 million cost of ITV's adaptation of *Emma*, made by the same production team the following year,[169] it stands in contrast to Joe Wright's 2005 film adaptation of the same novel, which cost twice as much at $28 million (roughly £12 million when adjusted for inflation and 2005 exchange rates).[170] These artistic and cost considerations may mean that different adaptions of the same novel, all believing they are giving an accurate reflection of the past, can have radically different interpretations of how that past looked. Just as authors, critics, and readers, as discussed above, can have differing views of the reality of the world and the world within a novel, so can each filmmaker, with the result that no two adaptations of a particular novel, no matter how good filmmakers' intentions are regarding authenticity, will ever look the same.

Moreover, one should not assume filmmakers are always interested in producing a faithful adaptation of a novel and by extension of the past world it portrays. Not all seek to adapt a novel by following its original time and setting, and there are many conscious decisions made when planning an adaptation that can affect any sense of absolute fidelity. Linda Hutcheon defines three distinct types of adaptation: a straight, literal adaptation of the source material with characters, time, place and the narrative thread essentially intact; one that takes the source material and, whilst remaining true to the spirit of the original, alters timelines, or introduces new characters and scenes in order to enhance dramatic effect; and one that takes the source material and reimagines it in the light of a different time or context, thus creating what is essentially a new work but one imbued with the spirit of the original.[171] Geoffrey Wagner describes the different adaptation types in the following way, but it is essentially the same list: 'transposition', in which a novel is shown on the screen with minimal apparent

---

167 Linda Troost, 'Filming Tourism, Portraying Pemberley', *Eighteenth Century Fiction*, 18 (2006), pp. 477-98.

168 Sue Birtwistle and Susie Conklin, *The Making of Pride and Prejudice* (London: Penguin Books/BBC Books, 1995), p. 27.

169 Clare Garner, 'TV drama kings fall out over Jane Austen', *Independent on Sunday*, July 14th, 1996.

170 *The Numbers – Pride and Prejudice (2005)*, (Beverly Hills: Nash Information Services, 2019) <https://www.the-numbers.com/movie/Pride-and-Prejudice-(2005)>. Wright's film was itself made on a relatively low budget – the same website lists the budget for *Harry Potter and the Goblet of Fire*, released in the same year, as being over $290 million.

171 Linda Hutcheon, *A Theory of Adaptation* (London: Routledge, 2006), pp. 7-9.

change; 'commentary', where an original is changed in some respects that expand on it but without total infidelity to the novel, and 'analogy', where the novel is the starting point but what results is a completely different work of art.[172]

The adaptations most of interest in terms of this study are those that fall into the first two of Wagner's categories, as they are most likely to be trying to recreate the historical context of the original novel. A number of films, though, demonstrate the analogy approach, for example the film *Clueless*, where Jane Austen's *Emma* is used as inspiration, but where the context is changed to that of the youth culture of late 20th century California, and *Bride and Prejudice*, where Austen's *Pride and Prejudice* is relocated to present-day Amritsar. These adaptations may not tell us directly about the world of the original source material but may be useful in drawing parallels between that world and the world in which the adaptation is set, for example allowing comparison between the courtship strategies of Hampshire at the turn of the 19th century with those of California and India at the turn of the 21st century.

A further consideration is that the most faithful of adaptations does not necessarily exist simply in relation to the source novel. Sarah Cardwell criticizes the idea of a 'centre-based conceptualisation of adaptation', that each adaptation of a novel holds 'a direct relationship with the culturally established original', and that 'each adaptation appears to sustain the original, and not to develop or improve it'. Rather, she believes that this approach ignores the relationship between an adaptation and other adaptations, which we will see in Section 3.4 is often an important influence on how consumers receive adaptations and also ignores the historical gap between the writing of the novel and the adaptation. She decries the attitude that, as she believes, 'sees the meanings expressed in both novel and adaptation as somehow trans-historical and unalterable'.[173] A consequence of Caldwell's historical gap is the degree to which filmmakers introduce researched historical elements from the period into the adaptations that may not appear directly in the source novel to enhance the dramatic and historical effect.

This is illustrated in Mireia Aragay's examination of Patricia Rozema's 1999 film adaptation of Jane Austen's *Mansfield Park*, where she looks at the way Rozema uses plot elements based around the contemporary slave trade that are not in the novel to provide extra background to Austen's actual plot as it unfolds.[174] Hutcheon cites the example of a film adaptation of Shakespeare's *Merchant of Venice*. She notes how Venetian Jews within the film are shown wearing red hats, and how prostitutes are shown bare-breasted, as they had to by law at the time the play is set.[175] There are other ways in which an adaptation can emphasize elements of the plot in order to make them resonate with the potential audience of the adaptation. For example, Aragay sees the 1995 BBC adaptation of Jane Austen's *Pride and Prejudice* as having a very late 20th century view of masculinity and courtship.[176] In a similar vein, de Groot describes

---

172   Geoffrey Wagner, *The Novel and the Cinema* (Teaneck, NJ: Fairleigh Dickinson University Press, 2012), pp. 224-6.
173   Sarah Cardwell, *Adaptation Revisited: Television and the Classic Novel* (Manchester: Manchester University Press, 2002), p. 14.
174   Mireia Aragay, 'Possessing Jane Austen: Fidelity, Authorship, and Patricia Rozema's Mansfield Park', *Literature/Film Quarterly*, 31 (2003), pp. 178-9.
175   Hutcheon (2006) p. 145.
176   Mireia Aragay, *Books in Motion: Adaptation, Intertextuality, Authorship, Contemporary cinema* (Amsterdam: Rodopi, 2005), p. 221.

this same adaption as being 'of a piece with contemporary academic rethinking of her work which emphasised the irony, the edgy challenge of her writing, and her self-dramatisation'.[177]

In a sense, we are seeing a two-way interaction at play here in the way some works are adapted; adaptations can use present-day understanding to illuminate the past, as in the *Merchant of Venice* and *Mansfield Park* examples, whilst at the same time using the past to illuminate present-day issues, as in the *Pride and Prejudice* example. It is possible to put the emphasis too much on one side of the interaction; Brian McFarlane warns of taking such ideas of authenticity too far, with the result that period fidelity distracts us from what at the time would have been a work of contemporary fiction, requiring little explanation for its readers.[178] This is echoed by Imelda Whelehan who warns that the search for 'historical veracity and authenticity of location and costume' in adaptations of 19th century literature may result in a situation where 'central characters may seem lost in the background'.[179] Keith Selby, Robert Giddings and Chris Wensley talk of a 'synthetic' historical realism 'in which everything must seem authentic and true to period'.[180] They warn of a strict adherence to reconstructing an 'authentic chronologically identifiable moment' that ignores the fact that at any point in time people may have worn clothes or owned artefacts that were *not* exactly of that particular moment, and comment also on the way that such authenticity does not extend to the state of the actors' teeth in comparison the normal dental health of the time, or to those same actors speaking in authentic accents of that time.[181]

Whichever way it is arrived at, the television or film adaptation of a novel can provide us with an immediate visual version of the world of the novel. J. Dudley Andrew describes this as film working from 'perception towards signification', from the outward appearance of the world as shown in the film to the inner meanings of the story set in that world. In contrast, literature works in the opposite direction, from words and propositions to a perception of the world.[182] The adaptation may or may not be faithful to the author's intention, it may bring in other reference points from the time of the novel itself or its adaptation, and it may relocate the essence of the story to another cultural setting entirely. Whichever way it is adapted, it provides us with vivid pictures to go with the imagined world that we may have in our heads if we have read the novel. Virginia Woolf, writing in 1926 at a time when films were still silent, was unhappy at this alliance between the eye and the brain; by making the world of the novel flesh, she saw the internal depth of the novel being lost to an external surface effect:

The eye says, 'Here is Anna Karenina'. A voluptuous lady in black velvet wearing pearls comes before us. But the brain says, 'That is no more Anna Karenina than it is Queen Victoria'. For the brain knows Anna almost entirely by the inside of her mind – her charm, her passion, her despair. All the emphasis is laid by the cinema upon her teeth, her pearls, and her velvet'.[183]

---

177   de Groot (2009) p. 190.

178   Brian McFarlane, *Novel to Film: An Introduction to the Theory of Adaptation* (Oxford: Clarendon Press, 1996), p. 9.

179   Imelda Whelehan, 'Adaptations: the contemporary dilemma', in *Adaptations : From Text to Screen, Screen to Text*, ed. by Deborah Cartmell and Imelda Whelehan (London: Routledge, 1999), p. 7.

180   Robert Giddings, Keith Selby, and Chris Wensley, *Screening the Novel: The Theory and Practice of Literary Dramatization* (Basingstoke: Macmillan, 1990), p. x.

181   Ibid. pp. x-xi.

182   J. Dudley Andrew, *Concepts in Film Theory* (Oxford: Oxford University Press, 1984), p. 101. Quoted in J. B. Bullen, 'Is Hardy a 'Cinematic Novelist'?: The Problem of Adaptation', *The Yearbook of English Studies*, 20 (1990), pp. 48-59.

183   Virginia Woolf, 'The Cinema (1926)', in *Collected Essays* (London: Hogarth Press, 1966), pp. 269-70.

Woolf's comment is apposite. Film and television provide us with the filmmakers' visual version of the imagined world of the novel that has an immediate effect on the viewer, in contrast with the slow build-up of a mental picture produced by reading the original novel. J.B. Bullen, quoting the above essay, also makes the point that Woolf might have thought differently of the film of *Anna Karenina* if she had not previously read the novel.[184] A film adaptation can interact with a previously held view of the novel gained by reading it, but it can also, like the vast majority of people who have never read, say, *Anna Karenina*, provide one with one's *only* view of the novel.

Any discussion of how novels and their adaptations can provide us with a view of history also needs to consider which novels are most likely to be read, and importantly given the relative consumption figures of novels and adaptation, which adaptations are most likely to be made and therefore viewed. To investigate this, Section 3.2 assesses evidence for the existence of a canon of 'classic' novels, and the degree to which, if such a canon exists, the choice of works for adaptation follows it. Just as a historian's understanding of a period may be limited by the number of extant sources for that period, so the existence of a select group of novels from a period that continue to be read and/or adapted may affect our understanding of that period as other alternative fictional views languish in obscurity. Data will show which novels from within the 19th century have been adapted, and how often, and the correlation between popular novels and popular adaptations will be examined.

Section 3.3 then looks at the adaptation process, and in particular at three adaptations of Thomas Hardy's *Far from the Madding Crowd*, all of which fit largely into Wagner's 'transposition' category. It examines how the respective filmmakers approached questions of authenticity, the extent to which other factors and influences may have affected the approaches taken to the adaptations, and how the sense of authenticity within the adaptations was received by reviewers. This novel has been chosen as an exemplar partly because of the descriptive power of Hardy's writing which fed into the many guidebooks to the links between the landscape of Dorset and the landscape of Hardy's Wessex (as is seen in Section 2.2), and which also led David Lodge to compare the filmic way he handled landscape directly with the way the film director John Ford used Monument Valley.[185] However, it was also chosen because the Dorset language and landscape being portrayed within the novel are still, as back at the time of publication, more remote to both critics and general consumers than the London of Dickens, portrayed multiple times in adaptations, and the novel is a test case for how authenticity is perceived from such a distance.[186] Section 3.4 introduces the consumer's perception of adaptations into the equation and how this may be influenced by factors external to the novel or the adaptation. It does this by comparing on-line consumer reviews of an adaptation of Gaskell's *North and* South with those of the novel itself. In conclusion, Section 3.5 discusses how these aspects of adaptation fit into the overall classic fiction process model.

---

184 Bullen (1990).

185 David Lodge, 'Thomas Hardy and Cinematographic Form', *NOVEL: A Forum on Fiction,* 7 (1974), pp. 246-54.

186 For example, as is shown below in Table 3.4, *Oliver Twist*, one of Dickens' archetypal London novels, had been adapted 25 times for film or television as of January 2016.

3.2 The 'Classic' Novel Canon and Film and TV adaptations

Walter Scott
Charles Dickens
W.H. Ainsworth
G.W.M. Reynolds
Harriet Beecher Stowe
Edward Bulwer-Lytton
Charles Kingsley
Charles Reade
James Grant
Thomas Hughes
Mrs Henry Wood
Hugh Conway
Mrs Humphry Ward
George du Maurier
R.D. Blackmore
Hall Caine
Marie Corelli

Table 3.1: Altick's List of Best-Selling 19th Century Authors.

Richard Altick's 1957 study of the development of mass reading in Britain through the 19th century includes an appendix which contains a list of novels published during the century that could be considered by the standards of the day to be 'bestsellers'.[187] Altick makes the proviso that no official sales figures exist from the period to provide true bestseller lists, and that these were simply novels and associated sales figures that he came across during his research. They do, however, give an indication of what sorts of writers achieved major sales during this period.

Dickens appears on the list (Table 3.1), and there are other writers on the list whose fame continued well into the 20th century, but whose eminence has since faded, writers such as Walter Scott, Charles Kingsley, and R.D. Blackmore. However, set against these are authors such as George Reynolds, Marie Corelli, Hugh Conway, and Mrs Humphry Ward, obscure now, but whose novels had at the time sales figures similar to the likes of Dickens. For example, the first two issues of the serialisation of Reynolds' *The Bronze Soldier* in 1854 sold 100,000 copies on the day of publication alone. By comparison, Altick quotes Dickens' *Little Dorrit,* first published in serial form at around the same time, achieving sales of '35,000 or more'.[188] Of these four writers, none, as far as can be ascertained, has had a filmed adaptation of their work produced in the last fifty years, and only Corelli has ever had *any* works adapted for film, and the last of those adaptations was in the 1920s.[189]

The question therefore arises as to how some authors achieve lasting fame, whilst others fade, and how some achieve posthumous fame following small beginnings, as was the case with Jane Austen. Robert Giddings and Keith Selby suggest that novels may have entered the classic canon simply through being chosen for adaptation by the BBC, such that 'the broadcast classic serial becomes a means by which past literature is identified as being worthy of classical status and this contributes to the construction and maintenance of the literary canon'.[190] Other contributing factors are hard to pin down, and the exact means by which novels enter the classic canon is outside the scope of the process model. However, the existence of a limited canon of classic novels, and the consequential restricted view of history through novels that that implies, can be demonstrated by examining the novels that the public enjoy reading, and those that are adapted for film and television.

To assess which novels are still available in mass market editions, the catalogues of five publishing imprints that specialise in the reprinting of classic novels were examined –

---

187 Richard D. Altick, The English Common Reader: A Social History of the Mass Reading Public, 1800-1900 (Columbus: Ohio State University Press, 1998), pp. 383-6.
188 Ibid.
189 *Sorrows of Satan*, filmed in 1926 by D.W. Griffith.
190 Robert Giddings and Keith Selby, *The Classic Serial on Television and Radio* (Basingstoke: Palgrave, 2001), pp. ix-x.

Penguin,[191] Vintage Classics,[192] Oxford World's Classics,[193] Everyman,[194] and the budget imprint Wordsworth Classics.[195] Each imprint's current catalogue was analysed during Summer 2016, and a list of novels written for an adult audience (*i.e.* excluding children's books or collections of short stories), written by British authors, or authors resident in Britain, during the period 1800 to 1939 was extracted. The selection criteria resulted in a combined list across the imprints of just 88 authors, shown in Table 3.2.[196] Of note is the number of authors shared across multiple catalogues. Of the 31 in the Everyman catalogue, 22 are shared with all of the other catalogues, and 26 with three of them.

To check whether this concentration within current print editions on a small number of authors is reflected in the relative popularity of these authors and their novels over others amongst the reading public use was made of the Goodreads.com website. This website allows readers to rate books they have read and engage in discussion forums about them.[197] Readers can also vote for their favourite books within specific lists where novels are ranked via a score based on the number of readers who have rated a book, its average rating, and the number of readers voting for the book within the list. Allowing for the fact that those voting are self-selecting, given the popularity of the website world-wide and the consequent quantity of data available for the most popular books (*Pride and Prejudice* had nearly 1.75 million ratings by early 2016), the website gives at least an indicative view of which books are most enjoyed by the reading public.

One of the Goodreads lists covers favourite books of the 19th century. From this data was extracted to draw up a table of the 75 favourite novels published between 1801 and 1900 (Table 3.3), ranked in Goodreads score order.[198] Note that all the authors in Table 3.3 are present in Table 3.2, and moreover that of the 75 novels listed in Table 3.3, all but Le Fanu's *Carmilla* are in the Penguin catalogue, and all but three are in the Oxford World Classics catalogue. What could not be ascertained from this analysis is whether these novels are in print because they are popular, popular because they are in print, or perhaps more pertinent to the later discussion, popular because they have been adapted. What we do see from examination of the five catalogues, however, are only 88 authors to represent the 139 years of the study period; and of the 53 of those 88 authors who were essentially 19th century writers, only 26 are represented in the 75 books included in the Goodreads favourites list. That number is small compared to the total number of novelists

---

191 *Penguin Press*, (London: Penguin Random House, 2016) <https://www.penguinrandomhouse.co.uk/publishers/penguin-press/>.

192 *Vintage Classics*, (London: Penguin Random House, 2016) <https://www.penguinrandomhouse.co.uk/publishers/vintage/vintage-classics/>.

193 *Oxford World's Classics*, (Oxford: Oxford University Dress, 2016) <https://global.oup.com/academic/content/series/o/oxford-worlds-classics-owc/?type=listing&lang=en&cc=gb>.

194 *Everyman's Library – Everyman Classics*, (London: Everyman's Library, 2016) <http://www.everymanslibrary.co.uk/classics.aspx>.

195 *Wordsworth Editions – Classics £1.99*, (Ware: Wordsworth Editions Ltd., 2016) <http://www.wordsworth-editions.com/collection/classics>.

196 A "Y" in the relevant column indicates a novel for adults in the specified catalogue published between 1800 and 1939, written by authors based within the British Isles.

197 *goodreads*, (San Francisco: Goodreads Inc.) <https://www.goodreads.com>.

198 The on-line lists include *all* books, so books were eliminated from the lists that did not fit the criteria used in selecting authors from the 'classic novel' catalogues, namely anything not specifically a novel for children and not a collection of short stories, published between 1801 and 1900, written by an author based within the British Isles.

Author	Wordsworth	Penguin	Vintage	Oxford	Everyman	Concordance
Edwin A Abbott	N	Y	N	Y	N	2
Eric Ambler	N	Y	N	N	N	1
Elizabeth von Arnim	N	Y	Y	N	N	2
Jane Austen	Y	Y	Y	Y	Y	5
William Beckford	Y	Y	N	Y	N	3
Arnold Bennett	N	Y	Y	Y	N	3
EF Benson	Y	Y	Y	N	N	3
RD Blackmore	Y	Y	N	Y	N	3
Elizabeth Bowen	N	N	Y	N	N	1
Mary Elizabeth Braddon	Y	Y	N	Y	N	3
Ernest Bramah	Y	N	N	N	N	1
Anne Brontë	Y	Y	Y	Y	Y	5
Charlotte Brontë	Y	Y	Y	Y	Y	5
Emily Brontë	Y	Y	Y	Y	Y	5
John Buchan	Y	Y	Y	Y	Y	5
Samuel Butler	N	Y	N	N	Y	2
GK Chesterton	Y	Y	N	N	Y	3
Erskine Childers	N	Y	Y	Y	N	3
Wilkie Collins	Y	Y	Y	Y	Y	5
Joseph Conrad	Y	Y	Y	Y	N	4
Charlotte Dacre	N	N	N	Y	N	1
EM Delafield	N	Y	N	N	N	1
Charles Dickens	Y	Y	Y	Y	Y	5
Benjamin Disraeli	Y	N	N	Y	N	2
Arthur Conan Doyle	Y	Y	Y	Y	Y	5
Maria Edgeworth	N	Y	N	Y	N	2
George Eliot	Y	Y	Y	Y	Y	5
Joseph Sheridan Le Fanu	N	Y	N	Y	N	2
J Meade Falkner	N	N	Y	N	N	1
Ford Madox Ford	Y	Y	Y	Y	Y	5
EM Forster	N	Y	N	N	Y	2
John Galsworthy	Y	Y	N	Y	N	3
Elizabeth Gaskell	Y	Y	Y	Y	Y	5
Stella Gibbons	N	Y	Y	N	N	2
George Gissing	N	Y	Y	Y	N	3
Edmund Gosse	N	Y	N	Y	N	2
Robert Graves	N	Y	N	N	N	1
Henry Green	N	N	Y	N	N	1
Graham Greene	N	Y	Y	N	Y	3
Walter Greenwood	N	N	Y	N	N	1
George Grossmith	N	Y	Y	N	N	2
H Rider Haggard	Y	Y	Y	Y	N	4
Radclyffe Hall	Y	Y	Y	N	N	3
Patrick Hamilton	N	N	Y	N	N	1
Thomas Hardy	Y	Y	Y	Y	Y	5
James Hilton	N	N	Y	N	N	1
Anthony Hope	N	Y	N	Y	N	2
Richard Hughes	N	N	Y	N	N	1

Table 3.2: Comparison of 'Classic' Book Imprints, Summer 2016.

Author	Wordsworth	Penguin	Vintage	Oxford	Everyman	Concordance
Aldous Huxley	N	N	Y	N	Y	2
Christopher Isherwood	N	N	Y	N	N	1
Henry James	Y	Y	Y	Y	Y	5
Jerome K Jerome	Y	Y	Y	Y	N	4
James Joyce	Y	Y	Y	Y	Y	5
Margaret Kennedy	N	N	Y	N	N	1
Charles Kingsley	Y	Y	N	Y	N	3
Rudyard Kipling	N	Y	Y	Y	Y	4
DH Lawrence	Y	Y	Y	Y	Y	5
Matthew Lewis	Y	Y	N	N	N	2
Wyndham Lewis	N	Y	N	Y	N	2
Charles Robert Maturin	N	Y	N	Y	N	2
W Somerset Maugham	N	Y	Y	N	Y	3
George du Maurier	N	Y	N	Y	N	2
George Moore	N	N	N	Y	N	1
Margaret Oliphant	N	Y	N	Y	N	2
Sydney Owenson	N	N	N	Y	N	1
George Orwell	N	Y	N	N	Y	2
Thomas Love Peacock	Y	Y	N	N	N	2
TF Powys	N	N	Y	N	N	1
Ann Radcliffe	Y	Y	N	Y	N	3
Rafael Sabatini	N	Y	Y	N	N	2
Vita Sackville-West	N	N	Y	N	N	1
Walter Scott	Y	Y	Y	Y	Y	5
Mary Shelley	Y	Y	Y	Y	Y	5
Nevil Shute	N	N	Y	N	N	1
Robert Louis Stevenson	Y	Y	Y	Y	Y	5
Bram Stoker	Y	Y	Y	Y	Y	5
William Makepeace Thackeray	Y	Y	Y	Y	Y	5
Robert Tressell	Y	Y	N	Y	N	3
Anthony Trollope	Y	Y	Y	Y	Y	5
Evelyn Waugh	N	Y	N	N	N	1
HG Wells	N	Y	Y	N	N	2
Ethel Lina White	Y	N	N	N	N	1
Patrick White	N	N	Y	N	N	1
Oscar Wilde	N	Y	Y	Y	N	3
PG Wodehouse	N	N	N	N	Y	1
Mrs Henry Wood	N	N	N	Y	N	1
Virginia Woolf	Y	Y	Y	Y	Y	5
Charlotte Mary Yonge	Y	N	N	N	N	1

Table 3.2: Continued.

Score Rank	Author	Novel	In Penguin catalogue	In Vintage catalogue	In Oxford catalogue	In Everyman catalogue	In Wordsworth catalogue	Number of catalogues
1	Jane Austen	Pride and Prejudice	Y	Y	Y	Y	Y	5
2	Charlotte Brontë	Jane Eyre	Y	Y	Y	Y	Y	5
3	Emily Brontë	Wuthering Heights	Y	Y	Y	Y	Y	5
4	Oscar Wilde	The Picture of Dorian Gray	Y	Y	Y	Y	N	4
5	Mary Shelley	Frankenstein	Y	Y	Y	Y	Y	5
6	Jane Austen	Emma	Y	Y	Y	Y	Y	5
7	Bram Stoker	Dracula	Y	Y	Y	Y	Y	5
8	Jane Austen	Persuasion	Y	Y	Y	Y	Y	5
9	Jane Austen	Sense and Sensibility	Y	Y	Y	Y	Y	5
10	Charles Dickens	A Tale of Two Cities	Y	Y	Y	Y	Y	5
11	Charles Dickens	Great Expectations	Y	Y	Y	Y	Y	5
12	Thomas Hardy	Tess of the D'Urbervilles	Y	Y	Y	Y	Y	5
13	Jane Austen	Mansfield Park	Y	Y	Y	Y	Y	5
14	Elizabeth Gaskell	North and South	Y	Y	Y	N	Y	4
15	Jane Austen	Northanger Abbey	Y	Y	Y	Y	Y	5
16	HG Wells	The Time Machine	Y	Y	Y	N	Y	4
17	Charles Dickens	Oliver Twist	Y	Y	Y	Y	Y	5
18	George Eliot	Middlemarch	Y	Y	Y	Y	Y	5
19	Arthur Conan Doyle	A Study in Scarlet	Y	Y	Y	Y	Y	5
20	Robert Louis Stevenson	Dr Jekyll and Mr Hyde	Y	Y	Y	Y	Y	5
21	Charles Dickens	David Copperfield	Y	Y	Y	Y	Y	5
22	Charles Dickens	Bleak House	Y	Y	Y	Y	Y	5
23	Wilkie Collins	The Woman in White	Y	Y	Y	Y	N	4
24	William Makepeace Thackeray	Vanity Fair	Y	Y	Y	Y	Y	5
25	HG Wells	The War of the Worlds	Y	Y	N	N	Y	3
26	Anne Brontë	The Tenant of Wildfell Hall	Y	Y	Y	Y	Y	5
27	Thomas Hardy	Far from the Madding Crowd	Y	Y	Y	Y	Y	5
28	Charlotte Brontë	Villette	Y	Y	Y	Y	Y	5
29	Wilkie Collins	The Moonstone	Y	Y	Y	Y	Y	5
30	Arthur Conan Doyle	The Sign of Four	Y	Y	N	Y	Y	4
31	Walter Scott	Ivanhoe	Y	Y	Y	N	Y	4
32	Elizabeth Gaskell	Wives and Daughters	Y	Y	Y	N	Y	4
33	Henry James	The Portrait of a Lady	Y	Y	Y	Y	Y	5
34	Henry James	The Turn of the Screw	Y	Y	Y	Y	Y	5
35	Thomas Hardy	The Mayor of Casterbridge	Y	Y	Y	Y	Y	5
36	Jerome K Jerome	Three Men in a Boat	Y	Y	Y	N	Y	4
37	George Eliot	The Mill on the Floss	Y	Y	Y	Y	Y	5
38	Charles Dickens	Our Mutual Friend	Y	Y	Y	Y	Y	5
39	Charles Dickens	Little Dorrit	Y	Y	Y	Y	Y	5
40	HG Wells	The Island of Dr. Moreau	Y	Y	Y	N	Y	4
41	Elizabeth Gaskell	Cranford	Y	Y	Y	N	Y	4
42	Anne Brontë	Agnes Grey	Y	Y	Y	Y	Y	5

Table 3.3: 'Goodreads' Top 75 British Novels 1801-1900, as at 20th January 2016.

Score Rank	Author	Novel	In Penguin catalogue	In Vintage catalogue	In Oxford catalogue	In Everyman catalogue	In Wordsworth catalogue	Number of catalogues
43	Thomas Hardy	The Return of the Native	Y	Y	Y	Y	Y	5
44	HG Wells	The Invisible Man	Y	Y	Y	N	Y	4
45	Charles Dickens	Nicholas Nickleby	Y	Y	Y	Y	Y	5
46	Joseph Conrad	Heart of Darkness	Y	Y	Y	Y	Y	5
47	Thomas Hardy	Jude the Obscure	Y	Y	Y	Y	Y	5
48	George Eliot	Silas Marner	Y	Y	Y	Y	Y	5
49	Robert Louis Stevenson	Kidnapped	Y	Y	Y	Y	N	4
50	H Rider Haggard	King Solomon's Mines	Y	Y	Y	N	N	3
51	Charles Dickens	The Pickwick Papers	Y	Y	Y	Y	Y	5
52	Anthony Trollope	Barchester Towers	Y	Y	Y	Y	N	4
53	Joseph Conrad	Lord Jim	Y	N	Y	Y	Y	4
54	Charles Dickens	Hard Times	Y	Y	Y	Y	Y	5
55	Anthony Trollope	The Way We Live Now	Y	Y	Y	N	Y	4
56	Joseph Sheridan Le Fanu	Carmilla	N	N	N	N	N	0
57	Anthony Trollope	The Warden	Y	Y	Y	Y	N	4
58	Jane Austen	Lady Susan	Y	N	Y	Y	Y	4
59	Henry James	Daisy Miller	Y	N	Y	Y	Y	4
60	Charles Dickens	Dombey and Son	Y	Y	Y	Y	Y	5
61	Henry James	Washington Square	Y	N	Y	Y	Y	4
62	Mary Elizabeth Braddon	Lady Audley's Secret	Y	N	Y	N	Y	3
63	Anthony Trollope	Can You Forgive Her?	Y	Y	Y	Y	N	4
64	Anthony Hope	The Prisoner of Zenda	Y	N	Y	N	N	2
65	Anthony Trollope	Dr. Thorne	Y	Y	Y	Y	Y	5
66	H Rider Haggard	She	Y	Y	Y	N	N	3
67	Charles Dickens	The Old Curiosity Shop	Y	Y	Y	Y	Y	5
68	Elizabeth Gaskell	Mary Barton	Y	Y	Y	Y	Y	5
69	Charlotte Brontë	Shirley	Y	N	Y	Y	Y	4
70	George Eliot	Adam Bede	Y	Y	Y	Y	Y	5
71	Walter Scott	Rob Roy	Y	N	Y	Y	Y	4
72	George Eliot	Daniel Deronda	Y	Y	Y	Y	Y	5
73	Anthony Trollope	Phineas Finn	Y	N	Y	Y	N	3
74	Anthony Trollope	The Small House at Allington	Y	N	Y	Y	N	3
75	RD Blackmore	Lorna Doone	Y	N	Y	N	N	2
% in catalogue			98.7%	84.0%	96.0%	78.7%	82.7%	

Table 3.3: continued.

Score Rank	Author	Novel	Film Adaptations	TV Adaptations	Total Adaptations	Last Film Adaptation	Last TV Adaptation
1	Jane Austen	Pride and Prejudice	2	6	8	2005	1995
2	Charlotte Brontë	Jane Eyre	12	17	29	2011	2006
3	Emily Brontë	Wuthering Heights	10	17	27	2016	2009
4	Oscar Wilde	The Picture of Dorian Gray	6	3	9	2015	1976
5	Mary Shelley	Frankenstein	12	10	22	2015	2004
6	Jane Austen	Emma	1	8	9	1996	2009
7	Bram Stoker	Dracula	10	10	20	2012	2013
8	Jane Austen	Persuasion	1	4	5	1995	2007
9	Jane Austen	Sense and Sensibility	1	4	5	1995	2008
10	Charles Dickens	A Tale of Two Cities	6	9	15	1958	1989
11	Charles Dickens	Great Expectations	7	8	15	2013	2011
12	Thomas Hardy	Tess of the D'Urbervilles	3	3	6	1979	2008
13	Jane Austen	Mansfield Park	1	2	3	1999	2007
14	Elizabeth Gaskell	North and South	0	2	2		2004
15	Jane Austen	Northanger Abbey	0	3	3		2007
16	HG Wells	The Time Machine	2	2	4	2002	1978
17	Charles Dickens	Oliver Twist	14	11	25	2005	2007
18	George Eliot	Middlemarch	0	2	2		1994
19	Arthur Conan Doyle	A Study in Scarlet	4	2	6	1983	2010
20	Robert Louis Stevenson	Dr Jekyll and Mr Hyde	15	15	30	2016	2008
21	Charles Dickens	David Copperfield	4	13	17	1935	2009
22	Charles Dickens	Bleak House	1	3	4	1920	2005
23	Wilkie Collins	The Woman in White	4	5	9	1982	1997
24	William Makepeace Thackeray	Vanity Fair	5	6	11	2004	1998
25	HG Wells	The War of the Worlds	3	0	3	2013	
26	Anne Brontë	The Tenant of Wildfell Hall	0	2	2		1996
27	Thomas Hardy	Far from the Madding Crowd	3	1	4	2014	1998
28	Charlotte Brontë	Villette	0	2	2		1970
29	Wilkie Collins	The Moonstone	2	5	7	1934	1997
30	Arthur Conan Doyle	The Sign of Four	4	6	10	1983	1999
31	Walter Scott	Ivanhoe	5	6	11	1983	1997
32	Elizabeth Gaskell	Wives and Daughters	0	2	2		1999
33	Henry James	The Portrait of a Lady	1	1	2	1996	1968
34	Henry James	The Turn of the Screw	4	8	12	2003	2009
35	Thomas Hardy	The Mayor of Casterbridge	1	2	3	1921	2003
36	Jerome K Jerome	Three Men in a Boat	3	1	4	1956	1975
37	George Eliot	The Mill on the Floss	2	3	5	1937	1997
38	Charles Dickens	Our Mutual Friend	0	3	3		1998
39	Charles Dickens	Little Dorrit	1	1	2	1977	2008
40	HG Wells	The Island of Dr. Moreau	3	0	3	1996	
41	Elizabeth Gaskell	Cranford	0	3	3		2007
42	Anne Brontë	Agnes Grey	0	0	0		
43	Thomas Hardy	The Return of the Native	1	1	2	2010	1994
44	HG Wells	The Invisible Man	3	2	5	1984	1984
45	Charles Dickens	Nicholas Nickleby	4	6	10	2002	2001

Table 3.4: 'Goodreads' Top 75 British Novels 1801-1900 – Summary of Adaptations, as at 20th January 2016.

Score Rank	Author	Novel	Film Adaptations	TV Adaptations	Total Adaptations	Last Film Adaptation	Last TV Adaptation
46	Joseph Conrad	Heart of Darkness	1	1	2	2016	1993
47	Thomas Hardy	Jude the Obscure	1	1	2	1996	1971
48	George Eliot	Silas Marner	5	2	7	1994	1985
49	Robert Louis Stevenson	Kidnapped	6	7	13	1986	2005
50	H Rider Haggard	King Solomon's Mines	4	2	6	1985	2004
51	Charles Dickens	The Pickwick Papers	2	3	5	1952	1985
52	Anthony Trollope	Barchester Towers	0	3	3		1982
53	Joseph Conrad	Lord Jim	2	0	2	1965	
54	Charles Dickens	Hard Times	0	2	2		1994
55	Anthony Trollope	The Way We Live Now	0	2	2		2001
56	Joseph Sheridan Le Fanu	Carmilla	4	3	7	2014	1989
57	Anthony Trollope	The Warden	0	2	2		1982
58	Jane Austen	Lady Susan	1	0	1	2016	
59	Henry James	Daisy Miller	1	2	3	1974	1972
60	Charles Dickens	Dombey and Son	1	4	5	1919	1983
61	Henry James	Washington Square	1	2	3	1997	1975
62	Mary Elizabeth Braddon	Lady Audley's Secret	6	2	8	1920	2000
63	Anthony Trollope	Can You Forgive Her?	0	0	0		
64	Anthony Hope	The Prisoner of Zenda	7	2	9	1988	1984
65	Anthony Trollope	Dr. Thorne	0	1	1		2016
66	H Rider Haggard	She	9	0	9	2001	
67	Charles Dickens	The Old Curiosity Shop	6	4	10	1984	2007
68	Elizabeth Gaskell	Mary Barton	0	1	1	1964	
69	Charlotte Brontë	Shirley	1	0	1	1922	
70	George Eliot	Adam Bede	2	1	3	1918	1992
71	Walter Scott	Rob Roy	3	2	5	1995	1977
72	George Eliot	Daniel Deronda	1	2	3	1921	2002
73	Anthony Trollope	Phineas Finn			0		
74	Anthony Trollope	The Small House at Allington	0	1	1		1960
75	RD Blackmore	Lorna Doone	5	4	9	1951	2000

Table 3.4: continued.

published during the study period. No definitive estimation can be found of the amount of fiction published during the 19th century, but sources give hints. William St Clair quotes the number of new works of fiction written between 1790 and 1830, before the growth in mass circulation of novels in book and periodical form that occurred through the rest of the 19th century, as being 3,000.[199] Michael Sadleir's bibliography of 19th century fiction, published in 1951, lists 3,392 items, though that contains largely just the items that were in his own collection, and is not exhaustive.[200] Finally, Melissa Van Vuuren talks of Robert Lee

199 Peter Garside and Rainer Schöwerling, The English Novel, 1770-1829: a Bibliographical Survey of Prose Fiction published in the British Isles. Vol. 2, 1800-1829 (Oxford: Oxford University Press, 2000), pp. 563-64. Quoted in William St. Clair, The Reading Nation in the Romantic Period (Cambridge, U.K. ; New York: Cambridge University Press, 2004), pp. 172-3.
200 Michael Sadleir, XIX Century fiction: a bibliographical record based on his own collection by Michael Sadleir (London: Constable ; Los Angeles : California University Press, 1951).

Novel	Initial Broadcast	Parts	Author	Adapter	Channel	In Good Reads list?
Adam Bede	01 January 1992	1	George Eliot	Maggie Wadey	BBC1	Y
Bleak House	30 October 2005	15	Charles Dickens	Andrew Davies	BBC1	Y
Cranford	18 November 2007	5	Elizabeth Gaskell	Heidi Thomas	BBC1	Y
Daniel Deronda	23 November 2002	3	George Eliot	Andrew Davies	BBC1	Y
David Copperfield	25 December 1999	2	Charles Dickens	Adrian Hodges	BBC1	Y
David Copperfield	10 December 2000	2	Charles Dickens	John Goldsmith	C4	Y
Diary of a Nobody	24 April 2007	4	George Grossmith	Andrew Davies	BBC4	N
Dr Thorne	06 March 2016	3	Anthony Trollope	Julian Fellowes	ITV1	N
Emma	24 November 1996	1	Jane Austen	Andrew Davies	ITV1	Y
Emma	04 October 2009	4	Jane Austen	Sandy Welch	BBC1	Y
Far from the Madding Crowd	06 July 1998	4	Thomas Hardy	Philomena McDonagh	ITV1	Y
Great Expectations	12 April 1999	2	Charles Dickens	Tony Marchant	BBC2	Y
Great Expectations	27 December 2011	3	Charles Dickens	Sarah Phelps	BBC1	Y
Hard Times	25 December 1994	1	Charles Dickens	Peter Barnes	BBC2	Y
He Knew He Was Right	18 April 2004	4	Anthony Trollope	Andrew Davies	BBC1	N
Jane Eyre	09 March 1997	1	Charlotte Bronte	Kay Mellor/Richard Hawley/Peter Wight	ITV1	Y
Jane Eyre	24 September 2006	4	Charlotte Bronte	Sandy Welch	BBC1	Y
Kidnapped	27 February 2005	3	Robert Louis Stevenson	Bev Doyle/Richard Kurti	BBC1	Y
King Solomon's Mines	09 July 2005	2	H Rider Haggard	Steven H Berman/Adam Armus/Kay Foster	C4	Y
Lady Audley's Secret	17 May 2000	1	Mary Elizabeth Braddon	Donald Hounam	ITV1	Y
Little Dorrit	26 October 2008	14	Charles Dickens	Andrew Davies	BBC1	Y
Lorna Doone	25 December 2000	2	R.D. Blackmore	Adrian Hodges	BBC1	Y
Mansfield Park	18 March 2007	1	Jane Austen	Maggie Wadey	ITV1	Y
Martin Chuzzlewit	07 November 1994	6	Charles Dickens	David Lodge	BBC2	N
Middlemarch	12 January 1994	6	George Eliot	Andrew Davies	BBC2	Y
Nicholas Nickleby	08 April 2001	2	Charles Dickens	Martyn Hesford	ITV1	Y
North and South	14 November 2004	4	Elizabeth Gaskell	Sandy Welch	BBC1	Y
Northanger Abbey	25 March 2007	1	Jane Austen	Andrew Davies	ITV1	Y
Oliver Twist	28 November 1999	4	Charles Dickens	Alan Bleasdale	ITV1	Y
Oliver Twist	18 December 2007	5	Charles Dickens	Sarah Phelps	BBC1	Y
Our Mutual Friend	09 March 1998	4	Charles Dickens	Sandy Welch	BBC2	Y
Persuasion	16 April 1995	1	Jane Austen	Nick Dear	BBC2	Y
Persuasion	01 April 2007	1	Jane Austen	Simon Burke	ITV1	Y
Pride and Prejudice	24 September 1995	6	Jane Austen	Andrew Davies	BBC1	Y
Sense and Sensibility	01 January 2008	3	Jane Austen	Andrew Davies	BBC1	Y
Tess of the D'Urbervilles	08 March 1998	2	Thomas Hardy	Ted Whitehead	ITV1	Y
Tess of the D'Urbervilles	14 September 2008	4	Thomas Hardy	David Nicholls	BBC1	Y
The Mayor of Casterbridge	28 December 2003	2	Thomas Hardy	Ted Whitehead	ITV1	Y
The Mill on the Floss	01 January 1997	1	George Eliot	Hugh Stoddart	BBC1	Y

Table 3.5: TV Adaptations since 1990 of Novels written between 1801 and 1900, as at 20th January 2016.

Novel	Initial Broadcast	Parts	Author	Adapter	Channel	In Good Reads list?
The Moonstone	29 December 1996	2	Wilkie Collins	Kevin Elyot	BBC2	Y
The Mystery of Edwin Drood	10 January 2012	2	Charles Dickens	Gwyneth Hughes	BBC2	N
The Old Curiosity Shop	26 December 2007	1	Charles Dickens	Martyn Hesford	ITV1	Y
The Tenant of Wildfell Hall	17 November 1996	3	Anne Bronte	David Nokes/Janet Barron	BBC1	Y
The Turn of the Screw	26 December 1999	1	Henry James	Nick Dear	ITV1	Y
The Turn of the Screw	30 December 2009	1	Henry James	Sandy Welch	BBC1	Y
The Way We Live Now	11 November 2001	4	Anthony Trollope	Andrew Davies	BBC1	Y
The Woman in White	28 December 1997	2	Wilkie Collins	David Pirie	BBC1	N
The Wyvern Mystery	05 March 2000	2	Joseph Sheridan Le Fanu	David Pirie	BBC1	N
Under the Greenwood Tree	26 December 2005	1	Thomas Hardy	Ashley Pharaoh	ITV1	N
Vanity Fair	01 November 1998	6	William Makepeace Thackeray	Andrew Davies	BBC1	Y
Wives and Daughters	26 November 1999	4	Elizabeth Gaskell	Andrew Davies	BBC1	Y
Wuthering Heights	05 April 1998	1	Emily Bronte	Neil McKay	ITV1	Y
Wuthering Heights	30 August 2009	2	Emily Bronte	Peter Bowker	ITV1	Y

Table 3.5: continued.

Adaptations of 19th Century Novels	53	19th Century Adapted Authors	18	
Adaptations in Good Reads list	45	Authors in Good Reads List	17	
% Adaptations in Good Reads list	84.9%	% Authors in Good Reads List	94.4%	

Table 3.6: Summary of 19th century TV Adaptations since 1990.

Wolff, a former Harvard history professor, having amassed a collection of 18,000 works of Victorian fiction prior to his death in 1980.[201]

To summarise thus far, examination of selected classic book catalogues suggests the existence of a limited canon of 'classic' authors from the study period who have remained in print. Examination of readers' favourite 19th century novels confirms that the authors selected comprise an even more limited subset of those within the classic book catalogues. What is clear is that the potential for us to view the past through fiction is limited, at least in terms of availability of new print editions, to what is a relatively small percentage of the total number of authors and novels published during the study period, though this percentage is obviously increased when one includes editions available in libraries and second-hand bookstores.

If we now look at the novels from the study period that have been adapted for film and television, we see evidence of a 'canon' of classic novels being reflected in the novels from the study period chosen for adaptation on film and television. Table 3.4 shows how often each of the novels within the Goodreads 19th century list have been adapted for film and television. The information on film and television adaptations in this and the preceding

---

201   Melissa S. Van Vuuren, Literary research and the Victorian and Edwardian ages, 1830-1910: strategies and sources (Lanham, Md. ; Plymouth: Scarecrow Press, 2011), p. 100.

table was obtained from a combination of the three sources listed in the footnote below. Whilst the listing is as comprehensive as possible given the nature of the data, there may be a few missing adaptations, especially from the early years of film and television.[202] All but three of the 75 Goodreads novels have been adapted at some time, and 39 had, at the time this list was compiled, been adapted in the last 15 years. 16 of the novels had been adapted more than ten times, and of these 16, 10 were in the top 25 most favourite novels.

Table 3.5 lists all television adaptations of 19th century novels from the study period produced since 1990. The analysis of this in Table 3.6 shows that a large majority of novels and authors adapted are also in the Goodreads list. The analysis therefore shows a close link between what is published, what is liked, and what is adapted. Judging by the many special editions of novels released to tie in with a specific film or television production, the publishers understand that the choice of classic fiction we read is in part influenced by us seeing an adaptation and being led to read the source material. Conversely, film and television producers, if return on investment is an issue, will want to ensure that their adaptations are guaranteed an audience and so choose novels that are in print, or can easily be made available in print, and are popular. Cardwell calls this 'convergence' between the classic fiction canon and the works chosen for adaptation 'multiple and complex', writing:

> Books that are adapted for television will sell more copies; books on school syllabuses and those that are most widely read are more likely to be adapted; and so on.[203]

The analysis above suggests the existence of a canon of established classic novels that are most likely to be kept in print, most likely to be favoured by the general readership, and most likely to be adapted for film and television. Close examination of the data reveals that there is also within this canon a group of writers who are especially favoured in this regard. Looking at the adaptations of 19th century novels in Table 3.5, only 18 authors are represented, and Charles Dickens (11 adaptations), and Jane Austen (6) alone provide nearly a third of the adaptations.

The exact causal process that may have produced this canon is the domain of literary researchers. What is important here is that it does appear to exist, and influences, and/or is influenced by, the choice of the reading public and of filmmakers. Where historians may search out all possible sources when researching a particular society in a particular place at a particular time, the choice of novel or literary adaptation describing that society, place, and time, as far as the casual reader is concerned, is largely limited to a preordained set of authors and novels. Thus, when we want a picture of Regency England, we are more likely to be drawn to Jane Austen than Fanny Burney, simply because Austen's novels are more available in print and in adaptations. For a view of Manchester during the Industrial Revolution we go to Elizabeth Gaskell rather than Elizabeth Stone whose novel *William Langshawe, the Cotton Lord* refers, in somewhat different tones, to the same real-life murder that Gaskell may have referenced in *Mary Barton* (see Section 5.3). As a chronicler

---

202 *Internet Movie Database*, (Seattle: IMDb.com, Inc.) <https://www.imdb.com>; British Universities Film & Video Council, *Television and Radio Index for Learning and Teaching*, (London: BUFVC) <http://bufvc. ac.uk/tvandradio/trilt/>; *BBC Genome Project*, (London: British Broadcasting Corporation) <http://genome. ch.bbc.co.uk>.

203 Cardwell (2002) p. 4.

of mid 19th century London Charles Dickens is pre-eminent, but such is the dominance of his novels in the canon, other London novelists such as George Gissing have slipped into relative obscurity.

The diligent reader can seek out alternatives to the canon of literature by visiting libraries and second-hand bookshops. However, such a choice is not available to the viewer of adaptations where, as is shown by the analysis above, the authors and novels being adapted tend to come from a restricted set, and unlike with novels, there are no alternative sources – we cannot see what has not been adapted. Thus, other than adaptations of historical novels by contemporary writers such as Sarah Waters, Philip Pullman and Michel Faber, or original fictional dramas such as *Ripper Street* that reimagine the period and place from a temporal distance, we mainly see mid 19th century London in filmic terms through the lens of Dickens.

An effect of this is that many novels get adapted many times. Table 3.4, for example, shows that Charlotte Brontë's *Jane Eyre* has been adapted for film and television at least 29 times over the years. Of the novels in Table 3.5 that have been adapted for television since 1990, 11 have been adapted more than once during that time. Successive adaptations of the same novel may have an effect on how the adaptations are developed, and how they are viewed, in the light of there being not just a novel to draw on, but also other adaptations. Thus, the following section looks at three adaptations of Thomas Hardy's *Far from the Madding Crowd*, to see what decisions were made by the filmmakers to ensure their productions had what they believed to be authenticity. It also assesses what effect previous adaptations have on subsequent productions and the degree to which these productions refer not just to an authentic past but to the filmic conventions that may have been established by those previous adaptations.

3.3 Far from the Madding Crowd – Recreating Wessex

Section 4.2 will describe the degree to which, in the form of 'Wessex', Thomas Hardy's depiction of rural Dorset within his novel *Far from the Madding Crowd* began to be accepted as 'realistic' by contemporary literary reviewers. Hardy himself acknowledged in his General Preface to the 1912 Wessex Edition of *Far from the Madding Crowd* the way in which his fictional world, through his writing career, had developed into something altogether more solid:

> Since then the appellation which I had thought to reserve to the horizons and landscapes of a partly real, partly dream-country, has become more and more popular as a practical provincial definition; and the dream-country has, by degrees, solidified into a utilitarian region which people can go to, take a house in, and write to the papers from.[204]

In Section 1.2 we saw mention of how Hardy's detailed landscape descriptions enabled Harold Darby to create a putative historical geography of fictional Wessex that could be placed alongside similar historical landscape descriptions of Dorset. Section 2.2 showed how this idea of a real, tangible Wessex took hold amongst literary tourists wishing to see, often with the active encouragement of Hardy, the Dorset world on which the fictional Wessex was based. In terms of the settings that so impressed the reviewers, therefore,

---

204   Thomas Hardy, *Far from the Madding Crowd* (London: Macmillan, 1874 (1912 edition)), p. General Preface.

Hardy's attention to detail should make him a very cinematic novelist. David Lodge saw Hardy as someone who 'wrote about the West of England and handled its landscape in a manner which often reminds me of, say, John Ford's way with Monument Valley'. He saw him paralleling the techniques of a film director, 'long shot, close-up, wide-angle, telephoto, zoom, etc.', using language to do what the filmmaker does with his camera.[205]

Despite this, the first sound film based on any Hardy novel was not made until 1967, the MGM production of *Far from the Madding Crowd*, adapted by Frederic Raphael and directed by John Schlesinger.[206] It was followed by Nicholas Renton's 1998 version of the novel for Granada TV, adapted by Philomena McDonagh.[207] The most recent adaptation in 2015 was the BBC Films version directed by Thomas Vinterberg and adapted by David Nicholls.[208] This section analyses these three adaptations to investigate how filmmakers treat ideas of 'authenticity', and how that authenticity was received by critics in the finished product. It looks particularly at the way the productions have approached both the spoken language of the novel's characters and the rural feel of the novel in terms of the Dorset/Wessex setting.

Issues of authenticity, in line with Whelehan's description above of a search for 'historical veracity and authenticity',[209] and Selby, Giddings and Wensley's of a reconstruction of an 'authentic chronologically identifiable moment' in adaptations,[210] were directly addressed in published comments made by filmmakers for two of these adaptations. The nature of Hardy's dialogue, which bothered some contemporary reviewers (as will be seen in Section 4.2), was addressed by John Schlesinger when he explained his and Frederic Raphael's approach in an interview in *The Times* at the time of the 1967 film's release. He talks of ditching some of the 'literary stuff', condensing and modifying dialogue, and removing archaisms, whilst at the same time looking to 'retain the formality of speech which is itself so charming and has such power to evoke the period'.[211] In these comments Schlesinger is directly addressing ideas of authenticity, and the need to retain the essential character of Hardy, and by extension, 'evoke the period', whilst at the same time ensuring that the film's dialogue was comprehensible for a 1960s audience. Listening to Thomas Vinterberg, director of the 2015 adaptation, you would expect that for him authenticity, and especially authenticity to the text, was also of paramount importance, as he refers to the novel as 'the Bible', with himself and the actors 'carrying the book under one arm and the script under the other'.[212] However, two comments by David Nicholls, the adapter of the 2015 film, suggest a less rigorous approach to language authenticity in practice. In a newspaper preview of the film, he describes the balancing act between being 'true' to the book and 'slavish', and the sacrifices he believed the complicated nature of the plot demanded.[213] A further comment suggests that his approach therefore might have been

205 Lodge (1974).
206 *Far from the Madding Crowd*, dir. by John Schlesinger (Metro-Goldwyn-Mayer, 1967).
207 *Far from the Madding Crowd*, dir. by Nicholas Renton (Granada, 1998).
208 *Far from the Madding Crowd*, dir. by Thomas Vinterberg (BBC Films/DNA Films/Fox Searchlight Pictures, 2015).
209 Whelehan (1999) p. 7.
210 Giddings, Selby, and Wensley (1990) p. x.
211 Ernest Betts, 'Filming Hardy's *Far from the Madding Crowd*', *The Times*, 19 August 1967.
212 Thomas Vinterberg, interviewed in 'Adapting *Far from the Madding Crowd*', (20th Century Fox Home Entertainment, 2015).
213 Quoted in Georgia Dehn, '*Far from the Madding Crowd*: behind the scenes', *Daily Telegraph*, April 18th, 2015.

somewhat different to Raphael's, describing Hardy as 'not always an easy writer' and talking of the prose being 'quite dense and difficult'.[214]

To examine how these attitudes affected the adapters' approach to Hardy's language, consider these lines from Gabriel Oak's first proposal to Bathsheba at the beginning of the book, which in Hardy's original reads:

> "I can make you happy," said he to the back of her head, across the bush. "You shall have a piano in a year or two – farmers' wives are getting to have pianos now – and I'll practise up the flute right well to play with you in the evenings."
>
> "Yes; I should like that."
>
> "And have one of those little ten-pound gigs for market – and nice flowers, and birds – cocks and hens I mean, because they be useful," continued Gabriel, feeling balanced between poetry and practicality.
>
> "I should like it very much."
>
> "And a frame for cucumbers – like a gentleman and lady."
>
> "Yes."
>
> "And when the wedding was over, we'd have it put in the newspaper list of marriages."
>
> "Dearly I should like that!"
>
> "And the babies in the births – every man jack of 'em! And at home by the fire, whenever you look up, there I shall be – and whenever I look up there will be you".[215]

In both the 1967 and 1998 productions the passage remained largely intact in terms of the idiom of Hardy's language. Here is Raphael's version from 1967:

> "I know I can make you happy. You shall have a piano in a year or two. Farmers' wives are getting to have pianos now".
>
> "Oh, I should like that".
>
> "And I could practice up a flute. Play for you in the evenings. You shall have one of those pound gigs for market".
>
> "Really?"

---

214 David Nicholls, interviewed in 'Adapting *Far from the Madding Crowd*', (20th Century Fox Home Entertainment, 2015).
215 Hardy (1874 (1993 edition)) p. 25.

"And a frame for cucumbers. We'll have the wedding put in the papers".

"Oh, I should love that".

"And the babies in the list of births. And at home by the fire, whenever I look up, there you will be. And whenever you look up, there I shall be".[216]

The 1998 production also came close to the sense of the original, with McDonagh rendering the words thus:

"You shall have a piano in a year or two when I've paid off the sheep. And I'll practise my flute so I can play with you in the evenings".

"I'd like that!"

"And we can announce the wedding in the newspaper".

"I'd dearly like that!"

"And the babies in the births, every one!"

"Don't talk so!"

"And at home by the fire, whenever you look up, there shall I be. And whenever I look up...there will you be".[217]

Whilst Nicholls in 2015 kept the essential structure of the scene as laid out in the novel, he took a far more drastic approach to the dialogue. It demonstrates how, as Graham Fuller says, where Raphael chose to keep much of Hardy's language intact, Nicholls chose to 'cut, condense and invent'.[218] The final line was more redolent of late 20th century television comedy than of 19th century Dorset:

"I have acres and sheep. If I pay off the money, the farm is ours. You could have a piano in a year or two. Flowers and birds and a frame for cucumbers. A baby or two".

"Mr. Oak..."

"Or more. I will always be there for you".[219]

---

216 Frederic Raphael, *Far from the Madding Crowd Script* (Metro-Goldwyn-Mayer, 1967) extracted from DVD.
217 Philomena McDonagh, *Far from the Madding Crowd Script* (Granada, 1998) extracted from DVD.
218 Graham Fuller, 'Wessex and the Single Girl', *Cineaste,* 40 (2015), pp. 12-16.
219 David Nicholls, *Far from the Madding Crowd Script* (20th Century Fox Home Entertainment, 2015) extracted from DVD. The theme song of the television comedy series *Friends* included the refrain 'I'll be there for you'.

Even on the few occasions where Nicholls quotes more directly from the novel, his resulting dialogue often dilutes the effect of the original, as in the adaptation of following speech near the beginning of the novel where Bathsheba explains to the farmworkers how she will approach her new responsibilities as mistress of Weatherbury:

'I shall be up before you are awake; I shall be afield before you are up, and I shall have breakfasted before you are afield. In short, I shall astonish you all'.[220]

Both the 1967 and 1998 adaptations use the dialogue verbatim (apart from McDonagh replacing 'shall' with 'will'), but Nicholls, by omitting one of the promises loses the tripartite rhythm of the original, and by replacing 'in short' with the bland 'it is my intention' turns a solemn promise into something more akin to a political campaign pledge:

'I shall be up before you're awake. I shall be afield before you are up. It is my intention to astonish you all'.[221]

These quotes typify the different approaches of the three adaptations. Raphael and McDonagh took much of the original dialogue, and whilst reducing and refining it in cinematic terms, left a strong sense of Hardy's novel and the Dorset antecedents of his language within it. Nicholls, whilst retaining the sense of the original story, used little of its dialogue directly and rewrote most of it in a more contemporary idiom. Whatever the reason for this on Nicholls' part, whether it be the much shorter running time of this adaptation compared to the others, or the need to connect with a 21st century cinema audience less in tune with Hardy's modes of speech, the effect of distancing the film from Hardy's dialogue and speech patterns is, by extension, to reduce the sense the dialogue gives of existing in a particular historical place at a particular historical time, and thereby insert a further layer between us and Hardy's perceived world.

Moving now to the settings of the adaptations, Raphael talked about it still being possible in the 1960s to find settings in Dorset unspoilt from Hardy's time, and by using such locations make a direct connection with Hardy's landscape. He believed it 'cohered' with Hardy's Wessex 'because it *was* Hardy's Wessex'.[222] Authentic locations were therefore sought, and a contemporary documentary made great play of the links between Hardy's Dorset and the Dorset of the film (even if some of the scenes portraying Casterbridge were filmed in Devizes, in the adjoining county of Wiltshire). The closing comments of the documentary describe how the 'mood and drama of Dorset' gave life to Hardy's novel and helped shape the film by 'providing an arresting setting' to what it calls Hardy's 'classic story of love'.[223]

Almost fifty years later Thomas Vinterberg, director of the 2015 film, thought it 'honest and truthful' that they should film in Dorset. As he said, 'I thought we had to be there to film it, in that countryside Hardy describes, and get under the skin of this landscape as much as the characters'.[224] Vinterberg's film used Dorset for most of the key framing

---

220 Hardy (1874 (1993 edition)) p. 66.
221 Nicholls (2015).
222 Schlesinger (1967). Frederic Raphael, quoted in DVD extra 'Interview with Frederic Raphael'.
223 Burt Sloane and Jay Anson, *Inside Far from the Madding Crowd: Script* (Professional Film Services, 1967).
224 Dehn (April 18th, 2015).

Figure 3.1: Weatherbury: Real-life model and film location. Top: Waterston Manor, Puddletown, Dorset; Bottom: Mapperton House, Dorset.

Figure 3.2: Little Weatherbury: Real-life model and film location. Top: Druce Farm, near Puddletown, Dorset; Bottom: Claydon, Bucks.

Figure 3.3: Far from the Madding Crowd (1998) – Bathsheba and Boldwood.

Figure 3.4: Far from the Madding Crowd (1998) – Fanny Robin's final journey. Filmed on Shipgate Street, Chester.

shots, and Mapperton House (Figure 3.1, bottom), the choice of house for Weatherbury, as with the houses chosen for the previous adaptations, strikes the same note of faded antiquity as that described by Hardy in his novel, which was based on Waterston Manor near Puddletown (Figure 3.1, top).[225] However, the location used for Little Weatherbury, Boldwood's farm, was Claydon (Figure 3.2, bottom), a substantial country house property in Buckinghamshire now owned by the National Trust.[226] This seems to miss the essence, both geographically and in terms of the social structure, of what Hardy is describing in the novel. Hardy's model for the farm, Druce Farm near Puddletown (Figure 3.2, top), whilst a substantial building, was, and still is, very much a working farm rather than a country house.[227] In choosing a much larger property the danger was that the filmmakers, when portraying the potential contract in marriage between Bathsheba and Boldwood, made it less between two Dorset yeoman farmers of equal standing, Hardy's original intention, and more in tune with the social differences of Jane Austen's Hampshire with Farmer Boldwood reinvented, at least in terms of social standing, as Mr Darcy.[228]

For the 1998 Granada production, most locations chosen were not in Dorset but close to Granada's home base in Manchester, with farming scenes being filmed on the fringes of the Peak District (Figure 3.3), and Chester being used for some of the Casterbridge scenes (Figure 3.4). The geographical shift still suggests an archetypal Wessex but is not as convincing as an evocation of a real Dorset, with dry-stone limestone walls in evidence and the hills rising much higher than the relatively modest chalk summits of Dorset. A similar sense of displacement can be felt when watching two other Hardy adaptations, Roman Polanski's *Tess*, which was filmed in Normandy, and the 2005 BBC adaptation of *Under the Greenwood Tree*, filmed in Jersey.

The use of a particular location in Chester is also an example of Cardwell's comment about there being relationships between an adaptation and previous adaptations in addition to that between the novel and the adaptation. In the still from the 1998 adaptation shown in Figure 3.4, Fanny Robin is seen struggling up a steep hill (Shipgate Street in Chester) on her final journey through Casterbridge to the workhouse, where she dies delivering a stillborn child. In the 1965 adaptation of the novel Fanny is shown ascending the similarly steep Gold Hill in Shaftesbury (Figure 3.5). However, in the novel she is simply described as circumnavigating the centre of Casterbridge along tree-lined

---

225 Hardy describes Weatherbury as follows: 'Fluted pilasters, worked from the solid stone, decorated its front, and above the roof the chimneys were panelled or columnar, some coped gables with finials and like features still retaining traces of their Gothic extraction. Soft brown mosses, like faded velveteen, formed cushions upon the stone tiling, and tufts of the houseleek or sengreen sprouted from the eaves of the low surrounding buildings'. Hardy (1874 (1993 edition)) pp. 56-57.

226 Hardy describes Little Weatherbury as follows: '"His house stood recessed from the road, and the stables, which are to a farm what a fireplace is to a room, were behind, their lower portions being lost amid bushes of laurel. Inside the blue door, open half-way down, were to be seen at this time the backs and tails of half-a-dozen warm and contented horses standing in their stalls..." Ibid. pp. 93-94.

227 The connection between Druce Farm and Little Weatherbury is made by Hermann Lea. Lea acknowledges the help of Hardy in the production of his book, stating in his introduction: 'I am indebted to Mr. Hardy himself for correcting me in a few identifications of some of the places which, owing to the meagre clues in the text, defied discovery by any other means'. Lea (1913) p. xx.

228 In the novel, following Boldwood's first proposal to Bathsheba, Hardy talks of the reasons why a woman would normally be happy to accept such an offer from a man of substance such as Boldwood. However, he makes clear that 'the understood incentive on the woman's part was wanting here. Besides, Bathsheba's position as absolute mistress of a farm and house was a novel one, and the novelty had not yet begun to wear off'. Hardy (1874 (1993 edition)) p. 102.

Figure 3.5: Far from the Madding Crowd (1967) – Fanny Robin's final journey. Filmed on Gold Hill, Shaftesbury.

Figure 3.6: West Walks, Dorchester. Probable model for Hardy's 'deserted avenue of chestnuts'.

avenues: '...they turned to the left into the dense shade of a deserted avenue of chestnuts, and so skirted the borough. Thus the town was passed, and the goal was reached'.[229] In the real-life Dorchester for which Casterbridge is the model these avenues, which follow the line of the original Roman walls of the town, are flat (Figure 3.6). The 1998 filmmakers appear, maybe subconsciously, to be referencing the previous adaptation by similarly

---

229   Ibid. p. 211.

amplifying the extent of Fanny's struggle through use of a physical obstacle that exists neither in the novel nor in the model for the novel.[230]

As with the novel, we can look to contemporary reviews to ascertain the general reaction to the filmmakers' attempts to evoke an authentic historical feel in their productions. Many reviews of the 1967 film praised the period settings. *Life* magazine perceived 'a view of life there in the 19th Century that is consistently fascinating'.[231] The *Times* praised the period detail as being presented 'with hardly an evident lapse in accuracy',[232] a sentiment echoed by the *Daily Telegraph* which noted the 'rural scenery and rustic characters, who are used as Hardy used them – to personify old ways and customs'.[233] *Film Quarterly* made an explicit connection between film and history, praising the film's 'evocation of nature, and the tenderness with which a vanished rural life is observed and recorded'.[234]

When assessing the film's language, the *Times* critic thought Hardy's original dialogue 'generally poor' and criticised Frederic Raphael for simply 'presenting gems from Hardy transcripted with literal directness from the book',[235] which is at least an admission that the dialogue seemed to him authentic Hardy. The *Spectator* and the *Daily Telegraph* both saw Raphael as being faithful to the novel, the latter catching Raphael's ideas about compression and refinement when talking about him 'selecting from lengthy conversations just the two or three lines which will forward the plot'.[236]

Though the film was not generally as well received by the critics in 1967 as it has been in retrospect, this praise for the film regarding its attention to period detail, in both the setting and, to a degree, the dialogue, suggest that the reviewers were seeking the same sorts of insights into the 'vivid descriptions of the physical setting' that Tosh described as being possible in fiction.[237] The very words used by the reviewers suggest a historical perspective at work, with a sense that they trust that what they are seeing is a reasonable facsimile of a historical past.

Within the reviews of the later adaptations there was one extra factor illustrating the way layers build up between us and the historical source, namely the 1967 film which, by 1998, had achieved something approaching a classic status. When Will Joyner in *The New York Times* assessed the 1998 serial's historical authenticity, he compared it to the earlier film, calling its language 'truer to Hardy's blend of poetry and natural speech', and in saying that some of the locations were identical to the 'original', the implication is that he meant to the earlier adaptation, not to the novel, despite the fact that most of it was *not* filmed in Dorset.[238] Andrew Billen in the *New Statesman* saw the serial as an 'antidote to Schlesinger', the earlier film seen as nostalgia not necessarily for a vanished rural England, but rather for what he called 'a generation of British actors who made

---

230 Note that the 2015 adaptation omits Fanny's progress through Casterbridge entirely.

231 Richard Schickel, '*Far from the Madding Crowd* Film Review: Blind Faith in Hardy Isn't Enough', *Life*, December 8th, 1967.

232 John Russell Taylor, 'Hardy film looks marvellous', *The Times*, October 17th, 1967.

233 Patrick Gibbs, '*Far from the Madding Crowd* Film Review: Hardy before the gloom', *Daily Telegraph*, October 20th, 1967.

234 Margot S. Kernan, '*Far from the Madding Crowd* Film Review', *Film Quarterly*, 21 (1967), p. 61.

235 Taylor (October 17th, 1967).

236 Gibbs (October 20th, 1967).

237 Tosh (2015) p. 79.

238 Will Joyner, '*Far from the Madding Crowd* TV Review: The 'Madding Crowd' Is Getting Crowded', *New York Times*, May 8th, 1998.

their names in the 1960s'. He praised the serial's period detail, comparing its portrayal of the 'precariousness of the casual hire-and-fire rural economy' favourably with the earlier film, and commenting how 'the unsentimental photography catches the grimness of their working days',[239] a point echoed by Peter Hillmore in *The Observer* who saw it, again comparing it to its predecessor, as 'a lot grimmer and less bucolic, just as Hardy visualized life down on the farm'.[240] Nearly all reviews made comparisons with the earlier cast, with the *Daily Mail* seeing Paloma Baeza, who played Bathsheba, as 'a distinctly more rustic and believable kind of girl for the Dorset countryside' than Julie Christie.[241]

The same comparisons arose when the 2015 film was reviewed. Peter Bradshaw's review in *The Guardian* began with the words 'John Schlesinger's 1967 adaptation of Thomas Hardy's Far from the Madding Crowd must be the hardest act to follow in cinema history',[242] and the *New Yorker* wondered aloud 'do we need a new film of "Far from the Madding Crowd"?'.[243] Bradshaw praised Carey Mulligan and Michael Sheen as Bathsheba and Boldwood, but offered brickbats to the Belgian actor Matthias Schoenarts as Oak, commenting that his 'Wessex accent has a strong tang of Antwerp'. In terms of the rustic setting he did not see 'the landscape and the textures of the outdoors' of Schlesinger's film and saw this as an intrinsic element that had gone missing: 'the countryside, the music, the madding crowd itself'.[244] The reviews in the *New Yorker* and the *Daily Telegraph* made similar points, the former commenting again on Schoenart's accent and on the diminished role of Hardy's rustics as a 'tragicomic chorus',[245] and the latter comparing the Schlesinger film which 'revelled in the details of rural life – its songs, rhythms and rituals – and sunk you up to the elbows in the community it depicted' with this film where 'the characters are lonelier, more isolated… specks on a hostile landscape'.[246]

So, throughout the critiques of the three adaptations we see the critics making assessments of how 'authentic' the film feels, to Hardy's novel, to his language, to the period and to Dorset. We do not know how much personal knowledge the reviewers have of these elements in creating these assessments, but if we assume it is very little, as they see it the elements 'look', 'feel' or 'sound' faithful to the period, or they do not. There is a received reality in the 'illusion', even though the adaptation may be viewed through several layers: author, critic, adapter, director, and ourselves. What is also evident is that we see adaptations in the context of the time in which they were made, especially when looking back at previous adaptations and comparing. Schlesinger's film is not just an evocation of Victorian Dorset, it is also a product of Britain in the 1960s, as the other adaptations are of their time. Filmmakers are producing adaptations at specific points in time for specific audiences, and whether consciously or

239   Andrew Billen, '*Far from the Madding Crowd* TV Review: Jolly fine sheepwork', *New Statesman*, July 10th, 1998.
240   Peter Hillmore, '*Far from the Madding Crowd* TV Review', *The Observer,* July 5th, 1998.
241   Peter Paterson, '*Far from the Madding Crowd* TV Review: Hell on trolley wheels', *Daily Mail*, July 7th, 1998.
242   Peter Bradshaw, '*Far from the Madding Crowd* Film Review: Carey Mulligan shines in Hardy perennial', *The Guardian,* April 2nd, 2015.
243   Anthony Lane, '*Far from the Madding Crowd* Film Review: Fighting On: "Avengers: Age of Ultron" and "Far from the Madding Crowd"', *The New Yorker*, May 4th, 2015. <http://www.newyorker.com/magazine/2015/05/04/fighting-on>.
244   Bradshaw (April 2nd, 2015).
245   Lane (May 4th, 2015).
246   Robbie Collin, '*Far from the Madding Crowd* Film Review: 'a mini-break on film'', *Daily Telegraph,* April 30th, 2015.

unconsciously this can influence the decisions they make in determining the look and feel of the adaptation.[247] Lane expresses this succinctly in his *New Yorker* review of the 2015 film:

> ...just as Schlesinger's film screams 1967 (check out Christie's hair), so Vinterberg's version will doubtless come to be viewed as a typical product of our time, in both its haste and its recurrent gloom.[248]

The ultimate arbiter of the success of an adaptation is not the reviewer of a newspaper or journal but the person watching the adaptation at home or in the cinema. When consumers receive a novel in this form, the imagined world that they create from it is as subjective and personal as their perception of the real world. The following section demonstrates how, when an adaptation moves beyond the filmmakers and the critics, its reception by consumers may also be affected by influences that sit outside of any specific reaction to period authenticity, in particular the influence of other period adaptations.

3.4 North and South – Consumer Perceptions of Milton

Consumers of adaptations may see authenticity in a novel or in an adaptation simply because they believe it is there, without any detailed background understanding of the period in which the novel is set. They may see authenticity in an adaptation simply because it fits the norms of other adaptations they have seen. Alternatively, their reception of a novel may involve no direct opinion as to its authenticity, but may be influenced more directly by other factors, such as their liking for an author, or for a particular actor.

These assertions can be demonstrated by examining the data in Table 3.7 and Table 3.8, which show how complex the reactions can be on the part of consumers when consuming a novel, especially when consuming it in the form of an adaptation. They also show that the reactions of consumers reading a classic novel are more tuned towards issues of historical information contained within than the reactions of those viewing an adaptation.

The data in Table 3.7 is taken from an analysis of 436 reviews posted on the UK Amazon website,[249] as at 23rd November 2017, for the DVD release of the 2004 BBC adaptation of Elizabeth Gaskell's *North and South*.[250] *North and South* sits alongside *Mary Barton* as one of Gaskell's Manchester novels, chronicling Margaret Hale's journey from rural southern England to the industrial north in the form of Milton, a thinly disguised Manchester. In its descriptions of Milton, it covers much the same ground as the earlier *Mary Barton*, namely mills and millowners, industrial unrest and the effect of strikes, and the poor working and living conditions prevalent at the time. The reviews were searched for certain keywords indicating the particular elements of the adaptation that the reviewers found most

---

247 Table 3.9 demonstrates how similar decisions were made for the 1995 television adaptation of *Pride and Prejudice*.

248 Lane (May 4th, 2015).

249 Data extracted from *North & South – Complete BBC Series With Extras (2 Disc Set) [DVD]*, (Amazon.co.uk, 2017) <https://www.amazon.co.uk/North-South-Complete-Extras-Disc/dp/B004QT0YR0>.

250 *North and South*, dir. by Brian Percival (BBC, 2004). The DVD had attracted 536 reviews at the time of the analysis, but the analysis excluded any cursory review (i.e., of 5 words or less), any review that commented on the physical DVD rather than its contents, and any review that referred to another format, such as a book or audiobook.

Words	Number of reviews	Percentage (of 436)
Richard Armitage	159	36.47%
Period/period drama	133	30.50%
Pride and Prejudice	102	23.39%
Elizabeth Gaskell	76	17.43%
Daniela Denby-Ashe	67	15.37%
Mill/mill-owner/millworker	67	15.37%
North/Northern/northerners (excluding title of book)	53	12.16%
Industry/industrial/industrialisation	48	11.01%
Mr. Darcy	45	10.32%
Reality/Realism/Realistic	42	9.63%
Setting/location	38	8.72%
Classic	37	8.49%
Jane Austen	36	8.26%
Cotton	34	7.80%
Social (divide/issue/conscience/concern etc.)	33	7.57%
Class (working-class/middle-class/class divide etc.)	31	7.11%
Faithful/faithfully/true	27	6.21%
History/historical	25	5.73%
Colin Firth	23	5.28%
Poverty/Poor	23	5.28%
Victorian	22	5.05%
Union	15	3.44%
19th century	13	2.98%
Insight	10	2.29%
Strike	9	2.06%
Conflict	5	1.15%
Authentic/authenticity	3	0.69%

Table 3.7: Analysis of Amazon reviews of North and South 2004 adaptation.

noteworthy. The keywords that crop up in the more considered reviews indicate a number of different influences at play within individual reviewer's reactions.

Examining the data, we see firstly that there is name recognition of the author of the original novel, and of the two stars of the adaptation, Daniela Denby-Ashe and, particularly, Richard Armitage, who is mentioned in over a third of the reviews. One might expect there to be comments on the main themes of the novel, and indeed there are mentions of mills, the class system, the North, social conditions, and of strikes, unions, and conflict. Many reviews also view the adaption in terms of its general historical insights, its settings, and its realism and faithfulness. However, there is also the recognition within the reviews that this is a period drama, in a long tradition of such dramas, with the word 'period', on its own or attached to 'drama', appearing in 30% of reviews. Also, the source novel's status as a 'classic' is recognized in over 8% of reviews. Linked to this, a large number of reviews view the adaptation not necessarily simply

Words	Number of reviews	Percentage (of 274)
Elizabeth Gaskell	82	29.93%
North/Northern/northerners (excluding title of book)	74	27.01%
Industry/industrial/industrialisation	57	20.80%
Social (divide/issue/conscience/concern etc.)	55	20.07%
Classic	54	19.71%
Mill/mill-owner/mill-worker	38	13.87%
Pride and Prejudice	36	13.14%
Class (working-class/middle-class/class divide etc.)	34	12.41%
Jane Austen	34	12.41%
Victorian	27	9.85%
Poverty/Poor	26	9.49%
Period/era	26	9.49%
History/historical	21	7.66%
19th century	21	7.66%
Insight	18	6.57%
Strike	14	5.11%
Mr Darcy	14	5.11%
Factory	12	4.38%
Reality/Realism/Realistic	12	4.38%
Cotton	12	4.38%
Faithful/faithfully/true	10	3.65%
Conflict	9	3.28%
Union	8	2.92%
Richard Armitage	8	2.92%
Setting/location	7	2.55%
Daniela Denby-Ashe	2	0.73%
Colin Firth	0	0.00%
Authentic/authenticity	0	0.00%

Table 3.8: Analysis of Amazon reviews of North and South 2004 Wordsworth edition.

in historical terms, but in comparison to other period dramas wholly unconnected to Gaskell or the subject matter of the source novel. In particular the 1995 BBC adaptation of *Pride and Prejudice* seems to be a significant influence, being mentioned in over 23% of the reviews. The name of Jane Austen appears in over 8% of the reviews. Austen's Mr Darcy appears in over 10%, mostly in terms of the comparison of the character to John Thornton in *North and South*; even Colin Firth, who played Mr Darcy in the 1995 adaptation, is mentioned in over 5% of the reviews.

The data in Table 3.8 is also extracted from Amazon,[251] this time from reviews of the novel itself, in particular 274 reviews attached to the listing of the Wordsworth edition of

---

251 Data extracted from *North and South by Gaskell, Elizabeth Cleghorn (AUTHOR) Apr-05-1993 Paperback*, (Amazon.co.uk, 2017) <https://www.amazon.co.uk/Gaskell-Elizabeth-Cleghorn-Apr-05-1993-Paperback/dp/B00C47I6LM>.

the book.[252] Within these reviews, the highest name recognition is awarded to the author herself, mentioned in 30% of reviews, rather than actors from an adaptation, with both Armitage and Denby-Ashe getting numbers of mentions that are much reduced from Table 3.7, though enough to suggest that to at least some the adaptation was the stimulus for buying the original novel. There is a perception within a number of reviews, as with the reviews of the adaptation, of the book's status as a classic novel. The word 'classic' appears more frequently than in Table 3.7, reflecting perhaps the novel's status as a member of the classic canon analysed in Section 3.2. Jane Austen and *Pride and Prejudice* are mentioned frequently, as in Table 3.7, both appearing in over 13% of reviews, suggesting many are, at least in part, reading the novel in the context of that author and that novel. What is significant, though, is that the words that relate specifically to the historical context of the novel appear more frequently in the reviews of the book than the reviews of the adaptation, for example words related to 'social', 'industry', 'northern', 'class', and 'mills'. What *do* appear more frequently in relation to the adaptation than the book, however, are words related to 'reality' and 'faithfulness', appearing in nearly 10% of reviews for the adaptation and less than 5% of reviews of the book, suggesting that the visual element of the adaptation may be assisting some viewers in creating an imagined world. Set against this it must be said that the words connected with 'authenticity' figure very rarely in reviews of the adaptation and not at all in reviews of the book. This suggests the concept of authenticity, in and of itself, may mean less to consumers than to the academic or filmmaker, that they have a more nebulous sense of the reality, truth, or faithfulness that the quest for authenticity within the book or the adaptation engenders.

These reviews of *North and South* show a number of different reactions at play in addition to the historical insights gained from the novel, such as comparisons with other classic novels, with other period adaptations, and recognition of the actors involved in the adaptation. What appears possible from this one analysis is that the book itself is more often perceived as providing historical insights than the adaptation, but that the visual elements framing those historical insights are more important in the adaptation.

3.5 Conclusion: Adaptation and the Classic Fiction Process Model

As is examined in detail in Chapter 4, contemporary reviews of novels from the 19th and early 20th were often predicated on perceptions of truth and reality, as the reviewers used their own experience of the contemporary world to comment on the author's view of the world as expressed in a novel. The novelist, affected by various internal and external influences, had his or her own perceptions of elements of their contemporary society and landscape that they used in the imagined world of the novel. The reviewers, with their own sets of influences, compared their own perceptions of the same world and the imagined world that they ascertained from the novel, and used them to validate the author's version. When it comes to the adaptation of novels that fall within the 'classic' canon, the adapters and filmmakers, and the consumers of their adaptations, do not have direct personal experience of the author's world to call upon but are affected by various influences when producing a visual and aural version of the imagined world of the novel. The filmmakers quoted in this chapter attempted to present an imagined world that was as

---

252 Elizabeth Gaskell, *North and South* (Ware: Wordsworth, 1855 (1994 Edition)) The data selection criteria were as for Table 3.7, such that an original 419 reviews were reduced to 274.

Adaptation Element	Filmmaker's comment
General period authenticity	'I became an instant expert on the Life and Times of 1813... How many servants would the Bennets have had?... I discovered an excellent book... published in 1825: *The Complete Servant*... Written for prospective servants, it outlined what tasks were performed by everyone in the household. 'Mrs Mavis Batey, the president of the Garden History Society, kindly filled me in on what plants were popular and available to the period... Chris Nicholson at the National Trust told me about the carriages and the number of postilions and footmen who would ride on them...' Claire Elliott, researcher, pp. 31-32
Dialogue	'Jane Austen writes wonderfully dramatic dialogue, so I was reluctant to cut it, but it was necessary in places to do so... to make it fit into the allotted fifty-five minutes, [and] because there can be an almost musical quality in the way scenes dovetail – a kind of rhythm and pace which one strives for – which scenes that are too dialogue-intensive can disrupt.' 'I wanted to make the dialogue sound like something that could be spoken in the early nineteenth century, but also something you wouldn't think terribly artificial if it were spoken now'. Andrew Davies, screenwriter, pp. 12-13
Locations	'We were all keen to establish a relationship between the sites and grandeur of the houses. Pemberley... has to be the grandest. Then, in descending order of importance, we placed Lady Catherine de Bourgh's house, Rosings Park, followed by Netherfield, which Bingley rents, Longbourn and finally Hunsford Parsonage, where Mr Collins lives'. Gerry Collins, production designer, p. 24
Production design	'Every author is portraying a specific world, and it's our job to recreate that world and make it accessible to an audience. Though I like to be as historically accurate as possible, I'm not prepared to be a slave to it. It's important to understand the way people lived in 1813, but we are not making an academic study of the period; it's much more important to grasp the spirit of the time'. Gerry Scott, production designer, p. 35
Costume design	'I started going to museums and collecting pictures straight way... I phoned various museums and worked out a plan of action... I visited many excellent collections in Bath, Brighton, Manchester and Worthing...' Dinah Collin, costume designer, pp. 47-48
Music	'My first job was to select the music that the television audience would see being played or danced or sung by the characters on screen... This is called the "source music", and it has to be authentic, in the same way that locations and costumes are...; the period was contemporary with Haydn and Beethoven, Mozart had just died, and Schubert was just starting to write music'. Carl Davis, composer, p. 62
Dance	'*Pride and Prejudice* was a fantastic job for me because it called for exactly those things which interest me, that is to say the social dimension of dance; how dance is both a reflection of a society and a clue to the way people think and feel... I knew a lot of the dances from the period already, but I started to do quite a lot of additional research'. Claire Elliott, researcher, p.31

Tab e 3.9: Pride and Prejudice (1995) Filmmaker comments.

faithful as possible to their concept of what the historical world looked and sounded like. At the same time there was also a perceived need on their part to create an adaptation that would be accessible to modern audiences, particularly with respect to spoken dialogue.

As additional evidence, the comments reproduced in Table 3.9 show how these twin concerns of authenticity and accessibility played out across all aspects of the 1995 television adaptation of *Pride and Prejudice*.[253] They show the care that was taken to research the period whilst the comments on dialogue and production design in particular show how the filmmakers were conscious that the adaptation would be put before a late 20th century television audience rather than an early 19th century literary audience who, as Claire Elliott says, 'were as familiar with the England that she was writing about as she [Austen] was.'[254]

Figure 3.7 illustrates how the work of filmmakers fits into the classic fiction process model. The adapter receives the imagined world of the author as expressed in the novel, and other artefacts such as the critical response to the novel and the literary places associated with the author and the novel, and blends them with other specific influences,

---

253   All quotes from Birtwistle and Conklin (1995).
254   Ibid. p. 31.

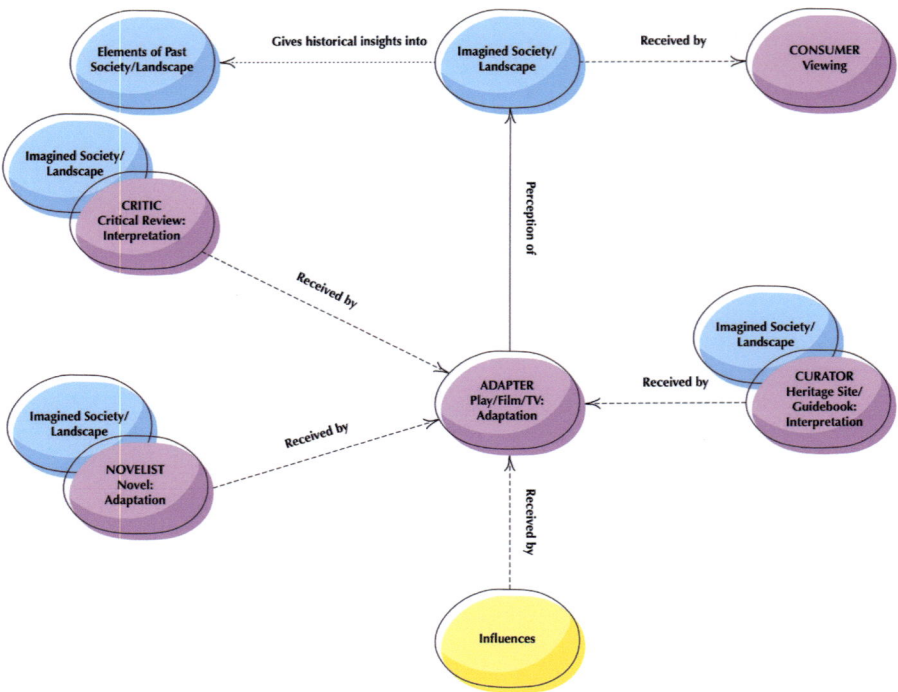

Figure 3.7: Classic Fiction Process Model – Adapting the novel.

most particularly around the imperative to produce an adaptation that is both authentic and commercially viable, to perceive the imagined world of the film or television adaptation which we then receive as consumers.

As an example of how these factors and influences blend together, the three adaptations of *Far from the Madding Crowd* all consciously interested themselves with ideas of authenticity in terms of the physical setting of the adaptation and the language used by the characters within the adaptations, authenticity to Hardy's novel itself and/ or the 19th century Dorset that was Hardy's inspiration for the novel. Other influences, however, affected the nature and degree of that authenticity, and these were mostly linked to the needs of the modern audience. In terms of dialogue, there was a need to provide language that was comprehensible to that audience. In the first two adaptations, that need was satisfied by a degree of simplification and streamlining of Hardy's original dialogue that retained the essential patterns and style of that dialogue, whereas in 2015 the decision was taken to undertake an almost wholesale rewrite of Hardy's dialogue in a modern idiom. In losing the link to the original dialogue, and by extension, the language of 19th century Dorset, the 2015 filmmakers seem to have traded a degree of authenticity to the novel and the period to the production of what feels like a much more 21st century romantic drama. In the terms of the setting, decisions made by the makers of the 1998 series to film in places like the Peak District and Chester, and by the makers of the 2015 film to place Boldwood in a setting that seemed to owe more to the tropes of Austenian period drama than the grittier demands of Hardy, had the effect of creating senses of geographical and social displacement. Within the 1967 film a more rigorously applied authenticity in terms of both language and setting was tempered by the casting of recognisably modern 1960s figures in

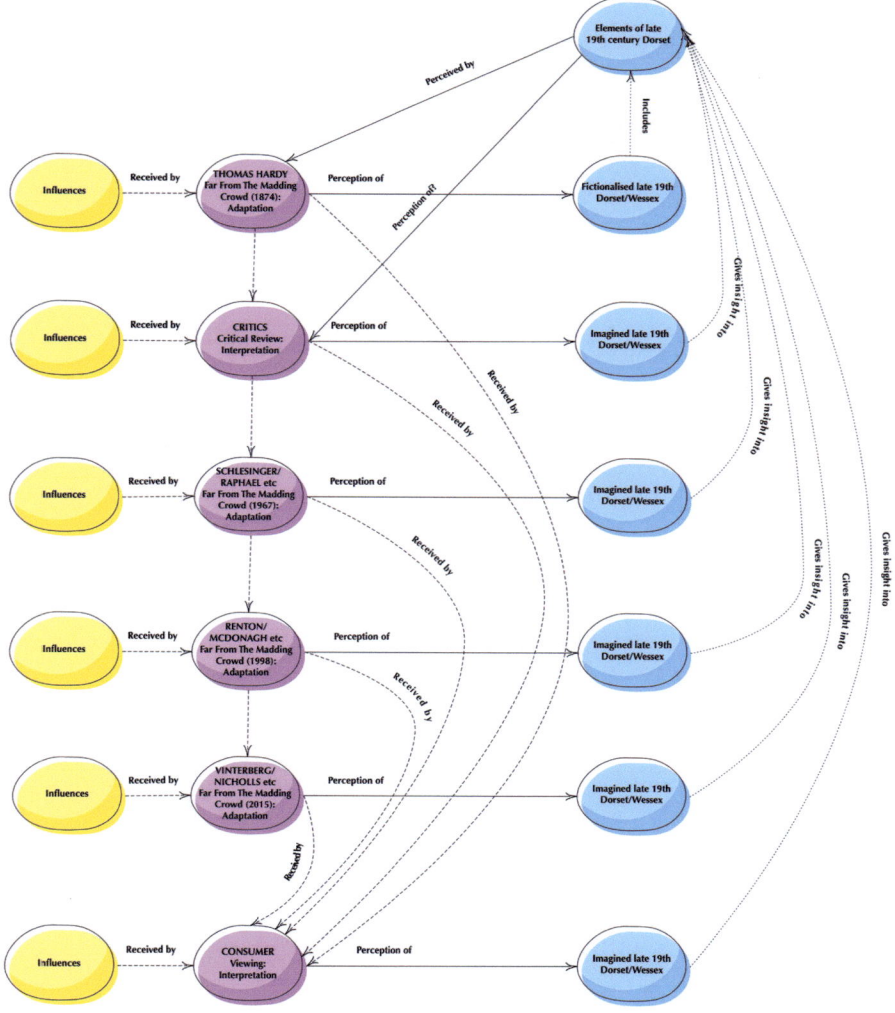

Figure 3.8: Far from the Madding Crowd Layering Process – Consumer View.

the form of Julie Christie and Terence Stamp, which for many proved a distraction that the 1998 series, in the mind of the *Daily Mail* reviewer at least, was seen to address.

This does not suggest a direct uncluttered line from the author's perceived world, to book, to film and to the consumer's perceived world. All through that process both internal and external influences act on the perception or reception of Hardy's world, the book, the adaptations, and our own acts of consumption. Figure 3.8 illustrates how the idea of internal and external influences within the fiction process model may work with regard to how a consumer perceives the world of *Far from the Madding Crowd*. The process begins with the historical Dorset society and landscape perceived by Hardy that is, subject to his particular influences, adapted by him into the imagined Wessex world of the novel. Influences specific to Hardy might include his upbringing, his education, the literary styles of the day, exposure to dialect writers such as William Barnes and the target audience for his work. Different actors then play a part within the ongoing process.

The diagram includes the critics who review the novel, the various filmmakers who take the novel and adapt it in visual terms, and the consumers who read the novel, absorb the critical analysis, or view the adaptation, but also included might be interpreters of literary places and compilers of literary guidebooks linked with Hardy. Each actor takes the novel and, governed in addition by their individual influences, imagines their own version of Hardy's imagined Wessex which then informs the artefact that they produce within the process model. Note therefore how, as time passes, potential layers of interpretation and adaptation build up, such that a reader of the novel or a viewer of an adaptation of the novel, in the present, may have awareness of the many other artefacts arising out of the novel.

The contemporary critics, as will be seen in the following chapter, judging by their reaction to the novel were in part influenced by a suspicion of a writer who was then little known, by their distance from, and unfamiliarity with, Dorset, and by preconceptions and prejudices about social classes. Each set of filmmakers then had their individual set of influences. To take the makers of the 2015 film as an example, they might have been affected by the requirements of the production in terms of locations chosen, the design, the optimum length for the production and the perceived target audience, and also by any detailed historical research they might have carried out, and by the two previous filmed adaptations in 1967 and 1998. We as consumers of that film, if we come with foreknowledge, might be affected by our knowledge of Hardy and his novels, by our historical understanding and familiarity with historical or present-day Dorset, by previous critical responses to the novel and the film, or by previous adaptations we might have seen.

This is demonstrated in the analysis of the reviews of *North and South* in Section 3.4, which shows how, in the eyes of consumers, the way they view adaptations can be affected by other adaptations in the same way that adapters themselves can be affected by previous adaptations. There is particular mention of the way many lay reviewers of the 2005 BBC adaptation of Elizabeth Gaskell's *North and South* saw the adaptation through the lens of the previous decade's adaptation of Austen's *Pride and Prejudice*, a novel set in a different time and in a different social environment. Another example below show how different influences may have affected adaptations of one of the other case study authors. Section 6.5 demonstrates how contemporary influences came into play in three filmed adaptations of J.B. Priestley's *The Good Companions*. In two of these adaptations the influence of Hollywood musicals of the day appeared an important influence on the filmmakers and had the effect of moving the adaptation away from a purely realist re-telling of the novel towards an attempt to compete with such musicals. In another adaptation, made for television, there is an acknowledgment from the adapters both of the need for an attempt to recreate the look and feel of the time, but also of the influence of the vogue at the time for television musicals in the musical numbers.

To conclude, the world created by filmmakers can be seen as but one of a succession of imagined worlds that are created during the classic fiction process model, each of which can provide us with insights back into the past world that lies behind an author's novel. The world the filmmaker creates is potentially more immediate and powerful because it is the printed page brought to visual and aural life. The amount of insight that the imagined world in the adaptation then gives us about the historical world perceived by the author depends on the degree to which the influences on the filmmakers, and the decisions they make as they adapt a novel, enhance, distort, or otherwise alter the perception of the author's world. The immediacy of adaptations becomes important if fiction is to be considered as a resource for the study of history.

The introduction to this chapter quoted Herlihy using the word 'illusion' to describe the nature of a period adaptation, a word defined by the Oxford English Dictionary as a 'wrong or misinterpreted perception of a sensory experience', which, if he meant to use the word in that way, suggests he sees adaptations as essentially unreliable.[255] However, relative consumption figures suggest we are more likely to get a view of history from adapted period dramas than from their source novels. If this is indeed the case, then it is important that we understand the dramas in the context of the means by which they were produced, the influences that affected those producing them, and decisions taken by the filmmakers as a result which may affect the historical pictures presented within the dramas. With such an understanding, adaptations have the capacity to provide us with valuable historical insights. Without such an understanding, the immediacy of adaptations has the potential to mislead us with its 'illusion' as, in Bartholeyns' terms, we see less 'historicity' and more 'authenticity'. We must also view the dramas with the understanding that the majority of adaptations come from the relatively small pool of source novels that have achieved 'classic' status and that the vast majority of fiction written in, and about, any given period in the past, is now lost to all but the most diligent reader. As with a historian who operates from a restricted, incomplete record of the past, so we are invited to base our vision of a period on an incomplete set of novels and adaptations from that period and must therefore balance our judgements accordingly.

---

255 *English Oxford Living Dictionaries: Illusion,* (Oxford: Oxford University Press, 2019) <https://en.oxforddictionaries.com/definition/illusion>.

4

The Critical Process

4.1 Introduction

The previous two chapters discussed how within the two forms through which the imagined worlds of classic fiction are often received by present-day consumers, namely adaptations and the interpretations at literary places, the multiplicity of inputs and influences combine to add a number of layers between the imagined world we create when we view the adaptation or interpretation and the imagined world originally created by an author based on their perception of their contemporary world. This chapter journeys back closer to the process whereby novelists take their experience of a contemporary or near-contemporary world and incorporate it into the imagined world of a novel, by looking at how, after a novel has been edited, published and marketed, especially in book form, it is read, analysed and reviewed by literary critics. The future success of the novel can often rest on what they then say. The primary purpose of a literary critic might normally be to judge on the literary merit of the novel, or on whether it is told in an interesting, entertaining, and satisfying way. The pure literary worth of any piece of fiction is not the primary concern here as such. However, contributing to that literary value of the novel is the way the characters are described and interact within the novel's setting. Those are therefore the main elements of reviews that this chapter examines.

Important with regard to the layering of the process model is the fact that contemporary critics of novels may have some of the same reference points as the author, simply by living in the same place at the same time and sharing the same educational, social and economic backgrounds, with the result that they can comprehend the cultural context and the physical setting of the novel. That does not necessarily mean that they will agree on whether or not the novel is a truthful reflection of the contemporary world that they share with the author, as is demonstrated in Section 4.3 in contrasting views of the veracity of Elizabeth Gaskell's portrayal of industrial life in Manchester in *Mary Barton*. Conversely, as is shown in Section 4.2, where critics may not have first-hand knowledge of the world of the author, authenticity may, or may not, be taken on trust. As discussed in Section 1.2, if each of us perceives our contemporary world differently, then each has a different conception of what the 'real world' is. Whether critics try to be dispassionate, to take the novel at face value and embrace the view of the world that the author describes, or alternatively read the novel with their own prejudices and interests to the fore, there are basic principles that Rod Allen, in describing the art of reviewing, believes should drive the act of reviewing. Firstly, critics should represent the interests of the reader rather than the writer of the novel being reviewed, and in this context, ensure reviews are written fairly. Secondly, critics need to be aware of the market served by the publication for which they are reviewing. Finally, critics need to provide their own opinions within a defined framework. Critics should therefore be conscious of the nature of both their own readership, and the potential readership of the novel, in terms of their levels of knowledge and cultural tastes and should pitch the tone of their review accordingly. Allen, for example, imagines that 'a review in *Socialist Worker* will be very different from one in *Loaded*'.[256]

The question then arises as to whether targeted literary reviews, in whatever form they take, affect sales of a novel, and thereby the number of people consuming the imagined world of that novel. Michael Clement, Dennis Proppe and Armin Rott define literary critics as being 'opinion leaders', whose reviews have a similar promotional effect to the efforts of the publisher, encouraging risk-averse potential customers to buy the book.[257] They analysed sales of new books following their appearance on the popular German TV book show *Das Literarische Quartett* and concluded that sales of books generally increased following a review on the show regardless of whether the opinions expressed on the show were favourable or not. Word-of-mouth contact made by the viewing public following a review was strong but may have been even stronger following a bad review.[258] This relationship between the critic, the review, and the author goes back to the earliest days of the English novel. Frank Donoghue writes of authors checking the two premier literary magazines of the 18th century, the *Monthly Review,* and the *Critical Review*, 'whenever they or someone they knew had just published a book'.[259] With the expansion of the readership of such journals and their growing importance as arbiters of taste in the latter half of that century, Donoghue believes that 'literary careers were chiefly described, and indeed made possible, by reviewers'.[260]

Within the period covered here, critical reviews would appear in many different types of publication, from daily newspapers such as *The Times*, and weekly political and current affairs journals like *The Spectator*, through to monthly magazines offering a general miscellany of news and views, such as *Blackwood's Edinburgh Magazine*. There was a large rise during the 19th century in the number of periodicals offering critical reviews of fiction, mirroring the growth in the production of fiction and the growth amongst the middle classes in the reading of fiction as a pastime. Joanne Shattock describes the rise of the periodical during this period, and how between 1815 and 1832 twenty new periodicals, and probably more, were published.[261] By the middle of the century the job of reviewer and

---

256 Rod Allen, 'The Art of Reviewing', in *Print Journalism: A Critical Introduction,* ed. by Richard Keeble (London and New York: Routledge, 2005), p. 180.

257 Michel Clement, Dennis Proppe, and Armin Rott, 'Do Critics Make Bestsellers? Opinion Leaders and the Success of Books', *Journal of Media Economics*, 20 (2007), pp. 77-105.

258 Ibid. p. 100.

259 Frank Donoghue, The Fame Machine: Book Reviewing and Eighteenth-Century Literary Careers (Stanford: Stanford University Press, 1996), p. 16.

260 Ibid. p. 3.

261 Joanne Shattock, 'The Culture of Criticism', in *The Cambridge Companion to English Literature, 1830-1914*, ed. by Joanne Shattock (Cambridge: Cambridge University Press, 2010), p. 72.

essayist for those periodicals had gradually become a respected and lucrative occupation. She quotes G.H. Lewes, writing in 1847, describing how 'literature', meaning the writing of reviews and essays for the expanding number of periodicals, had become a profession:

> In England, a journalist of 'ordinary ability' could hope to earn between £200 and £1,000 a year, a sum beyond the expectations of his counterparts in Germany and France where payments for articles were much smaller, and where the range of... publications open to the English journalist did not exist.[262]

Shattock also quotes the example of George Saintsbury, who spent a quarter of a century writing and reviewing for a number of periodicals, claiming that he could 'earn on average £3 10s for an evening's reading and a morning's writing'.[263] So where once critics either had to tout their articles around the periodicals, or wait for invitations from them to provide copy, increasingly the profession became one where one could make a good living. Many of the same names therefore come up across a variety of journals, names such as Lewes himself, Walter Bagehot, and Richard Holt Hutton. It was also a source of income for many women writers, including Marian Evans, who made her name as a critic before achieving fame as a novelist under the pseudonym of George Eliot.[264]

Especially in the periodicals, many of the reviews took the form of detailed essays, in which the review was often accompanied by a plot synopsis and extensive extracts from the novel. These longer reviews or essays took a considered view of the story and its worth, but also covered the characterisations and the setting, and a significant element of these reviews was consideration of how close these were to 'reality', or at least to reality as understood by the reviewer. Walter Bagehot coined the term 'review-like essay' or alternatively 'essay-like review' to describe these longer articles. The purpose of such reviews, according to Bagehot, was not to baffle or confuse the reader with 'the tedium of exhaustive discussion', but 'to speak to the many so that they will listen, – that they will like to listen, – that they will understand'.[265] Bagehot appreciated the claims on the reader's time in an increasingly fast-moving world and was of the opinion that the essay form was the ideal one to get a message across:

> The modern man must be told what to think – shortly, no doubt – but he **must** be told it. The essay-like criticism of modern times is about the length which he likes.[266]

The norm in the early part of the 19th century was for periodical articles to be unsigned, but as the century progressed so this practice gradually lessened. Shattock quotes a figure of 97% anonymity for articles written before 1865, a figure that dropped to 57% by the end of the century.[267] The general belief was that anonymity offered protection to the reviewer

---

262 Ibid.
263 Ibid. p. 71.
264 Ibid. p. 73.
265 Walter Bagehot, 'The First Edinburgh Reviewers (1855)', in *Literary Studies by the late Walter Bagehot, Vol. 1*, ed. by Richard Holt Hutton (London: Longmans, Green & Co., 1884), p. 147.
266 Ibid. p. 149.
267 Walter E. Houghton, *The Wellesley Index to Victorian periodicals, 1824-1900* (Toronto: University of Toronto Press, 1966), p. xvi., quoted in Shattock (2010) p. 81.

and gave them the freedom to express their views openly, as was the case with William Rathbone Greg's unsigned review of Elizabeth Gaskell's *Mary Barton* (see Section 4.3).

This chapter looks at how reviewers tackled the novels of Gaskell and Hardy, specifically Gaskell's *Mary Barton*, and Hardy's *Far from the Madding Crowd* and *Tess of the d'Urbervilles*. These particular novels were chosen to illustrate how the degree of familiarity the reviewers have with the elements of the contemporary world that inform the novel may have affected their perceptions of a novel's veracity. For example, many reviewers were personally acquainted with the authors whom they were reviewing. John Forster was a friend and biographer of Charles Dickens and reviewed many of his novels. He also recommended Elizabeth Gaskell's *Mary Barton* to its eventual publisher before reviewing the same in *The Examiner*. William Rathbone Greg, whose review of *Mary Barton* is discussed below, was a Unitarian and attended the chapel at which William Gaskell, Elizabeth's husband, was a minister. His father Samuel was, as was William, a member of the Manchester Literary and Philosophical society. Because Greg was also a member of a mill-owning family, he felt himself well placed to comment on the veracity of *Mary Barton*.

However, there were situations where there was not such a direct connection between the critic and the novelist, or between the critic and the subject matter of the novelist. Thomas Hardy, with his humble origins in rural Dorset and local grammar school education, began developing as a writer well away from the literary elite. At the beginning of this novel-writing career, certain aspects of the reviews may have exhibited a lack of empathy between the reviewer and author, both stylistically in terms of *how* he wrote, and culturally in terms of his subject matter.

The remainder of this chapter, therefore, considers how reviewers judged the descriptions of people and places in Gaskell and Hardy's novels. Both of these novelists were writing about a contemporary world with which they were familiar. From their own standpoint and bearing in mind the varieties of self-filtering that have been described in the previous chapters, they would have believed that they were writing to a large degree from life. The critics received this world portrayed by the novelist and filtered it via their own perception of the world, and their own prejudices and standpoints to produce their own judgement as to whether they considered that world to be truly 'authentic' in the sense of reflecting an actual world that they saw existing behind the fiction. With Gaskell, the focus is on William Rathbone Greg, a reviewer who had a wealth of personal information on which to base his consideration (Section 4.3). The first case study deals with Hardy and shows how an unfamiliarity with the subject matter in his early novel *Far from the Madding Crowd* may have affected the understanding of it on the part of his critics (Section 4.2). As the critics became more familiar with the author, his style, and his world in a later novel such as *Tess of the D'Urbervilles*, so the subject matter tended to get accepted as in some sense authentic, even though the critics may have been no closer to an understanding of the actual Dorset background of the novel than they were before.

4.2 Thomas Hardy and the London Critics

Thomas Hardy was born in 1840 in the Dorset hamlet of Higher Bockhampton, about four miles from the town of Dorchester. The thatched cottage where he was born and from where his father operated as a stonemason and builder still stands, lying within Thorncombe Wood close to the expanse of heathland that Hardy later fictionalised as

Egdon Heath.[268] After receiving a classical education at the British School in Dorchester,[269] he stayed in the town to begin training as an architect, a career he moved to London to pursue in 1862. However, school had given him a taste for literature and a possible career as a writer, and he soon returned to the family home to devote himself to writing professionally. Other than a brief spell in London after his first marriage in 1874, he remained in Dorset until his death in 1928, finally settling in Max Gate, a self-designed house built on the outskirts of Dorchester.[270] Hardy spent his early years immersed in a rural working-class community, and when he began writing novels, he soon he turned to this community as source material.[271] Much of his early work, including novels such as *Under the Greenwood Tree* and *Far from the Madding Crowd*, was created in the house in Higher Bockhampton in which he was born. The village of Mellstock, the fictional setting for his second published novel *Under the Greenwood Tree*, is modelled on Bockhampton and nearby Stinsford.[272] Later novels, including *Far from the Madding Crowd* and *Tess of the d'Urbervilles*, similarly use geographical settings based on actual Dorset models, a fact that Hardy eventually explicitly acknowledged.

Far from the Madding Crowd was Hardy's fourth published novel, serialised first in Cornhill Magazine, and then brought out in book form in November 1874.[273] It tells the story of a love quadrangle that apart from a few scenes in neighbouring Casterbridge (which is itself based on Dorchester), takes place within a rural community that is modelled on the area within which Hardy grew up; the house that was later recognized as the model for fictional Weatherbury is located close to present-day Puddletown a few miles north of Higher Bockhampton, on the edge of the same heath that also adjoins that village.[274]

When Hardy describes rural scenes, there is evidence of his close acquaintance with the physical landscape of rural Dorset in the latter half of the 19th century. The novel is full of descriptions of rural life and the major rituals of the farming year and also references folk songs and tunes such as 'The Seeds of Love'[275] and 'Soldier's Joy',[276] that he learned from his father and would have played at country dances in his youth.[277] The novel was also, in size, tone and subject matter, altogether on a larger scale than early novels such as

---

268 Hardy set most of his novel *The Return of the Native* on Egdon Heath.

269 The 'British Schools' were the non-conformist equivalent of the 'National Schools' set up by the Church of England. Both aimed to provide consistent free education in the basics of reading, writing, arithmetic and religion to children of less advantaged families before the introduction of universal state education. Derek Gillard, 'Towards Mass Education', in *Education in England: A History* (Derek Gillard, 2018). <http://www.educationengland.org.uk/history>.

270 Biographical information from Michael Millgate, 'Hardy, Thomas (1840-1928)', in *Oxford Dictionary of National Biography*, ed. by H.C.G. Matthew, Brian Harrison, and David (Online Editor) Cannadine (Oxford: Oxford University Press, 2004, online edition 2006). <http://www.oxforddnbcom/view/article/33708>.

271 Hardy's first published novel, *Desperate Remedies*, is a melodramatic tale of murder and intrigue set in a largely middle-class world, though one of the characters, like Hardy, was a young architect, an early example of Hardy writing from life.

272 Tomalin (2007) p. 116.

273 Thomas Hardy, *Far from the Madding Crowd* (London: Smith, Elder & Co., 1874).

274 The link between Waterston Manor and Weatherbury is made in many sources, one of the earliest being Bertram C. A. Windle, *The Wessex of Thomas Hardy* (London: John Lane: The Bodley Head, 1902), pp. 75-6.

275 Hardy (1874 (1993 edition)) p. 121.

276 Ibid. p. 190.

277 Tomalin (2007) pp. 19-20. The Dorset County Museum contains Hardy's own transcription of the tune for the song *O Jan! O Jan! O Jan!*, which he had remembered from childhood dances he had played and which he describes as being as suitable for 'any dance in 2/4 time'.

Under the Greenwood Tree, and was a pointer to the later, tragic, novels such as *The Mayor of Casterbridge* and *Tess of the d'Urbervilles*.

The volume of The Critical Heritage series devoted to Hardy quotes six contemporary reviews of the novel,[278] to which further searches have uncovered an additional review. In addition to these literary reviews, there were a number of press reviews of the initial serialisation of the novel as it progressed, much in the style of modern reviews assessing the latest instalment of a television serial. Whilst these often simply talked of the latest plot development, many of the comments looked ahead to the two main preoccupations of the literary reviews, namely praise for the depiction of the rural setting of the story and criticism of the nature of the language of Hardy's peasant chorus. Therefore, we have mentions of 'interesting glimpses of pastoral life',[279] 'a singularly original and clever story of rustic life',[280] a 'very amusing and pastoral tale'[281] on the one hand, and of dialogue being 'here and there being altogether unnatural',[282] and of the story's 'quaint Shakespearean clowns' on the other.[283]

When reading the critical reviews of the novel, these two main themes reappear. Firstly, there is the general praise for the aforementioned descriptions of rural life and customs. *The Graphic* compared the writing favourably to that of George Eliot, talking of being carried '"far from the madding crowd" of cities, with their varied and rapidly changing life, to West Country fields and farms' and their 'primitive and homely surroundings'.[284] *The Athenæum* could think of 'no other living author who could have described the burning rick-yard, or the approaching thunderstorm, or given us the wonderful comicalities of the supper at the malthouse'.[285] Richard Holt Hutton in *The Spectator* praised the various descriptions of farming practices and festivities, suggesting that Hardy was shedding light on an unfamiliar world:

> … from everything [the reader] reads he carries away new images, and as it were, new experience, taken from the life of a region before almost unknown. A book like this is, in relation to many of the scenes it describes, the nearest equivalent to actual experience which a great many of us are ever likely to boast of.[286]

Henry James, to whom the review in the American journal *The Nation* is attributed, was also impressed by the descriptions, seeing a man well-grounded in the settings he described:

> Mr. Hardy describes nature with a great deal of felicity, and is evidently very much at home among rural phenomena. The most genuine thing about his book, to our sense, is a certain aroma of the meadows and lanes – a natural relish for harvesting and sheep-washings.[287]

---

278   R. G. Cox, *Thomas Hardy: The Critical Heritage* (London: Routledge & Kegan Paul, 1970).
279   Anon, 'Literature of the Week – The Magazines, &c', *Hampshire Advertiser*, January 10th, 1874.
280   Anon, 'Roundabout. By The Square Man', *Judy*, January 28th, 1874.
281   Anon, 'Magazines for March', *Bell's Life in London and Sporting Chronicle*, March 7th, 1874.
282   Anon, 'Roundabout. By The Square Man', *Judy*, March 11th, 1874.
283   Anon, 'Monthly Mag-Pie', *Fun*, July 11th, 1874 p. 21.
284   Anon, 'New Novels – "Far From The Madding Crowd"', *The Graphic*, December 12th, 1874, p. 567.
285   Anon, '*Far from the Madding Crowd* Review', *The Athenæum*, December 5th, 1874, p. 747.
286   Richard Holt Hutton, '*Far from the Madding Crowd* Review', *The Spectator*, December 19th, 1874, pp. 1597-9.
287   Henry James, '*Far from the Madding Crowd* Review', *The Nation*, December 24th, 1874, pp. 423-4.

Andrew Lang, writing in *The Academy*, saw three main elements to the story: the descriptions of man and beast and their struggles with nature; the minor characters, who form the rural chorus that provide the backdrop to, and commentate on, the main story; and the major characters, Bathsheba and her suitors. Of these three he saw perfection in just the first, the setting: 'Of these three component parts of the tale, the first may be pronounced nearly perfect, and worthy of all praise'.[288]

So, there was general praise for the fictional world within which the novel is set. However, within this praise there was an implied note of unfamiliarity with this 'region before unknown', the Dorset/Wessex that Hardy described. This sense of unfamiliarity comes over strongly in two further reviews. Hutton wrote that 'the life of the agricultural districts in the South-Western counties – Dorsetshire probably – is a new field for the novelist',[289] and the *Saturday Review* talked of its setting being 'a part of the country that has not yet become hackneyed'.[290]

Of the three attributed reviewers here, all living in London, Hutton was a Yorkshireman, Lang was a Scotsman, and James was an American expatriate. It seems unlikely that their experience of Dorset would have been great, and nothing in their reviews suggests any intimate familiarity with the region. For example, Leon Edel's biography of James lists his many and varied travels throughout Europe and North America, but the closest he indicates James got to Dorset or Dorchester were short visits to Salisbury and Winchester during his first adult exploration of England in 1869.[291] The Salisbury area and Winchester both appear briefly at the end of *Tess of the d'Urbervilles*, when Tess is arrested at Stonehenge and later executed in Wintoncester (Winchester), but both are some distance from the Wessex heartlands around Dorchester. Lang was a Scottish anthropologist, classicist and historian who settled in London in the 1870s, but no evidence was found in his limited biographical record that, despite a life-long interest in folklore, he ever specifically investigated the regional folk history of South West England, or indeed ever visited the area.[292] Hutton was a journalist and theologian living and working in London, and again there is nothing in his brief biographical record that suggests familiarity with Dorset.[293] If they were indeed unfamiliar with the area, they would have been taking the descriptions offered them at face value, as read, with little in the way of their own experience with which to compare them. They believe what they read in the way it is described, and by using words such as 'genuine' and 'actual', suggest that they see a degree of authenticity in the descriptions.

A second element of the reviews is the attitude of the critics towards the novel's dialogue, especially the words that Hardy put into the mouth of his rustic chorus. A chief

288   Andrew Lang, '*Far from the Madding Crowd* Review', *The Academy*, January 2nd, 1875, pp. 9-10.
289   Hutton (December 19th, 1874).
290   Anon, '*Far from the Madding Crowd* Review', *Saturday Review*, January 9th, 1875, pp. 57-8. Reproduced in Cox (1970) p. 39.
291   Leon Edel, Henry James – A Life (London: Flamingo, 1996), p. 96.
292   William Donaldson, 'Lang, Andrew (1844-19120', in *Oxford Dictionary of National Biography*, ed. by H.C.G. Matthew, Brian Harrison, and David Cannadine (Oxford: Oxford University Press, 2004, online edition 2010). <http://www.oxforddnb.com/view/article/34396>.
293   Harold Orel, 'Hutton, Richard Holt (1826-1897)', in *Oxford Dictionary of National Biography*, ed. by H.C.G. Matthew, Brian Harrison, and David Cannadine (Oxford: Oxford University Press, 2004, online edition 2006). <http://www.oxforddnb.com/view/10.1093/ref:odnb/9780198614128.001.0001/odnb-9780198614128-e-14312>.

protagonist here is again Lang, whose review included criticism of the type of speech employed by the country people in the novel:

> Few men know the agricultural labourer at home, and it is possible that he is what Mr. Hardy describes him... Odd scraps of a kind of rural euphuism, misapplication of scripture, and fragments of modern mechanical wit, are stirred up into a queer mixture... Shepherds may talk in this way: we hope not; but if they do, it is a revelation; and if they don't, it is nonsense, and not very amusing nonsense.[294]

A particular interest of Lang's was the comparative study of customs and myths between different societies across the globe. He had a belief in the 'psychic unity' of societies, the development of similar myths and cultural practices in different societies despite there being no contact between them. He believed that 'European Society had a thin 'progressive' upper stratum in which alone true cultural change took place, and a sluggishly conservative underclass which had never seriously changed its ancient beliefs'.[295] While it appears he had the greatest respect for the intellect of the underclasses, it was for intellect in its own terms, and he may have approached the speech of the rustics in Hardy's novel with a certain prejudice against the very possibility of the high-flown dialogue Hardy puts in their mouths. He was not alone in this. The reviewer in *The Athenæum* put forward his views equally stridently:

> He is evidently a shrewd observer of the talk and habits of the Somersetshire [sic] rustics; and yet he puts such expressions into their mouth... which we simply cannot believe possible from the illiterate clods whom he describes.[296]

The Spectator's reviewer saw Hardy simply putting in his characters' mouths his own 'cultivated' thoughts 'to which he would himself have given utterance had he been in their place, but which come most unnaturally from the mouths from which they actually proceed'.[297] Even the American incomer Henry James criticised the way in which Hardy, when voicing his characters, 'fills their mouths with quaint turns of speech'.[298] The critic in *The Saturday Review* employed thinly veiled sarcasm to suggest that we had been misled in considering the 'farm-labourer of the Southern counties' as untaught and barely more intelligent than the beasts they tend. Such notions 'are ruthlessly overturned by Mr. Hardy's novel. Under his hand Bœtians became Athenians in acuteness, Germans in capacity for philosophic speculation, and Parisians in polish'.[299]

The reviewers' final conclusions on *Far from the Madding Crowd* were mixed. They saw a gifted writer, and they saw the power of his descriptive writing, but could not see past their dissatisfaction with his style and the nature of his dialogue. Lang put it simply: '...Far from the Madding Crowd displays undeniable talent, which has scarcely as yet

---

294 Lang (January 2nd, 1875).
295 Donaldson (2004, online edition 2010).
296 Anon (December 5th, 1874).
297 Hutton (December 19th, 1874).
298 James (December 24th, 1874).
299 Anon (January 9th, 1875) Reproduced in Cox (1970) pp. 40-1.

found its best and easiest and most natural expression'.[300] The review in *The Spectator* came to a similar conclusion:

> Mr. Hardy goes wrong by being too clever, preposterously clever where the world is stupid, too original where he ought to be accommodating himself to the monotonous habits of a world which is built on usage. It is a rare kind of mistake.[301]

There was therefore some encouragement for Hardy, but encouragement laced with a degree of condescension, perhaps the best example of which came in *The Athenæum's* review:

> He ought to hold his peace for at least two years, revise with extreme care, and refrain from publishing in magazines; then, though he has not done it yet, he may possibly write a nearly, if not quite, first-rate novel.[302]

These reviews tell us something about Hardy's novel and the authenticity of its descriptions of people and places, but they also tell us about the reviewers themselves and their own prejudices and preconceptions. Given their presumed unfamiliarity with Dorset one could query whether the reviewers' estimations of the accuracy of Hardy's descriptions of place and people is reliable. The question then arises as to whether, if reading the review persuaded people to read the novel, the reviewers could be influencing the process model by creating impressions and preconceptions in the readers' minds that may not have been there if they had read the novel according to just its own merits.

One further factor that becomes more relevant when discussing critics' reactions to *Tess of the d'Urbervilles*, is that critics and readers were still in the process of discovering this writer. After three relatively light and undemanding novels this was the first of his novels to be written at length and in depth. It was also Hardy's first true popular success, with the first printing of 1,000 copies selling out within two months, which emphasises the possibility that both his style and his subject matter were only just becoming familiar to many of the critics and most of the readers.[303] Whilst they were comfortable with the descriptions of country scenes, given their more stereotypical appeal, the one element of the novel that was truly unfamiliar could have been the Dorset dialect as rendered by Hardy.

One should also bear in mind the extent to which Hardy was at this time very much a provincial writer, and the reviews suggest he was viewed as such by the critics. The feeling of being a provincial outsider was something that Hardy himself had throughout his life. Ralph Pite writes of the conferment late in life of an Honorary Fellowship of Magdalene College, Cambridge, being what 'finally put to rest his sense of exclusion – his feeling that his working-class, provincial origins had condemned him to being a perpetual outsider'.[304] This sense of exclusion may have led to Hardy's sensitivity to bad reviews that Tomalin hints at when she says of an early negative review that 'Hardy never did forget it, any more than he developed a thick skin'.[305] There is a contrast with the way that critics

300   Lang (January 2nd, 1875).
301   Hutton (December 19th, 1874).
302   Anon (December 5th, 1874).
303   Tomalin (2007) p. 147.
304   Ralph Pite, *Thomas Hardy: The Guarded Life* (London: Picador, 2006), p. 445.
305   Tomalin (2007) p. 114.

approached the works of Charles Dickens, and in particular the way Dickens portrayed his home city of London. The following assessments of Dickens' characterisation of London were all written by writers, Walter Bagehot, John Forster, and Abraham Hayward, who were London-based and who were therefore presumably familiar with the real-world London that Dickens was using as the basis for his novels. They attest to the accuracy of his descriptions of both London life and London speech:

> Mr Dickens' genius is especially suited to the delineation of city life... He has, too, the peculiar alertness of observation that is observable in those who live by it. He describes London like a special correspondent for posterity.[306]

> With him, we pass along misty streets in some cold and foggy morning... we could not doubt that it was LONDON... At all times, and under every aspect, he gives us to feel and see the great city as it absolutely is. Its interior life is made as familiar to us as its exterior forms.[307]

> The primary cause, then, of this author's success, we take to be his felicity in working up the genuine mother-wit and unadulterated vernacular idioms of the lower classes of London...[308]

Such observations created a close association in the minds of many between the fictional world of Dickens' novels and the historical world of 19th century London. As Murray Baumgarten says, '[Dickens' fictions] stamp London with their characteristic perspectives. His contemporaries (like our own) saw the city through the eyes he provided'.[309]

Hayward's comments about Dickens' reporting of London speech remind us that the most pointed criticisms of Hardy's novel were for its reporting of the words uttered by Hardy's peasants, and the way he reacted to them is indicative of how he viewed his own sense of authenticity. Hardy spent all of his early life in rural Dorset and so would have been familiar with the Dorset vernacular. His grammar school education and architectural apprenticeship in Dorchester, as well as his own literary ambitions, would have ironed out the rough corners of his own mode of speech and given him a vocabulary far greater than that of most of his rural characters, but he would have known the speech patterns and sentence constructions of the Dorset peasantry with a degree of accuracy.

When assessing whether Hardy's peasants in the novel could have spoken like this in actuality one can compare Hardy's dialogue with the work of the poet William Barnes. Barnes had equally humble beginnings to Hardy, born a Dorset farmer's son in 1801, though he later became an Anglican priest. From 1862 until his death in 1886 he was

---

306 Walter Bagehot, *The Collected Works of Walter Bagehot*, ed. by Norman St. John-Stevas, Vol. II (London: The Economist, 1965), p. 87. Quoted in Rosemarie Bodenheimer, 'London in the Victorian Novel', in *The Cambridge Companion to the Literature of London*, ed. by Lawrence Manley (Cambridge: Cambridge University Press, 2011), p. 143.

307 John Forster, '*Nicholas Nickleby* Review', *The Examiner*, 27 Oct. 1839, p. 677.

308 Abraham Hayward, 'Review of *Pickwick Papers* Nos I-XVII ', *Quarterly Review*, (October 1837). Reproduced in Philip Collins, *Dickens: The Critical Heritage* (London: Routledge & Kegan Paul, 1971), p. 60.

309 Murray Baumgarten, 'Fictions of the city', in *The Cambridge Companion to Charles Dickens*, ed. by John O. Jordan (Cambridge: Cambridge University Press, 2001), p. 107.

Rector of Winterborne Came, a village close to Dorchester, and achieved fame for his poems written in the Dorset vernacular. Hardy knew Barnes well, and Tomalin reports how when practising poetry Hardy would write down in his notebook words and phrases that had caught his fancy, often copying chunks of Barnes' poems.[310] Hardy's affinity with both Barnes and Dorset speech was reflected in Hardy's obituary of Barnes in which he wrote that their shared dialect was 'a distinct branch of Teutonic speech... richer in many classes of words than any other tongue known to him'.[311] Defending his use of language against criticism in the *Athenaeum*, he talked of conveying 'the spirit of intelligent peasant talk' by retaining 'the idiom, compass and characteristic expressions', rather than recording precise inflections.[312] In a later essay, Hardy also defended the Dorset way of speaking against those who would make a 'caricature' of it. A visitor by rail from London would find that on encountering a Dorset native, that their language, far from being a 'vile corruption of cultivated speech, was a tongue with a grammatical inflection rarely disregarded by his entertainer'. He saw the mode of speech being a combination of a National School education and 'the unwritten, dying, Wessex English that they had learnt of their parents', with the result being 'a composite language without rule or harmony', similar in other words to the way Hardy himself would have learned to speak.[313] Leslie Howsam reported the publisher Charles Kegan Paul, born in Somerset and for many years a vicar in Dorset, praising Hardy's style as 'he was able, more so than a critic brought up in London, to judge Hardy's familiarity with Dorset customs and dialect'.[314] All this is circumstantial evidence for hearing at least the basic structure of the historical 19th century Dorset dialect in the reported dialogue of novels such as *Far from the Madding Crowd.* The main sticking point with the critics, however, appeared to be not so much the way the dialogue was structured, but its content, the words, and allusions, usually biblical, that Hardy put into the mouths of his characters. Lang drew particular attention to the following passage. Note the use of the words 'promiscuous' and 'conceive':

'However, I look round upon life quite **promiscuous**. Do you **conceive** me, neighbours? My words, though made as simple as I can, mid be rather deep for some heads'.

'O yes, Henery, we quite **conceive** ye'.[315]

This is indeed how this passage read when it originally appeared in the Cornhill magazine,[316] and also when it first appeared in book form published by Smith, Elder and Co. in 1874, the version that Lang would have been reviewing.[317] However, Hardy was throughout his life constantly revising his novels as new editions came out, and it is possible from the

310   Tomalin (2007) pp. 73-4.
311   Quoted in Raymond Chapman, *The Language of Thomas Hardy* (Basingstoke: Macmillan, 1990), p. 112.
312   Quoted in ibid. p. 113.
313   Thomas Hardy, 'The Dorsetshire Labourer', *Longman's Magazine*, July 1883, pp. 252-69.
314   Leslie Howsam, Kegan Paul, a Victorian Imprint: Publishers, Books and Cultural History (London: Kegan Paul International, 1998), p. 82.
315   As quoted in Lang (January 2nd, 1875).
316   Thomas Hardy, 'Far from the Madding Crowd', *Cornhill Magazine*, 1874.
317   Hardy (1874) p. 252.

evidence presented below that whilst railing against criticism of the authenticity of his novels' language on the one hand, on the other hand he may have taken note of some of the criticisms of the complexity of the language and made changes accordingly through time. Elizabeth James cites the many times *Far from the Madding Crowd* was revised, quoting revisions in 1895, 1901, 1902 and finally in 1912. Changes were made for a variety of reasons, to ensure topographical details were consistent across all of what came to be known as the Wessex novels, to change meanings, and, importantly in this context, to change certain words.[318] In the 1895 edition, the above passage now read as follows:

'However, I look round upon life quite **cool**. Do you **take** me, neighbours? My words, though made as simple as I can, mid be rather deep for some heads'.

'O yes, Henery, we quite **take** ye'.[319]

Hardy had changed the two Latinate words, 'promiscuous' and 'conceive', and replaced them with two simpler words of Anglo-Saxon origin, 'cool' and 'take'. Hardy did not stop there with this particular passage. The final version that appears in modern editions has a further revision, replacing the word 'take' with the word 'heed', as follows:

'However, I look round upon life quite cool. Do you **heed** me, neighbours? My words, though made as simple as I can, mid be rather deep for some heads'.

'O yes, Henery, we quite **heed** ye'.[320]

We cannot know if changes such as these were made in direct response to Lang's criticism of this particular passage. What they do seem to indicate, along with the updating of the Wessex elements within his novels, is a honing of his world into a more consistent form, both in terms of landscape and in terms of language and character.

In summary, therefore, in the critics' reaction to *Far from the Madding Crowd* evidence suggests that the critics would not have been making their judgements on the basis of detailed knowledge, as few would have ever been to rural Dorset, let alone have an intimate knowledge of it. The process therefore is continuing by which the landscape and people that Hardy used as inspiration for the novel, and which he himself then idealised within the novel, is further layered by the perceptions and prejudices of the critics. At this early stage in his career there is a sense within the reviews that the critics, however filtered their views might be, are implicitly comparing Hardy's world with reality, or at least their view of reality. It is therefore instructive to compare the critical reaction to this novel to the reaction to *Tess of the d'Urbervilles*, published nearly twenty years later in 1892.[321]

---

318 Elizabeth James, *Writing, Publishing and Revising Far from the Madding Crowd*, (London: British Library) <http://www.bl.uk/romantics-and-victorians/articles/writing-publishing-and-revising-far-from-the-madding-crowd>.

319 Thomas Hardy, *Far from the Madding Crowd* (New York and London: Harper & Brothers, 1874 (1895 edition)), p. 173.

320 Hardy (1874 (1993 edition)) p. 118.

321 Thomas Hardy, *Tess of the D'Urbervilles: A Pure Woman Faithfully Presented* (London: James R. Osgood, McIlvaine & Co., 1891).

Hardy by this time had experienced commercial success with *Far from the Madding Crow*d and had written a number of subsequent novels that also achieved success, such as *The Return of the Native* and *The Mayor of Casterbridge.* Though he had moved back to Dorset in 1867 and wrote *Far from the Madding Crowd* there, Hardy continued to have a presence in London, either renting property for periods or, towards the end of the 1870s, moving back to London full-time. The Oxford Dictionary of National Biography talks of him making the most of what we would now call networking opportunities with editors and fellow writers whilst in London.[322] Though he moved his base back to Dorset for good in 1882 he continued to involve himself with the Society of Authors and at least three London clubs, the Savile, the Athenaeum (which elected him as a member in 1891), and the Rabelais.[323] Hardy was no longer the rural outsider but increasingly a member of the literary establishment.[324]

Importantly, in *The Return of the Native* and *The Mayor of Casterbridge* especially, he had also been developing his idea of 'Wessex' as a coherent and consistent setting, based on locations in Dorset and its surrounding counties. This interest in a precise geographical backdrop to his novels was first suggested by the appearance as the frontispiece to the first edition of *The Return of the Native* of Hardy's 'Sketch map of the scene of the story', a topographical representation of the major places within the story.[325]

The process was extended in the first collected edition of the 'Wessex Novels' in 1895, which included an annotated map of Wessex based on the outline of the West Country of England, sanctioned by Hardy himself.[326] It reached a culmination in the Wessex Edition of 1912 in the General Preface of which Hardy gave a justification for the way in which he had continued to revise his novels to give what he hoped would be a consistent and above all accurate picture of this version of Dorset that he had created. He compared his endeavours authenticating the detail in his work to those of Boswell in saying:

> …I have instituted inquiries to correct tricks of memory, and striven against temptations to exaggerate, in order to preserve for my own satisfaction a fairly true record of a vanishing life.[327]

Tess of the d'Urbervilles, the tragic tale of Tess Durbeyfield, the 'pure woman' of the novel's full title,[328] is a novel fully imbued with the geography of Wessex that Hardy had developed. It presents a series of events through which Tess's purity is compromised by the realities of life, first when she is impregnated by her supposed kinsmen, Alec D'Urberville, for whom she has gone to work, subsequently losing the child, then when she is rejected on her wedding day by Angel Clare, the true love of her life, after he discovers the secret of her child, and finally, after she has murdered Alec and found reconciliation with Angel, when she is

---

322 Millgate (2004, online edition 2006).

323 Ibid.

324 How much so is evidenced by the fact that by the time of his death in 1928, Hardy's fame was sufficient that his body was buried in Poet's Corner in Westminster Abbey, though his heart was removed and buried in a separate grave in the graveyard of Stinsford Parish Church, close to his birthplace in Higher Bockhampton.

325 Thomas Hardy, *The Return of the Native* (London: Smith, Elder & Co., 1878).

326 Thomas Hardy, *A Pair of Blue Eyes* (London: Osgood & McIlvaine, 1873 (1895 edition)), p. 455.

327 Thomas Hardy, *Tess of the D'Urbervilles* (Toronto: Broadview Literary Text, 1891 (2007 edition)), p. 399.

328 "Tess of the D'Urbervilles: A Pure Woman Faithfully Presented".

arrested at Stonehenge and later executed. Aside from the drama of Tess's tragic journey, like *Far from the Madding Crowd* the novel immerses itself in a number of different Wessex landscapes which are portrayed through all of the seasons, often matching the rise and fall of Tess's fortunes. In so doing it also offers many detailed descriptions of different types of agriculture present across that landscape, such as the dairy farm at Talbothays where she first meets Angel,[329] and the 'starve-acre' farm at Flintcomb-Ash where, following her separation from Angel, she scrapes a living through harvesting swedes from flinty fields.[330]

The contemporary critical response was much more positive than that for *Far from the Madding Crowd*. As with the earlier novel there was general praise for the settings and for the descriptions of landscape. Typical of this is this extract from *The Saturday Review*:

> His description of life in a dairy farm in summer forms an admirable foil to his subsequent account of the terribly hard work both for males and females in an arable farm in winter, when swede-bashing, reed-drawing, or threshing occupied the hands from dawn to dark.[331]

Similarly, the critic of *Blackwood's Edinburgh Magazine* wanted to 'embrace Mr Hardy... in pure satisfaction with the good brown soil and substantial flesh and blood, the cows, and the mangel-wurzel, and the hard labour of the fields – which he makes us smell and see'.[332] There was a different note to some of these reviews, however, which signalled a changed attitude to Hardy to that displayed by the critics eighteen years previously. They suggested a growing familiarity with Hardy, with both his depictions of Wessex and with the darker tones of his mature novels. The review in *The Times* was typical of this, picking up on the tragic undertones of Hardy's work and how they are reflected in descriptions of place and of character:

> The craft of the field and the farm is described with a minute fidelity and a picturesqueness which sometimes approaches the idyllic, as in the scenes at Talbothays Dairy.... But as a rule Mr. Hardy does not paint in idyllic colours; he is too deeply tinged with the peasant's own fatalism and grim sense of fact. Viewing the lives of his 'workfolk' from a higher eminence than they occupy themselves, he feels the nobility of labour and makes us feel it too. But if his pictures sometimes throw a glamour over rustic industry and toil, they abound in reminders of its hard reality.[333]

In the *Illustrated London News*, Clementina Black praised his depictions of country toil and of the changing seasons, writing that 'perhaps no other English writer could have given precisely these impressions', a recognition perhaps that these impressions are reinforcing those created by previous Hardy novels.[334]

---

329   Hardy (1891 (2007 edition)) p. 129.
330   Ibid. p. 293.
331   Anon, '*Tess of the D'Urbervilles* Review', *Saturday Review*, January 16th, 1892, pp. 7-8. Reproduced in Cox (1970) p. 189.
332   Margaret Oliphant, '*Tess of the D'Urbervilles* Review: The Old Saloon', *Blackwood's Edinburgh Magazine*, Mar. 1892, pp. 464-74.
333   Anon, '*Tess of the D'Urbervilles* Review: Mr Hardy's New Novel', *The Times*, January 9th, 1892 p. 13.
334   Clementina Black, '*Tess of the D'Urbervilles* Review', *Illustrated London News*, January 9th, 1892, p. 50. Reproduced in Cox (1970) p. 187.

The aspect of *Far from the Madding Crowd* with which critics were particularly unhappy was the dialogue given to the peasant characters in the book. There were comments about the language of *Tess of the d'Urbervilles*, but they were comments about the prose style in general rather than the style of the reported dialogue. William Watson, writing in *The Academy*, talked of 'over-academic phraseology' and expressed 'a wish that it were absent'.[335] In similar fashion, Hutton, writing in *The Spectator*, was of the opinion that 'the only fault in Mr. Hardy's style is an excess of pedantic phraseology in various parts of the book'.[336]

There were comments praising Hardy's realistic depiction of the peasantry. The critic in *The Times* saw them as 'living, sentient characters, each with distinct mind, ambition, and dexterity', a function of 'Mr. Hardy's own intimate appreciation of the sons of the soil'.[337] However, while there were no adverse comments about peasant speech, the way some of the comments about the peasant characters were framed suggests that the critics are beginning to see them as belonging to a 'Hardy' landscape rather than a Dorset landscape, that they were authentic more in terms of the rules pertaining to Hardy's Wessex than in terms of anything truly of the authentic Dorset. For example, here are the comments of the reviewer in *Blackwood's Edinburgh Magazine*:

> Everybody knows what Mr Hardy's peasants in Wessex are. They are a quaint people, given to somewhat high-flown language, and confused and complicated reasoning... John Durbeyfield, the father of Tess, in an example of this somewhat artificial personage. If he is not good Dorsetshire, he is at least good Hardy, which answers just as well...[338]

'At least good Hardy' is the telling phrase, along with 'everybody knows'. The reviewer was able to enjoy 'Mr Hardy's peasants' not necessarily because they were true to life, that they were 'good Dorsetshire', but because they were familiar from Hardy's previous novels, that they were 'good Hardy'. It suggests that as certain writers such as Hardy became well known and their themes and obsessions became familiar, so the world that readers (and critics) perceived when they read their novels became increasingly not the *actual* world as such but more the *author's* version of the world. In this example, therefore, the reviewer was happy that the peasants were consistent with Hardy's established world, irrespective of whether they necessarily bore any resemblance to proper Dorset peasants. A parallel to this would be the way 19th century London, through its frequent appearances in his increasingly popular novels, came to be associated through those novels with this fictional version of itself which came to be known as 'Dickens' London', but there are two 20th century examples that also illustrate the point.

Graham Greene's novels, whilst usually based on his intimate knowledge of the various parts of the world in which they were set, were inhabited by a very particular type of character, flawed, insecure and often wracked by Catholic guilt, and set in a very particular type of landscape, seedy, decaying and often corrupt. In time, the term

---

335 William Watson, '*Tess of the D'Urbervilles* Review', *The Academy*, February 6th, 1892, pp. 125-6.
336 Richard Holt Hutton, '*Tess of the D'Urbervilles* Review', *The Spectator*, January 23rd, 1892, pp. 121-2.
337 Anon (January 9th, 1892).
338 Oliphant (Mar. 1892).

'Greeneland' was coined to describe this world and new novels were judged as to how they sat within *this* world.[339] Similarly, John le Carré's espionage novels, though based to a considerable degree on his own experiences in the British secret service, also contained much detail that came from his own imagination, structured with a detailed internal consistency of his own making.[340] In this instance, the popularity of the stories led to confusion between what was the authentic world of espionage and what was le Carré's elaboration of it, and the temptation on the part of many was to see his world as the authentic world of spies and spying.[341]

Thomas Hardy was therefore one of a particular class of novelist, like Dickens, Greene and le Carré, whose novels became associated, in the eyes of reviewers, just as much as readers, with the imagined version of their world. The verdict of the *Times* reviewer on *Tess of the d'Urbervilles* is a good example of this with its reference to Wessex, to 'unsophisticated folk' and to the common themes of Hardy's novels. At least part of his perception in reviewing the book is what he has read of Hardy before, and what he had come to expect of him:

> Amid his beloved Wessex valleys and uplands and among the unsophisticated folk in whose lives and labour we have learned from him to find unsuspected dignity and romance, he has founded a story, daring in its treatment of conventional ideas, pathetic in its sadness, and profoundly stirring by its tragic power.[342]

To some, a novelist's particular style can mean that what they did not like last time, they will not like this time, as in the case of Andrew Lang. What he considered the gloom of the text actually created a degree of depressed unreality. Here is a flavour of the opening remarks in his review in the New Review:

> ...the story is an excellent text for a sermon or subtly Spectatorial article on old times and new, on modern misery... That we should be depressed is very natural, all things considered; and indeed, I suppose we shall be no better till we have got the Revolution over, sunk to the nadir of humanity, and reached the middle barbarism again.[343]

To summarise, the likes of Lang aside, there were signs of a contrast between the attitude towards Hardy's writing at this point nearly 20 years on from the publication of *Far from the Madding Crowd*. Hardy's position as a leading Victorian novelist was now secure following the success of *Far from the Madding Crowd* and other subsequent novels such as *The Mayor of Casterbridge*. Critics appeared to have become used to both his style and manners of speech and the tragic nature of many of his plots, and saw them as part of Hardy's particular world,

---

339   'Greeneland', in *OED Online*, (Oxford: Oxford University Press, 2015).

340   John le Carré, whose real name was David Cornwell, worked in MI5 and MI6 between 1958 and 1964 before leaving the service to become a full-time writer.

341   An opinion expressed, for example, in David Denby, 'Which is the best John le Carré novel?', *The New Yorker*, August 5th, 2014. <http://www.newyorker.com/culture/cultural-comment/best-le-carre-novel>.

342   Anon (January 9th, 1892).

343   Andrew Lang, '*Tess of the D'Urbervilles* Review', *New Review*, February 1892, pp. 247-9. Reproduced in Cox (1970) p. 195.

'Hardy's Wessex' as it came to be known.[344] This allowed reviewers to concentrate more on the minutiae of the plot. Clementina Black, for example, saw in *Tess of the d'Urbervilles* a commentary on Victorian society's attitudes towards women, which is by extension a historical perspective on the same. She saw Tess as the victim of her place as a woman in society just as much as of her actions, with Hardy making a plea for society to judge women such as Tess by their overall character (hence his description of Tess as 'A Pure Woman'), not just by individual actions, in the same way that men would be judged by their overall character and not necessarily by the rightness or wrongness of any one of their actions:

> [The book's] essence lies in the perception that a woman's moral worth is measurable not by any deed, but by the whole aim and tendency of her life and nature. In regard to men the doctrine is no novelty; the writers who have had eyes to see and courage to declare the same truth about women are few indeed; and Mr. Hardy in this novel has shown himself to be one of that brave and clear-sighted minority.[345]

In the case of both *Far from the Madding Crowd* and *Tess of the d'Urbervilles*, the majority of the critics were receiving the novel as readers who were largely unaware of the detailed specifics of rural Dorset landscapes and society. When reviewing the earlier novel, at least in terms of the settings they were willing to take the descriptive power of Hardy's writing as an authentic description. Many found it difficult to approach Hardy's language and specifically the dialogue that he gives to his peasant characters, in the same manner. This affected both the way they viewed the novel as a piece of fictional storytelling, and the way they viewed the world that lies behind the novel. By the time of the publication of *Tess*, reviewers were reading the novel in the light of their own knowledge of, and familiarity with, Hardy's descriptive writing and his dialogue as displayed in what was by then a number of novels based around the same landscape and society. The reality of a specifically 'Dorset' landscape was becoming less important than an assessment of the novel's reality in terms of its specific 'Wessex' identity.

4.3 Elizabeth Gaskell and William Rathbone Greg

Section 4.2 described how reviewers of Thomas Hardy's novels made judgements on the veracity of the descriptions of the landscapes, settings and characters of those novels, judgements which in many instances may have been based on limited familiarity. The purpose of this section is to contrast this situation with the thinking of a reviewer who has far more detailed familiarity with the subject matter of the novel under review. It looks at contemporary reviews of Gaskell's *Mary Barton* and particularly a situation where one reviewer, William Rathbone Greg, had knowledge of the industrial Manchester settings and social structure that the author was using for inspiration. It looks at how Greg's experiences and research, and the fixed viewpoints and prejudices that came from those, may have affected his view of Gaskell's

---

344 According to Plietzsch, the order in which Hardy presented his novels in the Wessex Novels Edition of 1895-6 reflected the 'responses from the public' that Hardy had received, and that the public preferred the novels set most explicitly in South Wessex. To this end, the first three novels presented, in order, were *Tess of the d'Urbervilles, Far from the Madding Crowd,* and *The Mayor of Casterbridge*. Birgit Plietzsch, 'The Novels of Thomas Hardy as a Product of Nineteenth-Century Social, Economic, and Cultural Change', (PhD Thesis, Martin-Luther-Universität, Halle-Wittenberg, 2004), pp. 242-43.

345 Reproduced in Cox (1970) p. 187.

novel, how elements of Gaskell's novel were in fact based on similar research to Greg's, and finally how this writer's own prejudices affect his view of reviews like that of Greg.

Gaskell, though brought up in the country town of Knutsford, which she used as inspiration for her later *Cranford* stories, was when she wrote *Mary Barton* living close to the centre of Manchester, at the time one of the fastest growing cities in the industrial world, having married William Gaskell, a Unitarian minister at Manchester's Cross Street Chapel. She came from a devout Unitarian family and shared that movement's belief in social duty and reform. In Manchester, she observed at close hand the industrial life of the North – the strikes, riots, epidemics, depression, and poverty - and along with her husband she engaged in much social and charitable work aimed at alleviating the worst consequences of those conditions.[346]

Manchester was therefore a logical setting for her first published novel, *Mary Barton*.[347] It was set in the late 1830s and early 1840s, a period of manufacturing depression sparked by a financial crisis in the USA in 1837, which led to a fall in cotton prices and to the Lancashire mills being undercut by foreign competition.[348] This depression is crucial in providing the background to the stories of conflict within the novel. It was also the time of the beginnings of Chartism, the movement dedicated to political reform and greater representation for working people. Gaskell describes the rise of Chartism in some detail and makes Mary Barton's father John one of the delegates who present a Chartist petition to Parliament.[349] *Mary Barton* uses actual Manchester locations and institutions, such as Ancoats, Oxford Road, the Bridgewater Canal (in the guise of 'the Duke's Canal'), and the New Bailey courthouse and prison in Salford. Towards the end the novel also visits locations in Liverpool, including the docklands area and the Assize Court.

The main characters are as follows: John Barton, an unemployed factory worker, Chartist delegate and union activist; Mary Barton, the daughter of John Barton and a milliner; John Carson, a mill owner; and finally, Mary's two suitors, Jem Wilson, an apprentice engineer, and Harry Carson, the son and heir of John Carson and *de facto* leader of the owners' faction in their disputes with the millworkers. The relationship between owners and workers is crucial to the plot, and the book details the diverging paths of the owning and working classes. This is exemplified by the contrast between two generations of mill-owners. There is the older generation, typified by John Carson, who began as a worker himself before climbing the ladder to become a mill-owner, and who therefore retains a degree of empathy with the plight of the workers. Then there is the younger generation, typified by John's son and heir Harry Carson, who through their education and a degree of gentrification may have become more detached from the everyday concerns of working people.[350] The book also details the responses of owners to poor market conditions, such as the institution of wage cuts, part-time working and layoffs, and the modernisation of factory machinery and processes to reduce labour costs. Also important within the novel are the descriptions of how the workforce combined and agitated. As well as the coverage of Chartism, it covers the union system and the principles

---

346   Gaskell's place in the life of Manchester, and particularly its political, social and religious life, is described in detail in Jenny Uglow, *Elizabeth Gaskell: A Habit of Stories* (London: Faber, 1993), pp. 86-90.
347   Gaskell (1848).
348   Uglow (1993) p. 138.
349   Elizabeth Gaskell, *Mary Barton* (Ware: Wordsworth, 1848 (2012 Edition)), pp. 92-105.
350   Gaskell describes the younger Carson as follows: 'His dress was neat and well appointed, and his manners far more gentlemanly than his father's'. Ibid. p. 64.

of collective action, strikes (described as 'turn-outs') and the concept of strike pay, and of strike-breakers ('knob-sticks'). The process of negotiation between the Unions and the associations of mill-owners is a vital ingredient of the novel.[351]

To put Greg's review in context, the general tenor of many of the critical reviews immediately following the publication of *Mary Barton* was positive. In particular, in their summaries they emphasized the 'truth' that they felt when reading Gaskell's descriptions of Manchester and what they saw as the suffering of the working population. The reviewer for *The Athenæum* questioned if 'fiction' was the right vehicle for a treatise on 'social evils' but nonetheless went on to say that '...we have met with few pictures of life among the working classes at once so forcible and so fair as "Mary Barton". The truth of it is terrible'. In a parallel to the critical verdict on Hardy's dialogue he praised Gaskell's use of dialect 'with ease, spirit and nicety in selection'.[352] The reviewer in *The Economist* was also taken by the 'impress of truth' in what was seen as 'an appalling picture of the lives of the operatives in Manchester, and we fear in other manufacturing cities', with the hope that 'its pages may inspire [readers] with the wish to contribute their mite towards the lasting relief of the class depicted there'.[353]

Charles Kingsley, a novelist who also covered social themes in his fiction, reviewed *Mary Barton* for Fraser's Magazine and saw nothing but truth in it, believing the ills described within to be still current.[354] He was particularly strident in his comments on how the actions of the owners radicalised the operatives:

> The facts – the facts are all in all; for they are facts. ...a Manchester clergyman has just assured us, that his own eyes have seen the miseries there described..., not merely in the years in which the scene of the book is laid – 1839-1841, but now, in these very last years of 1847-9, when people on Turkey carpets, with their three meat meals a-day, are wondering, forsooth, why working men turn Chartists and Communists?[355]

Thomas Carlyle, who did much to promote the idea of social responsibility at this time, praised the novel's truthfulness in a letter to the author:

> On the side of "veracity", or devout earnestness of mind, I find you already strong; and that will tend well to help the other side of the matter if there be any defect there.[356]

Whilst some of these positive reviews may have been made from the safe distance of London or Edinburgh, the presence of Carlyle and Kingsley, who both wrote at length on similar subjects, suggests their perception of Gaskell's 'real world' was not as limited as the perception of many of Hardy's critics of his world.

---

351 Ibid. pp. 169-78.

352 Henry Fothergill Chorley, 'Mary Barton Review', The Athenæum, October 21st, 1848.

353 Anon, 'Mary Barton Review', The Economist, November 25th, 1848, pp. 1337-8. Reproduced in Angus Easson, Elizabeth Gaskell: The Critical Heritage (Routledge: 1991), p. 78.

354 As an example of Kingsley's social agenda, in his 1863 novel The Water Babies, he decried the evils of child labour, in particular the use of children to sweep chimneys. Charles Kingsley, The Water-Babies, A Fairy Tale for a Land Baby (London: Macmillan, 1863).

355 Charles Kingsley, 'Mary Barton Review', Fraser's Magazine, April 1849. Reproduced in Easson (1991) p. 153.

356 Manchester, John Rylands Library, Letter to Elizabeth Gaskell, MS 730/14.

However, set against such views were those of William Rathbone Greg, whose background aligned closely to that of the Carson family in *Mary Barton*. Like Harry Carson in the novel, he was the son of a mill owner, namely Samuel Greg, the founder of Quarry Bank Mill in Cheshire. This was considered a model for philanthropic industrial development in its time, with a planned community for its workers, and an Apprentice House for training younger members from the community and further afield.[357] Like Carson, he was made manager for a time of two of his father's other mills, in Bury and Bollington.[358] In his early years, he was a passionate advocate of industrial reform, speaking up for the concept of a 10-hour working day in an 1831 pamphlet.[359] He later retreated from that position when giving evidence to the Factory Commission. Appearing as proprietor of his father's Bury mill, he was quoted as saying that the cotton trade was in 'too precarious a state to make any further restrictions safe'.[360]

When he wrote a review of *Mary Barton* in *The Edinburgh Review* it was therefore from the standpoint of someone with experience of mill management, who had written about factory conditions and who had given evidence about the same to commissions, and who was also in a position to empathise with the main victim of the novel, Harry Carson, in terms of his position within a mill-owning family.[361] Greg also had another more personal connection with Gaskell herself. The Greg family were Unitarians, and worshipped at Cross Street Chapel, where the minister was Elizabeth Gaskell's husband William.[362] The two families were therefore known to each other, and indeed Jenny Uglow, when mentioning Greg's review of *Mary Barton* in her biography of Gaskell, describes it as coming from 'the Gaskells' Manchester friend'.[363]

Mary Barton is at heart a novel about the conflict between factory workers and owners in early 1840s Manchester. In her preface to the novel, Gaskell set out some of the thinking that led her to write the novel, and her sympathy with the workers, especially 'the careworn men, who looked as if doomed to struggle through their lives in strange alternations between work and want; tossed to and fro by circumstances'. She saw them as being 'sore and irritable against the rich, the even tenor of whose seemingly happy lives appeared to increase the anguish caused by the lottery-like nature of their own'. She was careful, however, to distance herself from any purely political motive in highlighting their plight:

> I know nothing of Political Economy, or the theories of trade. I have tried to write truthfully; and if my accounts agree or clash with any system, the agreement or disagreement is unintentional.[364]

---

357   Information about Quarry Bank mill was obtained from the National Trust website <http://www.nationaltrust.org.uk/quarry-bank/history/> and from a site visit to Quarry Bank in April 2014.

358   Anon, 'Obituary of William Rathbone Greg', *The Tablet*, 19 Nov. 1881, p. 823.

359   William Rathbone Greg, An Enquiry into the state of the Manufacturing Population, and the causes and cures of the evils therein existing (London: James Ridgway, 1831).

360   Quoted in Robert Q. Gray, *The Factory Question and Industrial England, 1830-1860* (Cambridge: Cambridge University Press, 1996), pp. 100-1.

361   The murder of Harry Carson by John Barton, and its possible links to a real-life incident, is described in detail in Chapter 5.

362   Uglow (1993) p. 89.

363   Ibid. p. 224.

364   Gaskell (1848 (2012 Edition)) pp. 3-4.

Greg's critique of the novel in *The Edinburgh Review* seemed particularly aimed at providing a riposte to this point.[365] Gaskell may know nothing of Political Economy, *unlike himself*, he appeared to be saying throughout his extremely long review, and he brought out a succession of facts and figures to support his contentions. So, unlike the situation with, for example, the reviews of Hardy's novels, here we have a reviewer prepared to provide what he believed to be concrete backing for his arguments. His review included two objections to Gaskell's novel that point to a belief in a variety of self-help. Firstly, he was wary of the idea that the onus fell on employers to assist workers when they fall on hard times, especially when those employers spent their wages on drink and union subscriptions. Secondly, he believed that because some fought their way up from the shopfloor to positions of management or even ownership (like, coincidentally, John Carson in *Mary Barton* and Mr. Thornton in Gaskell's later novel *North and South*), then there would be no reason others could not do the same.

Whilst he saw 'truthfulness displayed in the delineation of individual scenes', he believed the general impression that the book was likely to leave was 'imperfect, partial and erroneous'. He believed that 'without some corrective insight', those in the south of England who are ignorant of the conditions in the industrial towns of the North, might suffer from 'delusions', and regarding the employers, of whom he was of course one, 'ignorance and misconception of their true interests and position'.[366] He made it clear that his objections were based on his own knowledge, from 'our own observations, and the confirming views of others whose acquaintance with artisan life has been even more extensive and intimate than our own'.[367]

In what was a major element of Greg's argument, he chided John Barton, Harry Carson's assassin, for being a victim rather than a protagonist, such that when hard times come 'he is found cursing his masters instead of his own improvidence; spending his time and money on trades' unions, ...and wasting (as so many operatives do), in subscriptions for such objects, funds which, duly husbanded, would have saved his only son... from an early grave.[368] He contrasted this with employers who 'in the days of prosperity, had laid by a portion of their earnings' and could therefore in hard times 'subsist out of their previous savings', with the 'improvident' operatives who failed to show such thrift and had 'no savings to fall back on'.[369] He made estimates of the average family wage and believed it would be adequate were it not 'wasted at the ale-house... squandered in subscriptions to trades' unions and strikes... [and] gambling both by betting and at cards'.[370] He disabused any notion 'that the poor are to look to the rich, and not to themselves, for relief and rescue from their degraded condition and their social miseries'.[371] The only people who could help the poor were the poor themselves: '...the working classes, and they only, can raise their own condition'.[372]

---

365 Anon (19 Nov. 1881); William Rathbone Greg, '*Mary Barton* Review: Art. V. – Mary Barton; A Tale of Manchester Life', *The Edinburgh Review*, April 1849, pp. 402-35.
366 Greg (April 1849).
367 Ibid. p. 411.
368 Ibid. p. 413.
369 Ibid. p. 415.
370 Ibid. p. 417.
371 Ibid. p. 419.
372 Ibid. p. 420.

In his final summary, Greg seemed to suggest that the novel, rather than being an indictment of the state of relations between owner and worker is in fact a calumny on the working class, that Gaskell had not portrayed 'the real position of the operative classes', but rather 'the inaccurate and distorted view of that position as taken by the sour and envious among them'.[373] Greg therefore had his own view of the state of industrial relations that he saw as being in conflict with Gaskell's. Gaskell's comment about political economy may have encouraged him in his polemic, though in fact that particular comment by Gaskell may have been somewhat disingenuous. As we will see in Section 5.3 she was not averse to lifting sections from official reports and placing them almost verbatim in *Mary Barton*, emphasising that she understood the social conditions very well.

Despite the plethora of statistics that Greg throws at the author of *Mary Barton*, one can see that Gaskell, as that author, though coming at the subject from a different direction to Greg, was using both personal experience and a degree of research in much the same way as Greg. In the case of the two Thomas Hardy novels discussed earlier in this chapter there was a comparison between an author writing with knowledge and experience of his subject and reviewers assessing his fictional world with little of that knowledge and experience. Here we see that even where both novelist and reviewer have common background knowledge on which to establish a rapport, their different prejudices and preconceptions may create two different world views of the same social and economic situation. A footnote to the arguments between Gaskell and Greg is the evidence that, according to a letter Gaskell wrote to his wife, William Rathbone Greg's views were not shared by his elder brother Samuel Jr., another active participant in the family business started by their father Samuel. She talks of hearing much about 'the disapproval which Mr Greg's family have felt with regard to 'M.B.'', and of her gladness that 'Mr Sam Greg does not participate in it'. She goes on to surmise that such disapproval must come from those such as William Rathbone Greg seeing in her writing that she had 'misrepresented, or so presented, a part as the whole, as that people at a distance should be misled and prejudiced against the masters, and that class be estranged from class'.[374]

Greg was not alone, however, in questioning the veracity of Gaskell's descriptions of the state of working men and women in Manchester. The reviewer for the *Manchester Guardian*, like Greg, began by giving general praise. The novel, he believed, 'will be generally considered a faithful and true picture of Manchester life', that 'acknowledges that the interests of both masters and men are really the same'.[375] Then, as with Greg, the tone changed, as he questioned, based on his own investigations, whether there was a branch of industry that was able to pay its workers as well as the Manchester mills:

...I state it as my full belief, that there is no trade or calling, either in large towns or the agricultural districts, where a whole family can earn as much money, or procure more of the necessaries and comforts of life, than the millworkers can as a body.[376]

---

373   Ibid. p. 434.
374   Letter from Elizabeth Gaskell to Mrs Greg, quoted in J.A.V. Chapple and Arthur Pollard, 'The Letters of Elizabeth Gaskell', (Manchester: Manchester University Press, 1997), pp. 73-75.
375   Anon, '*Mary Barton* Review', *Manchester Guardian*, February 28th, 1849 p. 7. Reproduced in Easson (1991) p. 120.
376   Easson (1991) p. 124.

When it came to the murder of Harry Carson, he believed it both 'a libel on the workmen of Manchester' who 'never committed a murder under any such circumstances', and 'a libel on the masters, merchants, and gentlemen of this city, who have never been exceeded by those of any other part of the kingdom in acts of benevolence and charity, both public and private'.[377] Finally, he lamented the fact that the author had not 'taken account of what has been done by the masters for improving the condition of the workmen', in terms of improved education, libraries and mechanics institutions.[378]

The writer acknowledged, unlike Greg, that the novel's setting was 'during one of the great depressions in the cotton trade which no foresight of the masters can prevent, but the effects of which are most disastrous to all concerned', but neither he nor Greg made allowance for this in either of their critiques.[379] Between the time of the setting of the novel and the time of the publication of the novel, a continued stream of new Factory Acts had begun to take effect and improve the lot of working people in Manchester, albeit slowly, and trade conditions had also improved in the interim. In retrospect, Gaskell's subtitling of the novel as 'A Tale of Manchester Life', with its implied *contemporary* perspective, is maybe in part to blame, and the reaction of the two reviewers to the novel might have been different if the subtitle had acknowledged that the novel was about the recent past and not the present.

There is a third party in this conflict between the view of Gaskell and the Unitarian mission on the one side and Greg and the *Guardian* reviewer on the other, and that is this writer. It brings us back to the discussion of what influences one's reading of a novel set in the past without the contemporary insights of Gaskell or Greg. Taking a hermeneutical approach, for example, would suggest that when reading *Mary Barton* here in the 21st century one is reading Gaskell's novel through a whole mass of cultural assumptions that have built up around it through the years, from the influence of original critical analysis such as that of Greg's, further critical analysis of this and other Victorian novelists, the subsequent history of the textile industry in Manchester, the growth of heritage tourism around that industry in places such as Quarry Bank Mill, to recent film and television adaptations of novels with a similar period setting, such as Dickens' *Hard Times* and Gaskell's *North and South*. Having read the novel and read the review and trying to decide whether to find credence in either Gaskell's or Greg's as the view of Manchester industrial life one also has one's own cultural and political baggage. Just as Greg's review was contemporary but could not help but be influenced by his own knowledge and his own comparisons with his own experience, so any reading of both the novel and the review today is influenced by those of the reader.

This writer's view is one influenced by the industrial conflicts of the intervening years and specifically the events of the Thatcher years in the 1980s and of the period following the coming to power of the Conservative/Liberal Democrat coalition in 2010. Greg's declaration that 'the working classes, and they only, can raise their own condition' was a reminder of Norman Tebbit's comments in a speech made at the 1981 Conservative Party Conference: 'I grew up in the Thirties with our unemployed father. He did not

---

377 Ibid.
378 Ibid. p. 125.
379 Ibid. p. 121.

riot, he got on his bike and looked for work'.[380] It was also a reminder of a more recent exhortation to individuals to help themselves and not rely on centralised institutions to provide the help for them, namely David Cameron's speech in Liverpool soon after the 2010 coalition came to power:

> The Big Society is about a huge culture change… where people, in their everyday lives, in their homes, in their neighbourhoods, in their workplace…don't always turn to officials, local authorities or central government for answers to the problems they face… but instead feel both free and powerful enough to help themselves and their own communities.[381]

The world of Gaskell and Greg was long before the advent of the Welfare State, but if you replace 'official, local authorities or central government' with 'masters', then these words could reasonably have come out of Greg's mouth. The danger is that a lack of sympathy with both Tebbit and Cameron's statements might also lead one to find less sympathy with Greg's factually based and politically filtered review and more with Gaskell's factually based and fictionally filtered novel. If one reads the Gaskell novel and sympathises with its sentiment, one might be more inclined to find historical truth in it through its contemporary resonances and therefore believe in it as a version of 19th century Manchester. One might then find the present-day echoes of Greg's retort causing one to disagree with it, thus strengthening one's belief in the veracity of the original novel. There is therefore the danger that to cement a conviction one might have that Gaskell's description is a true one, one might concentrate when assessing contemporary reviews on those reviews that are themselves in sympathy with that picture. To use a 21st century analogy, it would be similar to the danger of going onto a review website for books, films or holiday destinations and only reading those reviews that agree with the point of view one wants confirming.

For example, if this discussion had concentrated on the positive reviews of *Mary Barton*, rather than Greg's views, acceptance of Gaskell's description of the world might have passed by without challenge. A more objective approach, reading *Mary Barton* in the context of all its reviews, is better able to validate the historical accuracy of the fictional descriptions within the novel.

4.4 Conclusion: Criticism and the Classic Fiction Process Model

Chapter 5 will include discussion of how authors perceive actual events and places and the structure of the landscape and society in which they live, filter them through their own experiences and prejudices, and then mould them to suit the purposes of the imagined world of their fiction. The contemporary critical reception of a novel marks the initial point at which it extends beyond the author's perception and is therefore subject to other perceptions. This chapter therefore involved discussion of the imagined world of a novel perceived by the critics following their reception of the and how closely that imagined

---

380 Speech by Norman Tebbit, at the time Employment Secretary in Margaret Thatcher's government, at the Conservative Party Conference, 15 October 1981, quoted in Susan Ratcliffe, *Oxford Dictionary of Quotations by Subject, Oxford Paperback Reference* (Oxford: Oxford University Press, 2010), p. 489.

381 David Cameron, *Big Society Speech – 19th July 2010*, (London: Cabinet Office, 2010) <https://www.gov.uk/government/speeches/pms-speech-on-big-society>.

world aligns with the critics' own perception of the elements of the contemporary world perceived by the author.

The critics may have knowledge of the same settings that the author uses, and of the same contemporary cultural sources that influence the author, so both the perception and reception actions come into play. They receive the author's view of the world in the novel as they read it, just as we do in the present day, but they also perceive that world themselves in a way that we cannot. The quality of that perception may vary; William Rathbone Greg reviewing Gaskell's *Mary Barton* as a manager of a Manchester textile mill should have a lot more depth to his perception than the metropolitan critics reviewing Hardy's *Far from the Madding Crowd* at a distance from Dorset. Where the reviewers are indeed perceiving the same world as the author, though they may be processing shared information, each of them has their own individual viewpoints, prejudices and predispositions that may differ from those of the author. They receive the novel and interpret the novel by comparing their own perception of the contemporary world with the author's. They may find themselves in sympathy with the novel, as with those who praised *Mary Barton*, or they may find themselves in conflict with it, as was the case with William Rathbone Greg or the reviewer from the *Manchester Guardian* reviewing the same novel.

Igor Webb makes some pertinent observations about the way contemporary readers of *Mary Barton* reacted to the truthfulness of novel. To Webb, the power the novel had over its initial contemporary audience was its ability to shock the reader with its factual detail, detail that 'they did not know… or wished not to know' or that shocked them 'because the distance between rich and poor was so vast that the usual routines of life made it extremely unlikely that they *would* know'.[382] He goes on, however, to ask what made a fact a fact for the reader, given that 'after all, Gaskell's original readers did not rush out to the Manchester working-class districts to confirm her facts; reading sufficed to persuade them that what she portrayed was actually so'.[383] He quotes the editor of a 20th century edition of the novel saying that 'reading convinces us that the author started from a thoroughly known reality that is neither exaggerated nor sentimentalized'.[384] He posits the idea of a 'self-evident truthfulness', a phrase used in a contemporary review of *Mary Barton*, explaining that 'something in the manner of the writing persuades readers, from 1848 to the present, that Gaskell's facts are facts', and that '[Gaskell] is experienced by the reader as telling the truth'.

Through this reasoning, we may believe aspects of a novel to be authentic, to be 'true to life', simply because they *read* as true, even if we are reading the novel at over 150 years' distance. Most of the reviews of *Mary Barton* praised Gaskell's urban Manchester settings, even those ultimately antipathetic to the novel. Webb warns us of the danger of this way of thinking. Whilst he believes the 'facts' in *Mary Barton* to be 'objective, in the old unregenerate sense of the term', 'the novel as novel cannot prove them to be so'.[385] As we will see in the next chapter, Gaskell did use factual material in the writing of her novel, as evidenced by her use of mission reports, and by her use of the local dialect. Though they were not present in the 1848 first edition, the 1854 edition and subsequent editions of

---

382 Igor Webb, Rereading the Nineteenth Century: Studies in the Old Criticism from Austen to Lawrence (New York: Palgrave Macmillan, 2010), p. 14.
383 Ibid. p. 15.
384 Ibid. p. 14.
385 Ibid. p. 15.

Mary Barton included as an appendix two lectures given by Elizabeth Gaskell's husband William on the subject of Lancashire dialect, something to which he devoted much study. Given the presence of the lectures in these later editions one might surmise that William's work informed Gaskell's use of dialect in the novel and that the lectures are included to act as a key for helping decipher it. Hardy used his knowledge of Dorset dialect and of the landscapes of rural Dorset to inform *Far from the Madding Crowd*. In both cases, however, as Webb tells us, their characters and plots only exist as 'reality' within the fictional world of the novel.

Issues of reality and authenticity were covered in reviews of the other novels highlighted herein, by Austen and Priestley. The *Critical Heritage* volume on Austen's works lists only three reviews of *Pride and Prejudice* written immediately after publication.[386] The reviewer in *The British Critic* spends most of the short review extolling the characters within the novel and their interactions, underlying a sense that is discussed in more detail in Section 5.2 that it is the social dynamic rather than the physical world that most interests the author, but there is one comment that suggests the reviewer senses a feeling of a social geography that mirrors real life:

> The picture of the younger Miss Bennets, their perpetual visits to the market town where officers are quartered, and the result, is perhaps exemplified in every provincial town in the kingdom.[387]

Emma attracted more reviews, most notably one from Sir Walter Scott, described by Brian Southam as the 'first major critical notice of Jane Austen',[388] in which, again concentrating on the social aspects of the novel, he praises Austen's 'knowledge of the world', though he makes no comment on what that world encompasses. He believed she presented 'characters that the reader cannot fail to recognize', reminding him of 'the merits of the Flemish school of painting'.[389] However that world may have been circumscribed by Austen, Scott therefore felt he saw truth in it, as did the critics of Priestley's *The Good Companions* in the much wider world that he described. These reviews are described in more detail in Section 6.2.

With regard to the classic fiction process model, as Figure 4.1 shows, these authors used their perceptions of elements of their contemporary world and adapted them into the imagined worlds of their fiction. Contemporary reviewers created their own imagined versions of these worlds following their reception of the fiction, sometimes, as with Greg, enhanced by their own knowledge of the author's real world. If contemporary reviewers believed their imagined worlds to be realistic, they did so because they saw them as validating the truthfulness, reality or authenticity of the real world that underpinned the fiction. Many, like the reviewer in *The Inquirer* whose 'self-evident truthfulness' comment Webb references, were able thus to take *Mary Barton* at face

---

386 Southam (1968). One further review surfaced following publication of this volume and was republished by Joukovsky: Nicholas A. Joukovsky, 'Another Unnoted Contemporary Review of Jane Austen', *Nineteenth-Century Fiction*, 29 (December 1974), pp. 393-96.

387 Anon, 'Review of *Pride and Prejudice*', *The British Critic*, February 1813, pp. 189-90.

388 Southam (1968) p. 58.

389 Sir Walter Scott, 'Unsigned Review of *Emma*', *Quarterly Review*, March 1816, pp. 188-201. Quoted in Southam (1968) p. 67.

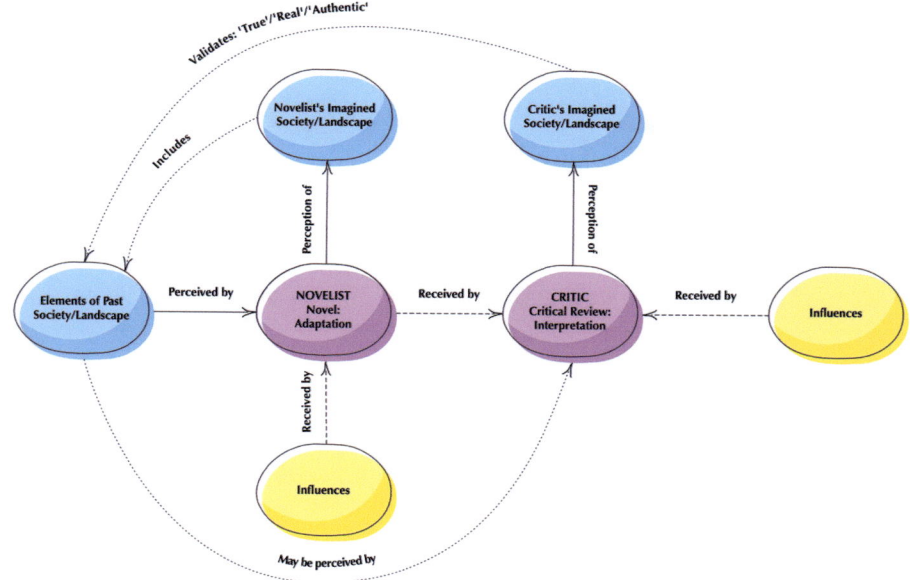

Figure 4.1: Classic Fiction Process Model – Reviewing the novel.

value and believe it as a depiction of something approaching real life. As the reviewer in *The Inquirer* goes on to say regarding what he sees as the moral of the book around the virtues and vices of the poor: 'we are firm believers in its truth and point'.[390] The reviewers of Hardy's *Far from the Madding Crowd* used similar language about Hardy's Dorset/Wessex setting, with their comments quoted above about it being 'genuine' and the 'nearest equivalent to actual experience'.

Where the trust of the reviewers is lacking, it can simply be because the reviewer does not experience any 'self-evident truthfulness'. The metropolitan reviewers did not see the language of Hardy's peasants as authentic. When we hear the reviewer in *The Athenæum* saying that he cannot believe such language should come from such 'illiterate clods' he is surely applying the same trust test as those reviewers assessing Gaskell's descriptions of Manchester, except that where Gaskell passed the test, Hardy did not. Where a reviewer's lack of trust comes from their own personal knowledge and research then we are seeing a conflict between two informed world views, two different perceptions of the same reality, whereby different interpretations of facts are used to reach different conclusions.

Figure 4.2 expands out the cultural sources at play on both Hardy's and the critics' reception filters in the case of *Far from the Madding Crowd*. Hardy's filtering of Dorset was influenced by memories of own family and its history and his rural upbringing within that family, by his later education at the Grammar School in Dorchester, by the literary styles and conventions he absorbed there and elsewhere which affected the way he chose to write, and by writers of dialect, such as his friend William Barnes and other writers who made use of dialect, such as George Eliot.

---

390   Anon, '*Mary Barton* Review', *The Inquirer*, November 11th, 1848, pp. 710-11. Reproduced in Easson (1991) p. 74.

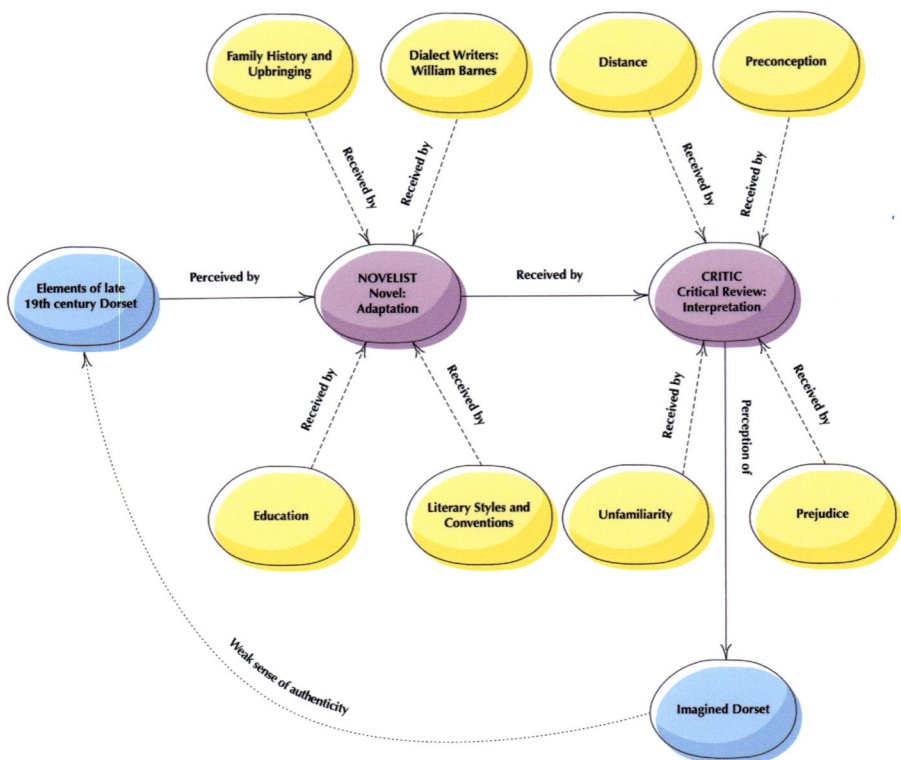

Figure 4.2: Processes at work in 'Far from the Madding Crowd'.

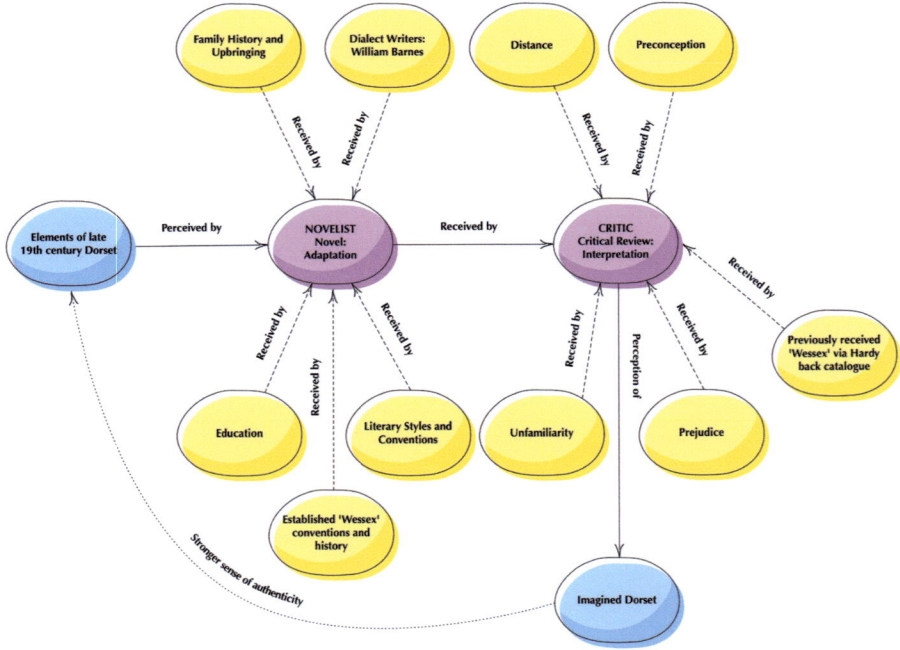

Figure 4.3: Processes at work in 'Tess of the d'Urbervilles'.

The critics' filtering of Hardy's novel may have been affected by their distance from Dorset, and their unfamiliarity with it and with the writing of Hardy at that point in his career. They may have had preconceptions about the dialect, speech patterns and vocabulary of rural Dorset, and possible prejudice against Hardy, the Dorset peasant class, or both. Note that the direct line from a 'perceived Dorset' to the critical review that is there in the general model has been removed; the London critics did not have a perceived view of the real Dorset to the same extent that Greg had a perceived view of industrial Manchester.

When *Tess of the d'Urbervilles* came to be reviewed, all of the above influences can be seen to be at work to a degree, but they are affected by the critics' increased familiarity with Hardy. This connects to the most important difference between the two novels. In the first novel, Wessex was still a largely unconstructed concept, but in the second Hardy had created a world that, whilst based on an existing model, had its own specific geography, social conventions, and history. When creating the novel, Hardy would have been referencing the rules of his fictional Wessex at the same time as referencing the true Dorset, and likewise the reviewers would have been imagining the fictional Wessex and comparing the world that was being described to them with that with which they were familiar from the previous novels. This is shown in the two extra boxes added in Figure 4.3.

In returning to the usefulness of fiction as an adjunct to historical investigation, novelists are first-hand witness to the past worlds underlying their novels in a way that historians can never be. However, a reviewer such as William Rathbone Greg can also be a first-hand witness to the same past world that the author perceives, and so should be used as a counterweight to any assessment of the usefulness of the novel in a way that a historian would balance conflicting contemporary sources. The argument then is as to whether the analysis of someone such as Greg should outweigh that of someone who is writing something that is fictional, even if both analyses are based on factual evidence.

We also read these novels ourselves now in the light of our own knowledge, preconceptions and prejudices which may affect whether we sympathise with the world view of the novelist. We also have the various layers of critical analysis that have grown up around the novels, from the contemporary reviews to more modern scholarship and received wisdom that may also affect how we view the veracity of novels. Finally, there are the views we get of the novels and their authors from the various film and television adaptations that have been produced over the years, and from the various literary houses and landscapes that have through time become associated with authors and their novels. We saw in Chapters 2 and 3 how literary tourism and literary adaptation add yet further layers between ourselves and the world of the novels and how the decisions that adapters, directors, curators and interpreters make regarding authors and their works can affect the way we view them.

5

The Writing Process

5.1 Introduction

The journey from novelist to consumer begins with the act of writing the novel, the process through which novelists can take their perceptions of the contemporary world and turn them into the imagined world of their fiction. In investigating this part of the classic fiction process model this chapter looks at the various external and internal influences that may have affected the author's perceptions. The findings are used in the construction of the final un-layering of the process model, and a pair of contrasting case studies both demonstrate aspects of this element of the model and amplify aspects of the academic arguments made in Section 1.2. The two case studies were chosen as examples of how two different approaches to descriptive writing within the two novels can provide the reader with two different perceptions of the historical context of the novels. The first case study looks at perceptions of Hampshire in Jane Austen's novels, examples of the type of fiction Tosh sees as providing social and intellectual insights into the author's world, and the second at perceptions of Manchester in the novels of Elizabeth Gaskell, examples of the type of fiction that Tosh sees as providing descriptive depth.[391] Both in their different ways provide an immersive experience, a sense of being in a world, providing Warren's knowledge *of* the past rather than simple facts about it – in White's terms filling in the gaps between the truths of history.[392] They also show that whilst it may be true, in White's words, that novelists invent stories rather than find them in the way that historians do, that invention is based on a kernel of truth about the past that the novelist may have experienced directly or otherwise had knowledge about.[393]

This section of the process model is therefore interested in the initial perception by novelists of elements of the contemporary world in which they live, the landscapes, social structures, and human relationships, and how those elements are adapted and transformed within the fictional work. If we take the philosophical view, outlined in Section 1.1, that novelists perceive the world in which they live in the light of their own knowledge and experience, then that knowledge and experience, and hence the perception of the world, can be affected by a number of influences that are addressed within herein. These include the time at which they were writing, their geographical location, their place in society, the prevailing social norms of

---

391   Tosh (2015) p. 79.
392   White (2005).
393   White (1987) p. 173.

the time, and their perception of their expected audience. At the beginning of the 19th century a novelist such as Jane Austen described a restricted geographical world, particularly in her early novels written in Steventon, a world that was very much the world of her upbringing, a rural landscape of scattered villages and big houses and the paths and rides connecting them. Section 5.2 shows how a novel such as *Pride and Prejudice* could be seen to reflect this world. In terms of the society she describes, it was largely that both of herself and of her readership, a select upper middle-class world. The huge industrial and economic changes taking place at the time in the Midlands and the North are barely referred to within her work, along with any significant reference to the working class. Whilst allowing that no author is under any obligation to portray the whole of the society in which they live, the world that Austen describes, whether by accident or design, was particularly circumscribed and limited, one where the very concept of 'work' hardly seems to exist, and life consists of an endless succession of social visits, parties, and balls. Austen's contemporary readership was equally restricted. Her first published novel was *Sense and Sensibility* (1811), in an initial printing of 1,000 copies. It was followed by *Pride and Prejudice* (initial printing 1,500 copies), *Mansfield Park* (1814, 1,500 copies), *Emma* (1815, 2,000 copies) and after Austen's death in Winchester, and *Northanger Abbey* and *Persuasion* (published together in 1817, 2,500 copies).[394]

As the 19th century progressed novels emerged that perceived a world outside of the narrow bands of class and society described by Austen. Thomas Carlyle's essay on Chartism, published in 1839, summed up the view of many that awareness of the conditions in which the poor working classes lived brought with it a social responsibility. He berated Parliament for avoiding discussing such issues, and in doing so gave a name to a new type of fictional literature: 'Surely Honourable Members ought to speak of the Condition-of-England question too'.[395]

In what became known as the 'Condition-of-England' novel, the living and working conditions of the industrial poor, along with the state of industrial relations between factory owners and their workers, were confronted head on. Many such novels, like those of Benjamin Disraeli and Charles Kingsley, are now largely forgotten, but some have remained in the popular canon. Novels by such authors as Elizabeth Gaskell with *Mary Barton* and *North and South*, Charlotte Brontë with *Shirley*, and Charles Dickens with *Hard Times*, are typical, with descriptions of the living conditions of the working people themselves, and of their manners and forms of speech, and of conflicts between workers and factory owners. They reflected their authors' personal perceptions of working-class life in contemporary England, Gaskell in her experiences as a Unitarian Minister's wife in Manchester (Section 5.3), Brontë in her family's experience of Luddite riots in early 19th century Yorkshire,[396] and Dickens in his early experiences of hardship on the streets of London and his later observations of working-class life as he travelled around the country (in particular to Preston before writing *Hard Times*).[397]

---

394 Print run figures from Southam (1968) p. 4 of Introduction. Sutherland calculates Austen's lifetime earnings as being £630 which she describes as 'modest by any contemporary standard' and not enough to give her financial independence. Kathryn Sutherland, 'Cents and sensibility: Jane Austen's world of risk', *Financial Times*, June 16th, 2017. The Bank of England inflation calculator estimates that a sum of £630 in 1817 would have been worth £57.425.45 in 2021. *Inflation Calculator*, (London: Bank of England, 2022) <https://www.bankofengland.co.uk/monetary-policy/inflation/inflation-calculator>.

395 Thomas Carlyle, *Chartism* (London: J. Fraser, 1840).

396 Lyndall Gordon, *Charlotte Brontë: A Passionate Life* (London: Virago, 2008), pp. 207-08.

397 Claire Tomalin, *Charles Dickens: A Life* (London: Penguin, 2012), p. 250., and Simon Callow, *Charles Dickens* (London: HarperPress, 2012), p. 235.

At the same time, however, the main characters of these novels were still largely of a type that Austen might have recognised, and as with Austen these characters reflected the social background of the authors themselves. Margaret Hale in *North and South*, and Caroline Helstone and Shirley Keeldar in *Shirley* are all women from a middle-class background drawn into the industrial world by circumstance. Even the eponymous heroine of *Mary Barton*, though from a working-class family, becomes a milliner as a means of bettering herself. Lynn Alexander makes the point that by moving Mary from her working-class origins 'Gaskell makes her a distanced observer and creates a sense of objectivity for the reader'.[398] The working classes were characters in the novels but not the nominal lead characters, though the actions of John Barton in *Mary Barton* are the catalyst that drives the narrative.[399]

As the subject matter of the novel opened out in the works of writers such as Gaskell and Brontë, so novels began to reach a wider audience. Walter Scott was one of the initial catalysts for the growth in the reading of fiction through the 19th century, first with narrative poems such as *Lady of the Lake*, and later with the 'Waverley' Novels. This is despite his early novels such as *Waverley* itself, costing around 30 shillings for the standard three-volume set, a sum that was more than the normal weekly wage for a working-class man.[400] Scott's *Rob Roy*, first published in 1817, sold 10,000 copies just in the first fortnight after publication, thereby dwarfing the sales of even the most popular of Austen's novels.[401] Up until 1852 there was a form of retail price maintenance on books which kept prices high, but after this was abandoned there was considerable discounting of novels.[402] Along with this many cheap 'railway editions' were published by retailers such as W.H. Smith.[403] With the growth of lending libraries such as Mudie's 'Select Library', which opened in Bloomsbury in 1842,[404] and the increasing phenomenon of novels first being serialised in journals such as Dickens' 'Household Words', which cost only twopence a week,[405] the market for fiction amongst the general public grew considerably. Kate Flint points to increases in literacy amongst men and women, especially after the Education Act of 1870, rising household incomes, and increased leisure time as additional contributory factors to the growth in the consumption of novels, and quotes Anthony Trollope in his 1883 autobiography describing this opening out of the reading process, with novels being read 'right and left, above stairs and below'.[406]

Again, hand in hand with this increase in readership, working-class authors of the later 19th century and early 20th century widened the scope of the novel further. In the novels of Thomas Hardy and D.H. Lawrence the subject matter became the lives of ordinary people, people such as Gabriel Oak in *Far from the Madding Crowd*, Tess Durbeyfield in *Tess of the*

---

398   Lynn M Alexander, 'Creating a Symbol: the Seamstress in Victorian Literature', *Tulsa Studies in Women's Literature*, 18 (1999), pp. 29-38.

399   Gaskell's first title for the novel was in fact *John Barton*. In consultation with her publisher Edward Chapman, she changed it to *Mary Barton* because, in Uglow's words, Chapman 'may have been reluctant to shock the public by having the name of a murderer, John Barton, as the title'. Uglow (1993) p. 186.

400   Simon Eliot, 'The Business of Victorian Publishing', in *The Cambridge Companion to the Victorian Novel*, ed. by Diedre David (Cambridge: Cambridge University Press, 2001), pp. 37-8.

401   Southam (1968) pp. 4-5.

402   Eliot (2001) pp. 38-9.

403   Kate Flint, 'The Victorian Novel and its Readers', in *The Cambridge Companion to the Victorian Novel*, ed. by Diedre David (Cambridge: Cambridge University Press, 2001), p. 21.

404   Eliot (2001) p. 39.

405   Ibid. p. 44.

406   Anthony Trollope, *An Autobiography* (Blackwood, 1883) Quoted in Flint (2001) p. 19.

D'Urbervilles, or Tom Brangwen in D.H. Lawrence's *The Rainbow*. Finally, in the 20th century works of writers such as Arnold Bennett, H.G. Wells and J.B. Priestley the world described became all-embracing, from the highest to the lowest level in society. Arnold Bennett in particular could set novels in working-class Stoke (*Anna of the Five Towns*) or in an upper-class luxury hotel (*The Grand Babylon Hotel*) or write novels that move between these two worlds (*The Card*) and appear comfortable writing about both. Priestley, in his novel *The Good Companions*, could in one novel provide descriptions of West Yorkshire mill towns, Cotswold villages, an East Anglian private preparatory school, the new industrial towns of the Midlands, and cosmopolitan London, and write them all from a degree of personal experience (see Chapter 6).

The way in which an author's own world and, moreover, their life enters their fiction is often clear. With some novelists you can trace their life through their fiction: Charlotte Brontë is sent to a boarding school in Brussels where she develops an infatuation for her tutor Constantin Héger,[407] and both her first and her fourth novels, *The Professor* and *Villette*, feature a girl's school in a French-speaking city run by a handsome and charismatic professor; Thomas Hardy is born and bought up in a small cottage set in woodland and heath,[408] and the characters in one of his early novels, *Under the Greenwood Tree*, live in small cottages set in woodland and heath; Charles Dickens' father spends time as a debtor in Marshalsea Prison and much of *Little Dorrit* is concerned with depicting the life of a debtor in Marshalsea Prison.[409] One's own life or the life of one's relatives may not require invention or large amounts of research, so is staple material for the novelist to transform into the imagined world of their novels.

What is also relevant in the context of this research are those events that are contemporary to novelists, and of which they have first- or second-hand experience, that find their way into the pages of their fiction. These contemporary events may sometimes be described straight, essentially as reportage, such as Benjamin Disraeli's description in his novel *Sybil* of the Bull Ring Riots that followed the rejection of the first Chartist Petition in 1839.[410] Whilst there are many such examples of novelists using detailed descriptions of the world in which they live in their novels, there are also examples where the picture that a novelist gives us of the world in which they live is subtler, where there is a sense that a picture of that world is implied or assumed within the novel, rather than being explicitly described. An example of these novelists, as is discussed below, would be Jane Austen. However, one might also cite a novelist such as Virginia Woolf, whose writing style fights against pure realist description but where, despite this, reading her novels can put you in the particular time and place in which she lived (Section 6.7).

For the authors themselves, their beliefs, their prejudices and the external influences and pressures on them, could also influence the choice of subject matter for the imagined worlds of their novels, and the way that subject matter is treated. Elizabeth Gaskell's concern for the working people and their conditions which is evident in her novels may have been informed by her faith, and what Jenny Uglow calls her 'Unitarian optimism'.[411] At the same time, she lived amongst, and worshipped with, fellow Unitarians who were members of the factory

---

407   Gordon (2008) pp. 116-17.
408   Higher Bockhampton, Dorset. See Tomalin (2007) p. 14.
409   Dickens' father's time in Marshalsea Prison is described in Tomalin (2012) p. 23.
410   Benjamin Disraeli, *Sybil or, The Two Nations, Volume 3* (Henry Colburn: London, 1845), pp. 8-11.
411   Uglow (1993) p. 506.

and mill owning classes, people from that stratum of society who were most likely to read her books.[412] As was discussed in the previous chapter, she received criticism from this quarter after the publication of *Mary Barton* particularly on the novel's position on the divide between mill-owners and mill-workers. This may explain why she was more careful in her second 'Manchester' novel, *North and South*, not to be seen to be taking sides in the industrial debate, even to the extent of fictionalising Manchester as 'Milton'.[413] Her desire to see mutual respect and conciliation between the classes may make for satisfying conclusions to novels for her readers but may also reflect an optimistic view of the reality of industrial relations at the time (see Section 5.3). An example would be the final rapprochement in *Mary Barton*, between John Barton, the union activist, and John Carson, the mill-owner whose son he has killed. In the preface to *Mary Barton* Gaskell talks about wishing to 'give some utterance to the agony which, from time to time, convulses this dumb people',[414] and yet pulls back from condemnation of the owning classes by also stating that she knows 'nothing of Political Economy, or the theories of trade', and that any disagreements are 'unintentional'.[415]

There are also the societal attitudes of the time that find expression in the literature, the more general prejudices, attitudes, and customs. There are, for example, attitudes towards race running through literature of the 19th and early 20th centuries that may have been socially acceptable at the time, but that we in the 21st century find unusual or offensive. Examples might include William Makepeace Thackeray's naming of a black servant as 'Sambo' in *Vanity Fair*,[416] Dickens' stereotypical characterisation of Fagin in *Oliver Twist*,[417] and in the early 20th century what would today be considered pejorative descriptions of black minstrel bands,[418] and Jewish music publishers,[419] in Priestley's *The Good Companions*.

Another external influence on novelists and their work is that of publishers and editors. The 19th century growth in the serialisation of novels required many authors to write in monthly instalments. As Laurel Brake explains, serialisation allowed the publisher and editor to control the direction of a story more easily than if they had been 'in receipt of a complete manuscript of a novel that had already found its characters, plot and narrative, without prior reference to an editor'.[420] This could result both in a need for melodramatic cliff-hangers to keep readers reading, or for the foreshortening of the final stages of the story to meet time and space constraints. Brake describes how authors often found the deadlines and the word count restrictions imposed by serialisation unwelcome,

---

412   As described in ibid. pp. 86-89.
413   Described in the novel by Margaret Hale in horror as 'Milton-Northern! The manufacturing town in Darkshire?' Gaskell (1855 (1994 Edition)) p. 34.
414   Gaskell (1848 (2012 Edition)) p. 3.
415   Ibid. p. 4.
416   William Makepeace Thackeray, *Vanity Fair: A Novel Without a Hero* (London: Bradbury & Evans, 1848), p. 1.
417   Dickens makes much of Fagin's appearance and stereotypical avariciousness and insists on calling him 'the Jew' throughout the novel. Charles Dickens, *Oliver Twist; or, The Parish Boy's Progress* (London: Richard Bentley, 1840).
418   The character Morton Mitcham talks of 'one of the Frenchified niggers you get in New Orleans [who] showed me one or two things about playing the banjo'. J.B. Priestley, *The Good Companions* (Ilkley: Great Northern Books, 1929 (2007 edition)), p. 209.
419   Priestley uses subtle stereotypical references to emphasize the Jewishness of both Mr Milbrau ('A young man with a masterful nose [and] wavy black hair') and of his boss Mr Pitsner ('a sort of super Milbrau, older, fatter and more Hebraic, with even blacker hair'). Ibid. p. 467/80.
420   Laurel Brake, 'The Serial and the Book in Nineteenth-Century Britain: Intersections, Extensions, Transformations', *Memoires du livre*, 8 (2017), pp. 1-16.

with George Eliot being one author in particular who refused to submit to such rigid constraints on her writing.[421] These constraints adversely affected Gaskell's *North and South* when it was serialised in Dickens' weekly magazine *Household Words*.[422] Gaskell actually apologises for this in a preface to the first published book-form edition of the novel, explaining that she has added new passages and whole new chapters towards the end of the novel, because within the periodical format she had 'found it impossible to develop the story in the manner originally intended, and... was compelled to hurry on events with an improbable rapidity towards the close'.[423]

Editors might also, through editing and/or censorship, affect the text finally shown to the reading public. Brake talks of how editors would interact with the writing process during the course of a serialisation and would demand changes if they thought there was material that would offend readers, and could, in extreme cases, discontinue the serialisation.[424] Thomas Hardy had considerable difficulty finding a periodical which was willing to serialise the original version of *Tess of the D'Urbervilles* due to the perceived frankness of its sexual content. Though the *Graphic* finally agreed to serialise it in 1891, it still required him to make a number of cuts and alterations.[425] The novel appeared in its originally intended form only when first published in book form.[426]

In summary, the novelist is influenced by his or her perception of the world, which is itself subject to limitations depending on factors such as the author's location, place in society, or political outlook. That view of the world can be reflected in the novels, broadening the canvas of the novel as the world view of the novelist increases. The novelist is however also subject to external influences that may affect their writing, either in the way they may mould their story to relate it to their audience, or in the way that they reflect contemporary social mores and attitudes. The method of publication affects the writing, especially with regard to serialised novels. Finally, the onus is always on the novelist to write a story that its contemporary readership finds satisfying. The author Kazuo Ishiguro, writing in 2014, railed against the conventional notion that novelists should simply 'write about what you know', as this can result in works that are simply 'dull autobiography'.[427] Therefore, the improbable becoming the actual, the unusual coincidence and the convenient juxtaposition were staples of 19th century fiction intended to heighten the drama and keep the story moving, even if this was at the expense of a degree of credibility. Viv Groskop, in a review of the 2019 BBC adaptation of Victor Hugo's *Les Misérables* describes these coincidences as 'the contradiction inherent in this kind of 19th-century classical literature' where despite claims to reality made by the author the story is 'told through a meticulously constructed narrative that can exist only in fiction'.[428] Dickens' novels are similarly full of such occurrences and his stories can

---

421   Ibid. pp. 6-7.
422   Elizabeth Gaskell, 'North and South', *Household Words*, September 2nd, 1854 to January 20th, 1855.
423   Elizabeth Gaskell, *North and South* (London: Chapman & Hall, 1855), Foreword.
424   Brake (2017).
425   As described by Sarah E. Maier, 'Introduction 1. In Defence of Tess', in *Tess of the D'Urbervilles (second edition)*, ed. by Sarah E. Maier (Toronto: Broadview Literary Text, 2007).
426   Hardy (1891).
427   Kazuo Ishiguro, 'Kazuo Ishiguro talks Zuckerberg, Game of Thrones and his new novel', *ShortList* (2014) <https://www.shortlist.com/entertainment/books/kazuo-ishiguro-talks-zuckerberg-game-of-thrones -and-his-new-novel/97003>.
428   Viv Groskop, '*Les Misérables* episode four recap – Les Coincidences, you mean?', *The Guardian*, January 20th, 2019.

take turns that no historical or biographical account would ever take. All of this affects our ability to separate out the story from the underlying historical context. John Hatcher puts it succinctly in an article on the use of fiction as history, saying that whereas historians would not admit to compromising 'their history in the pursuit of a good story, the novelist's chief aim it 'to tell entertaining stories rather than write accurate histories', and that their loyalty is to 'the book' rather than 'the facts'.[429]

The case studies below look at two instances of usage by the novelist of their contemporary worlds within their fiction that differ in the depth of description of those worlds. Section 5.2 looks at an example of an author whose detailed description of the physical world within which her fiction is set is limited, and where that fiction appears to rely on an implicit understanding of the world on the part of her readers. It uses two novels by Jane Austen, written at different stages of her life, namely *Pride and Prejudice*, and *Emma*. It examines how the novelist, whilst ostensibly setting the novels in Hertfordshire and Surrey respectively, may in fact have used elements of the localities in which she lived when writing the two novels to inform the social geography of those novels, such that we may be getting a clearer historical insight into the society and landscape of Austen's Hampshire than we do of Hertfordshire or Surrey.

Section 5.3 examines the more explicit way Elizabeth Gaskell's *Mary Barton* uses descriptions drawn from life. It demonstrates how Gaskell may have used a recent incident of real-life industrial violence to inform a key incident in the novel, and how, in spite of her efforts to dissemble it, the two incidents have become linked in the general imagination. Secondly, it examines how she used her knowledge of living and ministering with her husband in the centre of Manchester to inform descriptions of living conditions within her novels that mirror contemporary accounts both polemical, such as those by Friedrich Engels, and official, such as those by the Manchester Mission and the Manchester Sanitary Association. Finally, it suggests how her perception of Manchester was adapted when she fictionalised it for the novel, via such external influences as the need to provide a satisfying story for her implied audience and the need to be true to her Unitarian faith in the way in which she concluded the story.

5.2 Jane Austen and Hampshire

Pride and Prejudice was first written in draft form around 1796-7 but not finally published until 1813.[430] The significance of this is that although it was published when Austen was living in the village of Chawton, Hampshire, it was initially written when she still living in her birthplace, the village of Steventon, also in Hampshire. Within the novel Austen does not employ detailed descriptions of landscape, how her characters look or dress, the architecture of the houses or the furniture within them. Where a descriptive passage appears within the novel, it can feel perfunctory, as with this account of Pemberley:

> It was a large, handsome, stone building, standing well on rising ground, and backed by a ridge of high woody hills; – and in front, a stream of some natural importance was swelled into greater, but without any artificial appearance.[431]

---

429 John Hatcher, 'Fiction as History: The Black Death and Beyond', *History*, 97 (2012), pp. 3-23.
430 Jane Austen, *Pride and Prejudice: A Novel* (London: T. Egerton, 1813).
431 Jane Austen, *Pride and Prejudice* (Ware: Wordsworth, 1813 (2007 edition)), p. 206.

Her emphasis is very much on dialogue and the interplay of characters within a specific social structure. Bharat Tandon, in looking at the novel's historical background, picks up on two aspects of the novel that give particular insights. He emphasises the importance of money, and the part it plays in 'determining both the social climate of the novel and the permissible moves of the plot',[432] and also the significance that the mentions of the militia would have had for the contemporary readership, especially in the way Austen updated the original post-French Revolution 1790s context of the first draft of the novel to the Napoleonic era of 1813 in which she revised and finally published the novel.[433]

Herbert, whilst admitting that detailed description is not a strong feature of Austen's writing, details the ways in which fiction in general can be used to recreate a human geography of the period: to reconstruct actual and imaginary places; to understand how people with certain characteristics viewed their world; and to unravel the social order of the time and the influences upon it.[434] Because of the lack of descriptive detail, the first of these uses is problematic in Austen. However, one could contend that by examining the second and third uses, for which there is more ammunition in the novel, it is possible to use them to get a general idea of the spatial social geography of the places about which Austen was writing. By examining the social interaction of characters and the ways in which Austen describes them moving and intersecting within the landscape, it is possible to get an image of the past world Austen was perceiving.

What is significant in terms of the geography of *Pride and Prejudice* is the way that the various characters within the novel interact and come together, in formal and informal visits, in dinners and balls, and the way these interactions occur across a landscape. That landscape may itself be a blank in terms of its description, but a sense remains of something that needs to be journeyed across. The novel is fundamentally structured around a series of visits made across these spaces – person A visits person B who invites them to visit person C and they all meet later at a ball given by person D, and so on. The journeys they take to these meetings may take the form of, say, a short walk, a horse ride, or a longer carriage ride, but there is a sense of a distinct separation across space between the characters – these are not people living close together.

We see this idea of a visit at the very beginning of the book, when the Bennet family discover there is a new occupant of Netherfield House, Mr Bingley:

> Mr Bennet was among the earliest of those who waited on Mr Bingley. He had always
> intended to visit him, though to the last always assuring his wife that he should not go,
> and till the evening after the visit was paid, she had no knowledge of it.[435]

Two days later Bingley reciprocates and visits the Bennets who then formally invite him to dinner. Thus, the pattern begins. The idea of travelling across space to visit neighbours comes over strongly in Chapter 7 where Jane Bennet, having received a formal invitation, travels on horseback three miles to visit the Bingleys at Netherfield, becomes unwell, and her sister Elizabeth Bennet travels the same route on foot to visit her:

---

432 Bharat Tandon, 'The Historical Background', in *The Cambridge Companion to Pride and Prejudice*, ed. by
   Janet M. Todd (Cambridge: Cambridge University Press, 2013), p. 73.
433 Ibid.
434 Herbert (1991).
435 Austen (1813 (2007 edition)) p. 6.

...crossing field after field at a quick pace, jumping over stiles and springing over puddles with impatient activity, and finding herself at last within view of the house, with weary ankles, dirty stockings, and a face glowing with the warmth of exercise.[436]

The distance is emphasised by the fact that Elizabeth sends for a carriage to bring extra clothes when she decides to stay with her sick sister at Netherfield. Other such local visits occur through the novel – the Lucases to Longbourn, the Bennets to Netherfield, Mr Collins to Longbourn, the Bennets to the Lucases – a seemingly endless round of visiting and reciprocal visiting, punctuated by the formal balls at Meryton and Netherfield. In time the canvas broadens, with Elizabeth's trips to Rosings in Kent and Mr Darcy's Pemberley in the Derbyshire Peak, and Lydia Bennet's elopement with George Wickham to Brighton, but the basic landscape of the novel is this dispersed landscape of large houses around Meryton.

What does not emerge to any degree from the novel is what lies in the spaces between these houses. Other than a few cursory references to servants,[437] there are no appearances from the working people of the area, and few descriptions of the ordinary houses and cottages of those workers other than one.[438] The novel exists almost entirely within the world of these large houses and of this particular restricted section of society.[439]

Austen ostensibly sets the novel in Hertfordshire, in the area around the fictional town of Meryton. Austen enthusiasts have long been keen to pinpoint exactly where in Hertfordshire are the models for Meryton and Longbourn. Kenneth Smith spends much analytical effort trying to pinpoint the exact location for Longbourn, the home of the Bennet family. He uses the similarity of place names in the novel to ones in Hertfordshire, the distances measured from London in the novel, and the relative positions of the various houses mentioned in the novel to carry out this task and concludes that Longbourn was somewhere in the vicinity of Redbourn and Harpenden.[440] John Breihan takes a similar approach but expands it by exploring the role of the militia in the novel. One of the key characters in *Pride and Prejudice* is George Wickham, a soldier billeted in Meryton. Breihan notes that the Derbyshires, who he considers to be the likeliest regiment for Wickham to have belonged to, were billeted in the Hertford and Ware area during the winter of 1794-5, just before Austen began writing the first draft of what would become *Pride and Prejudice*. Like Smith, he also uses distances to triangulate where *Pride and Prejudice* might be set.[441] There is also speculation on the true location of Meryton on one of the many Austen fan websites, which tells us that Rev. Thomas Bathurst, cousin of Austen's father George, was until his death in 1797 working in the parish of Welwyn in Hertfordshire and may have passed intelligence about the militia back to his cousin which Austen may have read.[442]

---

436 Ibid. p. 30.
437 Ibid. p. 32.
438 Ibid. p. 143.
439 Jo Baker attempted to remedy this lack of balance between above and below stairs in her novel *Longbourn*, which describes the *Pride and Prejudice* universe from the servants' point of view, with a much-enhanced role for Mrs Hill, the Bennet's housekeeper at Longbourn. Jo Baker, *Longbourn* (London: Doubleday, 2013).
440 Kenneth Smith, 'The Probable Location of "Longbourn" in Jane Austen's Pride and Prejudice', *Persuasions*, 27 (2005), pp. 234-41.
441 John Breihan, 'Jane Austen and the Militia', *Persuasions*, 14 (1992), pp. 16-26.
442 Anon, *Ware is Meryton? Did Ware in Hertfordshire provide Jane Austen with the inspiration for her fictional market town?*, (2013) <http://austenonly.com/2013/02/08/ware-is-meryton-did-ware-in-hertfordshire-provide-jane-austen-with-the-inspiration-for-her-fictional-market-town/>.

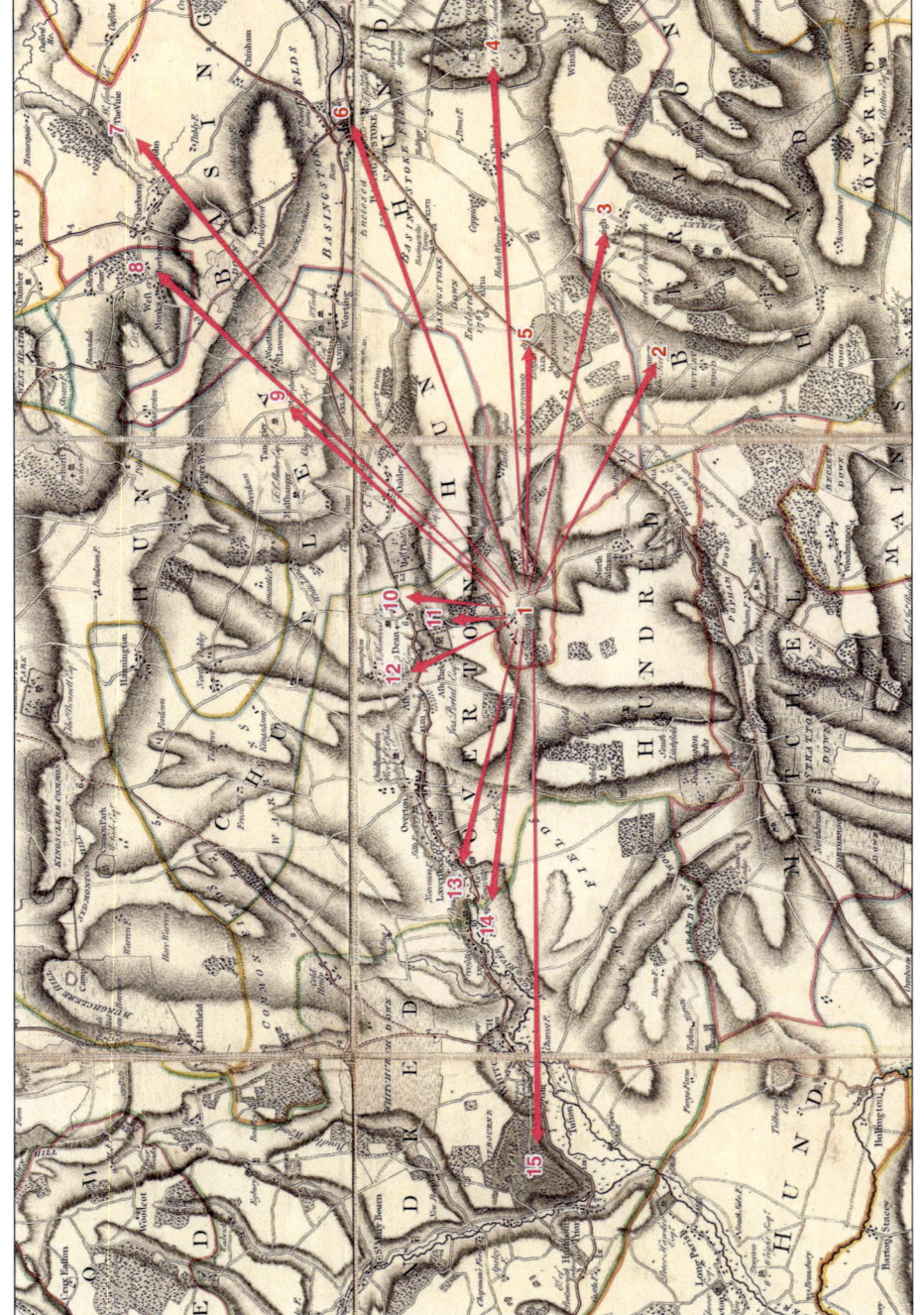

Figure 5.1: Steventon and its surroundings – 1791.

| STORIES OF THE PAST

Steventon and its surroundings

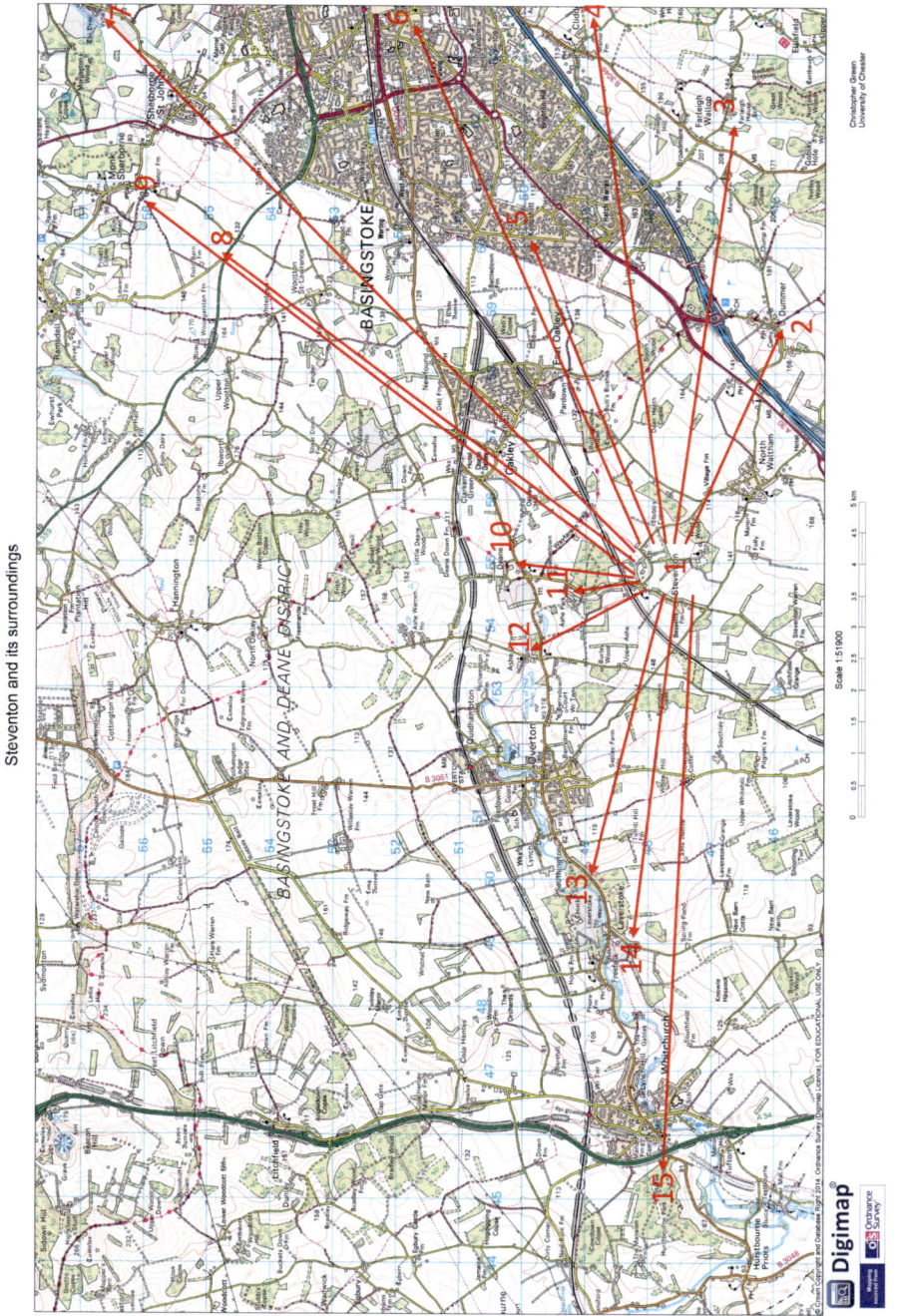

Figure 5.2: Steventon and its surroundings – present day.

Figure 5.3: Austen sites in Steventon, Hampshire. Top: St Nicholas' Church; Bottom: Site of the old Steventon Rectory.

Number	Name of house/location	Home of
1	Steventon Rectory	Jane Austen and family
2	Dummer	The Terrys
3	Farleigh House	The Hansons
4	Hackwood Park	Lord Bolton
5	Kempshott Park	Lord Dorchester
6	Town Hall Assembly Rooms	Dance venue
7	The Vyne	The Chutes
8	Manydown House	The Bigg-Withers
9	Monk Sherborne	George Austen (brother of Jane) Thomas Leigh (uncle of Jane)
10	Deane House	The Harwoods
11	Steventon Manor	The Digweeds
12	Ashe Rectory	The Lefroys
13	Laverstock House	The Portals
14	Freefolk Priors	General Mathew
15	Hurstbourne Park	Lord Portsmouth

Table 5.1: Key to Hampshire Austen locations as taken from Tomalin's biography of Austen.

Date of letter	Visit described
October 25th	Jane to Deane
	Jane to Oakley Hall & Oakley
	Jane to Deane (again)
	Mr Heathcote & Mr Harwood to 'Lord Carnarvon's Park'
November 1st	Jane to dine and sleep at Deane
	Jane to ball at Basingstoke
	Miss Harwood to Bath
	Miss Fonnereau to Ashe
	Martha Lloyd to Kintbury
November 8th	Jane to Basingstoke and back
	Jane to dine at Ash Park
November 20th	Jane to dine at Deane
	Jane to ball at Hurstbourne
	Jane to dinner at Ashe
	Digweeds to Steventon Rectory
November 30th	Jane to stay at Ibthrop

Table 5.2: Movements of people as described by Jane Austen Oct/ Nov 1800.

There is therefore at least some evidence to provide a location in Hertfordshire for Meryton and Longbourn. Christina Hardyment describes the lengths to which Austen went to ensure some measure of verisimilitude in her use of real locations, obtaining information about places from 'guides, books of engravings, almanacs, and road-books', as well as from friends.[443] She also explains how Austen ensured that distances between

---

443   Christina Hardyment, *Literary Trails: Writers in their Landscapes* (London: National Trust, 2000), p. 74.

real and imaginary places were consistent. Given this, it is perhaps no surprise that a determined investigator is able to pinpoint a specific real location on the map for a specific fictional Austen location. However, though a novel like *Pride and Prejudice* may be set *in* Hertfordshire, is there evidence to support any notion that it is *about* Hertfordshire? As stated above, Austen was not a great chronicler of the physical skin of the society that she described, be that the landscape, the architecture, the furnishings, or the clothes. One does not see the equivalents of the detailed descriptions of the industrial landscapes, and industrial and working conditions of Manchester that we see in Gaskell's *Mary Barton*. What does emerge from the novel, as described above, is the network of large houses and the social and physical connections between them. Based on readings of the novel and autobiographies of Austen, and a visit to her birthplace in Steventon, as this writer perceives it the world of *Pride and Prejudice* reflects most closely the landscape of that part of Hampshire where Jane Austen was born, grew up and wrote the novel.

Claire Tomalin's biography of Austen spends much of its initial chapters describing the social milieu within which the young Austen lived.[444] She was born in 1775 in the small Hampshire village of Steventon to the southwest of Basingstoke, where her father was Rector, and where she wrote the initial drafts of her first novels, including that of *Pride and Prejudice*. As the daughter of a clergyman, and with aristocratic roots on her mother's side, she belonged firmly to the Hampshire upper middle-classes, able to mix both with those on the same stratum as herself and with the Hampshire nobility.

Included within Tomalin's biography of Austen is a map of the Steventon and Basingstoke area showing the locations of her main social contacts.[445] Figure 5.1 maps these locations onto Thomas Milne's 1791 map of Hampshire,[446] and Figure 5.2 does the same with a present-day Ordnance Survey map. Table 5.1 provides the key for the numbers used in these maps, listing the house or the location and the names of Austen's acquaintances that lived there.[447] These are a mixture of rectories, comfortable middle-class homes, and the houses of the landed gentry. What is striking from the 1791 map is the dispersed nature of settlement in the area with a scattering of small villages in the valleys and Basingstoke the one town of any size. The modern map shows one or two villages that have expanded in size since then and also shows the enormous growth of Basingstoke, but away from these the pattern is very much the same with a dispersed pattern of settlement with small villages, hamlets and isolated farms scattered across the landscape.

A visit to Steventon in 2014 found this dispersed pattern to be emphasized on the ground. Away from the larger towns and villages and the main roads this still feels like deep countryside with small settlements hidden away down narrow lanes. On the 1791 map Steventon appears as a scattering of houses, barely more than a hamlet, and that is still true today, the main centre being just a handful of houses close to a small village green. The church then, as now, was set apart from the village about a mile down a narrow lane to the south of Steventon. The rectory was nearer to the 'centre' of the village but was still detached from other dwellings by some distance. Figure 5.3 shows pictures of St Nicholas' Church standing amongst fields, and of the field that was the site of the rectory in which

---

444 Tomalin (1997).
445 Ibid., frontispiece.
446 T. Milne, 1 inch to 1 mile map of Hampshire, (London: William Faden, 1791), from Hampshire CC Museums Service, item HMCMS:FA1998.124.
447 Information from Tomalin (1997) pp. xvi-xvii.

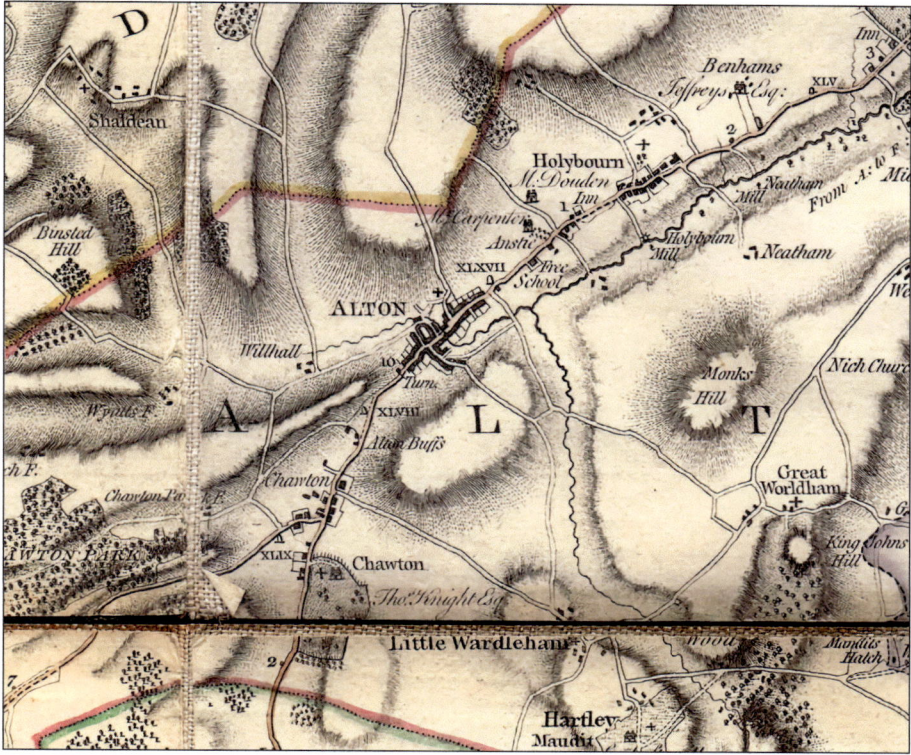

Figure 5.4: Alton and Chawton – 1791.

Jane was born. The rectory was demolished in the mid 19th century and is now a farmer's field. Now, as back in the late 18th century the nearest house is a field's width away.

In terms of interaction with their own social grouping therefore, the Austens lived in relative geographic isolation, and it appears from the maps that this was the case with most of their social contacts, few of whom lived in any sort of nucleated settlement, and who mostly lived at some distance from the Austens, at best a short walk, and at worst a day's ride away. There would have been opportunities for this stratum of society to meet together as a group, most notably at the regular balls held at the Assembly Rooms in Basingstoke, or at dances held in one of the big houses. Tomalin spends an entire chapter of her biography of Austen describing the various sorts of formal and informal dancing Austen would have enjoyed in her childhood and adolescence. She describes, for example, a ball that she attended in late 1793, 'when Henry[448] danced his six dances with Mrs Chute; Alethea and Harriet Bigg were there, the Lefroys, a Terry brother and sister, Coulson Wallop (Lord Portsmouth's brother) and Charles Powlett'.[449] If one analyses Austen's letters to her sister Cassandra late in 1800 one sees all of the trips, visits and events summarised in Table 5.2.[450] Many of these names here and in Tomalin's examples can be cross-referenced to the names on the maps.

---

448   Henry Austen, Jane's brother.
449   Tomalin (1997) pp. 102-3.
450   Jane Austen, *Jane Austen's Letters* (Oxford: Oxford University Press, 1995), pp. 49-66.

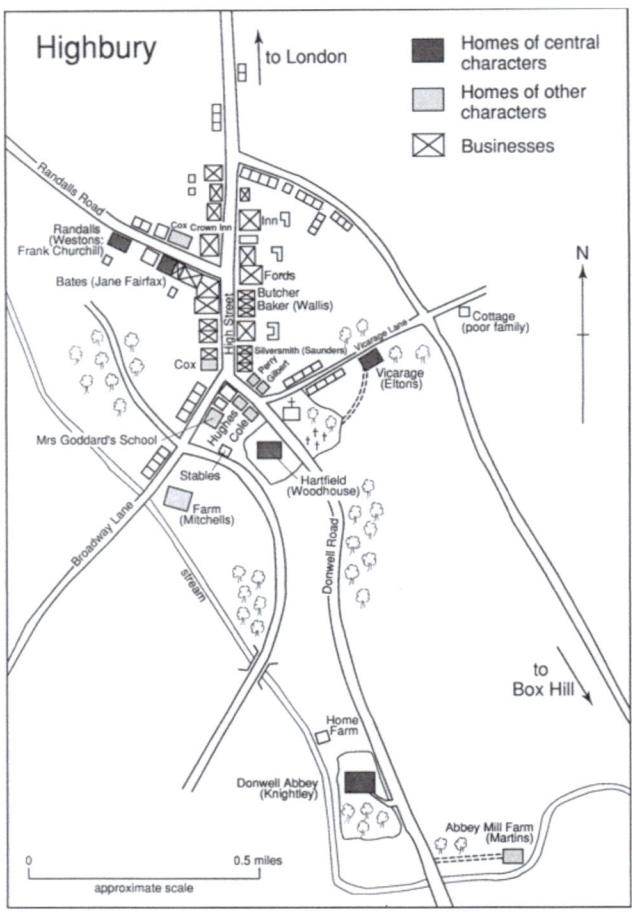

Figure 5.5: Herbert's map of Highbury.

Figure 5.6: Jane Austen's House Museum, Chawton.

STORIES OF THE PAST

The impression gained of Austen's mental map of her world during the time she lived in Steventon is therefore that of a widely spread network of interlinked places, the nodes being the homes of her acquaintances and the places where they would meet together socially, and the links between the nodes the routes between those places, be they paths, bridleways or turnpikes.

What strikes this writer is how similar this is to the world described in *Pride and Prejudice*. We see the same enclosed society, the same geographical dispersal across the landscape of the houses of the members of that society, the same forms of formal and informal social interaction. Austen was in her early twenties when she began writing what would become *Pride and Prejudice*, and apart from spells at boarding schools in Oxford, Southampton and Reading (none of these places anywhere near Hertfordshire), had lived all of her life in Steventon Rectory.

The fictional landscape of the novel may well also reflect that of Hertfordshire at the time, but she would not have known Hertfordshire in the intimate way she would have known this part of Hampshire in which she had grown up. If we assume she was writing at least to a degree from life, and Marilyn Butler typifies her as an 'exact' writer alluding to specific people and events,[451] then the landscape she knew could have infiltrated the novel.[452] For example, regarding the appearance of the militia in the novel, and the possible link between the militia in the novel and the Derbyshires being billeted in Hertford/Meryton, what is surely as pertinent is that there were militia officers in Basingstoke in 1794 and that, according to Tomalin, both her brother Henry and other friends appear to have given her tales of the behaviour of those officers.[453]

Comparing *Pride and Prejudice* with Austen's novel *Emma*,[454] within the later work we still see the idea of the visit to the fore, as shown by this extract describing the social circle of Emma Woodhouse's father:

> Mr. Woodhouse was fond of society in his own way. He liked very much to have his friends come and see him, and from various united causes... he would command the visits of his own little circle, in a great measure as he liked.[455]

Austen describes how he rarely ventured beyond that circle, but that living in a village such as Highbury there were many opportunities for 'intercourse' within that small location. As this writer perceives it, this brings out the major difference between the world of *Pride and Prejudice* and the world of *Emma*, namely the difference in Austen's own world between the writing of the two novels.

By the time Austen wrote *Emma*, in around 1815, she had moved to the house that is now the Jane Austen's House Museum in the village of Chawton, shown in Figure 5.6. This was at the centre of a much more substantial village than Steventon, and close to the small

---

451   Marilyn Butler, 'Austen, Jane (1775-1817), novelist', in *Oxford Dictionary of National Biography* (Oxford: Oxford University Press, 2004, online edition 2010). <http://www.oxforddnbcom/view/article/904>.

452   It should be noted here that whereas Austen describes Longbourn as being 'only one mile' from Meryton (Austen (1813 (2007 edition)) p. 26.), Steventon is about seven miles distant from Basingstoke. Further research would be required to determine whether this invalidates the argument being made here or whether this is simply Austen using geographic foreshortening for literary convenience. Either way, the point that this writer's initial perception was of links between Longbourn and Steventon, and Meryton and Basingstoke, is important in the context of this study.

453   Tomalin (1997) p. 164.

454   Jane Austen, *Emma: A Novel* (London: John Murray, 1816).

455   Jane Austen, *Emma* (London: Penguin, 1996), p. 19.

market town of Alton, and this change seems to be reflected in the geography of the novel. Figure 5.4 shows the relative locations of Chawton and Alton in Milne's map of 1791.[456]

Though both are small settlements by the standards of today, they show a more concentrated community than the dispersed landscape around Steventon seen in Figure 5.1. Herbert uses Austen's writings, and specifically *Emma*, to construct a social geography of the novel. He illustrates this by creating a plan of the imaginary village of Highbury in which the novel is set (Figure 5.5).[457] It shows how most of the main protagonists of the book, the Woodhouses, Knightley, Frank Churchill and the Eltons, live close to each other within the confines of this small community.[458] Herbert makes no mention of Chawton in his article and makes pains to explain his map in terms of distances and of sizes of properties as described in the novel. Indeed, rather than referencing Chawton, he quotes Park Honan as arguing that Austen may have based Highbury on Cobham in Surrey, close to Box Hill.[459] Whilst it appears there is no evidence that he might have been thinking of Chawton when drawing his plan, his Highbury does, at first sight, have a similar feel to the Chawton of Milne's map.

A similar exercise has been undertaken by Penny Gay, who whilst trying tentatively to locate Highbury in Surrey, where the novel, with its references to Kingston and Box Hill, is supposedly set, nonetheless makes the connection between Highbury and Alton, indicating that the geographical and social structure of Highbury reflects Austen's own environment during her time in Chawton.[460]

To conclude, *Emma* and *Pride and Prejudice* are ostensibly set respectively in Hertfordshire and Surrey but analysing the way that the characters interact across space, and the nature of those interactions, it is possible to see elements of Austen's own home worlds in Hampshire within the novel, firstly, in the dispersed landscape around Steventon, and secondly, in the more nucleated settlement of Chawton. Through such analysis it may therefore be possible to develop a historical and social geography of the two areas that may mirror the more descriptive historical landscape geography that Darby produced from Hardy's Wessex Novels.[461] This observation is based on a reading of the novel and observation of the relevant Hampshire landscapes and is therefore indicative of the way we perceive an imaginary world from our reception of a particular novel. At the same time, however, the observation suggests that there can be a way in which the contemporary world of the author infiltrates their novels in way that is largely indirect and removed from the direct references to landscapes and events in life made by authors such as Gaskell and Hardy.

5.3 Elizabeth Gaskell and Manchester

The second case study, involving direct usage of elements of the author's contemporary world, comes from the industrial life of 19th century Manchester as used by Elizabeth Gaskell in her novel *Mary Barton*, and in particular an incident of industrial-inspired violence in the novel that mirrors another, near-contemporary, real-life example of violence. In this the novel reflects the widening of the subject matter of British novels

---

456   Milne (1791).
457   From Herbert (1991).
458   Ibid.
459   Park Honan, *Jane Austen: her life* (London: Weidenfeld and Nicolson, 1987).
460   Penny Gay, 'A Hypothetical Map of Highbury', *Persuasions* (2015) <http://www.jasna.org/persuasions/on-line/vol36no1/gay.html>.
461   Darby (1948).

Manchester 1848

© Landmark Information Group Ltd and Crown copyright 2021. FOR EDUCATIONAL USE ONLY

Scale 1:20000

0 100 200 300 400 500 600 700 800 900 1000 m

Projection: British National Grid

Digimap

Chris Green
University of Chester

Figure 5.7: Manchester in 1848.

through the 19th century that was discussed in Section 5.1, and the greater descriptive depth that this implies. As was detailed in Section 4.3, *Mary Barton* contains large amounts of descriptive detail about the Manchester of the 1830s and 1840s in terms of its physical, social and political landscape. At the time of writing the novel, Gaskell and her husband were living in Upper Rumford Street in the Ardwick area of Manchester, which, though long since swallowed up by the expanding University of Manchester, was at the time a residential street within walking distance of both the city centre and Ancoats, so Gaskell was living close to the subject she was describing. She would have known the conditions in the mills and the industrial housing, and through her social contacts, especially in the Unitarian church via Cross Street Chapel, she would have mixed with many of the mill owners and other leaders of Manchester society such as 'corn millers, silk manufacturers, calico printers, patent-reed makers, engineers; bankers and barristers; founders of hospitals, libraries, educational institutes, charitable funds, missions to the poor'.[462]

Figure 5.7 shows how the elements of Gaskell's life and fiction came together in the geography of Manchester in the mid-19th century. It shows Manchester as it was depicted in the first Ordnance Survey map of 1848[463] and shows the location of the house in Rumford Street (labelled 1 on Figure 5.7) where the Gaskells lived at the time *Mary Barton* was written, and the house a short distance away in Plymouth Grove (2), where they moved soon after and which now forms the Elizabeth Gaskell House. Also marked are the industrial suburb of Ancoats (4) where key characters within *Mary Barton* lived, and the area of Green Heys Fields (3) where the novel starts. It can be seen from the scale that these locations are all within three kilometres of each other, suggesting that Gaskell's descriptions within the novel of these three locations was based on detailed local knowledge. A similar situation can be seen in London, where many of the sites used by Charles Dickens to inspire fictional locations in *Little Dorrit* and *Oliver Twist* are to be found within easy walking distance of the house in Doughty Street that was Dickens' home during the period when he was writing those novels. Simon Callow writes of Dickens 'incessantly walking the streets, learning London as he went, mastering it, memorizing the names of the roads, the local accents, noting the characteristic topographies of the many villages of which the city still consisted'.[464] Locations that entered his fiction include Bleeding Heart Yard, a key location in *Little Dorrit*, and the One Tun Pub, which on a visit in January 2015 advertised itself as the model for The Three Cripples in *Oliver Twist*.

The remainder of this section describes, using extracts from the novel and contemporary sources, firstly how Gaskell may have used a specific act of industrial violence to inform the main plot device of the novel, the murder of Harry Carson by John Barton, and secondly, how she used this local knowledge of Manchester more generally within the novel to inform her descriptions both of place and the social circumstances of the time.

The key plot development in *Mary Barton*, the violent murder of Harry Carson, comes about as an effect of a dispute between the mill-owners and the workers following wage cuts introduced by the owners, including John Carson, to combat foreign competitors who are undercutting their prices. A strike ensues:

> Class distrusted class, and their want of mutual confidence wrought sorrow to both. The masters would not be bullied, and compelled to reveal why they felt it wisest and best to offer only such low wages... And the workmen sat silent and stern with folded hands, refusing to work for such pay. There was a strike in Manchester.[465]

---

462 Valentine Cunningham, *Everywhere Spoken Against: Dissent in the Victorian Novel* (Oxford: Oxford University Press, 1975), pp. 131-2.

463 Ordnance Survey, County Series: Lancashire, (London: Ordnance Survey, 1848), County Series.

464 Callow (2012) p. 34.

465 Gaskell (1848 (2012 Edition)) p. 161.

As the dispute worsens there are threats of retribution on the owners' side, and cabals form on the union side. Negotiations break down amidst much recrimination. Harry Carson, the main spokesmen for the owners' faction, withdraws a compromise proposal, declaring:

> ...all communication between the masters and that particular Trades' Union at an end; secondly, declaring that no master would employ any workman in future, unless he signed a declaration that he did not belong to any Trades' Union, and pledge himself not to assist or subscribe to any society having for its object interference with the masters' powers; and thirdly, that the masters should pledge themselves to protect and encourage all workmen willing to accept employment on those conditions, and at the rate of wages first offered.[466]

Carson draws an unflattering caricature of the union negotiators on a scrap of paper and shows it, to general amusement, to other members of the owners' faction. The scrap of paper is later discovered by a union man and exacerbates union anger at the breakdown in negotiations, resulting in an oath being sworn by a group of disaffected workers to kill one of the owners. After discussion, they decide the obvious target is Harry Carson. Lots are drawn to determine who should be the murderer and John Barton draws the marked lot. He carries out the murder in Turner Street, a 'lonely unfrequented way'.[467] The victim is shot and killed at close range. Barton uses as wadding for the shot part of a Valentine sent by Jem Wilson to Barton's daughter Mary, unaware of its significance. This fact is later discovered by Mary's Aunt Esther who uses it to warn Mary that her father is the likely real culprit. Having been identified as a suspected culprit, Jem Wilson is arrested and charged with the murder, the alleged motive being an argument witnessed between him and Harry Carson over the girl they both love, Mary Barton. The trial takes place soon after at Liverpool Assizes, and Jem is eventually cleared following the late production of alibi evidence. In the final scenes of the book, the identity of killer is revealed to all (though the reader and Mary Barton have known it all along), reconciliation is finally reached between John Barton and John Carson, and John Barton dies of natural causes in Carson's arms before he can be brought to trial.

This murderous violence has a plausible real-life parallel in a specific incident that had occurred in the recent past in Hyde, less than five miles from the parts of Manchester where *Mary Barton* is set. Compare the following scenario with Gaskell's fictional incident of industrial violence. On 3rd January 1831, Thomas Ashton, son of millowner Samuel Ashton, was walking home from the mill he managed on behalf of his father. What the Stockport Advertiser later described as 'assassins' were lying in wait behind a hedge in Apethorn Lane, a quiet country byway.[468] They confronted Ashton and he was killed by a pistol shot delivered at close range. The wadding for the pistol shot was discovered and later used as evidence. Though the newspaper report claims the Ashtons were generally thought to be good employers, there had been a strike of cotton-spinners in the area, which had had repercussions at the Ashtons' mill. As James Ashton, brother of the deceased, said at the subsequent murder trial: 'at this

---

466 Ibid. p. 172.
467 Ibid. p. 195.
468 Stockport Advertiser, 7 January 1831, quoted in Thomas Middleton, Annals of Hyde and District. Containing historical reminiscences of Denton, Haughton, Dukinfield, Mottram, Longdendale, Bredbury, Marple, and the neighbouring townships (Manchester: Cartwright & Rattray, 1899), p. 85.

time there was considerable excitement amongst the workpeople in Ashton and Stalybridge. I had discharged one man the day before for belonging to the Union'.[469]

Looking at the actual and the fictional murders, several elements are present in both events: the murder of the son of mill-owning father; the idea of conspiracy and oath taking; an isolated location for the murder; a similar *modus operandi* for the murder, namely a gun shot at close range; and the significance of wadding.[470] However, Gaskell herself always fought shy of making a direct link between Ashton and Carson's murders. In a letter to Sir John Potter in August 1852, after he had commented on the perceived similarities, she says that 'of course I had heard of young Mr Ashton's murder' and that she 'knew none of the details, nothing about the family'. If the incident were in her mind at the time of writing it was done so 'unconsciously'. She suggests other incidents that might also have been in her mind, such as 'one or two similar cases at Glasgow' which 'were, I have no doubt, suggestive of the plot, as having shown me to what lengths the animosity of irritated workmen would go', a reference to the trial of five Glasgow Cotton-Spinners in 1838 on charges of murder, intimidation, and conspiracy. She ends by saying: 'I would rather never have written the book, than have been guilty of the want of all common feeling…. if I had made Mr Ashton's death into a mere subject for a story'.[471] There were indeed similarities between the Carson murder and the incidents in Glasgow, such as the alleged presence in the Glasgow incident of secret oath-taking between Trades Unionists, but in other details the Glasgow story differed. The Glasgow conspirators were accused of murdering a strike-breaker, not a member of the owning class, and though many of the accused were found guilty of intimidating strike-breakers, on the more specific charge of murder the jury reached the Scottish verdict of 'not proven'.[472]

Despite Gaskell's denial many critical articles and biographies have since made the link between the Ashton and Carson murders. To give a few examples, Nancy Weyant's chronology in the *Cambridge Companion to Elizabeth Gaskell* says under the entry for 1831: 'January 3 – Thomas Ashton murdered, an event… fictionalized in the death of Harry Carson in Mary Barton'[473]. Louis James in the *Encyclopedia of Literature & Criticism* states that 'The murder of a millowner's son by an embittered worker [in Mary Barton] is largely based on the notorious murder of Thomas Ashton'.[474] Jenny Uglow, in her 1993 biography of Gaskell, backs up her own attribution by describing how, when Thomas Ashton's sister read *Mary Barton* for the first time, 'on coming to the chapter of the murder she suddenly

---

469 Ibid. p. 90.

470 As an example of how the decisions taken within an adaptation can affect the nature of the author's original imagined world (covered in more detail in Chapter 3), Rona Munro's 2006 adaptation of *Mary Barton* for the Royal Exchange Theatre in Manchester, changed two of these pieces of evidence. Firstly, John Barton, rather than murdering Harry Carson because he drew the short straw as part of the conspiracy, does so simply of his own volition out of despair following the collapse of the strike (Elizabeth Gaskell and Rona Munro, *Elizabeth Gaskell's Mary Barton* (London: Nick Hern Books, 2006), p. 37.). Secondly, Esther recognises Barton as the likely culprit not by finding the Valentine card wadding but by finding a scarf that she has given Mary and that Barton has used to wipe the gun after use (ibid. p. 80.).

471 Extracts from letter from Elizabeth Gaskell to Sir John Potter, quoted in Chapple and Pollard (1997) p. 195.

472 Patrick Brantlinger, 'The Case Against Trade Unions in Early Victorian Fiction', *Victorian Studies*, 13 (1969), pp. 37-52.

473 Nancy Weyant, 'Chronology', in *The Cambridge Companion to Elizabeth Gaskell*, ed. by Jill L. Matus (Cambridge: Cambridge University Press, 2007), p. xii.

474 Louis James, 'The Nineteenth Century Social Novel', in *Encyclopedia of Literature & Criticism*, ed. by Martin Coyle, et al. (London: Routledge, 1990), p. 551.

realised that it was a description of her own brother's assassination, and she fainted'.[475] Finally, M.C. Rintoul records Ashton represented not only as Harry Carson, but as Henry Wolstenholme in Elizabeth Stone's novel *William Langshawe, the Cotton Lord*.[476]

If we look specifically at the issue of industrial violence, contemporary reportage suggests that whilst Gaskell may have been referencing just one real-life incident, she was writing against a contemporary backdrop of many instances of industrial violence. An article in the *Churchman* magazine for April 1841 described the Ashton murder as being one of many acts of violence that came out of the same industrial dispute. Within a fortnight of the Ashton murder, it reported, 'two other master spinners were severally shot at upon their own premises'. It also reported 'outrages' in Bolton in 1839 including a 'destruction committee' set up 'for the purpose of planning and superintending the execution of those outrages'.[477]

Another contemporary witness was Friedrich Engels, who lived in Manchester during this period whilst working for his father's textile firm. In *The Condition of the Working-Class in England in 1844* he quoted several examples of industrial violence at the time Gaskell was writing, including the Ashton and Glasgow Spinners incidents. He saw how conditions could excite such violence, exemplified by this quote that echoed similar passages in *Mary Barton*:

> That these Unions contribute greatly to nourish the bitter hatred of the workers against the property-holding class need hardly be said. From them proceed, therefore, with or without the connivance of the leading members, in times of unusual excitement, individual actions which can be explained only by hatred wrought to the pitch of despair, by a wild passion overwhelming all restraints.[478]

The Scottish thinker Thomas Carlyle quoted the example of the Glasgow Spinners Trial (or 'Glasgow Thuggery' as he calls it), and whilst he was sympathetic to the plight of the poor working classes, he decried those who used violence in attempting to get reform:

> The melancholy fact remains, that this thing known at present by the name Chartism does exist; has existed; and either 'put down' into secret treason, with rusty pistols, vitriol-bottle and match-box, or openly brandishing pike and torch (one knows not in which case more fatal-looking), is like to exist till quite other methods have been tried with it. What means this bitter discontent of the Working Classes? Whence comes it, whither goes it? Above all, at what price, on what terms, will it probably consent to depart from us and die into rest?[479]

Whether or not the Ashton murder was truly in Gaskell's mind at the time of writing the description of the Carson murder, the incident itself and its particulars as described in the novel were typical of the types of industrial violence prevalent at the time.

If the Barton murder was Gaskell writing using the inspiration of real-life events and mirroring the industrial situation of the time, then *Mary Barton* also provided many

---

475   Uglow (1993) p. 216.
476   M. C. Rintoul, *Dictionary of Real People and Places in Fiction* (London: Routledge, 1993), p. 162.
477   Anon, 'Trades' Unions and Strikes', The Churchman – A Magazine in support of the Church of England, April 1841.
478   Friedrich Engels, *The Condition of the Working Class in England in 1844*, trans. Florence Kelley Wischnewetzky (London: George Allen and Unwin, 1845 (1952 reprint)), pp. 219-20.
479   Carlyle (1840) p. 2.

Figure 5.8: Ancoats in 1851.

Figure 5.9: Manchester Court Dwellings in the early 20th century. Left: McWilliams Court, Ancoats; Right: Newgate, Corporation Street.

examples of Gaskell writing from life when describing place, which can be directly to compared to contemporary factual sources. As a first example, the novel begins with the Barton and Wilson families spending a Sunday off in Green Heys Fields, now part of the urban sprawl of Moss Side south of the centre of Manchester, but at that time a landscape of fields and scattered farms a three kilometre walk from the industrial suburb of Ancoats, where Gaskell describes John Barton as living, but much closer to Rumford Street, where Gaskell herself was living when writing the novel.[480] The novel's opening is deceptive, only slowly revealing that this is to be a novel set fairly and squarely in an industrial setting:

> There are some fields near Manchester, well known to the inhabitants as 'Green Heys Fields', through which runs a public footpath to a little village about two miles distant. In spite of these fields being flat, and low, nay, in spite of want of wood... there is a charm about them which strikes even the inhabitant of a mountainous district, who sees and feel the effect of contrast in these commonplace but thoroughly rural fields, with the busy, bustling manufacturing town he left but half an hour ago.[481]

Having established the contrast with the industrial Manchester she goes on to describe, Gaskell never returns to this rural setting within the novel.[482] Whether factory workers would actually have visited this setting is, however, open to question if one compares

---

480   The connection between place and novel is reinforced by a recent housing development in the Greenheys area of Moss Side that has been given the name 'Mary Barton Fields'.
481   Gaskell (1848 (2012 Edition)) p. 5.
482   Unlike Gaskell's later 'Manchester' novel *North and South*, whose initial premise is the contrasts that its heroine, Margaret Hale, finds between the rural south and the industrial north.

Gaskell's account with the testimony that J.L Hammond and Barbara Hammond quote of a Manchester doctor of the time decrying the lack of exercise taken by the working population:

> At present the entire labouring population of Manchester is without any season of recreation and is ignorant of all amusements... Healthful exercise in the open air is seldom or never taken by the artisans of this town, and their health certainly suffers considerable depression from this deprivation.[483]

Gaskell may have been exaggerating the extent to which working people might have visited Green Heys Fields, but at the same time she is giving us a vivid picture of the geography of Manchester at this time, of the close proximity of, and sharp contrast between, the rural and urban that is borne out by the Ordnance Survey map in Figure 5.7, which shows the distance between Green Heys Fields and the industrial suburb of Ancoats that the families return to after their Sunday out.

Following the Bartons' return journey Gaskell describes the court where they live thus:

> ...they turned out of one of these innumerable streets into a little paved court, having the backs of houses at the end opposite to the opening and a gutter running through the middle to carry of household slops, washing suds, etc. The women who lived in the court were busy taking in strings of caps, frocks, and various articles of linen, which hung from side to side...[484]

Courts were a particular type of housing development within industrial cities, whereby a number of houses opened out into an enclosed court with shared sanitary facilities and a gutter out of which all waste material flowed (not just the washing effluent that Gaskell describes). Adshead's 1851 map of Ancoats (Figure 5.8) shows a number of court developments lining the streets north of the mills that line the Rochdale Canal.[485] As can be seen from the map, some courts were almost completely enclosed with access via narrow alleys, whilst some had one end open to the streets. Though the courts shown in the map have long since been demolished, photographs exist in the Manchester City Council Local Image Collection, taken at the beginning of the 20th century, showing examples of court developments (Figure 5.9).[486] Note the gutter in both pictures, as well as the pump, washing vessels and washing lines in the picture to the right, all things that tie in with Gaskell's description above.

Friedrich Engels' contemporary account describes several types of court dwellings. He writes first of the more modern developments, consisting of small courts, open to the street, with dwellings that possessed the luxury of back doors, and which commanded the highest rent. To the rear of these dwellings ran an alley which led into an enclosed

483   Dr J.P. Kay, writing in 1833. Quoted in J. L. Hammond and Barbara Hammond, *The Age of the Chartists, 1832-1854. A study of discontent* (London: Longmans, 1930), p. 119.
484   Gaskell (1848 (2012 Edition)) p. 13. Gaskell talked of them returning home through 'many half-finished streets' emphasizing that this was a city that was still developing and growing.
485   Manchester, University of Manchester, Adshead's twenty four illustrated maps of the township of Manchester: New Cross Ward (1851), JRL1300179.
486   Manchester, Manchester City Council, *Ancoats, McWilliams Court (1902)*, GB127.m10285. Manchester, Manchester City Council, *Housing: Newgate, Corporation Street (1908)*, GB127.m08316.

courtyard where the dwellings shared their rear walls with dwellings facing a second street. These commanded the least rent.[487]

Engels' description seems to tally with that of the court where the Bartons lived, and the dwelling that Gaskell describes seems to fit the Engels' high rent cottage category. At the beginning of the novel, John Barton has a good job and is therefore able to live in relative comfort with his wife and daughter Mary. Gaskell portrays the Bartons' actual dwelling with an eye for detail that feels based on close observation:

> On the right of the door, as you entered, was a longish window, with a broad ledge. On each side of this, hung blue-and-white check curtains, which were now drawn, to shut in the friends met to enjoy themselves... In the corner between the window and the fire-side was a cupboard, apparently full of plates and dishes, cups and saucers, and some more nondescript articles, for which one would have fancied their possessors could find no use – such as triangular pieces of glass to save carving knives and forks from dirtying table-cloths. However, it was evident Mrs. Barton was proud of her crockery and glass, for she left her cupboard door open, with a glance round of satisfaction and pleasure.[488]

Engels also describes an older type of court, built in an unplanned manner and often below the level of the surrounding streets making drainage of the effluent from the court difficult. He emphasizes the unsanitary nature of these courts:

> The air simply cannot escape; the chimneys of the houses are the sole drains for the imprisoned atmosphere of the courts... Moreover the houses surrounding such courts are usually built back to back, having the rear wall in common; and this alone suffices to prevent any sufficient through ventilation... And as the police charged with care of the streets, does not trouble itself with the condition of these courts... there is no cause for wonder at the filth and heaps of ashes and offal to be found here.[489]

In Gaskell's novel events quickly take a turn for the worse as Barton's wife sickens and dies. Barton then loses his job as a result of worsening trade conditions. The tone of Gaskell's descriptions gradually darkens, especially when she describes a visit made by Barton and his friend Wilson to the cellar home of Ben Davenport, a former colleague suffering from fever, whose wife, as we discover, is dying of starvation. What soon becomes clear here is how closely Gaskell's descriptions of the house and its environs mirrored contemporary factual accounts. Here is Gaskell describing the approach to Davenport's house on Berry Street (labelled 5 on Figure 5.7).[490] Though she is not talking about a court *per se*, this was an older part of town and her description of the sanitary conditions mirrors that of Engels above:

> It was unpaved and down the middle a gutter forced it way, every now and then forming pools in the holes with which the street abounded. Never was the old Edinburgh cry of "Gardez l'eau!" more necessary than in this street. As they passed, women from their door

---

487   Engels (1845 (1952 reprint)) pp. 55-56.
488   Gaskell (1848 (2012 Edition)) pp. 14-15.
489   Engels (1845 (1952 reprint)) pp. 55-56.
490   Berry Street lay, and still lies, just to the south of Piccadilly Station, then known as London Road station, about a kilometre south of Ancoats.

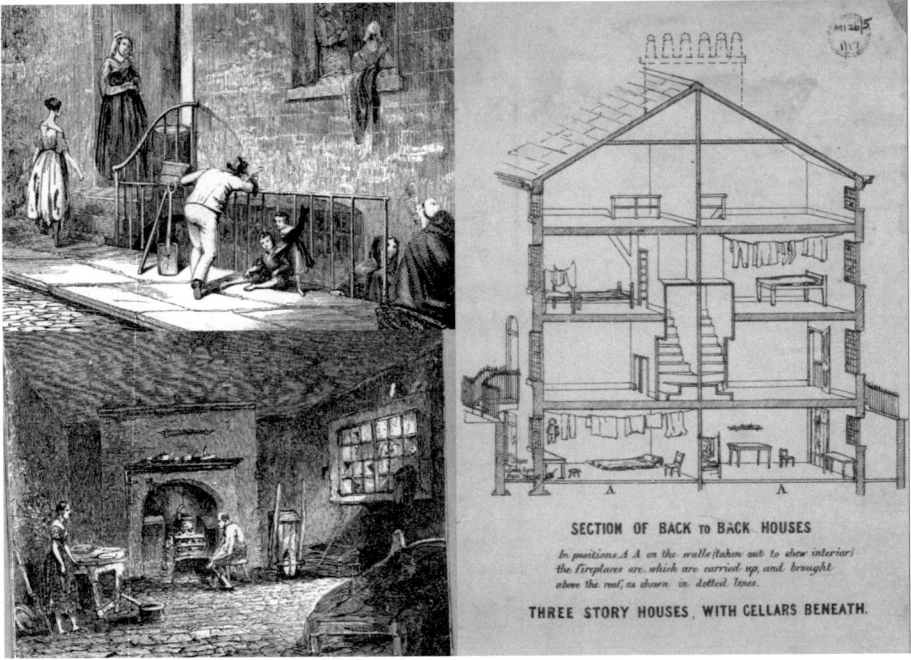

Figure 5.10: Slum conditions in mid-19th century Manchester. Top left: entrance to cellar dwelling; Bottom left: Interior of Manchester Cellar; Right: Plan of back-to-back houses.

tossed household slops of every description into the gutter; they ran into the next pool, which overflowed and stagnated. Heaps of ashes were the stepping-stones, on which the passer-by, who cared in the least for cleanliness, took care not to put his foot.[491]

Gaskell's description of the cellar dwelling itself also closely matches that of Engels. Here is Gaskell writing about Davenport's dwelling:

You went down one step even from the foul area into the cellar in which a family of human beings lived. It was very dark inside. The window-panes, many of them, were broken and stuffed with rags, which was reason enough for the dusky light that pervaded the place even at mid-day. ...the smell was so fœtid as almost to knock the two men down. Quickly recovering themselves, as those inured to such things do, they began to penetrate the thick darkness of the place, and to see three or four little children rolling on the damp, nay wet brick floor, through which the stagnant, filthy moisture of the street oozed up; the fireplace was empty and black; the wife sat on her husband's lair, and cried in the dark loneliness.[492]

Compare this with Engels writing about the 'Little Ireland' area of Manchester, close to the Berry Street that Gaskell is describing. He describes the area around Oldham Road and Great Ancoats Street where 'cellar dwellings are to be found under almost every

---

491   Gaskell (1848 (2012 Edition)) pp. 56-57.
492   Ibid. p. 57.

cottage',[493] and of a race living 'in dark, wet cellars, in measureless filth and stench, in this atmosphere penned in as if with a purpose' and proclaims that such a race 'must really have reached the lowest stage of humanity'.[494]

The illustrations reproduced in Figure 5.10 reflect the descriptions of cellar dwellings made by both Gaskell and Engels.[495] The illustrations on the left are from 1838, closely contemporary with Engels' research and with the period in which *Mary Barton* is set. They show the relationship between the cellar dwellings and the street, and the position of the windows shows how little light must have reached the cellar room below, the sparse nature of which is shown in the bottom illustration. This is borne out by illustration on the right, from around the time Gaskell was writing her second Manchester novel, *North and South*. It shows the relationship of the cellar dwellings to the rest of the buildings under which they sit and also shows the back-to-back method of construction to which Engels alludes. What the illustrations do *not* give is any sense of the squalid conditions emphasized by both Gaskell and Engels. They have little sense of the coldness, dampness, and darkness that the written descriptions convey.

Both Engels and Gaskell had a crusading intent in their writing, and this is reflected in the emotive way they describe the courts, alleys, and cellar dwellings. The colder language of official reports, however, provides corroborating evidence for their descriptions. The following is an extract from a report by the Manchester Sanitary Association on the Deansgate area of Manchester in 1854. The inspectors of the association assessed the area street by street and house by house, giving an impression of the living conditions in each dwelling, including the cellars described here in Jordan Street. This report too gives an idea of the dampness and lack of light within the cellars, as well as the vermin infesting the dwelling, and the overcrowding that could occur. Again, we see echoes of Gaskell's description of Davenport's cellar dwelling in *Mary Barton*:[496]

Cellar No 1 is a dwelling of two rooms 12ft x 10ft and 12ft x 9ft respectively each room is lighted by a sash window – 3ft x 2ft. The sleeping room has no fire place nor any means of ventilation except through the broken window. There are five people living in this cellar.

Cellar 3 is but one room about 12 feet by 14. There are two beds in the room. 7 people live & sleep in this one room. We could learn nothing more [because] a little girl only being in charge.

Cellar 5 has 2 rooms 12 ft by 14 & 12 by 12 respectively. The rooms are dark and damp. The approach to the cellar from the street is not more than 2ft 6in wide and the top of the window is rather below the level of the street. The tenant has been in it only a short time but complains of damp, rats, mice, etc.[497]

---

493   Engels (1845 (1952 reprint)) p. 57.
494   Ibid. p. 60.
495   Manchester, Manchester City Council Manchester Local Image Collection, *Cellar Dwellings (1838)*, GB127.m08387. Manchester, Manchester City Council Manchester Local Image Collection, *Interior of a Manchester Cellar (1838)*, GB127.m08388. Manchester, Manchester Central Library, *Section of back to back houses*, GB124.M126/5/1/17.
496   Cellar 3 houses 7 people in one room, which compares with the 6 (two adults and four children) that Gaskell describes as inhabiting Ben Davenport's small cellar room in *Mary Barton*.
497   Manchester, Manchester Central Library, Manchester Sanitary Association Report on the Deansgate District 1854, M126/2/3/21-1 & 2.

In Gaskell's descriptions of the streetscapes of industrial Manchester and the types of houses and living conditions therein, there are clear resonances with other contemporary documentary descriptions of the same things. Gaskell was also capable of using such descriptions in a far more direct fashion. Both Elizabeth Gaskell and her husband William were involved in charitable work amongst the poor of Manchester through the work of Cross Street Chapel, and especially through its involvement with the Manchester Domestic Missionary Society. William Gaskell was secretary of this society for many years, and whilst Elizabeth, according to Uglow, was not involved in the direct relief work of the society she was deeply involved in the Unitarian educational mission, helping to set up, and teaching in, Sunday Schools in Mosley Street, Manchester.[498] She would also have known of the annual reports produced by John Layhe on behalf of the Society, the 'Reports of the Ministry to the Poor, in Manchester'. Monica Frykstedt has shown how Gaskell took large chunks of John Layhe's reports in the 1840s and reproduced them almost verbatim (but without acknowledgement) in the pages of Mary Barton.[499] This is confirmed by Edward Royle, who in his introduction to the catalogue of the microfilm collection of these annual reports writes of the 'striking parallels between passages in the reports and descriptions of slum life in Mary Barton'.[500]

Take as an example, the following two extracts, the first from the mission report of 1842, and the second from Mary Barton. The two passages are practically identical, and suggest, considerations of plagiarism aside, that Gaskell wanted her descriptions of working life to be rooted in some kind of reality. As Frykstedt says, 'her anxiety to give a truthful account is noteworthy':[501]

At the present, however, I have reason to think, that the indigence and sufferings of the operatives of Manchester, with other concurring cases, have induced a suspicion in the minds of many persons, that their legislators, their magistrates, their employers, and even the ministers of religion, are, in general, their oppressors and enemies, and are in league for their prostration and enthralment.[502]

The indigence and sufferings of the operatives induced a suspicion in the minds of many of them that their legislators, their magistrates, their employees, and even the ministers of religion, were, in general, their oppressors and enemies; and were in league for their prostration and enthralment.[503]

Both the accounts of the Ashton murder, and other more general contemporary reportage, show us the basis that the events described within a novel such as Mary Barton have in historical mid-19th century Manchester and in Gaskell's perception of it. However, a work of fiction such as Mary Barton takes that perception and adapts it into an imagined story. It is therefore important to understand the choices Gaskell, and other writers in a similar

---

498   Uglow (1993) p. 90.
499   Monica C. Frykstedt, 'Mary Barton and the Reports of the Ministry to the Poor – A New Source', Studia Neophilologica, 52 (1980), pp. 333-36.
500   Edward Royle, Annual Reports of the Manchester Domestic Missionary Society, 1833-1908, (Wakefield: EP Microform Ltd).
501   Frykstedt (1980).
502   John Layhe, Reports of the Mission to the Poor, in Manchester (Manchester: 1842) Quoted in Kate Flint, The Victorian Novelist: Social Problems and Social Change (London: Croom Helm, 1987), p. 33.
503   Gaskell (1848 (2012 Edition)) p. 80.

situation, make when adapting their contemporary world into the imaginary world of the novel, because the way that world is described in the novel in turn influences the way we ourselves create our own imagined version of that original world through reading the literature or through watching adaptations of that literature. Three factors in particular were important in influencing the choices Gaskell made, whether knowingly or otherwise, in adapting the contemporary world into the imagined world.

Firstly, the social and political points of view of the author were important. Gaskell's Unitarian instincts, and her belief in compassion and reconciliation between the classes, were strong. At the end of *Mary Barton,* John Barton dies in the arms of John Carson, whose son he has murdered but who has forgiven him, and the novel then goes on to describe improvements made to the systems at Carson's factories because of his acknowledgement of some of the grievances against him:

> ...those that were admitted into his [John Carson's] confidence were aware that the wish that lay nearest to his heart was that none might suffer from the cause from which he had suffered; that a perfect understanding, and complete confidence and love, might exist between masters and men.[504]

Annette Hopkins relates this reconciliation squarely to Gaskell's Christian ethics and fundamental social philosophy, which resulted in 'her belief in the capacity of human beings to rise above their passions and meet on a plane of rational intercourse'.[505] Gaskell herself, in a letter to Mary Greg, the wife of Samuel Greg Jr., talked of 'the universality of some sort of suffering', and of the 'groping search' of men such as John Barton for the 'causes of suffering, and the reason why suffering is sent, and what they can do to lighten it'.[506] She sees suffering as part of a necessary process towards a good end, a belief typified by the reconciliation she describes at the end of the novel.

Secondly, Gaskell's reconciliatory approach suggests an element of recognition on her part of the likely consumers of her novel. Gaskell's intended readership would have included those with a similar background to herself, including many who would have been termed 'Masters', including indeed Ashton's own family. Whether this was a conscious influence or not, she does take care to produce an even-handed view of the industrial situation, emphasising good and bad aspects of the way both owners and workers organise themselves. In terms of whether this a true reflection of reality, as was seen in Section 4.3, William Rathbone Greg argued that it was too severe a picture and one can conjecture that Engels might have argued, if he had reviewed the novel, that it was too rosy a picture. Both, as Gaskell did, had their own points of view, their own prejudices and beliefs that coloured how they saw the world. Either way, Gaskell's conclusion is an imagined end to an imagined dispute rather than a real end to a real historical dispute.

Thirdly, and setting aside these considerations of reconciliation, the creation of a good story is also important to a novelist. The differences between the fictional murder account in *Mary Barton* and the factual account described above can be explained to an extent by the need to produce a dramatic narrative, and if this required Gaskell to compress and conflate the events,

---

504   Ibid. p. 361.
505   Annette B. Hopkins, '"Mary Barton": A Victorian Best Seller', *The Trollopian*, 3 (1948), pp. 1-18.
506   Letter from Elizabeth Gaskell to Mrs Greg, quoted in Chapple and Pollard (1997) pp. 73-75.

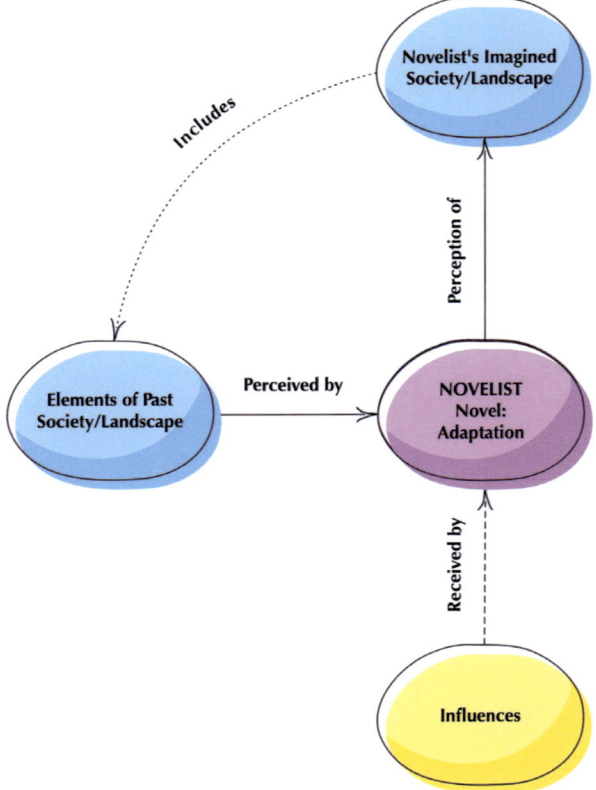

Figure 5.11: Classic Fiction Process Model – Writing the novel.

and to introduce elements of melodrama and suspense, then that was grist to the storytelling mill. And though tragic events occur throughout novels of this period, not least in *Mary Barton* where the body count is sometimes alarming, such novels, especially those serialised in regular instalments in popular magazines, such as Gaskell's other 'Manchester' novel, *North and South*, needed the solace of a happy ending. In *Mary Barton* though, the happy ending is somewhat ambivalent. Though we see the reconciliation between John Barton and John Carson and Carson's improvements in factory practices, it's telling that at the very end of the novel Mary Barton and her new husband Jem Wilson can only find true happiness by emigrating to Canada and starting a new life, away from the system that caused them so much pain.[507]

Gaskell, therefore, shows in *Mary Barton* how her perceptions of the Manchester in which she lived could find its way into the pages of the novel. As such, much of it is not at face value too dissimilar to the non-fictional contemporary accounts of Engels and the Manchester societies quoted above. Whilst there may be a polemical motive behind those accounts, particularly in the case of Engels, they are essentially real accounts of real situations. Gaskell, in contrast, is telling a story and in so doing adapting her perception through both her desire to be true to her faith and its doctrines of peace and conciliation and to her need to tell a story with dramatic tension and narrative drive.

---

507   Mary and Jem's new life in Canada is described in the final chapter of *Mary Barton*. Gaskell (1848 (2012 Edition)) pp. 362-66.

5.4 Conclusion: Writing and the Classic Fiction Process Model

As was discussed in Section 1.2, whilst both straight historical accounts and novels can be thought of as narrative stories, in the former the stories are found but, in the latter, they will normally be invented. However, many novels set in the author's contemporary world have a grounding in the direct life and experiences of the author, not just in generalised observation. In terms of other authors that are discussed in these pages, both Thomas Hardy and J.B. Priestley made frequent use of their own lives in specific places, Hardy of his life growing up in Higher Bockhampton in *Under the Greenwood Tree*, and Priestley of his time living and working in Bradford immediately before the First World War in *Bright Day*, and to a lesser extent in *The Good Companions*. Sometimes the experiences, though indirect, are still personal to the author, as in the previously cited example of Dickens' *Little Dorrit* and its use of Marshalsea Prison, or in the case of Charlotte Brontë's *Shirley*, where the author made use of her father Patrick's witnessing of Luddite industrial violence thirty years prior to the writing of the novel.[508] Gaskell and Austen show more directly how a sense of an actual contemporary world underpinning fiction can be had. Gaskell's use of a model for the murder of Harry Carson may or may not have been conscious and deliberate, but her descriptions of housing conditions, industrial unrest and industrial violence do appear to be. By contrast, Austen's depiction of a genuine social landscape in *Pride and Prejudice* and *Emma* is indirect, not explicitly addressed within the novel, but implied through the interactions described within it. Both, however, appear to be assimilating the world in which they live and using it in their fiction.

This brings into play two issues that are more relevant to Austen than to Gaskell. Firstly, the physical world as described by Austen is by its very nature harder to pin down than that described by Gaskell. Gaskell's descriptions of place have power, whereas a lack of any substantial descriptive element in Austen's writing makes any analysis of the world behind the novel more problematic; the emphasis in her novels is overwhelmingly on examining the interpersonal relationships between her characters rather than setting those in a descriptive frame. Many, as described above, have tried to place Austen's stories in specific real-world settings, but with varying degrees of success. This introduces a second issue, namely that in making assertions about *Pride and Prejudice* and *Emma*, this writer is perceiving the novel through his reading of the novel, biographies of Jane Austen, and academic articles on the subject, and on an examination of sources contemporary to Austen and of the present-day landscape of two specific parts of Hampshire that were home to Austen at different times, namely Steventon and Chawton. Essentially, whereas Gaskell *provides* a clear picture of the world in which she sets her novel, and by extension, her own world, Austen does not provide such a picture but rather, given a degree of effort and knowledge on the part of the reader, *enables* such a picture to be ascertained.

We are now back at the root of the classic fiction process model, the perception of elements of a past historical society and landscape by an author and its translation into the imagined world of a novel. As can be seen in Figure 5.11, novelists such as Gaskell and Austen are at root using direct first-hand perception of their contemporary world within novels such as *Mary Barton*, *Pride and Prejudice*, and *Emma*. The imagined version of the contemporary world that they create within the novels is then conditioned by their reception of particular influences, prejudices, and other social norms. At the same time,

---

508   Charlotte Brontë, *Shirley: A Tale* (London: Smith, Elder & Co., 1849).

there is the further element of reception in the taking in of other sources, the choice of which may be affected by the same conditioning, to enhance or corroborate the perceived world. Instances of this might include Gaskell's use of published reports on poverty in Manchester when writing *Mary Barton*. The author then takes the perceived world and the received influences and via adaptation, either subconscious governed by their conditioning, or conscious governed by their expected readership or simply the needs of good storytelling, produces the work of fiction that is the novel. At this initial stage in the classic fiction process therefore, these processes of perception, reception and adaptation change what would otherwise be raw data about the contemporary world, which could otherwise be turned into history, into what the author hopes will be compelling fiction, where the actual contemporary background provides the skeleton on which the skin of the drama hangs.

What is clear even right back here at the beginning of the process is that what we are seeing in the novel is not a true historical record as such, other than them being, as Marwick says, primary sources for a period simply because they are documents of that period. Indeed, as Paul Ricoeur argues, it would be dangerous for fictional people in fictional settings to have the same credence as recorded historical people in recorded historical settings: 'as soon as the idea of a debt to the dead, to people of flesh and blood to whom something really happened in the past, stops giving documentary research its highest end, history loses its meaning'.[509] The novel is a fictional adaptation of a perceived world rather than that world itself, even if the 'facts' contained within are redolent of situations in the world perceived by the author. As the novel moves beyond the printed page into criticism, adaptation and interpretation, as was explained in the previous chapters, so extra layers are added to the classic fiction process model on top of those that authors such as Austen and Gaskell built into their novels as they adapted the contemporary world in which they lived into the imagined world of their novel. However, as is expanded upon in the conclusion, the contention is that consciousness of the process by which the various artefacts within the process are produced, as per the model, may enable the novel to be used effectively as an immersive three-dimensional framework or background to conventionally derived historical sources. As an aid to developing such a consciousness, the following chapter discusses various ways in which a novel, specifically J.B. Priestley's *The Good Companions*, can be deconstructed to maximise its utility as an adjunct to historical discussion.

---

509   Paul Ricoeur, K Blamey (trans.), and D Pellauer (trans.), *Time and Narrative* (Chicago: University of Chicago Press, 1988), p. 118. Quoted in Simon Gunn and Lucy Faire, 'Introduction: Why Bother with Method?', in *Research Methods for History*, ed. by Simon Gunn and Lucy Faire (Edinburgh: Edinburgh University Press, 2012), p. 4.

6

J.B. Priestley's
The Good Companions –
Discerning History

6.1 Introduction

So far, we have discussed how fiction whose subject matter at the time was contemporary or near-contemporary may contain elements that can be of some use in the study of the history of that time. It has also discussed the ways in which the actions of perception, reception, adaptation, and interpretation can add layers that distance the world we believe we see when we receive the fiction in the form of the original book, an adaptation, or a tourist interpretation, from the elements of the past the original author perceived when he or she was writing the fiction. To be able to use fiction as an effective historical resource may require means whereby one can remove those layers that these actions have imposed over the author's perceived past.

This chapter discusses practical ways in which novels can be analysed or otherwise used to help them in this regard, either for the general reader, or more particularly for educational purposes. It looks at methods that could be used individually or collectively to deconstruct the novel and the world contained therein to draw out historical elements from the fictional text and thereby amplify any historical insights that might be gained simply from a straight reading of that text. It also examines how those historical insights, as with most of the insights discussed in previous chapters, should be viewed in the context of the personal influences that the authors and other agents bring to bear on their source material. Each method relates directly to particular elements of the process model, the writing of a novel and its critical reception, its adaptation for film and television, and its use within literary tourism. However, the list of methods as presented is not intended to be exhaustive but simply indicative of the type of techniques that could prove useful. Note also that the order in which the methods are presented moves from the original novel outwards, but although the first two might naturally be undertaken in tandem, as a whole they could be done in any order. The methods described are as follows:

- **Mind mapping**: Using mental maps as a method of brainstorming the main subject areas of the world described in the novel, following an initial reading,

- **Textual interpretation**: using footnoting to deconstruct the text and point up the specific historical parallels with elements of the text,
- **Adaptation analysis**: comparing the novel with its various adaptations to ascertain how much of the world of the novel makes its way into the adaptation and the degree to which the world we see in the adaptation enhances or alters the world of the novel,
- **Site visits**: visiting landscapes and locations that parallel those described in the novel to gain an understanding of the elements of the past that sit behind the novel *in situ* and to place that world in a continuum of historical change.

The book that is used predominantly is J.B. Priestley's *The Good Companions*.[510] The reasons for choosing this work are threefold. Firstly, Priestley was a self-aware author who understood the nature of the novels and plays he was producing, writing about the process extensively in his memoirs and in various interviews.[511] Secondly, the world he uses as his inspiration is recent enough for many traces of it to remain in the landscape, particularly in his hometown of Bradford, thus facilitating a dialogue between that world and the imagined world of his fiction. Finally, the novel has been adapted many times and participants in some of those adaptations have provided us with written and verbal insights into the process of recreating the world of the novel in their adaptations (Section 6.5). *The Good Companions* is however being used here as an exemplar. Other Priestley novels such as *Angel Pavement* could have been used, and the methods suggested could be also used on other novelists, for example to gain historical insights on London in the novels of Dickens, on Dorset in the novels of Hardy, or Manchester in the novels of Gaskell.

6.2 J.B. Priestley and *The Good Companions*

Priestley was born in the Yorkshire city of Bradford in 1894. After leaving school, he worked as a shipping house clerk for Helm and Co. of Bradford, supplementing his income with short pieces of local interest written for a local newspaper. He lived in Bradford until 1914 when he left to fight in the First World War, and following the war, where he saw active service on the Western Front and was twice seriously injured before being invalided out, he went to Cambridge on an officer's scholarship. After graduation and marriage, he moved to London to become a full-time writer of novels, plays, screenplays, essays, and literary criticism. He died in 1984, and whilst he never returned to Bradford to live, he often visited, and frequently returned to it as source material for his novels and plays.[512]

The first direct example of his use of Yorkshire in fiction was in the 'Bruddersford' sections of his third novel *The Good Companions*, written immediately prior to the Wall Street crash of 1929 and the depression that was catalogued in Priestley's later non-fiction work, *English Journey*, for which this work, with its detailed descriptions of the landscapes and customs of Middle England, acts as a kind of benign fictional precursor. The novel describes the changing fortunes of a travelling concert party travelling through

---

510   J.B. Priestley, *The Good Companions* (London: William Heinemann, 1929).

511   For example, Priestley wrote extensively about the act of writing in his memoir *Margin Released*, and particularly about the writing of *The Good Companions*. (Priestley (1962) pp. 181-86.). Use is made below of this and other instances of Priestley talking about his art, such as the interview he had with Alan Plater that was included in a documentary on the making of the 1980 adaptation of the novel. *On the Road with J.B. Priestley and The Good Companions*, dir. by Mervyn Cumming (Yorkshire Television, 1980).

512   Biographical detail from Judith Cook, *Priestley* (London: Bloomsbury, 1997).

the small towns and seaside resorts of late 1920s England. Middle-class spinster Elizabeth Trant uses the inheritance from her late father to revive the fortunes of the concert party, helped by odd-job man Jess Oakroyd, fleeing his family and job in the Yorkshire town of Bruddersford, and pianist, songwriter and schoolmaster, Inigo Jollifant. The concert party, newly renamed 'The Good Companions', achieve a modicum of success before Inigo and the two juvenile leads, Susie Dean and Jerry Jerningham, are tempted away to London's West End. Elizabeth Trant marries a former flame, Jess Oakroyd emigrates to Canada to be with his beloved daughter, and all ends happily. The style is picaresque, broad, and populist and the descriptive density of the book is evident from the very beginning. Priestley described the minutiae of life in great detail – the people, their modes of speech and ways of dressing, the shops, pubs, and hotels of small-town England, seaside piers and fairs, travelling shows, and the general landscape of a country on the brink of recession. A biographical background to Priestley in the 2007 edition extols the realistic power of the novel, praising its 'immense power of place with exact social realism and observation' in its descriptions of an England that 'Priestley knew better than any author of his day, and an England that still exists in forgotten corners of the country'.[513] In the same edition Priestley's son Tom saw the novel as 'a merry journey through the late '20s, through a world of concert parties, grim towns, bedraggled theatres, station waiting rooms, seaside piers, cafés and bars'.[514]

Contemporary reviews saw the novel as an essentially optimistic work. The *Fortnightly Review* praised 'the imaginative sweep and eloquence of the descriptive passages',[515] and L.P. Hartley saw in it an all-embracing view of society:

> ...it treats of every kind of life, and every quality of person, the rich and the poor, the happy and the wretched. Being an itinerant semi-picaresque novel, it moves about a great deal and gives representative pictures of England, both town and country-side. It is in fact a survey of contemporary life – its "note" being inclusiveness, it rejects nothing.[516]

Hartley's idea of it being a novel about 'England' in the broadest sense was echoed by other reviewers, such as Ralph Straus in the *Sunday Times* who called it 'a picaresque novel of present-day England'.[517] Praise in this regard came from both sides of the contemporary political divide, with the right-wing journal *The Spectator* noting that it 'sprawls like a map of England',[518] and the radical feminist and socialist Vera Brittain in *Time and Tide* commending 'this colossal *tour de force* to all who have travelled through unknown England'.[519]

---

513 Hanson and Joy (2007) p. 25.

514 Tom Priestley, 'Foreword', in *The Good Companions (2007 edition)*, ed. by Lee Hanson and David Joy (Ilkley: Great Northern Books, 2007), p. 13.

515 Gerald Bullett, 'Good Company', *Fortnightly Review*, 1929.

516 L.P. Hartley, 'New Fiction', *The Saturday Review*, 148 (1929), pp. 136-7.

517 Ralph Straus, '*The Good Companions* Review', *Sunday Times*, July 28th, 1929. Reprinted in Alan Plater, David Fanshawe, Leonard J Lewis, and J.B. Priestley, *The Good Companions – A Scrapbook*, (London: Trident Television Ltd., 1980).

518 Anon, '*The Good Companions* Review', *The Spectator*, August 3rd, 1929. Reprinted in Plater, Fanshawe, Lewis, and Priestley (1980) p. 6.

519 Vera Brittain, '*The Good Companions* Review', *Time and Tide*, August 9th, 1929. Reprinted in Plater, Fanshawe, Lewis, and Priestley (1980) p. 6.

Just as we saw with some of the reviews of novels by Elizabeth Gaskell and Thomas Hardy discussed in Sections 4.3 and 4.2, there was a sense in many of the reviews that the reviewers perceived a degree of 'truthfulness' in the descriptions within the novel, which came not just from the metropolitan reviewers quoted above, but also from Priestley's native Yorkshire, as in this review from the *Yorkshire Post*:

> Whether it be the attitude of occupants of semi-detached houses to tenants of back-to-back dwellings, or the conversation that fills the walk home from a football match, or the interior life of theatrical lodgings, or whether it be descriptions of English scenery or of the illogicality of trade unionism as seen by an old-fashioned trade unionist, Mr Priestley achieves astonishing verisimilitude.[520]

The book proved popular – Priestley would claim at the end of the year that the book 'has been breaking all Heinemann's records for daily sales'.[521] By Christmas of 1928 its publishers were shipping 5,000 copies a day and were still selling 1,000 copies a week a year after publication.[522] A West End stage adaptation was put together in 1931, followed in 1933 by the first filmed adaptation. In a case of life imitating art, some concert parties also began advertising themselves as 'The Good Companions'.[523] A theme in reviews of both adaptations, like the novel, was their Englishness, the *Daily Telegraph* commending the play for managing to 'preserve most of the gusto, the hearty English flavour, the atmosphere which gave the book its immense popularity',[524] and a cinema periodical calling the film 'a panorama of England; of the show business on tour, and the open roads leading from Yorkshire and Lancashire to the Midlands'.[525]

However, as John Baxendale says, 'the book's optimism was a one-off, a holiday from the gloom caused by war and family tragedy', A suggestion that Priestley's perception of the world had been filtered to remove elements that would conflict with the essential optimism of the novel.[526] Priestley alluded to this in 1980, viewing the writing of the novel as a release from a period of personal hardship, during which he had an affair with the woman who became his second wife, fathering a daughter with her whilst at the same time caring for his first wife who was dying of cancer. As he saw it, rather than take a holiday as relief, he 'kept on working, to earn the money I badly needed, but did it as best I could in a holiday mood'.[527] Indeed, Priestley's next novel, *Angel Pavement*, set in a post-slump London, offered a much bleaker view of the world with its story of a small family firm in the City being duped by a confidence trickster.[528] The same level of detail is there in

520   Collin Brooks, 'Book of the Day. Mr. J.B. Priestley strikes a Dickensian vein', *Yorkshire Post*, July 29th, 1929 (p. 6).
521   Letter from J.B. Priestley to Edward Davison on 28th December 1929, quoted in Cook (1997) p. 98.
522   Hanson and Joy (2007) pp. 23-25.
523   The listings in *The Stage* show resident companies called 'The Good Companions' playing in Ventnor, Boscombe and Newquay during the course of August 1933. 'On Tour', *The Stage*, August 10th, 1933 (p. 1).
524   Anon, '*The Good Companions* Play Review', *Daily Telegraph*, May 15th, 1931. Reprinted in Plater, Fanshawe, Lewis, and Priestley (1980) p. 8.
525   Anon, '*The Good Companions* Film Review', *Illustrated Topics of the Screen*, September 25th, 1933. Reprinted in Plater, Fanshawe, Lewis, and Priestley (1980) p. 10.
526   Baxendale (2007) p. 23.
527   J.B. Priestley in Plater, Fanshawe, Lewis, and Priestley (1980) p. 7.
528   J.B. Priestley, *Angel Pavement* (London: William Heinemann, 1930).

the descriptions of London streets and London society, particularly middle and working-class society, but also in the descriptions of the economic realities of the time. Though the writing style often approaches the humour of *The Good Companions,* the overall tone is considerably more pessimistic.

Whatever their tone, both *The Good Companions* and *Angel Pavement* place their characters and plot within carefully constructed contemporary frames. The remainder of this chapter details the methods chosen to analyse *The Good Companions* and the insights they may give us into both the historical world behind the novel and the ways that world may have been filtered by the author and, where relevant, by adapters and interpreters.

6.3 Mind Mapping the World of *The Good Companions*

6.3.1 Mind Maps as a technique

Mind mapping is a technique used extensively in business and education to brainstorm ideas. It involves placing the theme or topic being analysed at the centre of a chart and linking it using words and images with progressively more detailed sub-topics, thus effecting a top-down deconstruction of the topic.

The benefits of mind maps as an aid to understanding a topic are many. Seeing the topic in the form of one big picture enables links and associations to be made and spotted where they were not initially apparent. In terms of its use within education Martin Davies details how mind mapping can be used to 'help impart critical and analytical skills to students, [and] to enable students to see relationships between concepts'.[529] The BBC Active website discusses how mind mapping could be useful in terms of visualising concepts and the connections between them and improving the way in which students 'understand and absorb information'.[530] Nancy Margulies sees the benefits of the technique to facilitate this understanding and absorption, through its ability to 'see the parts and the whole and notice the relationship between them'.[531]

Therefore, given mind mapping has been used to understand both the totality and the interlinking detail of a diverse range of subject areas, one could use the technique to pull apart the internal structures and connections of a novel as they relate to the world described within the novel. By so doing one could see the whole world of the novel with all its constituent parts and relationships and have a means of cementing this world in our minds. In terms of the classic fiction process model, mind mapping might provide an indication of how both perception and reception work, perception in terms of assessing the elements of their contemporary world the author has put into the novel, and which elements have been omitted, and reception in terms of how we, as readers, read a novel and its author-perceived elements and form an image of the historical world that is the backdrop to the novel.

---

529   Martin Davies, 'Concept mapping, mind mapping and argument mapping: what are the differences and do they matter?', *Higher Education,* 62 (2011), pp. 279-301.

530   *Using Mind Mapping Tools to Promote Independent Learning and Study Skills,* (London: Educational Publishers LLP trading as BBC Active, n/a) <http://www.bbcactive.com/BBCActiveIdeasandResources/UsingMindMappingTools.aspx>.

531   Nancy Margulies, *Mindmapping and Learning,* (Baltimore: Johns Hopkins University School of Education, 2004) <http://education.jhu.edu/PD/newhorizons/strategies/topics/Graphic%20Tools%20for%20Learning/margulies_2.htm>.

The technique was used to gauge, following a reading of *The Good Companions*, this writer's personal view of the main themes, ideas, and representations within the novel. There are many mind mapping tools available, but this analysis was carried out using the on-line Coggle tool because of the simplicity and clarity of the breakdown it allows one to create. It allows one to deconstruct the basic 'item', in this case the novel, and link it by 'branches' to 'child' items, which in the context of a novel could be items such as places, events, institutions or concepts. As the tool is web-based, each diagram can be shared with other users of the tool who can themselves add comments and suggest changes, making Coggle useful both as an individual and a collaborative mind mapping tool. The remainder of this section discusses the use of mind mapping to deconstruct *The Good Companions* and outlines the historical insights that can be gained from carrying out such a deconstruction.

6.3.2 Mind Mapping – Analysis and Summary

Figure 6.1 shows the mind map of *The Good Companions* that was produced. Note that as well as recording what was discerned of the world of the novel, observations were also made of what was *not* seen, based on knowledge and understanding of the period and personal expectations of what ought to be seen, in the hope that this might provide an understanding of the factors affecting how Priestley turned the historical world into the fictional world of the novel. The Coggle mind map analysis was carried out directly after a reading of *The Good Companions*. Whilst it was intended that the mind map should be based predominantly on that reading of the book, there may be elements within it formed by previous readings of the book. Note also, however, that because this analysis was carried out before the footnoting exercise described in Section 6.4 and the analysis of the various adaptations of the novel described in Section 6.5, it was not influenced by any additional insights gained from carrying out those tasks.

What emerged predominantly from the analysis were the descriptive elements. Firstly, there are the descriptions of the physical landscape and of settlements large and small, both real, such as Sheffield and London, and imagined, such as the small towns and coastal resorts in which the company performs. There were the descriptions of elements of the entertainment industry – concert parties, cinemas, and musical revues – that were the subject matter of the novel. However, other aspects of the leisure industry were also described, such as pubs, cafés, hotels and boarding houses, and spectator sports such as football, horse racing and rugby. Finally, there were descriptions of the various modes of goods and passenger transport – motor cars, railways, lorries, charabancs, and of many of the industries that made up the economy of the time, from the mills and car factories to cottage industries like dressmaking and joinery.

Amongst the subject areas noted as being conspicuous by their relative absence were the following. Firstly, the still recent First World War is barely mentioned, and secondly, despite the novel being written shortly after the General Strike and being published only a few months before the beginning of the Great Depression, there is no mention of local or national politics or of the general state of the nation, other than a brief diatribe by Jess Oakroyd about his trade union as he tears up his National Insurance card prior to leaving home. These elements would all have been present in the contemporary world that Priestley was perceiving in 1929 as he wrote the novel, and as a committed Socialist he had views on the contemporary social and political climate (and frequently expressed them in print). However, despite the seemingly all-embracing world view of the novel, as

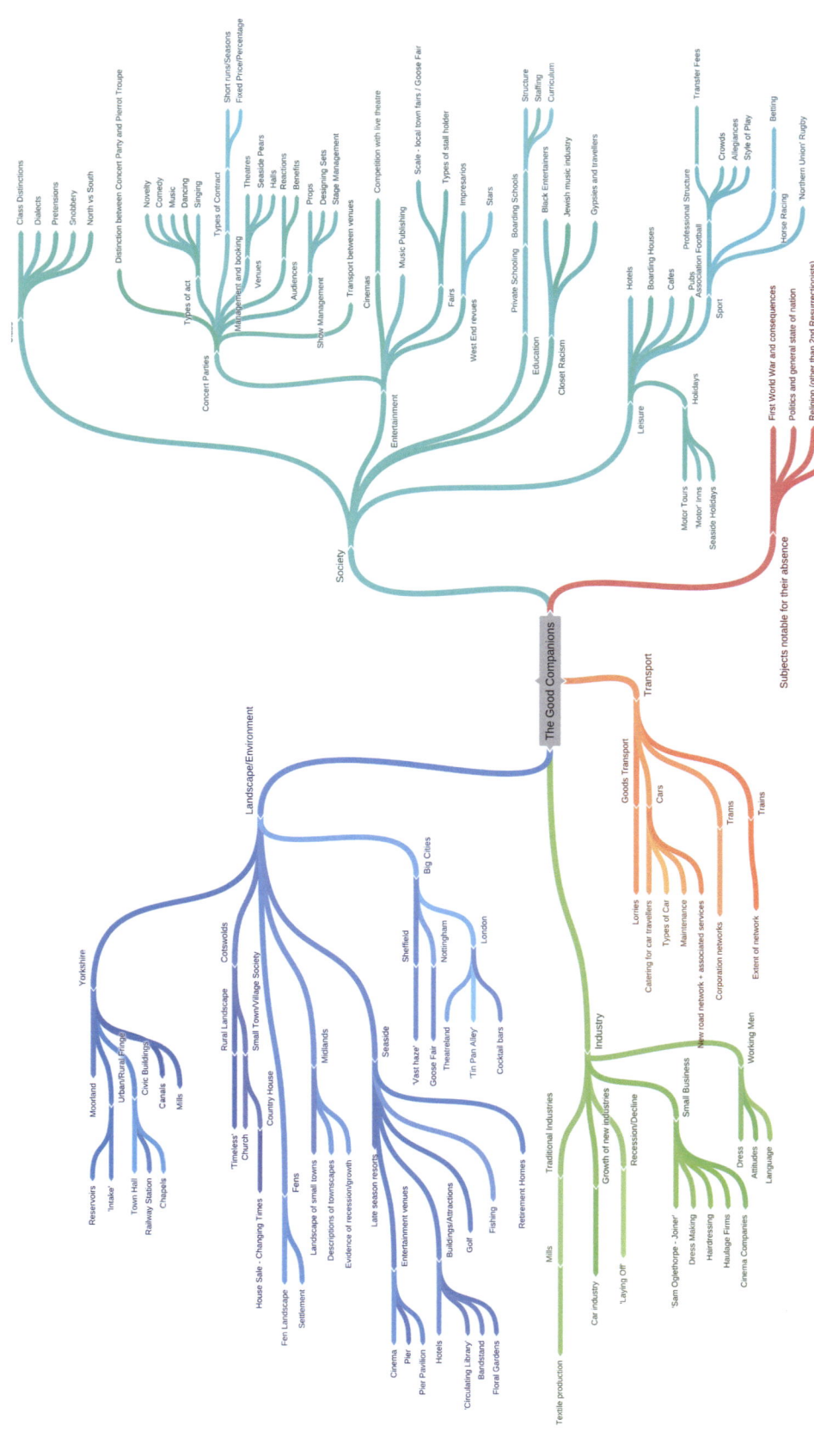

Figure 6.1: Mind Map of *The Good Companions*.

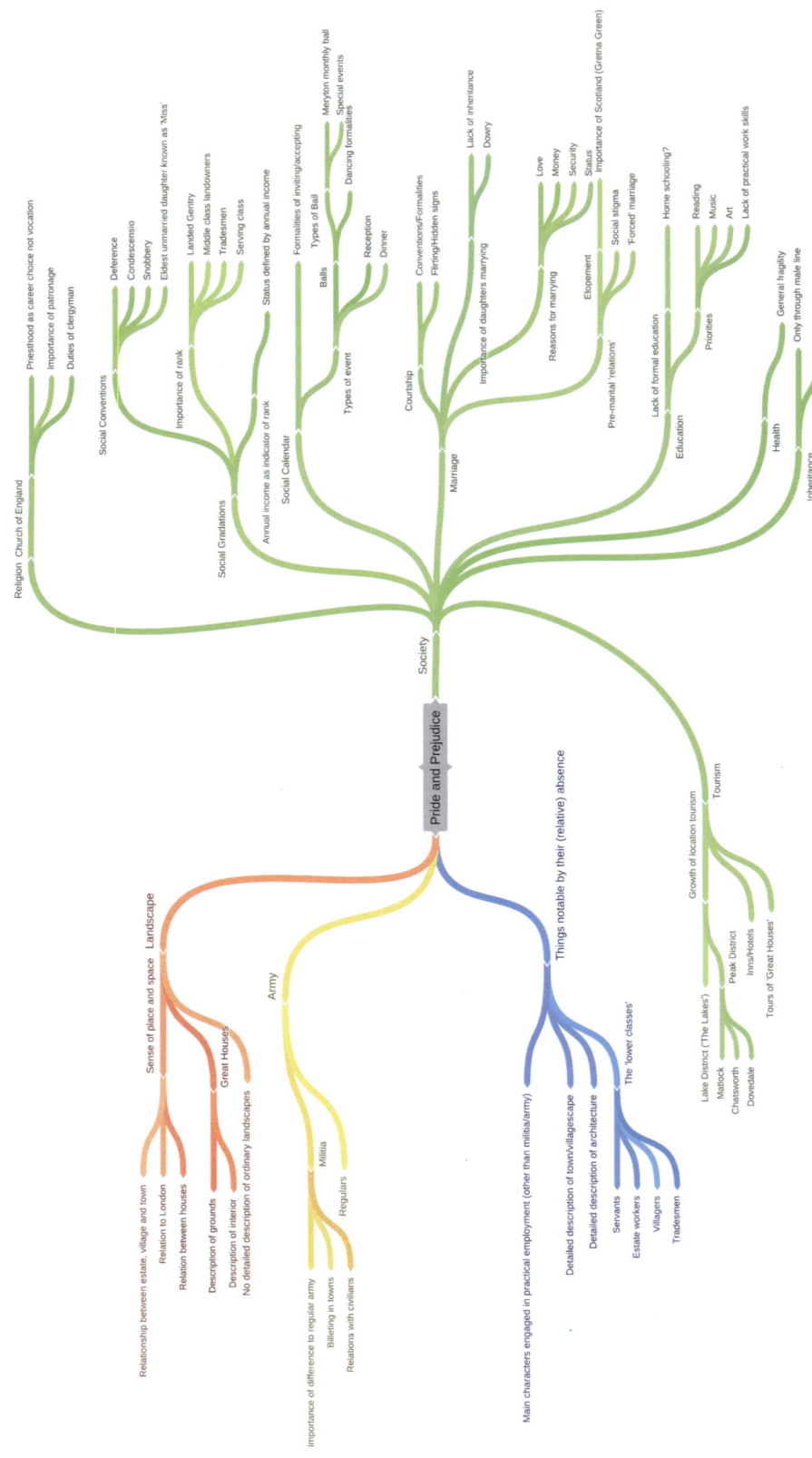

Figure 6.2: Mind Map of *Pride and Prejudice*.

he interpreted and adapted that perceived world while writing the novel, the elements did not form part of the world he wanted to portray within the novel, reflecting perhaps Baxendale's comment about the novel being a 'holiday from gloom'.[532]

Whilst bearing this in mind, one sees that what was important to Priestley in this novel was to root the narrative in a clearly described physical world. Mind mapping enables one to compare such an approach with the less physically descriptive approach of, say, Jane Austen as discussed in Section 5.2. A comparison with a mind map produced at the same time for Austen's *Pride and Prejudice* (Figure 6.2) shows that where Priestley's map is weighted towards the physical descriptions of the environment and the human structures and institutions that exist within that environment, the mind map of Austen's *Pride and Prejudice* is weighted much more strongly towards social rituals around love and money, and the interactions between people within that society, and includes very little actual description of the actual environments within which those rituals and interactions were transacted.

It should be noted that these mind maps are based on individual receptions of the novels and describe what this writer personally saw as being present within the imagined worlds that were perceived from the two novels, and that other readers may have different responses dependent on their differing reception of the novels. The writer's background in Geography may have predisposed a more favourable reaction to those descriptive elements within the text of *The Good Companions* that enabled the building up of a geography of the world that Priestley describes. This would be very like the way that Harold Darby used the descriptive elements in Thomas Hardy's novels to create a putative geography of Wessex (Section 1.2). To other readers coming to the novel from different perspectives, other elements may strike them as important in terms of the makeup of the world of the novel. Therefore, whilst one person's mind map might differ in many respects from another's, affected as they are by differing personal knowledge, experience, and outlook, combining mind maps from many individuals, or carrying out the exercise in a group, would produce an increasingly objective model of the novel. The items around which there was consensus would thereby help to measure how effectively the author's world as described within the novel has been transmitted and received. It may be, however, that even with a larger sample of mind maps, that there are elements that, as we receive the novel, we either do not see because we do not have the contemporary awareness to interpret successfully what we read, or that we see in a different way because layers of hermeneutic change have altered the way we assess what we read.

6.4 Textual Interpretation of the Yorkshire of *The Good Companions*

6.4.1 Interpretive Footnotes as a technique
Section 6.3 assessed how using a mind map to carry out a top-down deconstruction of a reader's reception of a novel such as *The Good Companions* can provide an overall picture of the important social, political, and geographical aspects of the world the author is describing within the novel and by extension the actual historical world which the author perceived when writing the novel. This section investigates how it could be possible to complement the top-down deconstruction with a bottom-up deconstruction that interprets individual sections of the actual text of a novel to produce an analysis of the novel that

---

532   Baxendale (2007) p. 23.

draws out historical references and parallels within the text from the descriptive fictional elements within it.

The descriptive energy within *The Good Companions* that might drive such an analysis is evident from the first chapter, which introduces us to Yorkshire labourer Jess Oakroyd. Priestley uses a filmic technique to zoom in from a broad overview of the North Country of England down to a detailed view of the streets of Oakroyd's hometown of Bruddersford. Though this is a world still within the living memory of some, there is much that Priestley describes that is now lost in the past, such that the passage may provide a valuable historical resource if one could provide a detailed real-world context for the descriptive elements within the novel.

What follows therefore is an attempt to analyse the novel in such a bottom-up fashion and present the information obtained in the form of interpretive footnotes, in a way often employed within modern editions of classic novels to provide commentary for those not familiar with the historical resonances of a novel. An extreme example of this technique, albeit using footnotes that are themselves fictional, can be found in Susanna Clarke's fantasy novel *Jonathan Strange and Mr Norrell*.[533] The novel was written in an approximation of an early 19th century Austenian style about an England during the Napoleonic Wars where magic is a practical reality. The pages are filled with footnotes purportedly written some years after the novel itself was supposedly written in order to provide detailed further information for the reader of that time. The effect is to heighten the sense of a historical reality underlying the novel, even as it delves into the realms of pure fantasy. Using such a technique in a *realist* novel such as *The Good Companions* could allow the reader to go beyond the fictional storytelling of the author to the specific historical elements that underpin the storytelling that would assist readers with their reception of the novel.

6.4.2 Textual interpretation – Analysis and Summary

The passage within *The Good Companions* chosen for the application of this technique was the opening of the first chapter of the book, our introduction to Jess Oakroyd's Bruddersford. Figure 6.3 shows the first page of the footnoting exercise. What follows is a summary both of what the exercise added to a general understanding of the historical world of the novel, and also of what are the benefits and pitfalls of carrying out such an exercise.

There were a few general considerations that arose from carrying out this analysis. Firstly, though he names Bradford as a separate town in the text, and the name could be seen as an amalgam of Bradford and Huddersfield, there is evidence that the description of Bruddersford is largely based on Bradford. Some of the evidence for this is circumstantial, in that Priestley was born and brought up in Bradford, his first work experience was in the Bradford textile industry and his first literary output was created for Bradford newspapers, so one might reasonably assume that he would use Bradford as a model for an industrial Yorkshire town. However, the descriptive elements themselves, though individually they could be taken as generic Yorkshire elements, when taken together point to Bradford as the likely model. For example: the particular textile industry specialities described as being present in Bruddersford were also present in Bradford; many of the major buildings described in this opening chapter have visual equivalents in Bradford, particularly a tune-playing clock on the Town Hall; the geographic setting on the edge of

---

533   Susanna Clarke, *Jonathan Strange & Mr Norrell* (London: Bloomsbury, 2004).

CHAPTER ONE

Mr Oakroyd Leaves Home

There, far below, is the knobbly backbone of England, the Pennine Range. At first, the whole dark length of it, from the Peak to Cross Fell, is visible.[1] Then the Derbyshire hills and the Cumberland fells disappear, for you are descending, somewhere about the middle of the range, where the high moorland thrusts itself between the woollen mills of Yorkshire and the cotton mills of Lancashire.[2] Great winds blow over miles and miles of ling and bog and black rock, and the curlews still go crying in the empty air as they did before the Romans came. There is a glitter of water here and there, from the moorland tarns that are now called reservoirs.[3] In summer you could wander here all day, listening to the larks, and never meet a soul. In winter you could lose your way in an hour or two and die of exposure perhaps, not a dozen miles from where the Bradford trams end or the Burnley trams begin.[4] Here are Bodkin Top and High Greave and Black Moor and Four Gates End, and though these are lonely places, almost unchanged since the Domesday Book was compiled,[5] you cannot understand industrial Yorkshire and Lancashire, the wool trade and the cotton trade and many other things beside, such as the popularity of Handel's Messiah[6] or the Northern Union Rugby game,[7] without having seen such places. They hide many secrets. Where the moor thins out are patches of ground called 'Intake', which means that they are land wrested from the grasp of the moor.[8] Over to the right is a long smudge of smoke, beneath which the towns of the West Riding[9] lie buried, and fleeces, tops, noils, yarns, and stuffs, come and go, in and out of the mills, down to the railways and canals and lorries. All this too, you may say, is a kind of intake.

---

[1] The Pennines is the name given to the range of hills separating the east and west sides of Northern England, running from the Peak District in the south to where the range meets the Cheviot Hills close to the Scottish border.

[2] Traditionally there was a contrast between the manufacture of cotton goods in Lancashire and of woollen goods in Yorkshire. Cotton spinning benefits from a more humid environment, as the thread is more workable in such conditions, and so production was concentrated on the wetter western slopes of the Pennines in Lancashire.

[3] Reservoirs were constructed in the Pennine hills from the mid 19th century onwards to provide a clean water supply for the burgeoning populations on both sides of the range.

[4] The tramcar was an electrically-powered mode of mass transport running on rails. The Bradford tram system ran from 1898 to 1950 and the Burnley system from 1901 to 1935. Both, as with nearly all tram systems of the time, were replaced by motor buses, though trams did make a comeback in the north of England in the late 20th century in places such as Manchester and Sheffield.

[5] A survey of land and property commissioned by William the Conqueror following the Norman invasion of England in 1066, completed in 1086.

[6] Messiah, an oratorio composed in 1741 by Georg Friedrich Handel, was a staple work in the repertoire of the choral societies of the north of England at this time. Particularly famous were the annual Christmas performances of the work by the Huddersfield Choral Society and the Hallé Orchestra and Choir of Manchester.

[7] Priestley is referring here to the professional version of the game of Rugby as played in the north of England. This version split away from the amateur version, now known as Rugby Union, in the late 19th century. Priestley appears to be being deliberately archaic here as the breakaway code, though indeed known as the Northern Rugby Football Union until 1922, had by the time of the writing of this book been renamed as the Rugby Football League. In the late 20th century Rugby Union also embraced professionalism, but the split between the two codes remained.

[8] The concept of intake land as described here by Priestley dates from medieval times and is common throughout the hill country of the north of England.

[9] The term 'riding' dates from Norse times and applied to the subdivision of land it means a 'third part'. Historically Yorkshire was divided into ridings, the North, East and West Ridings. Soon after the publication of The Good Companions, Winifred Holtby published the novel South Riding, set in the area of Yorkshire alongside the Humber estuary. As an administrative area, the West Riding County Council existed from 1889 to 1974, when it was largely replaced by the new administrative areas of South Yorkshire and West Yorkshire.

Figure 6.3: Textual Interpretation of Chapter One of *The Good Companions*.

the moors that mirrors that of Bradford; and the Leeds-Liverpool Canal that passes the northern outskirts of Bruddersford, just as it does Bradford.

What is clear from this opening chapter is the degree to which Priestley cares about description and about creating a detailed backdrop to his stories; the realism of the settings seems important to him in establishing both character and plot. Similar exercises could be carried out on other descriptive passages within the novel, particularly in the descriptions of fictional East Midlands towns such as Rawsley, Tewborough and Gatford, of the various theatres, music halls and cinemas visited during the novel, and of music publishing district of London. However, what is also evident is that in the context of a novel supposedly set around the end of the 1920s, the description of Bruddersford has an anachronistic element to it. As was found in the mind mapping exercise for the novel as a whole, there is no mention in the chapter of the First World War in its description of the town. A large war memorial was erected in the centre of Bradford in 1922 to commemorate the 37,000 men of Bradford who served in the First World War, of whom 5,000 were killed.[534] Such memorials were important civic elements in post-war Yorkshire towns, as elsewhere in Britain. In leaving out any mention of such a commemoration of the conflict that so deeply affected him, there is a sense that in his description of Bruddersford is to an extent a pre-conflict one, that what we see here is a post-war town viewed through a pre-war lens. Two minor elements in the text provide circumstantial evidence for this, his use of the term 'Northern Union' when describing the organisation running the game of Rugby League, which is very much a pre-war term, and his description of Bruddersford having a successful Division One football team, as Bradford had in the immediate pre-war years, but did not have in the late 1920s. Outside of the text itself, it should also be remembered that when writing about Yorkshire in his novels and plays, such as *Bright Day*, *An Inspector Calls*, and *When We Were Married*, he continually returned to the Yorkshire of the years preceding the First World War, the last years in which he was a permanent resident of Bradford. Rycroft and Jenness talk about Priestley's 'connection to Bradford and its landscape... affirming him as a Bradford and Yorkshire writer' but also talk about his belief in an 'ideal Edwardian industrial city [that] no longer existed'.[535]

Just as Charlotte Brontë wrote in *Shirley* about a version of the industrial landscape of the time of the Luddites known to her from her family history, so in *The Good Companions* Priestley appears to write, at least in part, about a version of the urban landscape that he knew before the First World War, but, unlike Brontë, without the acknowledgement that it is in the past. Even Priestley's descriptions of concert parties within the novel might have been informed to a degree by his experiences in Edwardian Bradford, judging by the following comments in a 1978 interview. Asked how he became so familiar with the 'life of theatricals', he replied:

> A lot was guesswork... though I did mix among them a little. I had an uncle who was a pro and I sometimes went to concert parties as a boy. Before the First World War they were all the rage, and there were at least three Resident Companies in Bradford.[536]

If we therefore accept the suggestion that Bruddersford is in large part Bradford, the kind of interpretive analysis carried out above can be seen as an aid to deconstructing the historical city that at this time sat behind this section of the novel, providing extra detail that allows to go beyond the surface gloss of the vivid cinematic images that Priestley provides us with. Even if Priestley were to tell us that Bruddersford is *not* Bradford, one may gain some insights into the generic features that characterised the Pennine Yorkshire towns of that time, whilst questioning whether that time is the 1910s or 1920s.

---

534 *Bradford War Memorial, including steps, screen wall and terminal blocks*, (London: Historic England) <https://historicengland.org.uk/listing/the-list/list-entry/1434527>.

535 Simon Rycroft and Roger Jenness, 'J.B. Priestley: Bradford and a provincial narrative of England, 1913-1933', *Social & Cultural Geography*, 13 (2012), pp. 957-76.

536 Keith Macdonald, 'The Gentle Wizard', *Manchester Evening News*, July 16th, 1979 (p. 7).

However, Priestley is not writing a guidebook in this opening chapter of *The Good Companions*, nor is he engaging in a piece of travel writing, even if the passage has resemblances to both genres. The places he is writing about, though influenced by actual places, and particularly by Bradford, are ultimately imaginary, both in space and time. Footnoting can help us see the individual elements of the contemporary world that provided the skeleton around which the author fleshed out this imagined world. This is not to suggest that a novel should be entirely deconstructed and interpreted in such a way and published as such. In Clarke's *Jonathan Strange and Mr Norrell*, the footnotes are part of the conceit of the novel and as such are integral to its enjoyment; were a novel such as *The Good Companions* to be deconstructed in its totality it might lose the very narrative thread that makes it entertaining.

What is therefore suggested is that a technique such as this could be used on selected passages within a novel or in conjunction with a normal reading of a novel *as* a novel without the footnotes. This would provide historical context for the novel if one were looking at the novel from the standpoint of the study of English Literature or would enhance the novel's use as a historical resource if one were looking at the novel from the standpoint of the study of History.

Finally, to compare the technique with mind mapping, where that technique starts with a broad view of the world and works its way down to the individual items that make up that world, the approach described here starts at the level of those individual items and attempts to build up a broader picture from them. It requires the person carrying out the analysis to be able to identify those items and to be able to research the historical models that lie behind them. If the purpose of the educational exercise is to use the *production* of these analyses to gain a view of the historical world of the novel, then an approach would be to complement the two methods, using the top-down mind map analysis to decompose the novel down into its individual elements, which can then be researched in detail and linked back to specific elements within the text of the novel in the form of footnotes. If such an approach is either not practical or not desired, then previously produced analyses could be presented to readers of the novels to assist with their understanding, though this would mean that the readers would then be viewing the historical world not via their own received understanding but via the understanding of those producing the analyses.

6.5 Analysing Adaptations of the World of *The Good Companions*

6.5.1 The Good Companions on Film

Thus far, this chapter has looked at how a novel such as *The Good Companions* can be deconstructed to extract information about the historical world upon which elements of the novel were based, and how the deconstruction can be used to help verify if the view of the world within the novel is a complete one. In the case of this novel, there is considerable descriptive detail, enabling us to paint a picture of the world Priestley is describing which via further analysis can be linked to elements of the historical world. We can also identify which elements of the historical world, such as the First World War, Priestley chose not to include in his fictional world, and thereby see where provision needs to be made for such omissions in using the novel as a historical resource.

As shown in Section 6.2, *The Good Companions* was a popular success in its day. However, it has lost much of that popular appeal over the years, such that it is now only available in print via a single hardback version.[537] However, the three filmed adaptations of the novel are all still commercially available. All the adaptations are framed as musicals, using music not just within the concert performances of the troupe, but also to turn many of the other scenes into musical numbers. Characters bursting into song in the middle of their everyday lives is by its nature unrealistic, but none of the adaptations is sung through in the manner of grand opera or of a musical such as *Les Misérables*, and in all three adaptations the musical numbers come between spoken scenes that follow, to varying extents, passages within the novel. As was discussed in Section 3.1, such adaptations can be how many of us consume our fiction. There was mention of Davis' view that, as long as we properly understand the elements of historical authenticity within an adaptation, they can be a good way to learn about the past.[538] How realistic those historical elements are in an adaption depends not just on the decisions taken by the novelist, but also on those taken by the various filmmakers. Section 3.3 examined how the way the spoken language and visual spread of a novel are adapted can affect how we view the authenticity of the adaptation. Another way in which adaptations can alter one's view of their authenticity is if the adapters take an intertextual approach and translate the story to another time, as is the case with one of the adaptations analysed below.

This section takes a comparative look at the three filmed adaptations of the novel that have been made, in 1933[539] and 1957[540] and 1980.[541] Both the 1933 and 1980 adaptations have a setting contemporaneous with the novel. The 1957 adaptation, though it retains the story structure of the novel, is set at the time the film was made, such that the troupe become a touring variety show of the 1950s rather than a concert party of the 1920s.

6.5.2 Comparing Adaptations – Faithfulness to the Novel

A primary indicator of the authenticity of an adaption, at least in the eyes of many of those who have read the novel, is how faithfully the adaption renders the characters, plots and scenes within the novel. To this end Priestley's novel was analysed and broken down into individual scenes, as if it were being deconstructed for a putative screenplay. For each scene in the novel a brief plot exposition was written along with a list of which characters, from the list shown in Table 6.1, were involved in the scene. The three filmed adaptations were then examined scene by scene, and the degree to which each of the adaptations followed the original novel's scenario assessed. If a scene from the novel was present within the adaptation with little alteration from the original novel the scene was marked green in the table. If the scene was present but had been significantly changed in terms of setting, plot or characterisation, it was marked amber. If the scene was omitted, or had been so altered that it bore little resemblance to the original scene, it was marked red. Where relevant a commentary was provided of how the score was arrived at for a scene.

To enable a more detailed analysis, the colour ratings were converted into numerical values, 0 for red, 1 for amber, and 2 for green. It should be stated at this point that this value scale, limited as it is to three values, provides a broad-brush view of the faithfulness of an adaptation, and that to obtain a more nuanced view it might be advantageous to use a wider scale with, say, a choice of 5 or 10 values. That said, adding up the scores created an

---

537 Priestley (1929 (2007 edition)).

538 Zemon Davis (2006).

539 *The Good Companions*, dir. by Victor Saville (Gaumont British Picture Corporation, 1933).

540 *The Good Companions*, dir. by J. Lee Thompson (Associated British Picture Corporation, 1957).

541 *The Good Companions*, dir. by Bill Hays and Leonard Lewis (Yorkshire Television, 1980).

	JO	Jess Oakroyd	Yorkshire Labourer. Becomes Good Companions' handyman, leaving wife and son at home in Bruddersford.
	ET	Elizabeth Trant	Cotswold spinster. Inherits father's estate and buys into Good Companions. Holds a candle for old flame Dr McFarlane.
	IJ	Inigo Jollifant	East Anglian schoolteacher. Becomes Good Companions' pianist and songwriter. Madly in love with SD.
	MM	Morton Mitcham	Itinterant banjo player and storyteller. Joins Good Companions. Given to hyperbole.
	JN	Jimmy Nunn	Comedian and leader of Good Companions. Estranged from wife.
Main Dramatis Personae	**SD**	Susie Dean	Comedienne, singer and dancer. Ambitious for stardom. May or may not be in love with IJ.
	EL	Elsie Longstaff	Singer and dancer with Good Companions. Not as young as she was.
	JJ	Jerry Jerningham	Singer and dancer. Good Companions' juvenile lead. Even more ambitious than SD.
	JB	Joe Brundit	Baritone singer and drummer with Good Companions. Goes by name of Courtney Brundit.
	MJB	Mrs Joe (Brundit)	Soprano singer with Good Companions. Goes by name of Stella Cavendish. Wife to JB. Mother to young son.
	LP	Lady Partlit	Wealthy widow. Admirer of Good Companions and especially JJ. Has connections with West End theatres.
	HM	Dr Hugh McFarlane	Edinburgh doctor, long posted overseas. Old flame of ET.

Table 6.1: List of main characters in The Good Companions.

overall 'adherence score', calculated as the percentage of the total possible mark that each adaptation could score, that attempted to measure the faithfulness of the adaptation to the novel, both in terms of general story elements and specific plot elements. The following section examines if the comparison, in conjunction with the two adherence scores that derive from it, can be used to inform the adaptation's usefulness as a historical resource.

In terms of calculating the adherence score for the detailed plot elements of *The Good Companions*, 73 different scenes were identified within the novel of which, as an example, the first 19 are shown in Table 6.2.[542] Table 6.3 gives a view of how each adaptation scored using the criteria outlined in the previous section, with the 1980 TV adaptation scoring considerably more than either of the film adaptations.

Analysing these results, the relative length of the adaptations appears to be important. Both film adaptations were less than two hours long, and scored less than 35%, but in contrast the TV adaptation lasted over seven hours and scored nearly 87%.[543] If more time is available, one would assume there is more chance that the adapters will adapt a greater proportion of the book and will go into more detail in the portions that they take from the book. A similar conclusion could be drawn from analysis of the two film adaptations of Hardy's *Far from the Madding Crowd* discussed in Section 3.3. The 1967 version is more than an hour longer than the 2015 version, and many of Hardy's scenes that were included in the earlier film are either omitted from the 2015 film or included only as DVD extras.[544]

---

542 This sample covers the following pages: Priestley (1929 (2007 edition)) pp. 39-165.

543 Though longer, the 1957 film had a lower score than the 1933 film, but as is seen below, this was largely due to the adaptation being transposed in time from the original novel.

544 For example, see the deleted scenes within *Far from the Madding Crowd*, dir. by Thomas Vinterberg (20th Century Fox Home Entertainment, 2015).

	The Good Companions	Element of Book	1933 Film
Book One	**Chapter One – Mr Oakroyd Leaves Home**	Panorama of Northern England. JO leaving football match.	Amber
		JO is late for tea. Leonard (JO's son) and Albert appear and discuss Albert moving into spare room.	Green
		JO visits Sam Oglethorpe in his pigeon loft. They discuss travel. Sam's nephew Ted turns up. He will be leaving soon from Merriweather's with lorry going down south.	Green
		On way home JO meets racegoer George Jobley who gives him money. There is misunderstanding when JO refuses money and policeman appears. JO leaves, but still with money.	Red
		Next day JO is laid off after argument about union responsibilities. Mrs Oakroyd says Albert will move in. In disgust JO packs his tools, rips up insurance card and leaves.	Green
	Chapter Two – Miss Trant takes a holiday	House sale at Old Hall, Hitherton on the Wold in the Cotswolds, following death of ET's father.	Green
		ET meets vicar Mr Chillingford and his wife for tea. They announce their daughter Dorothy's engagement. Dorothy is ET's best friend. Mr Chillingford suggests motoring tour of the English Cathedral towns. ET remembers past friendship with Scottish doctor Hugh McFarlane.	Red
		ET's nephew Hilary comes to stay. ET tells him her uncle has waived a bequest of £600 which now comes to her. Hilary tries to interest ET in financing the magazine of The Statics, the new philosophical group he has joined in Oxford. Instead ET offers to buy his car.	Amber
		The following Monday morning ET leaves home in the car	Green
	Chapter Three – Inigo Jollifant Quotes Shakespeare and Departs in the Night	IJ is talking to colleague Felton in his room at Waterbury Manor School. They discuss the school food, especially the prunes. Miss Callender, school matron, arrives asking about washing lists. They all go down to the schoolroom and IJ plays the piano for their entertainment. Mrs Tarvin, headmaster's wife, enters room and orders them to stop.	Amber
		IJ invites colleagues to his birthday party the next day. That evening IJ is eating dinner with all the staff – he rejects the prunes. IJ takes Daisy Callender out for nighttime walk. They kiss, but Daisy falls when surprised by noise and twists her ankle.	Red
		The following evening, his birthday, IJ engages in late night drinking and piano playing with Mr Fauntley and Mr Felton as Mr and Mrs Tarvin are dining out. They return early and surprise him. The Tarvins dismiss IJ who decides to leave that night, quoting Shakespeare at Mrs Tarvin ('secret black and midnight hag').	Green
		IJ meets Daisy Callender before leaving and kisses her. He leaves, heading west.	Red
	Chapter Four – Mr Oakroyd on t'Road	JO catches lorry thinking Ted is driver and it heads down Great North Road. Lorry stops and JO discovered by two men – neither is Ted. They start attaching false numberplates but agree to take JO with them.	Green
		They are taken in and fed at Big Annie's – the Kirkworth Inn. Overnight, JO sleeps on sofa. In the morning, the men are gone.	Green
		JO continues on his way by foot. He has breakfast at Pobbleby's Dining Rooms in Everwell. Mr Poppleby talks about being 'uman. When the bill comes JO finds he has been robbed and has no money to pay – Pobbleby's tone changes.	Red
		JO meets Joby Jackson and his motor van – he sells things at fairs, at the moment rubber animals. Joby tells him his assistant has gone off after a woman and Jo agrees to stand in for him.	Red
		They reach Ribsden and Joby sets up his pitch by 'The Professor'. Joby leaves JO in charge for a moment. JO is confronted by Summers who is looking for Joby's assistant, obviously about the woman. Joby's assistant appears, and a fight ensues with Summers, who is arrested by a policeman.	Red
		No longer required, JO sets off again on foot. JO sees a woman with a broken-down car. She will prove to be ET.	Green

Table 6.2: Comparison of specific plot elements in *The Good Companions*.

Notes	1957 Film	Notes	1980 TV	Notes
There is a general collage of industrial northern scenes but no mention of football match.	Red		Green	
	Red		Green	
	Red		Green	Ted is spoken of rather than actually being in the scene.
While later preparing to leave home, JO takes a £5 note out of a draw thus giving the later motive for robbery.	Red		Green	
	Green	There are elements of earlier scenes, such as JO being late for his tea which has been left on the stove.	Green	
Done quickly and silently, but includes ET gazing wistfully at picture of Hugh McFarlane, hence covering that plot point.	Red		Green	
	Red		Amber	No mention of Dorothy's engagement, which is one of the reasons in the book for ET going – a fear of becoming an Old Maid. No mention of Dr McFarlane at this point.
This is combined with the previous scene and ET is with Mr and Mrs Chillingford and Hilary. She buys Hilary's car and decides to go off 'out into the blue'.	Amber	The only element remaining is ET buying the car off her nephew, her renamed David.	Amber	There is no mention of the £600, another element in a) ET deciding to go and b) eventually taking over the GCs.
ET leaves in what one assumes is her own car.	Red		Green	
IJ is just shown toying with prunes at school dinner.	Red		Amber	Rather than having the discussion on food in his room, the prunes debate happens during a school dinner and is given musical treatment.
	Red		Amber	The only element left is the rejection of the prunes.
	Green	Party includes woman we presume to be Miss Callender.	Green	Because it wasn't set up in a previous scene, there is no mention of this being IJ's birthday party, but otherwise everything is present
	Red		Green	
	Red		Green	
The note that JO finds instead of his money at Pobbleby's is here simply placed on him by one of the men while he is sleeping.	Red		Green	
	Red		Green	
	Red		Green	
	Red		Amber	The Summers element is missing, and any mention of policemen. Joby's assistant simply turns up and JO goes on his way.
	Green	After leaving home, the first time we see JO is on foot approaching ET's car.	Green	

Adaptation	Red	Amber	Green	Score	Length
1933 Film	39	22	18	36.71%	1hr 33 mins
1957 Film	46	18	13	28.57%	1hr 41 mins
1980 TV	4	11	64	87.97%	7hrs 30mins

Table 6.3: Analysis of adherence to detailed plot elements in *The Good Companions*.

Susie Dean	I feel a bit of a pig about this – but, oh Mrs Joe, I don't – I really, honestly don't – want to spend the whole summer in C.P. work at Bournemouth –
Mrs. Joe	Just what I said to Joe about you. "Susie doesn't want to," I told him. I saw it at once. He didn't of course, but then he never notices anything, never. Now why don't you? Tell me'.
SD	Everybody's beginning to tell me I'm restless, and it's true. I am. The weather, I suppose – bit of nerves – swelled head, if you like. I've had too many good audiences this year, all of a sudden – not good for the little girl. Now she doesn't know when she's well off.
Mrs. J	Now don't be foolish, Susie. Nobody is saying anything about you.
SD	I wouldn't care if they were. It isn't that. I suppose I'm always thinking something absolutely marvellous is going to turn up, and then when you all come along and say "Hooray! Six months in Bournemouth! Susie will continue to sing Number Twenty-seven on the programme! Twice daily! Outside in the afternoon, but if wet in the shelter! Bring the children!" then I see the same old stick-in-the-mud business going on and on, and I think – oh, hell!
Mrs. J	Not hell!
SD	Yes – *Hell!* I just see myself stuck there. With those three numbers of Inigo's, I could go anywhere, anywhere. They're too good for concert-party audiences.
Mrs. J	Not too good, but in a different style perhaps.
SD	I'm sorry. I didn't mean too good really, but not what they want. Anyhow – Oh I am a fool. I'd forgotten what I slipped in to tell you. About Coral Crawford. Now this is what gets my goat, and you can't blame me. I brought the paper and put it down somewhere. Here we are. Now, you remember Coral Crawford, don't you? She was with the *Larks and Owls* Company with you, and left just after I joined, didn't she?
Mrs. J	I should think I do remember her. Coral Crawford. One of the most outrageous Borrowers I ever shared a dressing-room with.
SD	Well, then, what did you think of her, honestly?
Mrs. J	As a turn, hopeless. As a companion, a fellow-performer, a lady, no better, being deceitful, untrustworthy, given to lying, to say nothing of borrowing everything that could possibly be borrowed and some things that a self-respecting girl would never dream of wanting from anybody else, and never returning anything without being asked times without number. What about her?
SD	You remember she said she was fed up with C.P. work and left us to try and get into the chorus? She got in. I've never heard of her since – until this morning. Now read this. Starring, *starring*, mind you – in a new show at the Pall Mall! Doesn't it make you want to scream? Coral Crawford! Read it. Playing with Tommy Mawson and Leslie Wate and Virginia Washington! Great success! Should run for ever! I'm not jealous, honestly I'm not – it's nice seeing people you know getting there – but that girl – a star at the Pall Mall already! Help! When I read that this morning in bed I could feel myself going hot and cold and pink and yellow all at once. I wanted to gnaw the sheets and blankets. I really did.
Mrs. J	Well, well! Of course the girl may have improved a lot since we knew her. I've known it happen in the most surprising way.
SD	Och – tripe! Not possible. Improved! She'd nothing to improve. There wasn't anything there. Anyhow, there she is – Coral Crawford – Crawly – at the Pall Mall, and here I am, taking the tram out to Mundley every night to sing Number Thirty-three on the programme! Isn't it enough to make you sick? And then you talk to me about six months in Bournemouth, jogging on through the same old show! I know – I know – I oughtn't to grumble – I'm not grumbling. Miss Trant's an angel – you're all angels – and I suppose I ought to shut up. But there you are. And *now* do you understand?
Mrs. J	You think this isn't good enough for you?
SD	I don't mean exactly that. I don't really.
Mrs. J	Yes, you do. And you're right. You are too good, Susie. I used to think I was.
SD	And so, you are. Miles and miles.
Mrs. J	Do you think so, really? Well of course when I'm in voice, there's no doubt I am. It's the delicacy of my voice that kept me out of the big work. And after all good training and long experience, Taste and Interpretation – they must count for something, mustn't they?
SD	Course they must, you absurd thing!
Mrs. J	What you want, what you're pining for, Susie, is a big Chance. That's why you're restless. I know, my dear. Well keep on quietly, doing your best, and it'll come, that's what I say. I don't say *how* or *where* it'll come because I don't know, but come it will. I feel it. And you're still very young, aren't you?
SD	I suppose so, though at times I feel a thousand, I can tell you. And telling yourself how young you are doesn't seem to make much difference if you're not satisfied. Every time I hear about anybody in the profession suddenly doing so marvellously, like Crawly, I always try and find out their ages. So does Jerry, I discovered the other day. He's pretty poisonous, of course, but he does understand about things like that. Jerry'll get there soon, if it kills him.

Figure 6.4: Excerpt from Book 3, Chapter 1 of *The Good Companions* – 'A Wind in the Triangle'. The text in bold type was adapted by Plater.

Susie Dean	I feel an awful pig but, oh Mrs. Joe I don't *want* to spend the whole summer in concert party work at Bournemouth. Twice daily! Bring the children! Susie Dean will sing number 27 on the programme and I think "Oh, hell!"
Mrs. Joe	Not hell!
SD	Yes, hell! Do you remember Coral Crawford?
Mrs. J	Coral Crawford - *Larks and Owls* Company.
SD	Well, what did you think of her? Honestly?
Mrs. J	Well, as a performer hopeless. As a companion, a lady, no better, being deceitful, untrustworthy, given to lying and borrowing.
SD	She is starring, *starring*, mind you, in a new show at the Pall Mall. Look, at that, look. Should run for ever! Playing with Tommy Mawson and Leslie Wate.
Mrs. J	Well she may have improved.
SD	There's nothing *to* improve! Oh, I know I shouldn't grumble, and Miss Trant's an angel, and you're all angels.
Mrs. J	Oh, but it isn't good enough for you, is it Susie?
SD	No, I didn't mean that exactly.
Mrs. J	No, you're quite right. You *are* too good. I used to think that I was.
SD	So you are! Miles and miles!
Mrs. J	Do you really think so? Oh, Joe says it's the delicacy of my voice keeps me out of the big work, but taste and interpretation – they must count for something, mustn't they?
SD	Oh, course they do, you absurd thing.
Mrs. J	And you're still very young.
SD	But it doesn't seem to make much difference. Every time I hear about someone in the profession doing really well I try to find out how old they are and if I can't find out then I guess. Well, Jerry Jerningham does the same. Oh, he's pretty poisonous I know, but he understands about things like that. He'll get there soon, if it kills him!

Figure 6.5: Excerpt from Episode 7 of 1980 adaptation of *The Good Companions* – 'A Wind in the Triangle'. The text in light type is all that is invented by Plater.

To emphasise the depth of Alan Plater's 1980 adaptation, it included all but four of the novel's scenes in some form, with nearly 80% of the scenes essentially intact. According to Plater, he was offered 13 50-minute episodes by Yorkshire TV to tell the story, but after detailed analysis of the structure of the novel he decided he only needed nine.[545] Even with just nine episodes, Plater left himself a considerable amount of time per scene for substantial extracts from Priestley's dialogue to be included. This is illustrated by Figure 6.4, which shows a section of Priestley's original dialogue for a scene set in a Gatford Tea Room between Susie Dean and Mrs Joe extracted from Book 3, Chapter 1 of the novel,[546] and Figure 6.5, which shows the equivalent section of dialogue in Episode 7 of Alan Plater's adaptation.[547] Pieces of dialogue that are identical or close to identical in both sections are highlighted. Whilst the original dialogue is edited in the adapted version, the main thrusts of the exchange between the two characters have been left intact, and all but one short phrase in Plater's version is taken almost directly from the original, with much of the dialogue being lifted almost *verbatim* from the novel.

The result is that because the essence of dialogue remained intact Susie's description of the mundane nature of seaside concert party work, and the comparisons with the world of West End revues, are to be found in the 1980 adaptation almost as clearly as in the original, giving the viewer historical insights that are largely missing in the much more abbreviated version of the scene in the other two adaptations.

---

545 Alan Plater, *Alan Plater on Priestley* (Bingley: Moorside Words and Music, 2005). CD recording of an address given to the J.B. Priestley Society on April 23rd, 2005.
546 The passage comes from Priestley (1929 (2007 edition)) pp. 434-36.
547 Alan Plater, *The Good Companions Script* (Yorkshire TV, 1980).

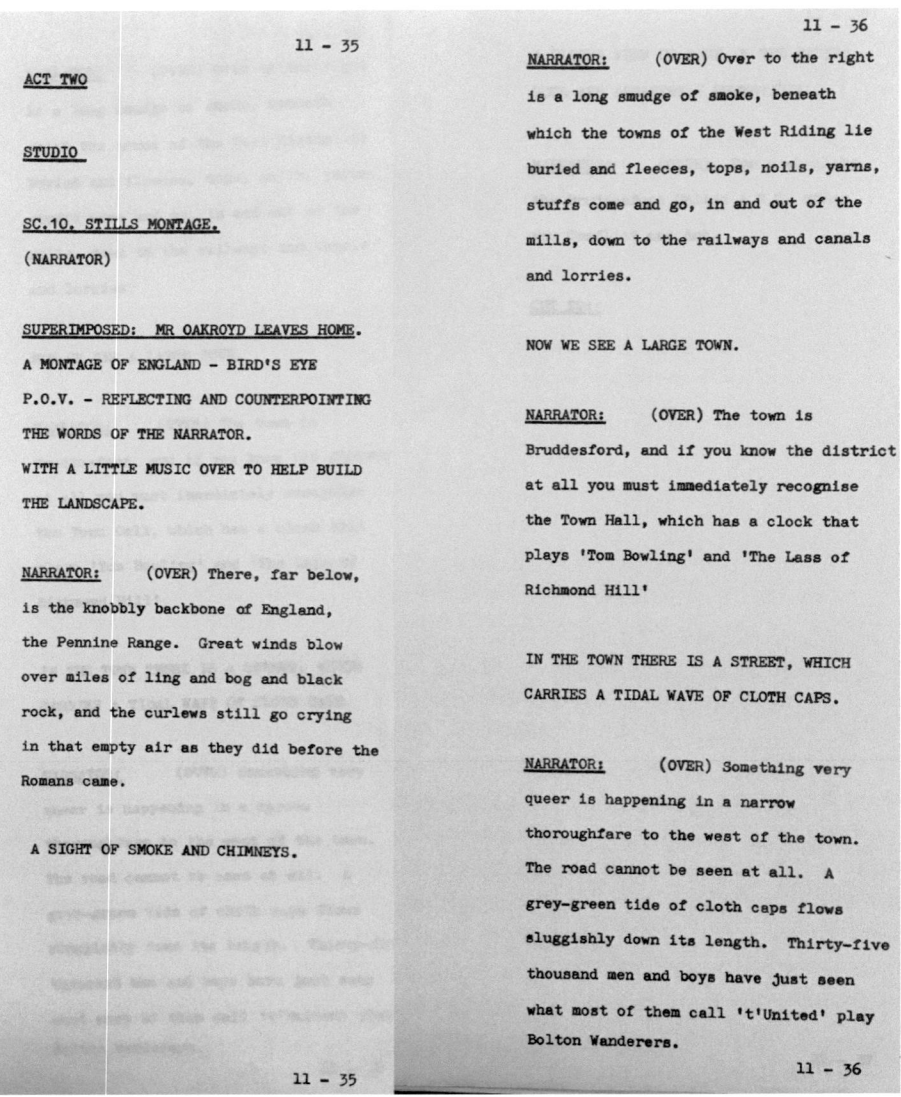

11 - 35

11 - 36

ACT TWO

STUDIO

SC.10. STILLS MONTAGE.
(NARRATOR)

SUPERIMPOSED: MR OAKROYD LEAVES HOME.
A MONTAGE OF ENGLAND - BIRD'S EYE
P.O.V. - REFLECTING AND COUNTERPOINTING
THE WORDS OF THE NARRATOR.
WITH A LITTLE MUSIC OVER TO HELP BUILD
THE LANDSCAPE.

NARRATOR: (OVER) There, far below,
is the knobbly backbone of England,
the Pennine Range. Great winds blow
over miles of ling and bog and black
rock, and the curlews still go crying
in that empty air as they did before the
Romans came.

A SIGHT OF SMOKE AND CHIMNEYS.

11 - 35

NARRATOR: (OVER) Over to the right
is a long smudge of smoke, beneath
which the towns of the West Riding lie
buried and fleeces, tops, noils, yarns,
stuffs come and go, in and out of the
mills, down to the railways and canals
and lorries.

NOW WE SEE A LARGE TOWN.

NARRATOR: (OVER) The town is
Bruddesford, and if you know the district
at all you must immediately recognise
the Town Hall, which has a clock that
plays 'Tom Bowling' and 'The Lass of
Richmond Hill'

IN THE TOWN THERE IS A STREET, WHICH
CARRIES A TIDAL WAVE OF CLOTH CAPS.

NARRATOR: (OVER) Something very
queer is happening in a narrow
thoroughfare to the west of the town.
The road cannot be seen at all. A
grey-green tide of cloth caps flows
sluggishly down its length. Thirty-five
thousand men and boys have just seen
what most of them call 't'United' play
Bolton Wanderers.

11 - 36

Figure 6.6: Excerpt from rehearsal script for 1980 adaptation of The Good Companions.

To take another example of Plater's attention to detail, Plater preserves some of the elements of Priestley's opening description of Bruddersford, using photographs of mountain and moor and archive photographs of a period Yorkshire townscape to reproduce the author's original zoom effect to complement, but not entirely replace, Priestley's original text. Compare the extract from the rehearsal script for Episode 1 of the adaptation, shown in Figure 6.6, with the original.[548] Most of the detail is of necessity missing, but the idea of a story rooted in a specific historical landscape at a specific historical time is preserved.

In a novel such as *The Good Companions*, where the historical insights are found within both the breadth and depth of the novel, this analysis suggests that in the hands of an

548   Hull, Hull History Centre/Alan Plater Archive, Rehearsal Script for "The Good Companions" Episode 1: "In Which We Meet The Company", U DPR/4/39.

Figure 6.7: The Good Companions' Opening Number (1933 film).

adapter such as Plater, who had both the time and, importantly, the inclination given his attitude towards adaptation to include the detail of the plot and the language of the novel, watching the resulting adaptation can provide an experience approaching that of reading the novel. However, as was shown in Chapter 3, decisions made by filmmakers regarding the look and feel of an adaptation can affect the way one views its authenticity. The following section looks how attention to period detail was treated in the three adaptations.

6.5.3 Comparing Adaptations – Faithfulness to the Period

Whilst faithfulness to the novel can be quantified by using a procedure such as the one followed above, determination of how faithful each adaptation is to the period setting of the novel involves a much more qualitative approach. It involves looking in detail at each of the adaptations with regard to the picture of Priestley's imagined world they showed on the screen, and how closely that aligned to historical world of the late 1920s, using histories of the real world within which the original novel was set, contemporary reviews of the adaptions, and the recorded opinions of those involved in the adaptations.

To begin with Victor Saville's 1933 film of *The Good Companions*, it was loosely adapted itself from the first stage production of the novel in 1931, and Priestley himself had one of the writing credits for both adaptations. The world they attempted to recreate, both in terms of concert parties and West End revues, was a contemporary one. For example, the film reflected the roots of the concert party in the pierrot tradition of performance. From its distant roots in Renaissance Italy this tradition evolved through time to become in 19th century Britain a distinct form of seaside entertainment, with, in John Walton's words,

PRESS PARS!

One of the most cheery, good-humoured and altogether entertaining musicals that have emerged from British studios over a long period . . . the cast is full to the seams with top talent . . . in fact, it is, as you gather, what I call first-rate screen entertainment.

WHAT'S ON IN LONDON

A bright British back-stage musical.

DAILY MIRROR

Saucy—that's the new Janette . . . starring in Britain's boldest reply to the Hollywood backstage musical.

DAILY MAIL

It is a human, likeable picture with attractive tunes and spectacular dancing . . .
LIVERPOOL DAILY POST

A warm-hearted and tuneful film.

THE PEOPLE

Janette . . . with her winsomeness wins all the way . . . a lavish musical spectacle.
NEWS OF THE WORLD

Gay, warmly human film. A British musical to be proud of.

*EMPIRE NEWS &
SUNDAY CHRONICLE*

New 'Companions' musical is great — And British.
THE NEW MUSICAL EXPRESS

Figure 6.8: Film reviews from Good Companions Pressbook.

'white-faced performers in clown costumes who provided songs, jokes and sketches on beaches and in parks as well as on the pier'.[549] Many concert parties acknowledged this heritage by including a number where they would dress in pierrot costumes, and the Good Companions company in both the novel and the 1933 film were no exception (Figure 6.7).[550]

In the novel Priestley describes the concert party's musical accompaniment being simply piano, banjo and drums, but in this particular scene we see Inigo playing the piano on stage, and Morton Mitcham holding his banjo, but also a conductor and orchestra in the pit. The norm for concert parties of this size, according to Bernard Ince, would have been relatively simple musical accompaniment, often from just a pianist.[551] To go the expense of hiring an orchestra would seem contrary to the shoestring nature of such ensembles, as Priestley and Ince describe them. However, given the *Reynold's Illustrated News* review talked proudly of the film being a 'British talkie production at its brightest and best', and the *Daily Herald* called it 'a landmark in British Studio production', this suggests the filmmakers felt they needed an expansion in staging and instrumentation beyond what was the norm to compete with other musicals from Britain and Hollywood.[552] This is echoed in the British Film Institute's summary of the film, which talks of the film's 'record 72 sets' and its 'hundred speaking parts', as well as the fact that it was honoured with a Royal Premiere screening.[553] The years since the novel's publication had seen the Crash of 1929 and the beginning of the Great Depression, and the publicity material for a recent DVD set of British musicals from this time explains how they were viewed by their audience as 'a source of much-needed escapism throughout the decade haunted by the Great Depression and the growing menace of war'.[554]

So, if the stage performances in the 1933 film only partly reflected authentic concert party conventions, they did give us some insight into the historical development of the British musical film in the 1930s as entertainment. As indeed does the 1957 adaptation of its era. In not even attempting to root the film in the era of its source material but relocating it to the 1950s, it gives us insights into influences specific to the 1950s, the variety circuit and the popularity of blockbuster musicals.

The selection of press reviews chosen by the film's publicists in Figure 6.8 seem to see it first and foremost as a musical, and crucially as a *British* musical, as the British film industry's response to the American musicals of the time, such as *The King and I* and *Oklahoma*.[555] Lush orchestrations were used throughout the musical numbers and many of the performances, especially those of Susie Dean, whilst starting out conventionally stage-bound, opened out beyond the stage into full-blown studio productions that owed

549 John K. Walton, *The British Seaside: Holidays and Resorts in the Twentieth Century* (Manchester: Manchester University Press, 2000), p. 94.

550 Bernard Ince, 'The Neglected Art: Trends and Transformations in British Concert Party Entertainment, 1850-1950', *New Theatre Quarterly*, 31 (2015), pp. 3-16.

551 Ibid. p. 7.

552 Both reviews are quoted in a contemporary publicity advertisement: '"The Good Companions" Starring Jessie Matthews, Edmund Gwenn, Mary Glynne, A.W. Baskcomb & John Gielgud', *The Era*, March 1st, 1933.

553 Janet Moat, *BFI screenonline: The Good Companions (1933)*, (London: British Film Institute, 2003-14) <http://www.screenonline.org.uk/film/id/439635/>.

554 *British Musicals of the 1930s: Volume 1*, (Network, 2016) <http://networkonair.com/shop/1798-british-musicals-of-the-1930s-volume-1-5027626396442.html>.

555 The Good Companions – Singing... Laughing... Dancing... They'll mean Good Business for you! (Press Book for Good Companions 1957 film), (London: Associated British-Pathé Ltd, 1957). Included as an extra on DVD of 1957 film of The Good Companions.

Figure 6.9: Finale of 1957 adaptation of The Good Companions.

more to the fantasy ballet sequences in films such as *The Red Shoes* or *An American in Paris* than to what might have been seen on an actual 1950s variety stage (Figure 6.9).

The Hollywood comparisons are clear, though as Chris Chibnall says, in trying to 'spruce up J.B. Priestley's tired old nag and turn it into a joy ride for teenagers', and creating a story of youthful talent, in the form of Susie Dean and Inigo Jollifant against the world, comparisons were more likely to be made not with Hollywood musicals but with contemporary rock-and-roll films such as *Blackboard Jungle* and *Rock Around the Clock*. In those respects, Chibnall says, the film's 'values, like its style, remain more rocking-chair than rock and roll'.[556] John Fraser, who played Inigo Jollifant, gave his view on how the film was pitched, believing it was a mistake to try to copy American musicals 'since the whole charm of the book is the utterly English, provincial charm of it'.[557]

For the 1980 adaptation, the setting was moved back to the 1920s. The adaptation was by Alan Plater, who had a long pedigree writing original dramas and comedies, and adaptations of works such as Trollope's *Barchester Chronicles*. Plater had a deep respect for Priestley, particularly his 'humanity, and the generosity of spirit that informs [his] work'.[558] He also believed in adaptation as an act of 'homage' wherein 'you take a great book and pay homage to it by doing it in such a way that you the adapter remain invisible', the implication being that *The Good Companions* falls into the 'great book' category, and that he saw it his duty to render the adaptation as faithfully as possible.[559] In creating just such an adaptation, Plater agreed the production should be a 'full-blooded musical', with music by the composer David Fanshawe. Tapping into a contemporary *zeitgeist* he

556   Steve Chibnall, *J. Lee Thompson* (Manchester ; New York: Manchester University Press, 2000), p. 129. Quoted in David Rolinson, 'The Good Companions (1980-81)', <http://www.britishtelevisiondrama.org.uk/?p=2934>.

557   John Fraser, quoted in Lee Hanson and David Joy, 'The Good Companions on Stage and Screen', in *The Good Companions (2007 edition)*, ed. by Lee Hanson and David Joy (Ilkley: Great Northern Books, 2007).

558   Plater (2005).

559   Ibid.

Figure 6.10: Manuscript of Main Titles music for 1980 adaptation of The Good Companions.

talked of television musicals being 'very much in the vogue', quoting the example of the television rock musical, *Rock Follies,* made four years earlier. A recent television drama by Denis Potter, *Pennies from Heaven,* which interwove a story about a 1930s sheet music salesman with fantasy sequences where the actors lip-synced to recordings of the period, may also have been in his mind. As Plater said: 'musical television was all the rage, and we said "OK, let's do it as a series with music"'.[560] The result was an adaptation which whilst it paid what Plater hoped was a faithful homage to the concert party tradition of the 1920s and early filmed musicals, also had contemporary influences, in this case from television.

Whilst the music for the production was largely a 1920s pastiche, it had anachronistic traits that Plater himself acknowledged, with his lyrics owing much to his love of jazz and of the complex rhyming schemes of lyricists such as Lorenz Hart and Ira Gershwin. There is also one number where Plater admits Fanshawe seems to be channelling late 1930s Benjamin Britten. Plater believed that in the process of creating the music he and Fanshawe 'got intoxicated with our own cleverness', moving away from the simple concert party fare that Priestley described in the novel.[561] That said, the music for the main titles (Figure 6.10) demonstrates how in its simplest form, in the songs they wrote for the company to sing in their actual performances, Fanshawe's music and Plater's lyrics echoed the authentic style of concert party music. We see the syncopated accompaniment when the voices first enter, and dynamic markings ('with charm and gay abandon',

---

560   Ibid.
561   Ibid.

Figure 6.11: The Good Companions' Opening Number (1980 TV series).

'comic bravado') that suggest the style in which the song should be sung.[562] Note that this sequence, when filmed (Figure 6.11), echoed the 1933 adaptation in acknowledging the pierrot roots of concert party performance. Plater's own comments summing up the series emphasized his commitment to authenticity:

> My hope is that by remaining true to the spirit of the book, while having a few adventures with the narrative style – knowing that Mr. Priestley would want us to live a little dangerously – we have ended up with a show that sings the right song in roughly the right key.[563]

6.5.4 Comparing Adaptations – Summary

All three of the adaptations of *The Good Companions* attempted to an extent, to follow the basic structure of the original novel. The 1980 adaptation followed the detailed scene structure much more closely, though Alan Plater as adapter had considerably more time at his disposal so to do. He often followed Priestley's dialogue very closely, as shown in the Tea Room scene reproduced in Figure 6.5. If one assumes that the dialogue in the novel is faithful to the period, and it can only be an assumption even if the contemporary critics, as described in Section 6.2, attested to the novel's verisimilitude, then the degree of faithfulness to the novel's dialogue in the adaptation is linked to the degree to which that dialogue is faithful to the period.

In terms of the success or otherwise of the adaptations in providing us with a glimpse of the past world that lay behind the original novel, the filmmakers for the 1933 adaptation, created only four years after the publication of its source material, had perceived the same world as Priestley when writing the novel, helping to create a world for the film that mirrored the real world of small theatres and touring concert parties. However, there

---

562 Hull, Hull History Centre, Main Titles music for 1980 adaptation of The Good Companions, U DPR/4/39.
563 Plater, Fanshawe, Lewis, and Priestley (1980) p. 4.

appear to have been other influences on the look of the film that were not taken directly from life or from the novel. Most important of these influences was the competition from other musical films from both Britain and Hollywood, films that had become increasingly popular since the advent of talking pictures a few years previously. Thus, certain choices were made in the way the musical numbers were staged that moved the feel of the adaptation away from that of an absolute recreation of a concert party from the late 1920s towards that of an early 1930s musical.

The makers of the 1957 adaptation lacked a direct connection to what for the 1933 adaptation had been the perceived contemporary England. In this adaptation the main connection with Priestley's original novel was through its storyline, rather than the setting, which was re-imagined in the context of the variety circuit of the 1950s, which although an inheritor of the earlier concert-party tradition, had its own look and feel that needed to be incorporated into the film. As with the 1933 film, there were the influences of the musical films of the time, both home-grown and those from Hollywood. The effect was therefore to add extra layers that further distanced the past behind the original novel, with new external influences to add to those that affected the previous adaptations.

As with the 1957 adaptation, the makers of the 1980 adaptation had largely lost the direct link with the world of 1920s England that was present for both the 1931 play and the 1933 film. However, the adaptation now had the novel, its various stage adaptations, and the film adaptations of both 1933 and 1957 as potential source material. Alan Plater spent a year reading the novel and researching the period.[564] He was also very aware of the novel's adaptation heritage. In the 'Making Of' documentary that accompanied the 1980 series he referenced the previous adaptations, and as well as showing excerpts from the new adaptation also included brief clips of the two previous film adaptations.[565] This awareness of previous adaptations is illustrated by one scene within the documentary, which showed how the adaptations treated scenes such as the one where Inigo Jollifant storms off into the night from the preparatory school in the Fens where he has been a teacher, pointing out how faithfully all three filmed adaptations follow both Priestley's setting and his dialogue.[566] The documentary also paid due attention to the original source by including the last television interview that J.B. Priestley ever gave. However, the attempt to strip the production back to a more authentic setting was occasionally compromised by contemporary influences such as those admitted to in the writings of Plater and Fanshawe, such as the 1970s fashion for musical television dramas, Plater's jazz leanings, and Fanshawe's predilection for the music of Britten.

If we look at this in terms of the classic fiction process model, we need to be aware when assessing the use of any of these adaptations as historical resources of the effect of all of the various adaptations layering on top of the original novel. To take just the 1980 adaptation, as Figure 6.12 shows, the adaptation had the novel, the play of 1931, and the film adaptations of both 1933 and 1957 as potential source material, and Plater was certainly conscious of them. This illustrates the way in which sources and reference

---

564   Ibid.
565   Cumming (1980).
566   Ibid.

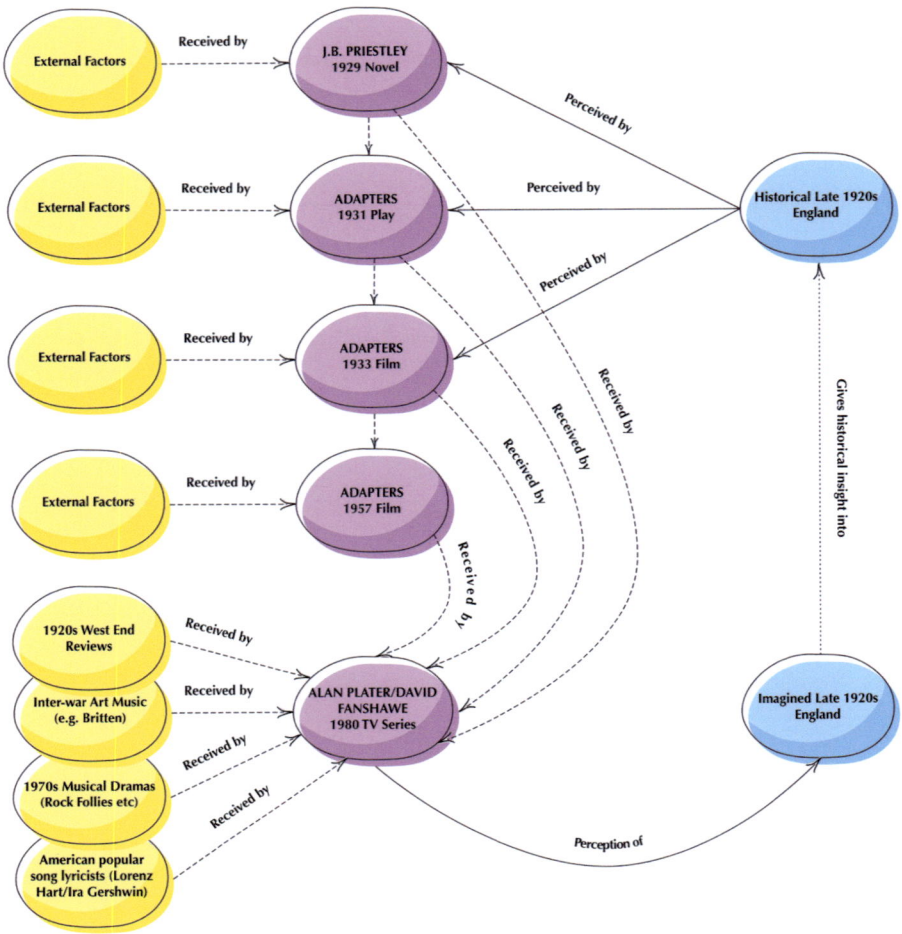

Figure 6.12: Classic Fiction Process Model for 1980 adaptation of *The Good Companions*.

points can grow in number the more often a novel is adapted. It also shows the way in which the cultural climates prevalent at the times of adaptations, or the distinct cultural standpoints of the adaptors, can dictate different influences and considerations. Finally, it shows how this makes the route back to the original perceived present of the novel more problematic, particularly when, as in the case of the 1957 film, an adaptation is recast in a different temporal context. All of this needs to be taken into account when considering the use of the adaptations as historical resources. The 1980 adaptation could, for example, be used in an academic context along with the deconstructions of the novel described above, but as with the novel, account need to be taken of the decisions taken as to how the adaptation is presented in its period setting in terms of any changes, omissions, or compromises that may have occurred.

Figure 6.13: Statue of J.B. Priestley outside the National Media Museum, Bradford.

6.6 Visiting Priestley's World

6.6.1 Priestley and Bradford

None of the approaches described thus far directly relate the historical past underpinning the novel to a present-day landscape or investigate the extent to which we can use the novel to recreate elements of a past landscape that has been lost, in the way that Hardy's pilgrims used his novels as a literary guidebook to Dorset. This section uses Bradford to provide an example of how one could investigate these relationships between a present-day world and a novel in Priestley's fiction.

Section 6.4 examined the ways in which Priestley used elements of Bradford to inform his description of the fictional town of Bruddersford in *The Good Companions*. Priestley wrote another Bruddersford novel, namely *Bright Day*.[567] It concerns a Hollywood scriptwriter, Gregory Dawson, in the aftermath of the Second World War, remembering his years before the First World War living and working in Bruddersford. Bruddersford is used in *The Good Companions* as one location of many. In *Bright Day*, Dawson's time in Bruddersford plays an integral part of the story and drives the dénouement of the tale in post-Second World War London. The area that was home to both Dawson, in *Bright Day*, and Jess Oakroyd, in *The Good Companions*, can be linked specifically to the Bradford suburb of Manningham, where Priestley was born and grew up, and the area running north from Manningham to Shipley. We will therefore look at descriptions of Bruddersford in both novels whilst visiting Bradford locations that can be linked with those descriptions. We will examine the extent to which the area has changed since Priestley's time and, if it has

---

567   J.B. Priestley, *Bright Day* (London: William Heinemann, 1946).

changed significantly, whether it is possible to use the fictional descriptions to produce an on-the-ground recreation of the landscape that informed Priestley's fictional descriptions.

Priestley's books, as shown in Section 6.5.1, no longer have the mass-market appeal that they once had. On visiting Bradford, it becomes apparent that his loss of appeal is mirrored in the degree to which the city celebrates Priestley. The most visible symbol of his presence as a Bradfordian is the statue of Priestley, erected in 1986 by Bradford City Council, that sits outside the entrance to the National Media Museum (Figure 6.13). Into the base of the statue is inscribed a passage from *Bright Day* where Priestley contrasts the ugliness of Bruddersford, 'lost in its smoky valley among the Pennine hills, bristling with tall mill chimneys, with its face of blackened stone', with the adjoining moors, where a Bruddersford man could travel the short distance from the city by paying 'tuppence on the tram... to hear the larks and curlews, to feel the old rocks warming in the sun, to see the harebells trembling in the shade'.[568] What is relevant to this current study is that by including this quote the statue makes a direct connection between Priestley the novelist, his Bradford origins, and his fictional descriptions of places that can be linked back to a real-world Bradford at a specific period in the early 20th century. This was a period before the Clean Air Act when the city was smoky and blackened from the now largely derelict mills, a period before mass car ownership when travel by tram was the norm, and a period when city dwellers would escape from the drudgery of the city to ramble on the moors at weekends, as indeed Gregory Dawson does in *Bright Day*.[569]

Other symbols of commemoration for Priestley in Bradford are few. Bradford Playhouse, founded in 1929 with Priestley as its first president, following periods when it was known as the Priestley Centre for the Arts and simply The Priestley, is now known again by its original name. It contains the Priestley Coffee Lounge and Bar, but the Playhouse's website has no mention of the origin of this name, or indeed of the history of the theatre and its connection with Priestley, other than a brief mention in a promotional video.[570] Stephen Daldry's touring production of *An Inspector Calls,* originally produced for the National Theatre, did visit the Alhambra Theatre for a week in May 2016. It was enthusiastically reviewed in the local newspaper by a reviewer who acknowledged the local connection, talking about passing Priestley's statue after the performance and thinking 'he'd have approved', though her acknowledgement of the youthful audience suggested that the play's significance to its audience might have had more to do with its place on the National Curriculum than its author's local origins.[571] The council's official Bradford Guide for 2021 included no mention of Priestley, though as the council's area includes Haworth, there was much mention within the guide of the Brontës, and also of another of Bradford's famous sons, David Hockney.[572] A further link between Priestley and his home city is the J.B. Priestley Library at the University of Bradford, opened by Priestley in 1975, which now houses the J.B. Priestley Archive. The final physical reminders of Priestley within Bradford

---

568   J.B. Priestley, *Bright Day* (Ilkley: Great Northern Books, 1946 (2006 edition)), p. 51.

569   In *Bright Day* Priestley describes a visit to 'Pikeley Scar', 'a famous lime-stone cliff, not quite as wild as so many artists have pretended it is in their landscapes but a good place for a day's outing.' ibid. p. 219.

570   Clare Davenport, *The Bradford Playhouse. An introduction to the Playhouse.,* (Bradford: Bradford Playhouse, 2015) <https://youtu.be/x7sm1Htag6I>.

571   Emma Clayton, 'Urban thriller twist on JB Priestley classic delights young Alhambra audience', *Bradford Telegraph and Argus,* May 4th, 2016.

572   *Bradford & District Visitor Guide 2021*, (Bradford: City of Bradford MDC, 2021).

are the houses in Manningham where Priestley was born, and where he was later brought up. Both have small blue plaques but are private residences (Figure 6.15).

There is therefore very little for a visitor to Bradford to latch onto in terms of connecting the place, Bradford, with the author, Priestley, certainly nothing approaching the links connecting Dickens with London, the Brontës with Haworth, or Jane Austen with Winchester, Bath or Chawton. There are no author-themed walking tours for Priestley such as you would get in Bath, Haworth, or London for their respective authors. However, continuing the theme within this chapter of investigating how, educationally, we can use novels in different ways to gain historical insights into the periods in which they were written, the following section uses Priestley's Bruddersford novels in conjunction with visits to the real locations associated with them to compare the fictional descriptions with present-day observations, and in conjunction with ancillary research to strip back the contemporary landscape to its historical antecedent and attempt to see the historical skeleton beneath the present-day skin.

6.6.2 Visiting the Bradford of The Good Companions and Bright Day

The most obvious change from the descriptions within Priestley's novels is the decline of the textile industry. No longer do you see a 'host of tall chimneys, the rows and rows of little houses, built of blackening stone, that are like tiny sharp ridges on the hills'.[573] Many of the mills and their chimneys have disappeared, and of those that remain, the majority have been put to new uses. For example, Lister Mills have now been converted into flats. They were the model for Higden's Mill, which appears as Jess Oakroyd's workplace in *The Good Companions*, and in *Bright Day*, where it dominates the landscape around Gregory Dawson's lodgings. The description of house and mill in *Bright Day* gives a feel for an enclosed landscape of mills cheek-by-jowl with houses, all against a backdrop of high moorland, that because of the replacement of old housing stock by newer housing developments is not as evident today:

> The house was unpretentious and very snug... I recalled the view outside my two windows: first a rather melancholy prospect of back gardens and sooty privet and clothes-lines, and of some stacks of builders' timber in a ruined field; and then to one side there was a constant sight of the vast square chimney of Higdens' giant mill, the largest chimney and the largest mill of their kind, it was said, in the world then; and on the other side, above the clustered roofs, there was an occasional hazy glimpse of the moorland skyline.[574]

Figure 6.14 shows a view of the chimney of Lister Mills taken from the suburb of Manningham, where Priestley was born and brought up. The juxtaposition of the two also brings to mind the home of Jess Oakroyd in *The Good Companions*, close to his workplace at Higden's Mill. Within *The Good Companions* Priestley offers the following description of his fictional Ogden Street, the home of Jess Oakroyd:

---

573   Priestley (1929 (2007 edition)) p. 39.
574   Priestley (1946 (2006 edition)) p. 46.

Figure 6.14: Former chimney of Lister Mills, seen from Manningham.

Figure 6.15: Priestley's homes in Manningham. Left: Priestley's birthplace – 34, Mannheim Road, Manningham. Right: Priestley's second home – 5, Saltburn Place, Manningham.

Figure 6.16: Abingdon Street, Manningham.

Nobody could consider Ogden Street very attractive; it was very long and very drab, and contained two rows of singularly ugly black little houses; yet Ogden Street had its boasts, and its residents could claim to have both feet on the social ladder... Then too, it was composed of proper houses, all with doors opening on to the street; and in this respect it was unlike its neighbours at the back, Velvet Street and Merino Street, which had nothing but 'passage' or 'back to back' houses, the product of an ingenious architectural scheme that crammed four dwelling-places into the space of two and enabled some past citizens to drive a carriage-and-pair and take their wives and daughters to the Paris Exhibition in 1867.[575]

This description suggests that Priestley's birthplace in Mannheim Road (Figure 6.15, left), because of its small front garden, was not the model for Oakroyd's house, but in the neighbourhood there are many terraced streets similar in appearance to Ogden Street, such as Abingdon Street (Figure 6.16), though there are no longer any examples of the back-to-back housing from which Ogden Street was a step up. These only remain today within Priestley's description and the historical record.

---

575   Priestley (1929 (2007 edition)) p. 48.

Figure 6.17: Private house near Lister Park, Manningham, Bradford.

Simon Taylor and Kathryn Gibson write of Manningham at the end of the 19th century having a mix of housing that went from the grand houses of closed communities of wealthy merchants and factory owners to, 'open streets... often grouped in micro-communities of four households, dictated by the design of tunnel back-to-back houses and the shared facilities that these entailed' for the factory workers.[576] The grander houses are fictionalised in the form of the well-to-do district of 'Merton Park':

> ...Merton Park, Bruddersford's best suburb, where the wool merchants and manufacturers and the bank managers had their detached villas. These pleasant avenues were full of leafy shadows, for there were trees in the gardens and trees alternating with street-lamps on the pavement itself.[577]

This progression up the social scale between the Ogden Street area and Merton Park is still evident on the ground today in Manningham when travelling from Mannheim Road towards Shipley. Within two miles of the terraced houses of Mannheim Road are villas such as that shown in Figure 6.17, very similar in feel to those of Priestley's Merton Park. They are reminiscent both of the area Jess Oakroyd walks through returning from visiting Sam Oglethorpe in *The Good Companions*, and the area where the Alingtons lived in *Bright Day*.

This idea of social progression also crops up in *Bright Day*. Priestley's father was a teacher, and on becoming the headmaster of a local school he moved the family the short distance from Mannheim Road to 5, Saltburn Place, also a terraced house but 'what was

---

576   Simon Taylor and Kathryn Gibson, *Manningham: character and diversity in a Bradford suburb* (Swindon: English Heritage, 2010), p. 73.
577   Priestley (1929 (2007 edition)) p. 59.

considered in the Bradford of the day a "posh" address'.[578] On visiting Saltburn Place (Figure 6.15, right), and reading the passage from *Bright Day* quoted earlier about the house in Brigg Terrace, there is a hint that Priestley might have been remembering this when describing Gregory Dawson's lodgings.[579] Dawson also describes in the novel his walks to his friends the Alingtons who lived 'somewhere farther along the Wabley Road than the turning I took up to Brigg Terrace... in a wilderness of suburban Drives and Groves'.[580] When he finally finds the house, he describes it as 'a square detached villa',[581] which suggests that it sits in the same social relationship to Brigg Terrace as you see between Merton Park and Ogden Street in *The Good Companions*, and as you still see on the ground today when travelling from Manningham to Shipley.

There are other comparisons with Priestley's Bruddersford that one could make when visiting Bradford that help to see beyond the Bradford of today and visualise what Bradford/Bruddersford might have looked like in the first 30 years of the 20th century. The 2006 reprint of *Bright Day* includes an appendix that uses the Bradford models for various Bruddersford buildings mentioned in the novel to create a kind of literary tour.[582] It includes buildings that still exist, such as St. George's Hall, the model for Gladstone Hall where Priestley describes Gregory Dawson listening to the Hallé Orchestra.[583] It also describes areas that have changed markedly, such as the area around the Wool Exchange, including Swan Arcade, where Priestley worked as a junior wool clerk before the First World War, just as Gregory Dawson does in *Bright Day*.[584] Swan Arcade itself was demolished in the 1960s, and the buildings that survive, including the Wool Exchange itself, have long since lost their connection to the textile industry. Hanson and Joy, through describing these changes in detail and relating them back to the novel and its descriptions of how these buildings were used, have provided a brief historical geography for certain parts of Bradford that is informed by the fictional source of *Bright Day*.

In one respect more than any other, Bradford has changed significantly since Priestley portrayed it as Bruddersford. The Bruddersford that Priestley describes in *The Good Companions* and *Bright Day* is the archetypal Yorkshire working town of popular imagination peopled with solid northern surnames like Oakroyd, Oglethorpe, Clough and Buttershaw. While this may have been true of the Bradford of the early 20th century (though there are provisos that are expanded on later), Taylor and Gibson in their study of Manningham detail how since the Second World War there have been successive waves of immigration into the area, initially in the 1940s from the West Indies, but from the 1950s onwards predominantly from India, Pakistan, and Bangladesh.[585] The result is that 20.3% of the population of Bradford Metropolitan District identify themselves as being of

---

578   Cook (1997) p. 9.

579   This assertion is also made in an appendix to the 2006 edition of *Bright Day*: "it is this house that was the main Priestley residence during his time in Bradford and it is the Brigg Terrace home of Gregory Dawson in Bright Day". Lee Hanson and David Joy, 'Bright Day Literary Tour', in *Bright Day (2006 edition)*, ed. by Lee Hanson and David Joy (Ilkley: Great Northern Books, 2006), p. 295.

580   Priestley (1946 (2006 edition)) p. 53.

581   Ibid. p. 72.

582   Hanson and Joy (2006) pp. 289-311.

583   Priestley (1946 (2006 edition)) p. 68.

584   Ibid. p. 55.

585   Taylor and Gibson (2010) p. 80.

Figure 6.18: Duckworth Lane, Manningham.

Pakistani ethnic origin and 24.7% as Muslim.[586] It becomes clear when moving from the centre of Bradford out to Manningham that this whole area is now predominantly Asian, including the streets around the two houses in which Priestley lived in the early part of the 20th century.

The Manningham one sees today is therefore very different culturally from Priestley's Ogden Street area in the 1920s and given the decline of the mills very different in terms of the working life of its inhabitants. What seems to have remained from Priestley's time is a sense of being a community. The impression one gets of Manningham today is that most shops in the area are small and privately owned and include many geared specifically to the needs of the Asian community, such as food shops and fashion retailers (Figure 6.18). These are reminiscent of shops like 'Buttershaws', described by Priestley in *The Good Companions* as follows: 'It catered to both body and soul, one half of it given up to tripe and cow-heels and the other half to music, chiefly sixpenny songs and cheap gramophone records'.[587] Given the absence there of many national chain stores or franchised corner shops, Manningham today may resemble the Bruddersford suburbs Priestley describes and their shops like Buttershaws. In *The Good Companions*, there is evidence of a community that is interdependent, as shown by the scene near the end of the book where Jess Oakroyd discovers his neighbour Mrs Sugden spring-cleaning his house following the death of his

---

586 *City of Bradford MDC: Population*, (Bradford: City of Bradford MDC, 2017) <https://www.bradford.gov.uk/open-data/our-datasets/population/>.
587 Priestley (1929 (2007 edition)) p. 44.

wife.[588] The impression gained in walking around the Manningham of today was of a high number of open doors, and of a large amount of neighbourly discourse going on in the street. This suggests that despite the changed cultural mix and working environment of Manningham, there are surviving elements within the neighbourhood that would strike a chord with Priestley, and that in turn we can see an echo of the streets surrounding Priestley's Ogden Street not just in the physical infrastructure of Manningham but in the social structure.

The Asian influence in the Manningham of today is, however, evidence of just one phase in the economic and cultural growth and development of Manningham, which probably goes back to the time of the Domesday Book.[589] Taylor and Gibson describe Manningham in the 17th century as being 'probably the least populous of the Bradford manor townships' with only 65 houses in 1672, and it still had less than 1,000 inhabitants in 1780.[590] However, by the 1830s new mills were being built in Manningham and growth continued exponentially until by the end of the century Manningham was a single contiguous suburb of Bradford.[591]

A major element of the growth of Bradford in the 19th century was an influx of German merchants, many of them Jewish, their contribution to the growth of the city becoming so important that an area of warehouses near the centre of the city became known as 'Little Germany'. This influx was also reflected in Manningham. Priestley himself was born in Mannheim Road, part of a complex of streets that reflects German influence and includes Heidelberg Road and Bonn Road. In his travelogue *English Journey* Priestley visited Bradford and remembered the influence of the German population on Bradford:

> ...during the early and mid-Victorian periods, a number of German and German-Jewish merchants, with German banks behind them, came to settle in the town... Bradford became – as it still remained when I was a boy there – at once one of the most provincial and yet one of the most cosmopolitan of English provincial cities.[592]

Later comments suggest that the foreign populations were so well integrated as to be barely worthy of note:

> ...there was this curious leaven of intelligent aliens, chiefly German-Jews and mostly affluent. They were so much a part of the place when I was a boy that it never occurred to me to ask why they were there.[593]

However, the picture Priestley painted of the fictional Bruddersford in *The Good Companions* was firmly anglocentric, with no mention of any world beyond. In *Bright Day*, for all that the two 20th century wars with Germany are the shadows that lie behind the story of the novel, any Germanic influence on pre-First World War Bruddersford is limited to German customers and agents visiting the company for whom Gregory Dawson works,

---

588 Ibid. p. 566.
589 Taylor and Gibson (2010) p. 7.
590 Ibid. p. 11/13.
591 Ibid. pp. 26-28.
592 J.B. Priestley, *English Journey* (London: William Heinemann; Victor Gollancz, 1934), p. 158.
593 Ibid. p. 160.

and the Germanic composers played at the musical parties that Dawson attends and in concerts at the Gladstone Hall. In neither novel is there any mention of any German or Jewish influence on the social makeup of Bruddersford, despite Priestley's stated view of Bradford as 'cosmopolitan' leavened with 'intelligent aliens'. This absence within *The Good Companions* may have been driven by Priestley's reluctance to talk about the First World War and, by extension, the Germans. Priestley said that in *Bright Day* he was looking 'to recreate... something of the life I had known before 1914, and not, I believe, without colour, warmth and tenderness'.[594] One should assume that it suited Priestley's purpose to portray the fictional Bruddersford in both novels, despite all of its clear connections with Bradford, as more of a cultural *Yorkshire* archetype, without some of the societal subtleties that existed within that city.

What one gets from considering this brief history of the parts of Bradford with which Priestley was most intimate, is that the picture of Bruddersford/Bradford that he gives us is in retrospect only a brief snapshot in the evolving story of Manningham and Bradford. The white working-class industrial Bradford of mills, smoky chimneys, tramcars, terraced streets and the like in which Priestley grew up, and which he described in these two novels, had only existed in that exact form since around the middle of 19th century, and would change not long after as the textile industry declined, housing was improved, the air was cleaned up and waves of immigration changed the cultural mix of the city and of Manningham in particular. As has been described, elements of Priestley's Bradford/ Bruddersford do still exist, but the descriptions within the novel are of a world and a society that has been in large part lost to us, and as such the Bruddersford novels can exist as a historical document for a specific place in a specific point in time that provide us with context for what we see physically on the ground today.

This idea of the novels giving us a snapshot in time is underlined by consideration of a film that Priestley made for the BBC in the late 1950s. *Lost City* was filmed in Bradford during March 1958 by the documentary filmmaker Richard Cawston.[595] The film followed Priestley on a visit to Bradford as he revisited many of the old haunts of his time spent growing up and working in the city, many of which found their way in some form or another into the pages of *The Good Companions* and *Bright Day*. The film was not a portrait of Bradford in 1958 *per se*, but rather a film about the shadows of Priestley's past that inhabited the Bradford of 1958. Priestley described it as 'a sentimental journey' to 'a city lost to me through sheer lapse of time',[596] whereas Cawston described the title as referring to 'the passage of time and to Mr. Priestley's memories of his boyhood'.[597] To that end Priestley was seen visiting locations connected with his early life, portraying Priestley as a wanderer returned after a long absence and lamenting what the intervening years had done to the city of his youth, commenting critically on the dereliction of the Theatre Royal and on the threat to the continued existence of the Swan Arcade building, both times

---

594 Priestley (1962) p. 192.
595 *Lost City*, dir. by Richard Cawston (BBC Television, 1958).
596 Bradford, J.B. Priestley Library, Cutting from Radio Times of October 24th, 1958: 'In Search of the Bradford I Knew', (GB 0532) PRI 19/9.
597 Bradford, J.B. Priestley Library, Letter received by Mavis Dean from Richard Cawston on the making of Lost City, (GB 0532) PRI 19/9.

Figure 6.19: Stills from *Lost City*.

harking back to major elements of the two Bruddersford novels.[598] In one early scene he looked through the 1958 Bradford telephone directory for names of old acquaintances only to find when he tried to ring them that they had died or otherwise vanished from the scene. In a conscious link to one of the novels, an anonymous critic writing in the Bradford Telegraph & Argus made a telling comment on this section of the film:

> From his hotel room, Mr. Priestley vainly tried to contact by telephone Mr. Mothergill (dead, alas!), Mrs. Lugden (poorly for months) and Mr. Oldenroyd (doesn't live here anymore!). Did they ever exist J.B., or were they names left over from *The Good Companions*?[599]

Priestley was searching for his lost Bradford in the then present-day Bradford, but there is a sense of him looking for a lost *Bruddersford* as well, for the archetypal Yorkshire city of the two novels with its archetypal Yorkshire names and customs, rather than the more, to use Priestley's own word, 'cosmopolitan' city of which it was a fictional image. Priestley had lost the direct link with the Bradford / Bruddersford of his past and was using his memories to reimagine it within the Bradford of the present.

Figure 6.19 shows stills of *Lost City*, including shots of Priestley visiting his old home in Saltburn Place, Swan Arcade, and Theatre Royal. What they picture is a city that is further distant in time from the Bradford of today than Priestley's Bradford was from the Bradford of 1958. A film like *Lost City* fixes an image of Bradford in the mind from within that evolutionary continuum, specifically March 1958, and provides us with something with which to make comparisons with the present day. Similarly, whilst *The Good Companions* and *Bright Day* cannot be traced back to as specific a point in time as *Lost City*, they can also provide us with an image of Bradford at a period in time, via their descriptions of Bruddersford, that we can use to make comparisons with both the Bradford of today and the Bradford of *Lost City*. We, as readers of the two novels, do not have that link with the Bradford of the past, but we can use the descriptions of Bruddersford within those novels, and through that link with Priestley's memories of Bradford, out of which he created those descriptions, also reimagine past Bradford within the Bradford of the present.

6.6.3 Visiting Priestley's World – Summary

Just as Bradford in 1958 was a city with which Priestley felt he had lost his links, so Bradford today is a city that has lost many of its links with Priestley. One large reminder remains in the form of the Priestley statue, which in its inscription explicitly links his fictional view of Bradford in *Bright Day* with the city itself. Other than that, however, memorials are limited and often pass unacknowledged. Priestley's birthplace has been gutted and the house where he grew up has a uPVC front door. Look for Priestley on the official tourist website for Bradford and there is nothing that will lead you to the author and his connections with Bradford. The comparisons with Haworth, which also lies within

---

598 During the late 1950s leases within Swan Arcade were being bought up by Arndale Property Trust in preparation for future redevelopment of the site. Swan Arcade closed in 1962 and was demolished, and a new shopping precinct, the Arndale Centre, was built in its place. Jim Greenhalf, 'When Bradford's city bosses bet the house...', *Telegraph & Argus*, October 20th, 1967.

599 Anon, 'Review of 'Lost City'', *Bradford Telegraph and Argus*, October 27th, 1958. Quoted in Peter Holdsworth, *The Rebel Tyke: Bradford and J.B. Priestley* (Bradford: Bradford Libraries, 1994), p. 111.

the Metropolitan Borough of Bradford, are telling given that there is a whole section of the same website devoted to Haworth and the Brontë Country.[600]

Much of this discrepancy is obviously to do with the relative fame of Priestley and the Brontës, but it also could be a function of the difference in size between Haworth and Bradford. Haworth still seems in parts to be sufficiently unaltered as to have the power to evoke the life and times of the Brontë sisters. Indeed, Sally Wainwright's 2016 BBC dramatisation of the life of the sisters, *To Walk Invisble*, used Main Street and the Black Bull pub as filming locations, though because the church and parsonage have been rebuilt and enlarged respectively since the time of the Brontës, the church, graveyard and parsonage were recreated on a nearby moor.[601] Haworth is still a relatively small village, and long ago embraced its key role in the history of the Brontës and its central position in the tourist industry that has grown up around them. With Haworth and Brontës intrinsically linked in the public imagination it is a straightforward task for City of Bradford Council to promote 'Brontë Country' via a website or a brochure, or even for the neighbouring Kirklees Council to promote locations associated with Charlotte Brontë's *Shirley* by publishing the brochure 'Shirley Country'.[602] This identification of Haworth with the Brontës and their novels is reinforced by the fact that of the top five 'things to do' in Haworth in February 2019 as chosen by contributors to the on-line travel reviewing site TripAdvisor, four had a connection with the Brontës.[603]

Searching for Priestley in Bradford is, as was shown above, a much more difficult task than searching for the Brontës in Haworth, but that is not to say that Priestley and his novels could not play an important part in illuminating the past landscapes of Bradford and Manningham. Visiting Bradford and Manningham with copies of *The Good Companions* and *Bright Day* can help set in motion a two-way conversation with the past. On the one hand, the visible traces of the city that Priestley knew and wrote about in the two novels help to provide a realistic context for the novels' fictional descriptions of Bruddersford, and on the other, where there has been significant change since Priestley's time, the descriptions within the novels can assist in filling in detail of what is not visible today on the ground, such as the long since demolished back-to-back houses. Priestley may not always provide the full picture, as in his decision not to include any Germanic influence in his descriptions of Bruddersford, but at their best his descriptions can be viewed as a snapshot of a place in time that can help us peel back the layers from the present-day landscape to that place in time. The word snapshot is used advisedly, however. The real history of Bradford, and indeed the fictional history of Bruddersford, is an ever-evolving continuum. Though Priestley hints at a historical background to Bruddersford in the first chapter of *The Good Companions*, the detail of his description in *Bright Day* and even to an extent in *The Good Companions*, despite its late-1920s setting, is very much based in his time in Bradford immediately before the First World War. Comparisons with the Bradford of *Lost City* and between that Bradford and the present-day show that in terms of the total history of Bradford and Manningham since the Middle Ages, 'Bruddersford' is but a momentary instant.

---

600 *Discover Haworth and Brontë Country*, (Bradford: Bradford Visitor Information Centre, 2021) <http://www.visitbradford.com/discover/Haworth.aspx>.

601 Huw Fullerton, 'Where was To Walk Invisible: The Brontë sisters filmed?', *Radio Times*, December 29th, 2016. <http://www.radiotimes.com/news/2016-12-29/where-was-to-walk-invisible-the-bront-sisters-filmed>.

602 *The Brontës in Pennine Yorkshire*, (Huddersfield: Kirklees Council, 2008).

603 *Things to do in Haworth*, (TripAdvisor, 2019) <https://www.tripadvisor.co.uk/Attractions-g186409-Activities-Haworth_Keighley_West_Yorkshire_England.html>.

6.7 Conclusion: *The Good Companions* as a Historical Resource

In *The Good Companions*, Priestley provides us with clearly defined settings for the story within. From the very first chapter of the novel, and the zoom in to the city of Bruddersford, we see clear attention to detail in his descriptions of place. Priestley wanted the world of his novel to come alive in the minds of his readers in the same way as Dickens with London and Hardy with Dorset. This sense of detail lends itself well to dramatic representation, either on film or in the theatre, as the many adaptations of the novel testify.

This chapter has attempted to show a number of ways in which the fictional world of *The Good Companions* can be taken apart and used to provide historical insights into Bradford at a particular point in time and thereby supplement the conventional historical sources of the period. Firstly, the novel lends itself to carrying out textual deconstruction and analysis from a historical perspective. The use of mind maps gives us a broad top-down view of the main themes and subject areas within the novel and helps us gain a general impression of the world that the author is perceiving when writing the novel. The more detailed bottom-up deconstruction of the text obtained from a technique such as footnoting allows us to drill down into the historical detail of elements of the novel and elucidate some areas that might not have been apparent to the general reader when producing their mind maps. Secondly, carrying out detailed analysis of adaptations of the novel helps us assess how much those adaptations either add to, or take away from, the structure of the novel and the understanding of the world of the novel, and how much they might tell us as well about the period in which the adaptation was made. Finally, visiting the present-day sites that formed the historical backdrop to the fictional places described in the novel and Priestley's other Bruddersford novel, *Bright Day*, can help us to equate the fictional/historical landscape with the modern one and understand the development of that landscape through time.

Before summarising the historical picture that Priestley's novels can give us, what has been emphasised throughout this study is also important when analysing Priestley, namely that his novels are imagined works of fiction, not true historical sources, and that any analysis of the novels in historical terms should take account of the decisions Priestley made when adapting real-world Yorkshire and the wider England into the world of the novels. Similar provisos must be made when assessing the value of adaptations in this regard, given the choices filmmakers make in their turn when adapting Priestley's imagined world into the imagined world of their adaptations. For example, in the textual analyses of *The Good Companions*, we saw that what is conspicuously missing from the descriptions of England in the late 1920s, is any mention, other than a couple of brief references in passing, to the event that cast a shadow over the 1920s and 1930s, namely the First World War. The effect on Priestley of his war service was devastating, as he acknowledges when writing about *The Good Companions* in his memoir *Margin Released*. Describing the genesis of the novel, whilst calling the background of the novel 'contemporary and realistic', he admitted it also had a 'cosy fairy-tale atmosphere'. This atmosphere was due, as he saw it, to needing to find 'some release, [to] give myself a holiday of the spirit while writing this novel of 250,000 words' after suffering personal crises after a war in which 'almost every man I had known and liked had been killed'.[604] Priestley was therefore very much aware of the dichotomy in the novel between the realistic and the imagined. What he wrote

---

604   Priestley (1962) p. 182.

might be imagined, a 'fairy tale', but still be grounded in reality. The last words of *The Good Companions* sum this feeling up as he describes what has come before as 'stumbling chronicles of a dream of life'.[605] A dream, yes, but a dream of life, of something real. In an interview with Alan Plater for the 'making of' documentary that accompanied the 1980 adaptation of the novel Priestley aligned himself with Charles Dickens in this regard:

> Dickens is a very good example. Of course, I mean his sense of reality was tremendous… He walked down the street and noticed every name… and yet at the same time as soon as he began writing about it this curious fairy tale feeling came. Partly because, of course, in his case he made everything alive, you know. He could make a piece of furniture alive, and this is very much a fairy tale quality, that, you know, the dresser may answer back if you're not careful.[606]

It was not until the aftermath of the *Second* World War, in 1946, that Priestley could address his feelings about the war in his fiction, in the novel *Bright Day*. Even here, the subject is addressed obliquely, as Gregory Dawson looks back from the 1940s to the Bruddersford of 1912 in which he had grown up, the same Bruddersford depicted in *The Good Companions*, with a sense of it being a golden era before the Fall. Gregory talks about how in the intervening years, amongst other things, he had 'lived for weeks in waterlogged trenches, [and had] been machined-gunned, gassed and bombed'.[607] The war seems to stand as a watershed moment between a golden past and an uncertain present, too devastating to describe in detail but too awful in its consequences to ignore.

One final observation on Priestley and his attitude to the war comes from comparison with another novelist writing about the 1920s, namely Virginia Woolf. Baxendale saw Priestley as belonging to a social realist tradition stretching back to the previous century and the novels of those such as Gaskell, Dickens, and Hardy, defining them as '…novels which make social and physical reality their subject matter, dealing with real events and offering a recognisable account of the social world', and which focus on 'externals, on actions and settings, on social, political and moral issues, on social relationships.[608] This seems diametrically opposed to the approach of Virginia Woolf, a novelist contemporary to Priestley who wrote about the world in a very different way. Woolf was critical of realist writers such as Priestley and Arnold Bennett who took their perceived contemporary worlds and adapted them into something solid and structured in the imagined worlds of their fiction, writing:

> Life is not a series of gig lamps symmetrically arranged; life is a luminous halo, a semi-transparent envelope surrounding us from the beginning of consciousness to the end.[609]

---

605 Priestley (1929 (2007 edition)) p. 573.
606 *A Dream of Life*, dir. by Mervyn Cumming (Yorkshire Television, 1980).
607 Priestley (1946 (2006 edition)) p. 45.
608 Baxendale (2007) pp. 13-4.
609 Virginia Woolf, 'Modern Fiction (1925)', in *The Essays of Virginia Woolf. Volume 4: 1925-1928*, ed. by Andrew McNeillie (London: The Hogarth Press, 1984), p. 160.

To her, writing was a matter of describing the perceived sensations of the moment in a way contrary to the narrative emphasis of conventional fiction:

> ...the moment is a combination of thought; sensation; the voice of the sea. Waste, deadness come from inclusion of things that don't belong to the moment; this appalling narrative business of the realist: getting on from lunch to dinner.[610]

However, at root both Priestley and Woolf were writing about a perceived contemporary world, interpreted, and adapted through their imagination, which suggests that it is not just through the realist novels of the period such as *The Good Companions* that one can gain historical insights. Woolf's *Mrs Dalloway*, as well as being an intellectual exercise that can both infuriate and enthral the reader, can also be seen as a rich evocation of the London of 1923 in its geographical, commercial and socio-cultural descriptions, as rich in its way as Priestley's descriptions of the England of 1928 in *The Good Companions* and of the London of 1930 in *Angel Pavement*, and indeed of James Joyce's descriptions of Dublin in *Ulysses*, at face value equally as 'difficult' a novel as *Mrs Dalloway*.

Mrs Dalloway might not be as immediate and as clearly defined as, say, the first chapter of *The Good Companions* but a passage such as the following, which describes the aftermath of a passage of a car down Bond Street in which passers-by believe they can see the Queen, can give several insights into the London of 1923:

> The car had gone, but it had left a slight ripple which flowed through glove shops and hat shops and tailors' shops on both sides of Bond Street. For thirty seconds all heads were inclined the same way – to the window. Choosing a pair of gloves – should they be to the elbow or above it, lemon or pale grey? – ladies stopped; when the sentence was finished something had happened. Something so trifling in single instances that no mathematical instrument, though capable of transmitting shocks in China, could register the vibration; yet in its fullness rather formidable and in its common appeal emotional; for in all the hat shops and tailor's shops strangers looked at each other and thought of the dead; of the flag; of Empire. In a public house in a back street a Colonial insulted the House of Windsor which led to words, broken beer glasses, and a general shindy, which echoed strangely across the way in the ears of girls buying white underlinen threaded with pure white ribbon for their weddings. For the surface agitation of the passing car as it sunk grazed something very profound.[611]

Whether or not it was Woolf's intention for a reader to react in such a way when reading this passage, one could carry out a footnoting exercise on it that might provide the following insights into the real world of post-First World War London. One sees a picture of the types of shops that lined Bond Street at the time and the fact that they were clearly delineated around specific specialisms, such as hats, gloves, and tailors, that would not be as apparent today, even in London. One sees the importance of gloves as a fashion item in the 1920s. One sees a very early reference to the royal family being the House of Windsor,

---

610 1928 diary entry by Virginia Woolf, quoted in Uzma Hameed, 'Woolfian Perspectives', in *Royal Ballet: Woolf Works* (London: Royal Opera House Covent Garden Ltd, 2017), p. 8.

611 Virginia Woolf, *Mrs Dalloway* (London: Vintage Classics, 1925 (2004 edition)), p. 14.

which had only been founded eight years prior to this novel being published and six years prior to the events described within it, and one sees evidence of the deference that was paid to the concept of royalty and that a 'colonial' (itself a term which places the novel in a certain historical context) insulting it could lead to violence. Most importantly one sees the way that the simple act of a member of this family passing by could bring about intense emotional memories of the recent war and of 'the dead'. The shadow of the recent war that Priestley avoids is also apparent in this vivid description of the flashback suffered by ex-soldier Septimus Smith on hearing a street musician that today would invite a diagnosis of Post-Traumatic Stress Disorder, and would presumably be readily understood by an ex-soldier such as Priestley:

> Or he was hearing music. Really it was only a barrel organ or some man crying in the street. But "Lovely!" he used to cry, and the tears would run down his cheeks, which was to her [Rezia, Septimus' wife] the most dreadful thing of all, to see a man like Septimus, who had fought, who was brave, crying. And he would lie listening until suddenly he would cry that he was falling down, down into the flames, it was so vivid. But there was nothing. They were alone in the room.[612]

Unlike with Woolf, however, if you go to *The Good Companions* for an idea of how the aftermath of the First World War lingered on into the succeeding decade, you may find little to enlighten you there. And yet in the subject areas picked up in the mind map of the novel, and in the references uncovered in the annotation of the first chapter of the novel, in his descriptions of things as varied as the burgeoning road network and the haulage and catering industries growing up around it, the rise of the new Art Deco cinemas and the fall of the old Victorian theatres, the contrast between new and old industries, and last but not least, the many and varied ways in which people were entertained, from the traditional pierrot shows to the bright new West End revues, he gives a picture of an England on the cusp of the modern age that has historical value.

If we look specifically at Priestley's descriptions of Bruddersford, we should also consider Priestley's circumstances when writing the novel when assessing the use of those descriptions as a historical resource. Priestley had left Bradford, the model for Bruddersford, in 1914, and apart from a short spell after demobilisation he was never to live there again. The Bradford he knew best, the Bradford in which he was born, grew up and worked, was the one that existed in the immediate pre-war years, the Edwardian period he returned to frequently in his novels and plays, as for example in *Bright Day*, *An Inspector Calls* and *When We Were Married*. It is also the Bradford that Priestley was returning to in the film *Lost City*. If one looks at the way *The Good Companions* describes Bruddersford, and the way it avoids detailed mention of the war that had so affected Priestley, there is a suggestion that this element of the novel fits into this pre-war Priestley canon, even as elements of the rest of the novel appear to more accurately reflect the England of the late 1920s.

Trying to uncover that historical world of the 1920s in present-day Bradford through the lens of *The Good Companions* one is immediately aware of how much has changed since Priestley lived here before the First World War. The Bradford of his childhood and

---

612   Ibid. p. 124.

adolescence, and particularly the suburb of Manningham, with its German heritage and its then predominantly white working-class population, now presents a completely different cultural face to the world following successive waves of immigration from the Indian sub-continent. The mills that dominated the economy of the city are now largely silent, and the post-industrial landscape that Bradford presents today provides only echoes of the past world Priestley would have known. Thus, the Bradford/Bruddersford of novels such as *The Good Companions* and *Bright Day* are in historical terms, despite the novels' seemingly archetypal and timeless 'northern ness', a valuable snapshot of what has turned out to be merely one stage in the development of the city.

7

Stories of the Past: Conclusions

This study began with a discussion of the links between history and fiction and of current thinking about the worth of novels as resources for the study of history, not simply for their status as artefacts of that period, but for their historical content. Marwick's assertion that novels should never be accounted secondary sources was balanced by a concern that, in line with White's view that a historian 'finds' stories and a novelist 'invents' them,[613] fictional description should not take precedence over verifiable real-world facts,[614] a concern echoed by Allen's warning about historians mistaking the detail within novels for facts.[615] However, Lowenthal[616] and White[617] both attested to the incomplete nature of the historical record, that historians fill in through the use of narrative techniques akin to those of a novelist. Warren,[618] de Certeau,[619] and de Groot[620] all saw how that same novelist, in providing us with an immersive way into an imagined version of the past in which the verifiable facts exist, may add to those facts what de Certeau calls the 'reality' of fiction, and what Warren calls 'knowledge of' the past. Tosh summed up the two sides of the argument – novels and plays should not be taken as being strictly factual, but they can provide insights into the physical, social, and intellectual worlds in which the author lived.[621] Spiegel talked of how we need to find procedures to help us find the past that is 'out there' in a manner that retained the integrity of that past.[622]

The initial aim of this study was therefore to examine Tosh's 'insights' and to investigate the details of a classic fiction process model which begins with writers taking their knowledge of the reality of the world in which they live and incorporating that knowledge into the imagined world of novels, and which could provide at least one procedure to assist with finding Spiegel's 'past'. This model could be used to assess a novel's utility and

---

613   White (1975) p. ix.
614   Marwick (2001) p. 187.
615   Allen (1983).
616   Lowenthal (2015) pp. 336-37.
617   White (1975) p. ix.
618   Ellison, Styron, Warren, and Woodward (1969).
619   White (2005).
620   de Groot (2009) p. 217.
621   Tosh (2015) p. 79.
622   Spiegel (1990).

reliability as a historical resource, as supplemental data to a pure fact-based study of history. Gaskell's descriptions of living conditions in Ancoats and the spatial geography of Manchester in the 1840s in *Mary Barton* stand out as vivid examples of an imagined world being created as a backdrop to an imagined story that can also be used to provide background for the historical world that was the inspiration for the story. Similar examples include Hardy's descriptions of rural Dorset as Wessex and Priestley's of the Yorkshire urban landscape and the middle England of the 1920s. Even where the descriptive content of a novel does not give us an obvious picture of the physical world, such as with Austen's *Pride and Prejudice* and *Emma*, close study of the text can give us insights into the nature of the society and the landscapes in which those novels were written and set.

The proviso that the process model brings out is that authors are adapting what are perceptions of their contemporary world and creating stories in an imagined version of that world – they do not necessarily set out to write factual chronicles of the times. This and other influences, such as the social and political outlook of the novelist and the expected readership of the novel, mean that whilst the imagined world of the novel may have a direct relationship with these now past worlds, account must also be made of such factors and influences when assessing their historical utility. For example, Greg's issues with the depiction of industrial troubles in Gaskell's *Mary Barton*, or those of contemporary reviewers with the language of the peasantry in Hardy's *Far from the Madding Crowd* show examples where those receiving a novel do so from a different standpoint from that of the author and reach different views as to its veracity.

Such critical disagreements regarding novels demonstrate that consideration of the links between fiction and history has to go beyond simple consideration of the novelist using real-world settings to create the imagined world of the novel itself. Additionally, the novels that have ascended to the classic fiction canon can now be found within artefacts other than the original novel, such as film and television adaptations, or tourist interpretations, and indeed may be more likely to be consumed in such a form, with each new artefact adding extra layers of adaptation and interpretation that sit between the consumer and the past that inspired the author. The further aim of this study was therefore to show how a classic fiction process model extends beyond the original author's creation to include the actors that create these additional artefacts.

Figure 7.1 brings together all of the individual elements of the classic fiction process model, the actors, actions, artefacts, external influences, and past and imagined worlds, that were described in the preceding chapters. The line connecting novelist and consumer shows that the most direct method of discerning historical insights from fiction, given that the consumer is directly interfacing with the author, is reading the actual source artefact, the novel itself, though even here the author may be using processes of adaptation to turn elements of their contemporary world into the imagined world of the novel. Further down the process model, each subsequent actor, be they critic, adapter, or interpreter, receives some or all of the previous artefacts within the process model, beginning with the original novel, and perceives a further imagined world around which they construct their own artefact, governed by their own specific set of external influences. For example, initial reviewers of a novel, such as Greg and Forster reading *Mary Barton*, use their own perception of the same world in which the author lived to validate the truthfulness or otherwise of the imagined world they create in their minds from reading the novel.

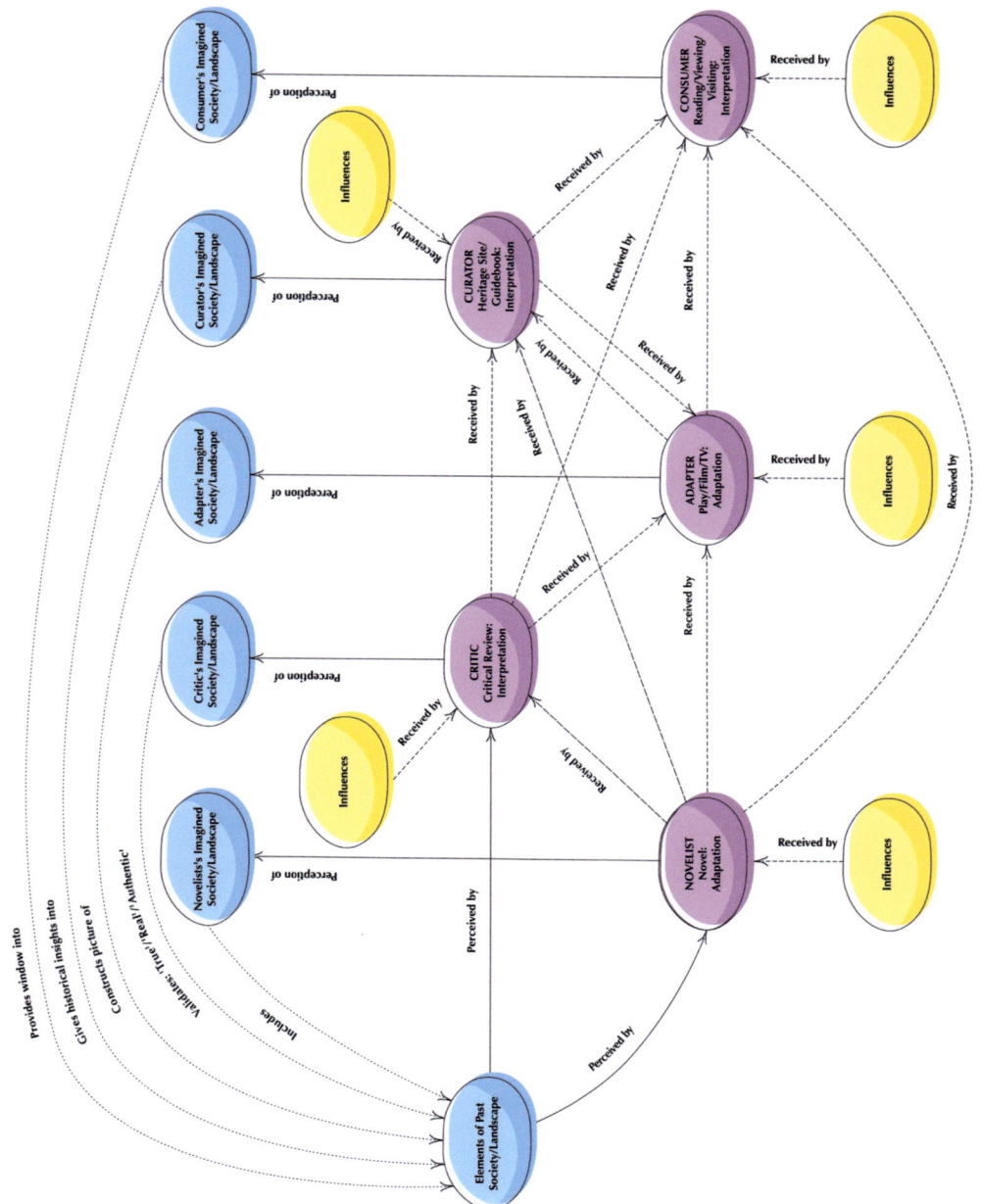

Figure 7.1: Overall Classic Fiction Process Model.

Contemporary filmmakers, such as those adapting Hardy's *Far from the Madding Crowd*, lack that direct perception of the past with which to validate their imagined worlds but have many other available historical and biographical sources that influence the visual world they imagine within their adaptations, though equally important may be such things as the demands of their audience and the influence of previous adaptations of the novel and other similar novels.

Within literary places there is potential for the greatest number of influences to come to bear on the way they are presented to consumers – the novel, critical responses to the author, adaptations of the novels and other biographical, historical and geographical considerations. The influences that affect those interpreters of literary places such as Hardy's Casterbridge and the Jane Austen's House Museum can then be seen as creating tourist interpretations split between those that are predominantly author-based, where interpreters use biographical information to place the author in an imagined historical setting, and those that are predominantly novel-based, where interpreters use an author's fictional descriptions, and relevant historical sources, to produce an imagined historical world where the one informs the other. The interpretations can also be seen as split between those with a desire to appeal on the one hand to dedicated literary pilgrims and on the other to the general tourist, with consequent differences in the type and depth of interpretive information on offer. At the same time, the influences of adaptations such as Austen's *Pride and Prejudice* on a tourist site such as Lyme can mean the creation of imagined worlds that have little or no direct connection to the author or the novel other than through their being a location within such an adaptation.

The impressions we then get from viewing a Hardy adaptation or an Austen literary location have the potential to be influenced by the decisions made by adapters and interpreters. Indeed we, as the passive consumers of the novel in whatever form, are the final actors in the process model, subject to external influences in the same way as the other actors within the process model as we perceive our own imagined world from our consumption of the novel. For example, if we read a particular novel having already seen an adaptation or having visited a literary place associated with the author or the novel, we may read the novel entirely differently to if we had read the novel without such inputs, and the insights we obtain may be subtly different. This propensity for a reader of a novel to be influenced by artefacts other than the novel itself was demonstrated in the analysis of *North and South* reviews. If we simply consume the novel via an adaptation, our imagined worlds are affected by the visual world of the adaptation which is itself affected by the decisions and compromises made by the adapters. This may result in misleading conflations such as those present at Lyme.

The idea of an objective past world and of imagined worlds layered upon it ran as a thread throughout the body of this study, as within each chapter an actor in the process model received the past and/or imagined worlds observed and created previously, and fashioned elements of them into a newly imagined world that then may have provided further input for actors later in the process model. The root of the process model is the historical past that provided the backdrop for the novel originally created by the author, and the initial question within this study was whether such a past can ever be objectively viewed, *and described*, by an actor such as a novelist. Perception is therefore the other important thread running through the study. If we perceive the world through our senses, and if each individual person's perception is different, then through the process model that has been described the original contemporary world of the author has the propensity to be transformed, to a greater or lesser extent, at each stage in that process model.

The novel in its original form contains an imagined world perceived by the author that may be based on elements of the contemporary world of the author that were adapted for the purposes of fiction. Later imagined worlds can move us closer to or further away from that world. It is important when assessing the historical information that we can get from novels, that we understand the processes that are at work in the production of the imagined world of the particular artefact we are consuming, such as the external influences affecting the adaptation itself, and the influences of previous artefacts in the process model derived from the same source material. Whilst, as was said above, consuming the novel itself gives the most direct access to the author's imagined world, even this can be affected by the imagined world of other artefacts in the process model, as in the example above of reading a novel after viewing an adaptation.

Historians' perceptions are also important in influencing how they describe the past, and of necessity they are also operating at a temporal distance from the events they are attempting to describe. Hence historians can make conclusions about the past, based on their own perception of the historical facts, governed by their own experiences, prejudices, and state of mind, that can be at odds with those of other historians. As such they operate within a process like that described within this study but without the direct contact with the contemporary world that is available to the contemporary novelist of any period. What is described within a history of the past at a particular point in time may therefore, as an imagined world, show similarities to the imagined worlds created within a novel by an author who actually lived and worked at that time.

Both history and contemporary fiction of a particular period can therefore provide us with stories of the past. The stories within history are set within a framework of known facts. Those within contemporary fiction are set within a framework that is largely invented by the author, but which may, at its core, contain a kernel of reality in its setting and in the detail of its descriptions that can provide true historical insight. The danger is that the complexity of the process model and the potential for modification in those insights from the various actors within the process model caused by their varying source artefacts, knowledge and influences, may result in us gaining an incomplete, misleading, or inaccurate picture of the historical past, as we try to relate the imagined world we create when we consume the novel back to that past. When the novels and the other associated artefacts are used within an academic context, however, consciousness of the context in which the artefact was created, and the processes that helped produce it, would help peel back the filtering layers that lie between it and the historical past of which it contains echoes. Some examples of ways in which this un-layering could be achieved were shown in Chapter 6.

In introducing the concept of a process model in Chapter 1 mention was made of its origins in the field of Quality Management Systems. In such systems all inputs, outputs and processes should be identifiable and quantifiable. In applying such a model to the life cycle of a novel we are dealing with something much more nebulous because firstly, most of what we are investigating sits in the past and is therefore subject to the same problem of incompleteness that is encountered in conventional historical investigation and secondly, we may never know the totality of the influences that may have been present in the mind of an actor in creating an artefact, be that the novelist creating the novel, a critic writing a review, an adapter making an adaptation or an interpreter setting an interpretive scheme at a literary place. Despite this, it is the contention here that by setting each artefact in the context of a process and all of the *potential* influences on the creation of that artefact within that process and by using investigative methods such as those described in Chapter 6, the model provides us with a template for assessing the utility of the artefacts as historical resources by highlighting how the imagined worlds that these influences create may add or subtract from our ability to perceive the historical world behind the novel.

A general conclusion would therefore be that, as a rule, as long as there is an awareness of the process model elements described above, novels written with a backdrop of the contemporary world lived in by the author can be valid resources for historical studies. If thus used, fiction has the potential to provide a detailed canvas to fill in the gaps between individual items of factual historical knowledge, a canvas that is produced through the perception of elements of a historical world by someone actually living and working in that world.

To take this conclusion further, a direction forward from this research would be to investigate ways in which fiction can be used more actively, albeit in a controlled way with knowledge of and reference to the process model, in the teaching of History or of English Literature, building on the ideas and methods discussed in Chapter 6. What the complexity of the complete model in Figure 7.1 and the analyses within Tables 3.7 and 3.8 both suggest is that consumers will probably derive their most direct historical insights from fiction when reading the source novel given that it gives them the shortest route back to the world perceived by the author, insights that may change as further layers of critical analysis, adaptation and interpretation are placed on the original novel. In terms of control, the historical insights within fiction would need to be assessed in the context of the specific influences on the particular artefact being used, along with that artefact's relation within the process model to other artefacts related to the source novel, thus limiting the danger of making false or misleading historical conclusions from a consumption of the artefact.

A fruitful avenue for future research would therefore be to look more closely into the reactions of both academics and students to the use of fiction in historical research. Combined with further studies into non-academic consumer reactions to novels and adaptations of, and literary places linked to, those novels, one would hope to do two things. Firstly, to demonstrate how, in what form and in what context, fiction could most advantageously be used in the academic sphere to supplement conventional historical sources in studying a particular period. Secondly, by analysing the degree of any false or misleading historical insights that may be present in the imagined worlds that we create, outside of the academic environment, when we, as lay consumers, read the novels of the past, watch adaptations of those novels, or visit literary places, one could propose means to improve the historical context in which we present novels in their various forms. For example, one could propose means of improving historical commentary within new editions of novels and new interpretative schemes at literary places. One could also suggest ways of providing more detailed historical contexts within the features produced to support a television or video release of the adaptation of a classic novel.

The beginning of Chapter 1 quoted Sparshott's question as to whether truth can be found in works of fiction. As works of the imagination we should not use novels to find historical truth *per se* – they are primary sources not because of the descriptive elements within them, even if those elements have their origin in a real past experienced by the author, but only insofar as they are documents of a particular period. However, this study has attempted to understand the processes by which authors engaged with elements of the actual historical worlds within which they created their novels, and the process by which subsequent actors in the process engaged with the original novel and other fictional artefacts related to it. It is to be hoped that by developing ways in which the artefacts can be deconstructed and analysed we can properly bring out the historical information that helped create them, and that we might thereby substantially improve their usefulness as historical resources. This utility would extend both to those actors creating artefacts, such as those creating a new filmed adaptation or a new interpretive scheme at a literary place, and also to those consuming the novel and subsequent artefacts built from it. In this way we may see novels as true stories of the past.

Bibliography

Alexander, Lynn M, 'Creating a Symbol: the Seamstress in Victorian Literature', *Tulsa Studies in Women's Literature*, 18 (1999), pp. 29-38.

Allen, James Smith, 'History and the Novel: Mentalité in Modern Popular Fiction', *History and Theory*, 22 (1983), pp. 233-52.

Allen, Rod, 'The Art of Reviewing', in *Print Journalism: A Critical Introduction*, ed. by Richard Keeble (London and New York: Routledge, 2005).

Altick, Richard D., The English Common Reader: A Social History of the Mass Reading Public, 1800-1900 (Columbus: Ohio State University Press, 1998).

Andrew, J. Dudley, *Concepts in Film Theory* (Oxford: Oxford University Press, 1984).

Anon, Manchester City Council Manchester Local Image Collection, *Cellar Dwellings (1838)*, GB127.m08387.

——, '*Far from the Madding Crowd* Review', *Saturday Review*, January 9th, 1875, pp. 57-8.

——, '*Far from the Madding Crowd* Review', *The Athenæum*, December 5th, 1874, p. 747.

——, 'The Good Companions Film Review', Illustrated Topics of the Screen, September 25th, 1933.

——, '*The Good Companions* Play Review', *Daily Telegraph*, May 15th, 1931.

——, '*The Good Companions* Review', *The Spectator*, August 3rd, 1929.

——, Manchester City Council, *Housing: Newgate, Corporation Street (1908)*, GB127. m08316.

——, 'Literature of the Week – The Magazines, &c', *Hampshire Advertiser*, January 10th, 1874.

——, 'Magazines for March', *Bell's Life in London and Sporting Chronicle*, March 7th, 1874.

——, Manchester Central Library, Manchester Sanitary Association Report on the Deansgate District 1854, M126/2/3/21-1 & 2.

——, '*Mary Barton* Review', *Manchester Guardian*, February 28th, 1849, p. 7.

——, '*Mary Barton* Review', *The Inquirer*, November 11th, 1848, pp. 710-11.

——, '*Mary Barton* Review', *The Economist*, November 25th, 1848, pp. 1337-8.

——, 'Monthly Mag-Pie', *Fun*, July 11th, 1874, p. 21.

——, 'New Novels – "Far From The Madding Crowd"', *The Graphic*, December 12th, 1874, p. 567.

——, 'Obituary of William Rathbone Greg', *The Tablet*, 19 Nov. 1881, p. 823.

——, 'Review of 'Lost City'', *Bradford Telegraph and Argus*, October 27th, 1958.

——, 'Review of *Pride and Prejudice*', *The British Critic*, February 1813, pp. 189-90.

——, 'Roundabout. By The Square Man', *Judy*, March 11th, 1874.

——, 'Roundabout. By The Square Man', *Judy*, January 28th, 1874.

——, 'Tess of the D'Urbervilles Review', *Saturday Review*, January 16th, 1892, pp. 7-8.

——, 'Tess of the D'Urbervilles Review: Mr Hardy's New Novel', *The Times*, January 9th, 1892, p. 13.

——, 'Trades' Unions and Strikes', The Churchman – A Magazine in support of the Church of England, April 1841.

——, *Ware is Meryton? Did Ware in Hertfordshire provide Jane Austen with the inspiration for her fictional market town?*, (2013) <http://austenonly.com/2013/02/08/ware-is-meryton-did-ware-in-hertfordshire-provide-jane-austen-with-the-inspiration-for-her-fictional-market-town/>.

Aragay, Mireia, Books in Motion: Adaptation, Intertextuality, Authorship, Contemporary cinema (Amsterdam: Rodopi, 2005).

——, 'Possessing Jane Austen: Fidelity, Authorship, and Patricia Rozema's Mansfield Park', *Literature/Film Quarterly*, 31 (2003), pp. 178-9.

Austen, Jane, *Emma* (London: Penguin, 1996).

——, *Emma: A Novel* (London: John Murray, 1816).

——, *Jane Austen's Letters* (Oxford: Oxford University Press, 1995).

——, *Northanger Abbey and Persuasion* (London: John Murray, 1818).

——, *Pride and Prejudice* (Ware: Wordsworth, 1813 (2007 edition)).

——, *Pride and Prejudice: A Novel* (London: T. Egerton, 1813).

Austen-Leigh, James Edward, *A Memoir of Jane Austen by Her Nephew* (London: Folio Society, 1870 (1989 edition)).

Bagehot, Walter, *The Collected Works of Walter Bagehot*, ed. by Norman St. John-Stevas, Vol. II (London: The Economist, 1965).

——, 'The First Edinburgh Reviewers (1855)', in *Literary Studies by the late Walter Bagehot, Vol. 1*, ed. by Richard Holt Hutton (London: Longmans, Green & Co., 1884).

Baker, Jo, *Longbourn* (London: Doubleday, 2013).

Bakewell, Sarah, At the Existentialist Café: Freedom, Being & Apricot Cocktails (London: Chatto & Windus, 2016).

Barber, Nicholas, *Pride and Prejudice at 20: The scene that changed everything*, (London: BBC, 2015) <http://www.bbc.com/culture/story/20150922-pride-and-prejudice-at-20-the-scene-that-changed-everything>.

Bartholeyns, Gil, 'Representation of the Past in Films: Between Historicity and Authenticity', *Diogenes*, 48 (2000), pp. 31-44.

Battershill, Claire, and Ross, Shawna, Using Digital Humanities in the Classroom : A Practical Introduction for Teachers, Lecturers and Students (London: Bloomsbury, 2017).

Baumgarten, Murray, 'Fictions of the city', in *The Cambridge Companion to Charles Dickens*, ed. by John O. Jordan (Cambridge: Cambridge University Press, 2001).

Baxendale, John, *Priestley's England: J.B. Priestley and English Culture* (Manchester: Manchester University Press, 2007).

BBC Genome Project, (London: British Broadcasting Corporation) <http://genome.ch.bbc.co.uk>.

Bell, Amy, 'Landscapes of Fear: Wartime London, 1939-1945', *The Journal of British Studies*, 48 (2004), pp. 153-75.

Berkeley, George, *A Treatise concerning the Principles of Human Knowledge* (Philadelphia: J.B. Lippincot & Co., 1710 (1881 edition)).

Betts, Ernest, 'Filming Hardy's *Far from the Madding Crowd*', *The Times*, 19 August 1967.

Billen, Andrew, '*Far from the Madding Crowd* TV Review: Jolly fine sheepwork', *New Statesman*, July 10th, 1998.

Birtwistle, Sue, and Conklin, Susie, *The Making of Pride and Prejudice* (London: Penguin Books/BBC Books, 1995).

Black, Clementina, '*Tess of the D'Urbervilles* Review', *Illustrated London News*, January 9th, 1892, p. 50.

Bloch, Marc, and Putnam (trans.), Peter, *The Historian's Craft* (Manchester: Manchester University Press, 1954 (1992 reprint)).

Bodenheimer, Rosemarie, 'London in the Victorian Novel', in *The Cambridge Companion to the Literature of London*, ed. by Lawrence Manley (Cambridge: Cambridge University Press, 2011).

Bradburn, A, Manchester City Council, *Ancoats, McWilliams Court (1902)*, GB127.m10285.

'Bradford & District Visitor Guide 2021', (Bradford: City of Bradford MDC, 2021).

Bradford War Memorial, including steps, screen wall and terminal blocks, (London: Historic England) <https://historicengland.org.uk/listing/the-list/list-entry/1434527>.

Bradshaw, Peter, '*Far from the Madding Crowd* Film Review: Carey Mulligan shines in Hardy perennial', *The Guardian*, April 2nd, 2015.

Brake, Laurel, 'The Serial and the Book in Nineteenth-Century Britain: Intersections, Extensions, Transformations', *Memoires du livre*, 8 (2017), pp. 1-16.

Brantlinger, Patrick, 'The Case Against Trade Unions in Early Victorian Fiction', *Victorian Studies*, 13 (1969), pp. 37-52.

Braudy, Leo, *Narrative Form in History and Fiction: Hume, Fielding & Gibbon* (Princeton, N.J: Princeton University Press, 1970).

Breihan, John, 'Jane Austen and the Militia', *Persuasions*, 14 (1992), pp. 16-26.

British Musicals of the 1930s: Volume 1, (Network, 2016) <http://networkonair.com/shop/1798-british-musicals-of-the-1930s-volume-1-5027626396442.html>.

British Universities Film & Video Council, *Television and Radio Index for Learning and Teaching*, (London: BUFVC) <http://bufvc.ac.uk/tvandradio/trilt/>.

Brittain, Vera, '*The Good Companions* Review', *Time and Tide*, August 9th, 1929.

Brontë, Charlotte, *Shirley: A Tale* (London: Smith, Elder & Co., 1849).

The Brontës and Haworth – Brontë Places, (Haworth: The Brontë Society) <https://www.bronte.org.uk/the-brontes-and-haworth>.

'The Brontës in Pennine Yorkshire', (Huddersfield: Kirklees Council, 2008).

Brooks, Collin, 'Book of the Day. Mr. J.B. Priestley strikes a Dickensian vein', *Yorkshire Post*, July 29th, 1929.

Buckle, Henry Thomas, *History of Civilisation in England* (London: John W. Parker & Son, 1857).

Bullen, J. B., 'Is Hardy a 'Cinematic Novelist'?: The Problem of Adaptation', *The Yearbook of English Studies*, 20 (1990), pp. 48-59.

Bullett, Gerald, 'Good Company', *Fortnightly Review*, 1929.

Butler, Marilyn, 'Austen, Jane (1775-1817), novelist', in *Oxford Dictionary of National Biography* (Oxford: Oxford University Press, 2004, online edition 2010). <http://www.oxforddnbcom/view/article/904>.

Callow, Simon, *Charles Dickens* (London: HarperPress, 2012).

Calvert, Dave, 'From Pedrolino to a Pierrot: The Origin, Ancestry and Ambivalence of the British Pierrot Troupe', *Popular Entertainment Studies*, 4 (2013), pp. 6-23.

Cambridge Dictionary: Authentic, (Oxford: Cambridge University Press, 2019) <https://dictionary.cambridge.org/dictionary/english/authentic>.

Cameron, David, *Big Society Speech – 19th July 2010*, (London: Cabinet Office, 2010) <https://www.gov.uk/government/speeches/pms-speech-on-big-society>.

Cardwell, Sarah, *Adaptation Revisited: Television and the Classic Novel* (Manchester: Manchester University Press, 2002).

Carlyle, Thomas, *Chartism* (London: J. Fraser, 1840).

——, John Rylands Library, *Letter to Elizabeth Gaskell*, MS 730/14.

Carr, David, 'Reflections on Temporal Perspective: The Use and Abuse of Hindsight', *History and Theory*, 57 (2018), pp. 71-80.

Cawston, Richard, J.B. Priestley Library, Letter received by Mavis Dean from Richard Cawston on the making of Lost City, (GB 0532) PRI 19/9.

——, dir. by, *Lost City* (BBC Television, 1958).

Chapman, Raymond, *The Language of Thomas Hardy* (Basingstoke: Macmillan, 1990).

Chappell, Vere, 'Locke's Theory of Ideas', in *The Cambridge Companion to Locke*, ed. by Vere Chappell (Cambridge: Cambridge University Press, 1994).

Chapple, J.A.V., and Pollard, Arthur, ed., *The Letters of Elizabeth Gaskell* (Manchester: Manchester University Press, 1997).

Chatsworth on Film – Pride and Prejudice, (Chatsworth: Chatsworth.org, 2018) <https://www.chatsworth.org/news-media/chatsworth-on-film/pride-and-prejudice/>.

Chibnall, Steve, *J. Lee Thompson* (Manchester ; New York: Manchester University Press, 2000).

Chorley, Henry Fothergill, '*Mary Barton* Review', *The Athenæum*, October 21st, 1848.

City of Bradford MDC: Population, (Bradford: City of Bradford MDC, 2017) <https://www.bradford.gov.uk/open-data/our-datasets/population/>.

Clarke, Susanna, *Jonathan Strange & Mr Norrell* (London: Bloomsbury, 2004).

Clayton, Emma, 'Urban thriller twist on JB Priestley classic delights young Alhambra audience', *Bradford Telegraph and Argus*, May 4th, 2016.

Clement, Michel, Proppe, Dennis, and Rott, Armin, 'Do Critics Make Bestsellers? Opinion Leaders and the Success of Books', *Journal of Media Economics*, 20 (2007), pp. 77-105.

Cohn, Dorrit, 'Signposts of Fictionality: A Narratological Perspective', *Poetics Today*, 11 (1990), pp. 775-804.

Collin, Robbie, '*Far from the Madding Crowd* Film Review: 'a mini-break on film'', *Daily Telegraph*, April 30th, 2015.

Collingwood, R. G., *The Idea of History* (Oxford: Clarendon Press, 1946).

Collins, Philip, *Dickens: The Critical Heritage* (London: Routledge & Kegan Paul, 1971).

Cook, Judith, *Priestley* (London: Bloomsbury, 1997).

Cox, R. G., *Thomas Hardy: The Critical Heritage* (London: Routledge & Kegan Paul, 1970).

Cumming, Mervyn, dir. by, *A Dream of Life* (Yorkshire Television, 1980).

——, dir. by, On the Road with J.B. Priestley and The Good Companions (Yorkshire Television, 1980).

Cunningham, Valentine, *Everywhere Spoken Against: Dissent in the Victorian Novel* (Oxford: Oxford University Press, 1975).

Darby, H.C., 'The Regional Geography of Thomas Hardy's Wessex', *Geographical Review*, 38 (1948), pp. 426-43.

Davenport, Clare, *The Bradford Playhouse. An introduction to the Playhouse.*, (Bradford: Bradford Playhouse, 2015) <https://youtu.be/x7sm1Htag6I>.

Davies, Martin, 'Concept mapping, mind mapping and argument mapping: what are the differences and do they matter?', *Higher Education,* 62 (2011), pp. 279-301.

de Groot, Jerome, 'Affect and empathy: re-enactment and performance as/in history', *Rethinking History,* 15 (2011), pp. 587-99.

——, Consuming History: Historians and Heritage in Contemporary Popular Culture (London: Routledge, 2009).

——, *The Historical Novel* (Abingdon: Routledge, 2010).

——, 'The power of the past: how historical fiction has regained its gravitas', *The Guardian,* 30th September, 2009.

Dehn, Georgia, '*Far from the Madding Crowd*: behind the scenes', *Daily Telegraph,* April 18th, 2015.

Denby, David, 'Which is the best John le Carré novel?', *The New Yorker,* August 5th, 2014.

Dickens, Charles, *Oliver Twist; or, The Parish Boy's Progress* (London: Richard Bentley, 1840).

Discover Haworth and Brontë Country, (Bradford: Bradford Visitor Information Centre, 2021) <http://www.visitbradford.com/discover/Haworth.aspx>.

Disraeli, Benjamin, *Sybil or, The Two Nations, Volume 3* (Henry Colburn: London, 1845).

Donaldson, William, 'Lang, Andrew (1844-19120', in *Oxford Dictionary of National Biography,* ed. by H.C.G. Matthew, Brian Harrison and David Cannadine (Oxford: Oxford University Press, 2004, online edition 2010). <http://www.oxforddnb.com/view/article/34396>.

Donoghue, Frank, The Fame Machine: Book Reviewing and Eighteenth-Century Literary Careers (Stanford: Stanford University Press, 1996).

Drabble, Margaret, 'Thomas Hardy and Wessex', in *The Oxford Guide to Literary Britain & Ireland,* ed. by Daniel Hahn and Nicholas Robins (Oxford: Oxford University Press, 2009). <https://www.oxfordreference.com/view/10.1093/acref/9780198614609.001.0001/acref-9780198614609-e-2794>.

Drucker, Johanna, 'Graphical Approaches to the Digital Humanities', in *A New Companion to Digital Humanities,* ed. by Susan Schreibman, Ray Siemens and John Unsworth (New York,: John Wiley, 2016). <http://ebookcentral.proquest.com/lib/uocuk/detail.action?docID=4093339>.

Eagleton, Terry, *Literary Theory: An Introduction* (Oxford: Blackwell, 1996).

Easson, Angus, Elizabeth Gaskell: The Critical Heritage (Routledge: 1991).

Eliot, George, 'The Natural History of German Life', *Westminster Review,* XIX (1856), pp. 51-79.

Eliot, Simon, 'The Business of Victorian Publishing', in *The Cambridge Companion to the Victorian Novel,* ed. by Diedre David (Cambridge: Cambridge University Press, 2001).

Ellison, Ralph, Styron, William, Warren, Robert Penn, and Woodward, C. Vann, 'A Discussion: The Uses of History in Fiction', *The Southern Literary Journal,* 1 (1969), pp. 57-90.

Engels, Friedrich, *The Condition of the Working Class in England in 1844,* trans. Florence Kelley Wischnewetzky (London: George Allen and Unwin, 1845 (1952 reprint)).

English Oxford Living Dictionaries: Illusion, (Oxford: Oxford University Press, 2019) <https://en.oxforddictionaries.com/definition/illusion>

Everyman's Library – Everyman Classics, (London: Everyman's Library, 2016) <http://www.everymanslibrary.co.uk/classics.aspx>>.

Explore Sudbury Hall, (London: National Trust) <https://www.nationaltrust.org.uk/features/highlights-of-sudbury-hall>.

'Exploring Thomas Hardy's West Dorset', (Dorchester: West Dorset District Council and Weymouth & Portland Borough Council / Thomas Hardy Society, 2014).

Fincham, Tony, *Exploring Thomas Hardy's Wessex* (Wimborne, Dorset: Dovecote Press, 2016).

Flint, Kate, 'The Victorian Novel and its Readers', in *The Cambridge Companion to the Victorian Novel*, ed. by Diedre David (Cambridge: Cambridge University Press, 2001).

——, The Victorian Novelist: Social Problems and Social Change (London: Croom Helm, 1987).

Forster, John, '*Mary Barton* Review', *The Examiner*, Nov. 1848, pp. 708-9.

——, '*Nicholas Nickleby* Review', *The Examiner*, 27 Oct. 1839, p. 677.

Fourcade, Francoise, 'The Look of *Far from the Madding Crowd*', (20th Century Fox Home Entertainment, 2015).

Frykstedt, Monica C., 'Mary Barton and the Reports of the Ministry to the Poor – A New Source', *Studia Neophilologica,* 52 (1980), pp. 333-36.

Fuller, Graham, 'Wessex and the Single Girl', *Cineaste,* 40 (2015), pp. 12-16.

Fullerton, Huw, 'Where was To Walk Invisible: The Brontë sisters filmed?', *Radio Times*, December 29th, 2016.

Garner, Clare, 'TV drama kings fall out over Jane Austen', *Independent on Sunday*, July 14th, 1996.

Garside, Peter, and Schöwerling, Rainer, The English Novel, 1770-1829: a Bibliographical Survey of Prose Fiction published in the British Isles. Vol. 2, 1800-1829 (Oxford: Oxford University Press, 2000).

Gaskell, Elizabeth, *The Life of Charlotte Brontë* (London: Smith, Elder & Co., 1857).

——, *Mary Barton* (Ware: Wordsworth, 1848 (2012 Edition)).

——, *Mary Barton: A Tale of Manchester Life* (London: Chapman and Hall, 1848).

——, 'North and South', *Household Words*, September 2nd, 1854 to January 20th, 1855.

——, *North and South* (London: Chapman & Hall, 1855).

——, *North and South* (Ware: Wordsworth, 1855 (1994 Edition)).

Gaskell, Elizabeth, and Munro, Rona, *Elizabeth Gaskell's Mary Barton* (London: Nick Hern Books, 2006).

Gattrell, Simon, 'Wessex', in *The Cambridge Companion to Thomas Hardy*, ed. by Dale Kramer (Cambridge: Cambridge University Press, 1999).

Gay, Penny, 'A Hypothetical Map of Highbury', *Persuasions* (2015) <http://www.jasna.org/persuasions/on-line/vol36no1/gay.html>.

Gibbs, Patrick, '*Far from the Madding Crowd* Film Review: Hardy before the gloom', *Daily Telegraph*, October 20th, 1967.

Giddings, Robert, and Selby, Keith, *The Classic Serial on Television and Radio* (Basingstoke: Palgrave, 2001).

Giddings, Robert, Selby, Keith, and Wensley, Chris, *Screening the Novel: The Theory and Practice of Literary Dramatization* (Basingstoke: Macmillan, 1990).

Gillard, Derek, 'Towards Mass Education', in *Education in England: A History* (Derek Gillard, 2018). <http://www.educationengland.org.uk/history>.

'The Good Companions – Singing... Laughing... Dancing... They'll mean Good Business for you! (Press Book for Good Companions 1957 film)', (London: Associated British-Pathé Ltd, 1957).

'"The Good Companions" Starring Jessie Matthews, Edmund Gwenn, Mary Glynne, A.W. Baskcomb & John Gielgud', *The Era*, March 1st, 1933.

goodreads, (San Francisco: Goodreads Inc.) <https://www.goodreads.com>.

Gordon, Lyndall, *Charlotte Brontë: A Passionate Life* (London: Virago, 2008).

Gray, Robert Q., *The Factory Question and Industrial England, 1830-1860* (Cambridge: Cambridge University Press, 1996).

'Greeneland', in *OED Online* (Oxford: Oxford University Press, 2015).

Greenhalf, Jim, 'When Bradford's city bosses bet the house...', *Telegraph & Argus*, October 20th, 1967.

Greg, William Rathbone, An Enquiry into the state of the Manufacturing Population, and the causes and cures of the evils therein existing (London: James Ridgway, 1831).

——, '*Mary Barton* Review: Art. V. – Mary Barton; A Tale of Manchester Life', *The Edinburgh Review*, April 1849, pp. 402-35.

Greiner, Rae, *Sympathetic Realism in Nineteenth-Century British Fiction* (Baltimore: Johns Hopkins University Press, 2012).

Griggs, Yvonne, The Bloomsbury Introduction to Adaptation Studies: Adapting the Canon in Film, TV, Novels and Popular Culture (London: Bloomsbury, 2016).

Groskop, Viv, '*Les Misérables* episode four recap – Les Coincidences, you mean?', *The Guardian*, January 20th, 2019.

Gunn, Simon, and Faire, Lucy, 'Introduction: Why Bother with Method?', in *Research Methods for History*, ed. by Simon Gunn and Lucy Faire (Edinburgh: Edinburgh University Press, 2012).

Hameed, Uzma, 'Woolfian Perspectives', in *Royal Ballet: Woolf Works* (London: Royal Opera House Covent Garden Ltd, 2017).

Hammond, J. L., and Hammond, Barbara, *The Age of the Chartists, 1832-1854. A study of discontent* (London: Longmans, 1930).

Hanson, Lee, and Joy, David, 'Bright Day Literary Tour', in *Bright Day (2006 edition)*, ed. by Lee Hanson and David Joy (Ilkley: Great Northern Books, 2006).

——, 'The Good Companions on Stage and Screen', in *The Good Companions (2007 edition)*, ed. by Lee Hanson and David Joy (Ilkley: Great Northern Books, 2007).

——, 'Priestley's 'Happy Daydream' – Biographical Background', in *The Good Companions (2007 edition)*, ed. by Lee Hanson and David Joy (Ilkley: Great Northern Books, 2007).

Hardy, Thomas, 'The Dorsetshire Labourer', *Longman's Magazine*, July 1883, pp. 252-69.

——, *Far from the Madding Crowd* (London: Macmillan, 1874 (1912 edition)).

——, 'Far from the Madding Crowd', *Cornhill Magazine*, 1874a.

——, *Far from the Madding Crowd* (Ware: Wordsworth, 1874 (1993 edition)).

——, *Far from the Madding Crowd* (London: Smith, Elder & Co., 1874).

——, *Far from the Madding Crowd* (New York and London: Harper & Brothers, 1874 (1895 edition)).

——, *The Mayor of Casterbridge* (London: CRW Publishing Ltd, 1886 (2003 edition)).

——, *A Pair of Blue Eyes* (London: Osgood & McIlvaine, 1873 (1895 edition)).

——, *The Return of the Native* (London: Smith, Elder & Co., 1878).

——, *Tess of the D'Urbervilles* (Toronto: Broadview Literary Text, 1891 (2007 edition)).

——, Tess of the D'Urbervilles: A Pure Woman Faithfully Presented (London: James R. Osgood, McIlvaine & Co., 1891).

——, *Under The Greenwood Tree* (Ware: Wordsworth, 1872 (1994 edition)).

——, *Wessex Poems and Other Verses* (London: Harper, 1898).

Hardy's Cottage: evocative cob and thatch cottage – birthplace of Thomas Hardy, (London: National Trust) <https://www.nationaltrust.org.uk/hardys-cottage>.

Hardyment, Christina, *Literary Trails: Writers in their Landscapes* (London: National Trust, 2000).

Harmon, William, and Holman, C. Hugh, *A Handbook to Literature* (New York: Macmillan, 1992).

Harper, Charles G., *The Hardy Country: Literary Landmarks of the Wessex Novels* (London: Adam & Charles Black, 1904).

Hart, Jonathan, *Fictional and Historical Worlds* (New York: Palgrave Macmillan, 2012).

Hartley, L.P., 'New Fiction', *The Saturday Review*, 148 (1929), pp. 136-7.

Hatcher, John, 'Fiction as History: The Black Death and Beyond', *History*, 97 (2012), pp. 3-23.

Hays, Bill, and Lewis, Leonard, dir. by, *The Good Companions* (Yorkshire Television, 1980).

Hayward, Abraham, 'Review of *Pickwick Papers* Nos I-XVII ', *Quarterly Review* (October 1837).

Hendrix, Harald, 'From Early Modern to Romantic Literary Tourism: A Diachronical Perspective', in *Literary Tourism and Nineteenth-Century Culture*, ed. by Nicola J. Watson (Basingstoke: Palgrave Macmillan, 2009).

Herbert, David, 'Literary Places, Tourism and the Heritage Experience', *Annals of Tourism Research*, 28 (2001), pp. 312-33.

——, 'Place and Society in Jane Austen's England', *Geography*, 76 (1991), pp. 193-208.

Herlihy, David, 'Am I a Camera? Other Reflections on Films and History', *The American Historical Review*, 93 (1988), pp. 1186-92.

Hillmore, Peter, '*Far from the Madding Crowd* TV Review', *The Observer*, July 5th, 1998.

Holdsworth, Peter, *The Rebel Tyke: Bradford and J.B. Priestley* (Bradford: Bradford Libraries, 1994).

Honan, Park, *Jane Austen: her life* (London: Weidenfeld and Nicolson, 1987).

Hopkins, Annette B., '"Mary Barton": A Victorian Best Seller', *The Trollopian*, 3 (1948), pp. 1-18.

Hopkins, R. Thurston, *Thomas Hardy's Dorset* (London: Cecil Palmer, 1922).

Houghton, Walter E., *The Wellesley Index to Victorian periodicals, 1824-1900* (Toronto: University of Toronto Press, 1966).

Howsam, Leslie, Kegan Paul, a Victorian Imprint: Publishers, Books and Cultural History (London: Kegan Paul International, 1998).

Hutcheon, Linda, *A Theory of Adaptation* (London: Routledge, 2006).

Hutton, Richard Holt, '*Far from the Madding Crowd* Review', *The Spectator*, December 19th, 1874, pp. 1597-9.

——, '*Tess of the D'Urbervilles* Review', *The Spectator*, January 23rd, 1892, pp. 121-2.

Ince, Bernard, 'The Neglected Art: Trends and Transformations in British Concert Party Entertainment, 1850-1950', *New Theatre Quarterly*, 31 (2015), pp. 3-16.

Inflation Calculator, (London: Bank of England, 2019) <https://www.bankofengland.co.uk/monetary-policy/inflation/inflation-calculator>.

Interior of a Manchester Cellar (1838), Manchester City Council Manchester Local Image Collection, GB127.m08388.

Internet Movie Database, (Seattle: IMDb.com, Inc.) <https://www.imdb.com>.

Ishiguro, Kazuo, 'Kazuo Ishiguro talks Zuckerberg, Game of Thrones and his new novel', *ShortList* (2014) <https://www.shortlist.com/entertainment/books/kazuo-ishiguro-talks-zuckerberg-game-of-thrones-and-his-new-novel/97003>.

James, Elizabeth, *Writing, Publishing and Revising Far from the Madding Crowd*, (London: British Library) <http://www.bl.uk/romantics-and-victorians/articles/writing-publishing-and-revising-far-from-the-madding-crowd>.

James, Henry, '*Far from the Madding Crowd* Review', *The Nation*, December 24th, 1874, pp. 423-4.

James, Louis, 'The Nineteenth Century Social Novel', in *Encyclopedia of Literature & Criticism*, ed. by Martin Coyle, Peter Garside, Malcolm Kelsall and John Peck (London: Routledge, 1990).

Jewell-Lapan, Waldo, 'Perception and Reality', *The Journal of Philosophy*, xxxiii (1936), pp. 365-73.

Joukovsky, Nicholas A., 'Another Unnoted Contemporary Review of Jane Austen', *Nineteenth-Century Fiction*, 29 (December 1974), pp. 393-96.

Joyner, Will, '*Far from the Madding Crowd* TV Review: The 'Madding Crowd' Is Getting Crowded', *New York Times*, May 8th, 1998.

Kelleher, Michael, 'Images of the Past: Historical Authenticity and Inauthenticity from Disney to Times Square', *CRM: The Journal of Heritage Stewardship*, 1 (2004), pp. 6-19.

Kernan, Margot S., '*Far from the Madding Crowd* Film Review', *Film Quarterly*, 21 (1967), p. 61.

Kierkegaard, Søren, 'Concluding Scientific Postscript (1846)', in *Philosophic Classics: From Plato to Nietzsche*, ed. by Walter Arnold Kaufmann and Forrest E. Baird (Upper Saddle River, N.J.: Prentice Hall, 1997).

Kingsley, Charles, '*Mary Barton* Review', *Fraser's Magazine*, April 1849.

——, The Water-Babies, A Fairy Tale for a Land Baby (London: Macmillan, 1863).

Knutsford Heritage Centre: Walks, (Knutsford: Knutsford Heritage Centre) <http://www.knutsfordheritage.co.uk/visitor-info/bookings/walks/>.

Lane, Anthony, '*Far from the Madding Crowd* Film Review: Fighting On: "Avengers: Age of Ultron" and "Far from the Madding Crowd"', *The New Yorker*, May 4th, 2015.

Lang, Andrew, '*Far from the Madding Crowd* Review', *The Academy*, January 2nd, 1875, pp. 9-10.

——, '*Tess of the D'Urbervilles* Review', *New Review*, February 1892, pp. 247-9.

Langton, Simon, dir. by, *Pride and Prejudice* (BBC / Chestermead, 1995).

Layhe, John, Reports of the Mission to the Poor, in Manchester (Manchester: 1842)

Lea, Hermann, *Thomas Hardy's Wessex* (London: Macmillan & Co., 1913).

Legg, Rodney, *Thomas Hardy's Dorset* (Wellington: Halsgrove, 2011).

Lockhart, J. G., *Memoirs of the life of Sir Walter Scott, Bart* (Edinburgh: Robert Cadell, 1837).

Lodge, David, 'Thomas Hardy and Cinematographic Form', *NOVEL: A Forum on Fiction*, 7 (1974), pp. 246-54.

Lowenthal, David, *The Past is a Foreign Country* (Cambridge: Cambridge University Press, 1985).

——, *The Past is a Foreign Country – Revisited* (Cambridge: Cambridge University Press, 2015).

MacCannell, Dean, 'Staged Authenticity – Arrangements of Social Space in Tourist Settings', *American Journal of Sociology*, 79 (1973), pp. 589-603.

Macdonald, Keith, 'The Gentle Wizard', *Manchester Evening News*, July 16th, 1979.

Maier, Sarah E., 'Introduction 1. In Defence of Tess', in *Tess of the D'Urbervilles (second edition)*, ed. by Sarah E. Maier (Toronto: Broadview Literary Text, 2007).

Manzoni, Alessandro, *On the Historical Novel*, trans. Sandra Bermann (Lincoln: University of Nebraska Press, 1984).

Margolis, Joseph, The Language of Art & Art Criticism: Analytic Questions in Aesthetics (Detroit: Wayne State University Press, 1965).

——, 'The Logic and Structures of Fictional Narrative', *Philosophy and Literature*, 7 (1983), pp. 162-81.

Margulies, Nancy, *Mindmapping and Learning*, (Baltimore: Johns Hopkins University School of Education, 2004) <http://education.jhu.edu/PD/newhorizons/strategies/topics/Graphic%20Tools%20for%20Learning/margulies_2.htm>.

Marwick, Arthur, The New Nature of History: Knowledge, Evidence, Language (Basingstoke: Palgrave, 2001).

McCormick, Peter, 'Real Fictions', *The Journal of Aesthetics and Art Criticism*, 46 (1987), pp. 259-70.

McDonagh, Philomena, '*Far from the Madding Crowd* Script', (Granada, 1998).

McEwan, Ian, *Saturday* (London: Jonathan Cape, 2005).

McFarlane, Brian, Novel to Film: An Introduction to the Theory of Adaptation (Oxford: Clarendon Press, 1996).

McGann, Stephen, 'From how to who: accuracy and authenticity in the portrayal of the medic in TV drama', *Journal of the Royal Society of Medicine*, 108 (2015), pp. 123-26.

McIntosh, Alison J., and C. Prentice, Richard, 'Affirming Authenticity: Consuming Cultural Heritage', *Annals of Tourism Research*, 26 (1999), pp. 589-612.

Michie, Ranald, 'The City of London in Literature: Place, People and Pursuits', (London: Gresham College, 2013).

Middleton, Thomas, Annals of Hyde and District. Containing historical reminiscences of Denton, Haughton, Dukinfield, Mottram, Longdendale, Bredbury, Marple, and the neighbouring townships (Manchester: Cartwright & Rattray, 1899).

Miller, Alexander, *Realism*, (Stanford: Stanford University, 2016) <https://plato.stanford.edu/archives/win2016/entries/realism/>.

Millgate, Michael, 'Hardy, Thomas (1840-1928)', in *Oxford Dictionary of National Biography*, ed. by H.C.G. Matthew, Brian Harrison and David (Online Editor) Cannadine (Oxford: Oxford University Press, 2004, online edition 2006). <http://www.oxforddnbcom/view/article/33708>.

Milne, T., '1 inch to 1 mile map of Hampshire', (London: William Faden, 1791).

Mink, Louis O, 'History and Fiction as Modes of Comprehension', *New Literary History*, 1 (1970), pp. 541-58.

Moat, Janet, *BFI screenonline: The Good Companions (1933)*, (London: British Film Institute, 2003-14) <http://www.screenonline.org.uk/film/id/439635/>.

Morgan, Rosemarie, and Rode, Scott, 'The Evolution of Wessex', in *The Ashgate Research Companion to Thomas Hardy*, ed. by Rosemarie Morgan (Farnham: Ashgate, 2010).

National Trust 2019 Handbook, (London: National Trust, 2019).

Nicholls, David, 'Adapting *Far from the Madding Crowd*', (20th Century Fox Home Entertainment, 2015).

——, '*Far from the Madding Crowd* Script', (20th Century Fox Home Entertainment, 2015).

North & South – Complete BBC Series With Extras (2 Disc Set) [DVD], (Amazon.co.uk, 2017) <https://www.amazon.co.uk/North-South-Complete-Extras-Disc/dp/B004QT0YR0>.

North and South by Gaskell, Elizabeth Cleghorn (AUTHOR) Apr-05-1993 Paperback, (Amazon.co.uk, 2017) <https://www.amazon.co.uk/Gaskell-Elizabeth-Cleghorn-Apr-05-1993-Paperback/dp/B00C47I6LM>.

Noton, Amy, *20 famous film locations in Derbyshire and the Peak District*, (Derby: Derbyshire Life and Countryside, October 19th, 2015) <http://www.derbyshirelife.co.uk/out-about/places/20-famous-film-locations-in-derbyshire-and-the-peak-district-1-4148349>.

The Numbers – Pride and Prejudice (2005), (Beverly Hills: Nash Information Services, 2019) <https://www.the-numbers.com/movie/Pride-and-Prejudice-(2005)>.

Oliphant, Margaret, '*Tess of the D'Urbervilles* Review: The Old Saloon', *Blackwood's Edinburgh Magazine*, Mar. 1892, pp. 464-74.

'On Tour', *The Stage*, August 10th, 1933.

Ordnance Survey, 'County Series: Lancashire', (London: Ordnance Survey, 1848).

Orel, Harold, 'Hutton, Richard Holt (1826-1897)', in *Oxford Dictionary of National Biography*, ed. by H.C.G. Matthew, Brian Harrison and David Cannadine (Oxford: Oxford University Press, 2004, online edition 2006). <http://www.oxforddnb.com/view/10.1093/ref:odnb/9780198614128.001.0001/odnb-9780198614128-e-14312>.

Oxford World's Classics, (Oxford: Oxford University Dress, 2016) <https://global.oup.com/academic/content/series/o/oxford-worlds-classics-owc/?type=listing&lang=en&cc=gb>.

Parrish, Timothy, 'History and Fiction', in *The Cambridge Companion to Postmodern American Fiction*, ed. by Paula Geyh (New York: Cambridge University Press, 2017).

Paterson, Peter, '*Far from the Madding Crowd* TV Review: Hell on trolley wheels', *Daily Mail*, July 7th, 1998.

Payne, George A., *Mrs. Gaskell and Knutsford* (Manchester: Clarkson & Griffiths, 1900).

Pemberley Walk at Lyme, (London: National Trust) <https://www.nationaltrust.org.uk/lyme/trails/pemberley-walk-at-lyme->.

Penguin Press, (London: Penguin Random House, 2016) <https://www.penguinrandomhouse.co.uk/publishers/penguin-press/>.

Péoux, Gérald 'To Visualize Past Communities: A Solution from Contemporary Practices in the Industry for the Digital Humanities', *Digital Humanities Quarterly*, 11 (2017).

Percival, Brian, dir. by, *North and South* (BBC, 2004).

Pite, Ralph, *Thomas Hardy: The Guarded Life* (London: Picador, 2006).

Plater, Alan, *Alan Plater on Priestley* (Bingley: Moorside Words and Music, 2005).

——, *The Good Companions Script* (Yorkshire TV, 1980).

——, Hull History Centre/Alan Plater Archive, Rehearsal Script for "The Good Companions" Episode 1: "In Which We Meet The Company", U DPR/4/39.

Plater, Alan, and Fanshawe, David, Hull History Centre, *Main Titles music for 1980 adaptation of The Good Companions*, U DPR/4/39.

Plater, Alan, Fanshawe, David, Lewis, Leonard J, and Priestley, J.B., 'The Good Companions – A Scrapbook', (London: Trident Television Ltd., 1980).

Plietzsch, Birgit, 'The Novels of Thomas Hardy as a Product of Nineteenth-Century Social, Economic, and Cultural Change' (PhD Thesis, Martin-Luther-Universität, Halle-Wittenberg, 2004)

Priestley, J.B., *Angel Pavement* (London: William Heinemann, 1930).

——, *Bright Day* (London: William Heinemann, 1946).

——, *Bright Day* (Ilkley: Great Northern Books, 1946 (2006 edition)).

——, J.B. Priestley Library, Cutting from Radio Times of October 24th, 1958: 'In Search of the Bradford I Knew', (GB 0532) PRI 19/9.

——, *English Journey* (London: William Heinemann; Victor Gollancz, 1934).

——, *The Good Companions* (London: William Heinemann, 1929).

——, *The Good Companions* (Ilkley: Great Northern Books, 1929 (2007 edition)).

——, Margin Released: A Writer's Reminiscences and Reflections (London: William Heinemann, 1962).

Priestley, Tom, 'Foreword', in *The Good Companions (2007 edition)*, ed. by Lee Hanson and David Joy (Ilkley: Great Northern Books, 2007).

'The Process Approach in ISO 9001:2015', (Geneva: International Organisation for Standardization, 2015).

Raphael, Frederic, '*Far from the Madding Crowd* Script', (Metro-Goldwyn-Mayer, 1967).

Ratcliffe, Susan, Oxford Dictionary of Quotations by Subject, Oxford Paperback Reference (Oxford: Oxford University Press, 2010).

Renton, Nicholas, dir. by, *Far from the Madding Crowd* (Granada, 1998).

Ricoeur, Paul, Blamey (trans.), K, and Pellauer (trans.), D, *Time and Narrative* (Chicago: University of Chicago Press, 1988).

Rintoul, M. C., Dictionary of Real People and Places in Fiction (London: Routledge, 1993).

Robinson, Mike, 'Literature-Tourism Relationships', in *Literature and Tourism: Essays in the Reading and Writing of Tourism*, ed. by Mike Robinson and Hans Christian Andersen (London: Continuum, 2002).

Rolinson, David, 'The Good Companions (1980-81)', <http://www.britishtelevisiondrama.org.uk/?p=2934>.

Royle, Edward, 'Annual Reports of the Manchester Domestic Missionary Society, 1833-1908', (Wakefield: EP Microform Ltd).

Rycroft, Simon, and Jenness, Roger, 'J.B. Priestley: Bradford and a provincial narrative of England, 1913-1933', *Social & Cultural Geography*, 13 (2012), pp. 957-76.

Sadleir, Michael, XIX Century fiction: a bibliographical record based on his own collection by Michael Sadleir (London: Constable ; Los Angeles : California University Press, 1951).

Saville, Victor, dir. by, *The Good Companions* (Gaumont British Picture Corporation, 1933).

Schickel, Richard, '*Far from the Madding Crowd* Film Review: Blind Faith in Hardy Isn't Enough', *Life*, December 8th, 1967.

Schlesinger, John, dir. by, *Far from the Madding Crowd* (Metro-Goldwyn-Mayer, 1967).

Scott, Sir Walter, 'Unsigned Review of *Emma*', *Quarterly Review*, March 1816, pp. 188-201.

Section of back to back houses, Manchester Central Library, GB124.M126/5/1/17.

Sharp, William, *Literary Geography* (London: Offices of the Pall Mall Publications, 1904).

Shattock, Joanne, 'The Culture of Criticism', in *The Cambridge Companion to English Literature, 1830-1914*, ed. by Joanne Shattock (Cambridge: Cambridge University Press, 2010).

Sloane, Burt, and Anson, Jay, *Inside Far from the Madding Crowd: Script* (Professional Film Services, 1967).

Smith, Kenneth, 'The Probable Location of "Longbourn" in Jane Austen's Pride and Prejudice', *Persuasions*, 27 (2005), pp. 234-41.

Sokol, Ronnie Jo, 'The Importance of Being Married: Adapting Pride and Prejudice', in *Nineteenth-Century Woman at the Movies: Adapting Classic Women's Fiction to Film*, ed. by Barbara Tepa Lupack (Bowling Green: Bowling Green State University Popular Press, 1999).

Southam, B. C., Jane Austen: The Critical Heritage Volume 1 1811-1870 (London: Routledge, 1968).

Southgate, Beverley C., *History meets Fiction* (Harlow: Longman, 2009).

Sparshott, Francis E., 'Truth in Fiction', *The Journal of Aesthetics and Art Criticism*, 26 (1967), pp. 3-7.

Spiegel, Gabrielle M., 'History, Historicism, and the Social Logic of the Text in the Middle Ages', *Speculum*, 65 (1990), pp. 59-86.

St. Clair, William, *The Reading Nation in the Romantic Period* (Cambridge, U.K. ; New York: Cambridge University Press, 2004).

Stern, Fritz, 'Introduction', in *The Varieties of History : From Voltaire to the Present*, ed. by Fritz Stern (Cleveland: Meridian Books, 1956).

Stone, Lawrence, and Spiegel, Gabrielle M., 'History and Post-Modernism', *Past & Present* (1992), pp. 189-208.

Straus, Ralph, '*The Good Companions* Review', *Sunday Times*, July 28th, 1929.

Strauss, A.L., and Glaser, B.G., *The Discovery of Grounded Theory: Strategies for Qualitative Research* (New York: Aldine de Gruyter, 1967).

Sutherland, Kathryn, 'Cents and sensibility: Jane Austen's world of risk', *Financial Times*, June 16th, 2017.

Tandon, Bharat, 'The Historical Background', in *The Cambridge Companion to Pride and Prejudice*, ed. by Janet M. Todd (Cambridge: Cambridge University Press, 2013).

Taylor, John Russell, 'Hardy film looks marvellous', *The Times*, October 17th, 1967.

Taylor, Simon, and Gibson, Kathryn, *Manningham: character and diversity in a Bradford suburb* (Swindon: English Heritage, 2010).

Tetley, Sarah, and Bramwell, Bill, 'Tourists and the Cultural Construction of Haworth's Literary Landscapes', in *Literature and Tourism: Essays in the Reading and Writing of Tourism*, ed. by Mike Robinson and Hans Christian Andersen (London: Continuum, 2002).

Thackeray, William Makepeace, *Vanity Fair: A Novel Without a Hero* (London: Bradbury & Evans, 1848).

Things to do in Haworth, (TripAdvisor, 2019) <https://www.tripadvisor.co.uk/Attractions-g186409-Activities-Haworth_Keighley_West_Yorkshire_England.html>.

Thomas Vinterberg, dir. by, *Far from the Madding Crowd* (20th Century Fox Home Entertainment, 2015).

Thompson, J. Lee, dir. by, *The Good Companions* (Associated British Picture Corporation, 1957).

Thornton, Richard, University of Manchester, Adshead's twenty four illustrated maps of the township of Manchester: New Cross Ward (1851), JRL1300179.

Timothy, Dallen J., *Cultural Heritage and Tourism: An Introduction, Aspects of tourism texts* (Bristol ; Buffalo: Channel View Publications, 2011).

Timothy, Dallen J., and Boyd, Stephen W., *Heritage Tourism, Themes in tourism* (New York: Prentice Hall, 2003).

Tomalin, Claire, *Charles Dickens: A Life* (London: Penguin, 2012).

——, *Jane Austen: A Life* (London: Viking, 1997).

——, Thomas Hardy: The Time-Torn Man (London: Penguin, 2007).

Top Withens – Withins – Bronte Country, (Haworth: haworth-village.org.uk) <http://www.haworth-village.org.uk/brontes/places/top_withens.asp>

Tosh, John, *The Pursuit of History* (Harlow: Longman, 2015).

Towner, John, An Historical Geography of Recreation and Tourism in the Western World, 1540-1940 (Chichester: Wiley, 1996).

Tribe, John, 'The Indiscipline of Tourism', *Annals of Tourism Research*, 24 (1997), pp. 638-57.

Trollope, Anthony, *An Autobiography* (Blackwood, 1883).

Troost, Linda, 'Filming Tourism, Portraying Pemberley', *Eighteenth Century Fiction*, 18 (2006), pp. 477-98.

Uglow, Jenny, *Elizabeth Gaskell: A Habit of Stories* (London: Faber, 1993).

Using Mind Mapping Tools to Promote Independent Learning and Study Skills, (London: Educational Publishers LLP trading as BBC Active, n/a) <http://www.bbcactive.com/BBCActiveIdeasandResources/UsingMindMappingTools.aspx>.

Van Vuuren, Melissa S., Literary research and the Victorian and Edwardian ages, 1830-1910: strategies and sources (Lanham, Md. ; Plymouth: Scarecrow Press, 2011).

Various, *A Literary Atlas of Europe*, (Zurich: Institute of Cartography, ETH Zurich, 2018) <http://www.literaturatlas.eu/en/index.html>.

Veeser, H. Aram, 'Introduction', in *The New Historicism*, ed. by H. Aram Veeser (London & New York: Routledge, 1989).

Vintage Classics, (London: Penguin Random House, 2016) <https://www.penguinrandom-house.co.uk/publishers/vintage/vintage-classics/>.

Vinterberg, Thomas, 'Adapting *Far from the Madding Crowd*', (20th Century Fox Home Entertainment, 2015).

——, dir. by, *Far from the Madding Crowd* (BBC Films/DNA Films/Fox Searchlight Pictures, 2015).

Wagner, Geoffrey, *The Novel and the Cinema* (Teaneck, NJ: Fairleigh Dickinson University Press, 2012).

Walder, Dennis, 'The Genre Approach', in *The Realist Novel*, ed. by Dennis Walder (London: Routledge in association with the Open University, 1995).

Wallis, Steve, *Thomas Hardy's Dorset Through Time* (Stroud: Amberley, 2012).

Walton, John K., *The British Seaside: Holidays and Resorts in the Twentieth Century* (Manchester: Manchester University Press, 2000).

Watson, Nicola J., *The Literary Tourist* (Basingstoke: Palgrave Macmillan, 2008).

Watson, William, '*Tess of the D'Urbervilles* Review', *The Academy*, February 6th, 1892, pp. 125-6.

Webb, Igor, Rereading the Nineteenth Century: Studies in the Old Criticism from Austen to Lawrence (New York: Palgrave Macmillan, 2010).

Weyant, Nancy, 'Chronology', in *The Cambridge Companion to Elizabeth Gaskell*, ed. by Jill L. Matus (Cambridge: Cambridge University Press, 2007).

Whelehan, Imelda, 'Adaptations: the contemporary dilemma', in *Adaptations : From Text to Screen, Screen to Text*, ed. by Deborah Cartmell and Imelda Whelehan (London: Routledge, 1999).

White, Hayden V., The Content of the Form: Narrative Discourse and Historical Representation (Baltimore: Johns Hopkins University Press, 1987).

——, 'Introduction: Historical Fiction, Fictional History, and Historical Reality', *Rethinking History*, 9 (2005), pp. 147-57.

——, Metahistory. The Historical Imagination in Nineteenth-Century Europe (Baltimore and London: John Hopkins University Press, 1975).

Williams, Tony, 'Dickens's 'Magic Lantern' – Discover the city that was his home and inspiration', (London: City of London / Charles Dickens Museum, 2017).

Wilson, Cheryl A., *Jane Austen and the Victorian Heroine* (London: Palgrave Macmillan, 2017).

Windle, Bertram C. A., *The Wessex of Thomas Hardy* (London: John Lane: The Bodley Head, 1902).

——, *The Wessex of Thomas Hardy* (London & New York: John Lane: The Bodley Head, 1901).

Woolf, Virginia, 'The Cinema (1926)', in *Collected Essays* (London: Hogarth Press, 1966).

——, 'Modern Fiction (1925)', in *The Essays of Virginia Woolf. Volume 4: 1925-1928*, ed. by Andrew McNeillie (London: The Hogarth Press, 1984).

——, *Mrs Dalloway* (London: Vintage Classics, 1925 (2004 edition)).

Wordsworth Editions – Classics £1.99, (Ware: Wordsworth Editions Ltd., 2016) <http://www.wordsworth-editions.com/collection/classics>.

Zemon Davis, Natalie, '"Any resemblance to persons living or dead": film and the challenge of authenticity', *Historical Journal of Film, Radio and Television*, 8 (2006), pp. 269-83.